The Legacy of Fairbairn and Sutherland

The Legacy of Fairbairn and Sutherland provides the first comprehensive review of W. R. D. Fairbairn's and John Sutherland's theories on psycho-social development. It gathers Fairbairn's and Sutherland's ideas, traces the philosophical roots of their thinking, explores their legacy, and demonstrates their relevance to contemporary practice.

International contributors set these psychoanalytic theories in their philosophical and cultural context. They discuss the growing acceptance of Fairbairn's and Sutherland's work in Europe and the Americas. They discuss the theories' impact on current thinking in subjects such as sexuality, hysteria, autonomy and repression. They re-examine the theories in the light of current clinical experience, illuminate them with reference to contemporary psychoanalytic theories and illustrate them with examples from work with children, adults, groups and families.

This book presents an original fusion of the ideas of two of the most noteworthy figures in recent psychoanalysis. It will prove fascinating reading for all practising and training psychotherapists and psychoanalysts.

Jill Savege Scharff, MD, is Co-Director of the International Psychotherapy Institute, Clinical Professor of Psychiatry at Georgetown University, and Teaching Analyst at the Washington Psychoanalytic Institute.

David E. Scharff, MD, is Co-Director of the International Psychotherapy Institute, Clinical Professor of Psychiatry at Georgetown University and at the Uniformed Services University of the Health Sciences, and Teaching Analyst at the Washington Psychoanalytic Institute.

The Legacy of Fairbairn and Sutherland

Psychotherapeutic applications

Edited by Jill Savege Scharff and David E. Scharff

Routledge
Taylor & Francis Group

LONDON AND NEW YORK

First published 2005
by Routledge
27 Church Road, Hove, East Sussex, BN3 2FA

Simultaneously published in the USA and Canada
by Routledge
270 Madison Avenue, New York NY 10016

Routledge is an imprint of the Taylor & Francis Group

Typeset in Times by RefineCatch Ltd, Bungay, Suffolk
Printed and bound in Great Britain by
TJ International Ltd, Padstow, Cornwall
Paperback cover design by Lisa Dynan

This publication has been produced with paper manufactured
to strict environmental standards and with pulp derived from
sustainable forests.

British Library Cataloguing in Publication Data
A catalogue record for this book is available from the British Library

Library of Congress Cataloging-in-Publication Data
The legacy of Fairbairn and Sutherland / edited by Jill Savege Scharff
and David E. Scharff.
      p.   cm.
   Includes bibliographical references and index.
   ISBN 1-58391-731-4 (hbk.: alk. paper) – ISBN 1-58391-732-2
(pbk.: alk. paper)
   1.Psychoanalysis—Philosophy.   2.Psychoanalysis—Methodology.
3. Psychotherapy.   I. Scharff, Jill Savege.   II. Scharff, David E., 1941–.
III. Title.
   RC506.L427 2005
   616.89′17–dc22   2004020813

ISBN 1-58391-731-4 (hbk)
ISBN 1-58391-732-2 (pbk)

For Ellinor Fairbairn Birtles and Anne Sutherland

Contents

PART II
Sutherland and Fairbairn   185

Contributors

Editors

Jill Savege Scharff, MD, Washington DC, USA. Co-Director, International Psychotherapy Institute (IPI) and Chair of the IPI Psychoanalytic Training Program. Clinical Professor of Psychiatry at Georgetown University, Teaching Analyst at the Washington Psychoanalytic Institute. She is in private practice in psychoanalysis and psychotherapy with adults and children in Chevy Chase, MD. She is the author of *Projective and Introjective Identification and the Use of the Therapist's Self* (1992), and senior author with David E. Scharff on *Tuning the Therapeutic Instrument: Affective Learning of Psychotherapy* (2000), *Object Relations Individual Therapy* (1998), *Object Relations Therapy of Physical and Sexual Trauma* (1996), and *A Primer of Object Relations Therapy* (1992). She edited *The Autonomous Self: The Work of John D. Sutherland* (1994) and *Foundations of Object Relations Family Therapy* (1992). Formerly Chair, Object Relations Theory and Therapy Program Washington School of Psychiatry (1993–1994).

David E. Scharff, MD, Washington DC, USA. Co-Director International Psychotherapy Institute (IPI), Chevy Chase Maryland, and Chair of the IPI Object Relations Training Program. Clinical Professor of Psychiatry Georgetown University and at the Uniformed Services University of the Health Sciences, Teaching Analyst, Washington Psychoanalytic Institute. Past Director of the Washington School of Psychiatry (1987–1994). He is in private practice in psychoanalysis and psychotherapy in Chevy Chase, MD. His books include *Fairbairn and Relational Theory Today* (ed. with F. Perreira 2001), *The Psychoanalytic Century: Freud's Legacy for the Future (ed. 2000)*, *Fairbairn Then and Now* (ed. with N. Skolnick 1998), *From Instinct to Self* (ed. with E. Birtles 1994), *Object Relations Theory and Practice* (ed. 1994), *Refinding the Object and Reclaiming the Self* (1992), *The Sexual Relationship* (1982). He is senior co-author with Jill Savege Scharff of *Object Relations Couple Therapy* (1991), and *Object Relations Family Therapy* (1987).

Contributors

Theresa Aiello, PhD, New York, USA. Associate Professor, New York University Ehrenkrantz School of Social Work, recipient of NYU distinguished teaching award; supervisor, Child and Adolescent Analytic Training Program at National Institute for the Psychotherapies. Publications: *Child and Adolescent Treatment for Social Work Practices: A Relational Perspective for Beginning Clinicians*. Co-editor: *Love and Attachment: Contemporary Issues and Treatment Considerations*.

Ron B. Aviram, PhD, New York, USA. Licensed clinical psychologist. Published journal articles on prejudice, social identity theory, substance abuse and attention deficit disorder. William Allanson White Institute and private practice in New York City.

Carl Bagnini, MSW, BCD, Long Island, USA. Clinical social worker on the faculties of St John's University Post-doctoral Program in Couple and Family Therapy and the Suffolk Institute of Psychoanalysis and Psychotherapy and is in private practice in Port Washington, New York. He contributed to *Tuning the Therapeutic Instrument: Affective Learning of Psychotherapy* (2000). He is Chair of the Couple, Child and Family Therapy Program at IPI Washington and Chair of IPI Long Island.

Rubén Mario Basili, MD, Buenos Aires, Argentina. Psychiatrist, Training and Supervising Analyst, Associación Psicoanalítica, Argentina. Professor of Psychiatry (Faculty of Medicine, Universidad de Buenos Aires-UBA). Professor in the seminars of the Argentine Psychoanalytical Association. Publications in Spanish on the English school of psychoanalysis, and on borderline and narcissistic conditions.

Ellinor Fairbairn Birtles, BA, Edinburgh, Scotland. Scholar of the history of ideas, especially the origins of Fairbairn's thinking. Daughter of W. R. D. Fairbairn.

Torbjörn Borgegård, Uppsala, Sweden. Head of the Uppsala office of St Luke 1998–2004; Marriage Counsellor 1972–1978; Rector for the St Luke Educational Institute 1979–1997; Licensed psychologist and psychotherapist at the office of St Luke in Uppsala 1976–2004.

Judith Brearley, BA, AIMSW, Edinburgh, Scotland. Senior Lecturer in Social Work, Edinburgh University for 20 years. Psychoanalytic psychotherapist and medical social worker treating individuals, families, and groups. Teacher of child psychotherapy, supervisor of couple counsellors, and organizational consultant to health, education, and social services, volunteer agencies, and churches. Publications include *Counselling and Social Work*, and chapters and journal articles on application of psychodynamic concepts, abuse in the workplace, anxiety and the management of change.

Graham Clarke, PhD, Colchester, England. Works in the Department of Computer Science at the University of Essex and does some teaching in the Centre for Psychoanalytic Studies where he completed his doctorate on 'Fairbairn's Psychology of Dynamic Structure: Psychic Change, Creativity and Mature Dependence' (2002). He has an MA in Psychoanalytic Studies (1995) from the Tavistock/University of East London, an MSc in Computing (1977) and a BSc in Architecture (1964). He has published papers on an object relations approach to cinema in *Free Associations* (1994) and the *British Journal of Psychotherapy* (2003), and on Fairbairn and Macmurray published in the *Journal of Critical Realism*.

Hope Cooper, MSW, Williamsburg, USA. Clinical social worker specializing in child therapy and infant observation. Publications on infant development. Fellow of International Psychotherapy Institute.

Bernhard F. Hensel, MD, Giessen, Germany. Psychiatrist, psychotherapist and psychoanalyst. Member, training analyst and supervisor of the German Psychoanalytical Society (DPV), IPA and the Institute of Psychoanalysis and Psychotherapy in Giessen. Publications: Foreword to the German edition of Fairbairn's *Psychoanalytic Studies*, co-editor of Fairbairn's writing in German, author of journal articles on psychoanalysis in German.

Colin Kirkwood, MA Hons, MSc, Senior Lecturer in Counselling and Coordinator of the Centre for Counselling Studies, Moray House School of Education, University of Edinburgh; Psychoanalytic Psychotherapist, Marriage Counsellor. Member of: Scottish Institute of Human Relations; Scottish Association of Psychoanalytical Psychotherapists; British Confederation of Psychotherapists; COSCA (Counselling and Psychotherapy Scotland); British Association for Counselling and Psychotherapy. Publications on counselling and society, attunement, persons-in-relation perspective in counselling.

Una McCluskey, D Phil (York), BSocSc (UCD), DipSW, CQSW (Edinburgh), York, England. Senior Lecturer in Social Work, University of York, UK. Publications on Individual, Family, Couple and Group Therapy, Attachment, Abuse and Neglect.

Stephen Plumlee, PhD, Sarasota, USA. Psychologist, mental health counsellor, marriage and family therapist, Imago relationship therapy clinician, and ordained orthodox priest.

Peter Potthoff, MD, Ratingen, Germany. Psychiatrist, training and supervising psychoanalyst of German Psychoanalytical Association. Group Analyst. Teaches Fairbairn and Sutherland at the Köln-Düsseldorf Psychoanalytic Institute and to the German Psychoanalytical Association (together with Sabine Wollnik). Publications on Fairbairn, Sutherland,

Negative Therapeutic Reaction (together with Sabine Wollnik), Group Dynamics, Supervision in the Psychiatric Hospital, Self Support Groups.

Rainer Rehberger, MD, Seefelden, Germany. Internist, psychoanalyst, member IPA, GPA, private practice in Frankfurt/Main until 1995, now in Seefelden, Germany, teacher at the Sigmund Freud Institute and at conferences of the German Psychoanalytical Association. Co-worker in psychoanalytical research projects on heart infarction and rheumatoid arthritis at the Sigmund Freud Institute and the University Clinic Department for Psychotherapy and Psychosomatics, Frankfurt. Publications include journal articles on psychoanalytical training, psychotherapy and psychosomatics, and the second generation of Shoah; author in German of *Fear of Abandonment and Separation Anxiety* (1999), co-editor of Fairbairn's writings in German (2000), author of *Fear of Mourning* (2004).

Ricardo Juan Rey, MD, Buenos Aires, Argentina. Physician, Associate Professor of Internal Medicine, Fundación Barceló School of Medicine, Buenos Aires; Candidate, Psychoanalytical Association of Buenos Aires.

Ute Rupprecht-Schampera, DP, Tübingen, Germany. Psychologist and psychoanalyst, teaching member of the Institute of Stuttgart-Tubingen. Publications on hysteria and hypochondria. Paper on early triangulation in *International Journal of Psychoanalysis*.

Lea de Setton, PhD, Panamá City, Republic of Panamá. Clinical psychologist, Faculty International Psychotherapy Institute Panamá and Washington. Chapter on time and endurance in psychotherapy (in press).

Isabel Sharpin de Basili, Buenos Aires, Argentina. Licensed clinical psychologist specializing in borderline phenomena. Associate member of the International Psychoanalytical Association and the Argentine Psychoanalytical Association, and full member of the Latin American Psychoanalytical Federation. Staff member of the Adventist Sanatorium of Belgrano District (Buenos Aires, Argentina). Regular member of the Argentine Psychoanalytical Congress in Rosario (Argentina, APA, IPA), and of other Latin American Congresses of FEPAL (Montevideo, Uruguay; Guadalajara, Mexico). Her written papers have appeared in the "Revista de Psicoanálisis," "Comunicaciones científicas preliminares," and yearly symposia, all published by the Argentine Psychoanalytical Association.

Neville Singh, RMN, Edinburgh, Scotland. Staff Counsellor to Lothian Primary Care NHS Trust. Formerly Senior Nurse, Psychotherapy and Support Staff to Mental Health Unit, Royal Edinburgh Hospital. Publications on psychotherapy and family therapy with adolescents, and psychoanalysis in the post-industrial society.

John D. Sutherland (1905–1991) was a psychoanalyst working in Great Britain with individuals, groups and communities. He was co-founder, Scottish Institute of Human Relations, Edinburgh, 1970; Consultant Psychotherapist, Royal Edinburgh Hospital, 1968–1974; Editor, *International Journal of Psycho-Analysis*, 1960; Medical Director of the Tavistock Clinic, London, 1947–1968; and author of *Fairbairn's Journey to the Interior*.

Carol Tosone, PhD, New York, USA. Associate Professor New York University Ehrenkrantz School of Social Work. Publications on feminine masochism.

Yolanda de Varela, MA, PhD is a clinical psychologist whose PhD thesis is on research into learning object relations concepts. She is in the private practice of individual, child, and couple psychotherapy in Panamá City, Republic of Panamá. She is a Past President of the Panamanian Psychological Association. Publications: chapters in *Tuning the Therapeutic Instrument: Affective Learning of Psychotherapy* (2000) and *Comparative Treatments for Relationship Dysfunction* (2000). Past Chair of the International Psychotherapy Institute (IPI) Panamá, and faculty member of IPI Washington.

Henri Vermorel, MD, PhD, Chambéry, France. Psychiatrist, clinical psychologist, and training psychoanalyst, Paris Psychoanalytic Society; teacher, University of Savoie, Chambéry, France. He is a former President of the Groupe Lyonnais de Psychanalyse, and former editor of Revue Française de Psychanalyse.

Sabine Vuaillat, PhD, Paris, France. Psychologist and psychotherapist, research psychologist and supervisor, University of Paris. Publication: *La personalité schizoide: l'apport original de Fairbairn*.

Sabine Wollnik, MD, Köln, Germany. Phychiatrist, psychotherapist, psychoanalyst, associate member German Psychoanalytical Society where she teaches Fairbairn course with P. Potthoff. Training psychotherapist and supervisor at the Köln-Düsseldorf Psychoanalytic Institute. Publications in German on Freud, Fairbairn, and negative therapeutic reaction.

Acknowledgements

The chapters in this volume have been created mainly from papers delivered at the Legacy of Fairbairn and Sutherland, a conference co-sponsored by the International Institute of Object Relations Therapy (now the International Psychotherapy Institute) of Chevy Chase, Maryland, USA and the Scottish Institute of Human Relations, Edinburgh, Scotland. The conference chairs were Jill Savege Scharff, David E. Scharff and Christine J. Wilson. We are tremendously grateful to Christine Wilson as the on-site conference chair: she took all the heat and all the hard decisions. We would like to thank the anonymous donor who provided scholarship assistance in support of the conference.

Chapter 16 is adapted from *The Handbook of Addiction Treatment for Women: Theory and Practice* edited by S. L. A. Straussner and S. Brown; Copyright © 2002 Jossey-Bass. Reprinted with permission of John Wiley & Sons, Inc.

Credit goes to the foreign language translators including Elizabeth Vorspohl who translated Dr Hensel's paper. Jill Scharff supervised the rewriting. Many thanks to our superb administrators Anna Innes in Chevy Chase and Pamela Sinclair in Edinburgh; without them, that conference, and this book, would not have happened. Jill's colleague Dr Michael Field of Perth surprised her by producing an unpublished paper by John D. Sutherland, which Jock had entrusted to him after one of his last seminars. Jock's daughter Anne was delighted by the idea of publishing this lost work and thinks that her late mother, Molly, would have been pleased too. We are grateful to Anne and to Mike for this precious gift. Lastly we would like to acknowledge Otto Kernberg and James Grotstein whose appreciation for the contributions of Fairbairn and Sutherland has been a source of inspiration and encouragement.

Part I

Fairbairn

Introduction to Part I

David E. Scharff

Fairbairn has been at the center of my interest since the beginning of my career. As a young psychiatric resident in Boston, I was being immersed in ego psychology, but I managed to find colleagues to introduce me to object relations theory. That interest was cemented on meeting Jill, who was working with Jock Sutherland at the time, and later on meeting members of the Fairbairn family, Cosmo, Annabel, and especially Ellinor with whom I have worked closely on editing some of Fairbairn's uncollected work over the last ten years.

Part I begins with my overview of Fairbairn's contributions to psychoanalytic theory and practice. Kirkwood and Birtles follow with scholarly papers placing Fairbairn in the philosophical context. Vermorel and Rehberger describe the impact that Fairbairn has had in France and Germany. Hensel demonstrates how he applies Fairbairn's views to understanding sexual dysfunction and perversion treated in individual psychoanalysis. The editors complement that chapter with a discussion of the role of satisfactory, rejecting and exciting objects in sexuality as they are revealed in analytic couple and sex therapy. Two German women authors revisit the topics of hysteria and dissociation. American child therapists match their clinical illustrations to Fairbairn's paper on child assault and to motivational systems theory respectively. The Argentinians use Fairbairn's endopsychic structure as the basis for a new systematization of psychopathology. A German and a French author discuss the analyst as an accepted or refuted object, real and in the transference. Part I concludes with an American paper on the tie to the bad object in couple relationships and a Swedish riff on Fairbairn's theories of art as objects of art themselves.

Chapter 1

The development of Fairbairn's theory

David E. Scharff

Fairbairn was a devoted psychoanalyst, original in his thinking, yet diligent in his study of Freud. He was interested in Freudian theory from early in his career, as we can see from the lecture notes he prepared for a psychology discussion class on "The Ego and the Id" at the University of Edinburgh (1928 in Birtles & Scharff 1994). The seeds of change are already there in his notes on his points for criticism, including the problem of how the superego could be repressed and at the same time be an agent of repression, a topic he explored in two papers, now printed together (1929a). In his thesis submitted for the MD degree in 1929 (1929b) he explored the relationship between the defenses of repression and dissociation in an original and scholarly way that is the forerunner of his thinking on the theory of the personality introduced 15 years later. Of particular interest is his study of Freud's libido theory (1930), in which he noted the difference between appetitive and reactive tendencies, a precursor to his idea of *aggression as a reactive tendency* (an aggressive reaction to frustration) as opposed to Freud's idea of *aggression as a drive* that was inbuilt from the beginning and not at all dependent on the reaction of the environment (1939a).

Very early on, Fairbairn saw the role of affects as having to do with giving meaning to relationships, and being determined by the relationship between the self and the environment. This was a different slant on affect than Freud's. Fairbairn's clinical papers were always couched in terms of object relations – beginning more than a decade in advance of the time that he actually formulated his object relations theory (1927). During the 1930s he wrote a number of interesting papers that he did not later see as having been central to his eventual contribution, but they were very substantial in themselves. For instance, his paper on child abuse (1935) and sexual assault (1939b), from the standpoint of both victim and perpetrator, are in advance of their time, and clinically useful today (see Chapter 15). Through the years, Fairbairn applied psychoanalysis to child development, education, general psychology, dentistry, and social issues.

The last major papers before object relations theory to come on to his screen were on the psychology of art, in one of which his point is that art is *"making something for fun"* (1938a: 384) and in the other, he speaks of the work of art as a restored object (1938b). As best I can understand it, Fairbairn's (1938a) aim in describing art as fun is to fit in with Freud's idea of the pleasure principle, but at the same time he includes Melanie Klein's idea about restitution, and draws heavily on her ideas of esthetics. Fairbairn (1938b) talks about the genesis of art as "the found object," which on the one hand connects emotionally with the object relations of the artist especially, and on the other hand elicits an aesthetic response from the beholder, with whose unconscious object relations it resonates. He has an idea of the artistic object itself being located at a transitional point between creator and perceiver (see Chapter 18).

Fairbairn's model of development

Then, we come to a great period of about five years of productivity, from 1940 to 1944, during which four seminal papers show Fairbairn's ideas moving steadily towards his final theory of object relations.

In the first paper on schizoid factors in the personality (1940), Fairbairn makes the hypothesis that the splitting of the object leads to splitting of the ego – a totally new idea in analytic thinking. He gives one of his really fine clinical descriptions characterizing the schizoid personality by its secret withdrawal from the world of external objects, overevaluation of the internal world, and fear that its love (not its hate as Klein thought) will destroy or damage the object. He was the first to identify the affect of the schizoid problem as one of futility connected to the hopelessness of ever being able to reach or remain connected to the object, Fairbairn concludes that schizoid people are unable to love or be loved for themselves. Splitting of the self to various degrees is found not only in pathology: Splitting is universal.

The second of these four central papers revises the psychopathology of psychosis and neurosis (1941). Fairbairn begins by restating the centrality of splitting, and goes on to give, for the first time, a fundamental revision of Freudian analysis. He asserts that libido is object seeking, not pleasure seeking as Freud thought, and that what is central to the developing infant and the person going through life is the need for relationships, not the need for gratification. This paper is unique in that he brings on line issues that he does not talk much about thereafter, although they remain important on their own. He conceptualizes growth as the movement from infantile dependence to mature dependence, rather than towards the development of a genital personality.

Fairbairn breaks up development into the stages of early oral development, represented by an attitude of taking in, sucking, and rejecting, and a later oral phase of biting alternating with sucking. The early oral phase is the pre-ambivalent stage, in which the object is a part object, the breast of the mother. Here he shows a marked influence of Klein's language of part objects. The late oral phase then is the one where ambivalence becomes possible. This corresponds to Klein's depressive position in which sucking and biting alternate. At this stage, the object is the mother who has the breast, not the breast itself. The whole mother gets *treated* at times as part object, but it is the whole mother who *is* the object.

Fairbairn then moves to a discussion of what he calls *a transitional process*. (When Winnicott (1951) later borrowed the term *transitional* and gave it a very different set of meanings, he still included the idea of the transition from the earliest aspects of dependence to later aspects.) In this transition, there is a dichotomy of the object. The object is split into good and bad, and is treated in unconscious fantasy as if it is inside or outside the self, or it may be regarded simply as internal contents. Mature dependence is the attitude of giving, in which accepted and rejected objects are both exteriorized. The outside world is recognized as having an independent life: It is not simply a function of a person's internal life. The person accepts the other as being a whole person with genitals who is capable of genital aspects of relationships. He writes: "The real point about the mature individual is not that the libidinal attitude is essentially genital, but that the genital relationship is essentially libidinal" (p. 32). This is quite different from Freud's view that the object is genitalized by the Oedipal child's sexual curiosity and desire. Fairbairn's insight asks us to rethink Freud's notion of sexual zones as being at the center of development. Fairbairn says that anality is not a stage of sexual development, but a frequent conversion phenomenon. He writes: "It is not a case of the individual being preoccupied with disposal at this stage because he is anal, but of his being anal because he is preoccupied at this stage with the disposal of contents" (p. 43). Body areas lend themselves to the expression of internal ways of handling relationships because they have similarity to the child's way of handling relationships at a given stage.

Fairbairn identifies four techniques of relating to the object during the transition from infantile to mature dependence. These are not developmentally sequenced: they are not linear syndromes, or phenomena. They are alternative ways of handling internal object relations, depending on whether the object is thought of as inside or outside the self. For instance, in the obsessional character or syndrome, the good, accepted object and the rejected object are both felt to be internal. The obsessional personality controls good and bad objects inside the self, and tries to order the world in accordance with this internal situation. In the paranoid syndrome or character, the good, accepted object is inside and the bad is outside, and so the person avoids the badness of the outside world that is felt as being aimed at the self. In the hysterical personality, the good object is outside and the bad object is inside, and so the person feels like a bad person who is constantly trying to reach the elusive good object which is out there. In the phobic person, both good objects and bad objects are outside the self and so aspects of the environment feel unsafe and must be avoided, because there is no security inside the self, but at the same time the person wants to find the good that is out there in the dangerous world by locating it in a person or place and clinging to it for safety.

The return of the repressed object

In the third paper on the repression and return of bad objects (1943a), Fairbairn manages a much tighter formulation. This paper is famous for its description of moral issues in dynamic form, and for his description of the repression and return of bad objects. The term "bad" used in reference to internal objects means that the objects are felt as libidinally bad: It is not that they are actually bad. The badness of objects is not, in the first instance, a moral issue, although it leads to the development of aspects of morality. The child takes in what is too painful to bear, does not accept the object because it feels bad, splits it off from the good part of the object, and represses the unaccepted, bad part in the individual unconscious. The fate of the repressed bad objects, however, is to return from the inside, but, through the frequently used defense of projection, the person feels as if they are coming back from the outside.

In this paper Fairbairn develops his famous idea of *conditional badness* as opposed to *unconditional badness*. This unique contribution is especially relevant now as therapists are called upon more and more to deal with forms of abuse. Abused children prefer to see themselves as bad, and their parental persecutors as good, because if the parent is acknowledged to be bad, then the child lives in a universe where there is no hope; but if the persecutor is good and the child is bad, then the child can try to reform, and be good so that there is hope of improvement. The situation is one of conditional badness, meaning that the child meets the conditions of being bad and deserving a bad situation. If the child were to recognize that the parent is bad regardless of the child's behavior, then the child's attempts to be good and create a good response would not change the situation at all, and there would be no hope of anything better. In that case, the badness is said to be unconditional: In effect the child says, "If I can't be good, then I'll make evil my good," expressing attachment to a bad object that is libidinized.

Fairbairn illustrates this point with reference to Freud's (1923) story of a destitute artist who, when he fell into a melancholic state on the death of his father, made a pact with the Devil as a father substitute. Sutherland, who was the one to recognize the relevance of Freud's case for Fairbairn's point that the attraction to evil reflects the attachment to the bad object, advised Fairbairn that he "would find it a good story" (Sutherland 1989: 121). Fairbairn certainly found the story useful to support his line of thinking, and also noted that the man in the story was relieved of his demoniacal possession only when he invoked the aid of a good object. Fairbairn uses Freud's example to prove his point that it is the libidinal tie to the bad object that resists analysis, and that giving up that attachment to the bad object cannot happen until the analyst becomes installed as a good object.

Fairbairn's model of psychic structure

In the fourth paper, on endopsychic structure, Fairbairn's formulation of the organization of the personality now comes into view. Here is Fairbairn's own diagram given in that paper (1944: 105; see Figure 1.1). Fairbairn's ideas come together in, and are illustrated by, the dream of a patient, which displays the five parts of the ego that he identified that year. Incidentally, he uses the term ego throughout, keeping intact his lineage from Freud, even though early in his writing he had coined the term "the organized self." But when Guntrip said later that he believed that Fairbairn really did mean the self, Fairbairn agreed. (In my way of thinking, I tend to use the term *ego* when I'm talking about mechanisms of psychic organization, and to use the term *self* when talking about the person's internal experience.)

In Fairbairn's terms, there is the *central ego*, the part most associated with consciousness and preconscious organization, which splits parts off into unconscious space organized into two categories of bad objects – the rejecting and exciting constellations. The persecuting or *rejecting object*, which feels bad because it is based on experience with a mother who is neglectful, does not respond, or responds in an angry, persecutory way, pulls with it into repression an *antilibidinal ego*. Fairbairn introduces the term *the internal saboteur* which even more vividly and parsimoniously conveys the essence of the antilibidinal ego, which because of its tie to the rejecting object, repeatedly undermines the efforts of the self.

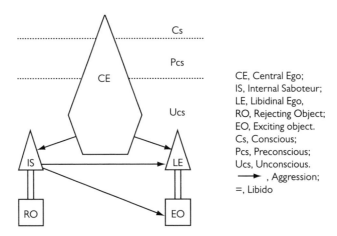

Figure 1.1 Fairbairn's original depiction of his object relations theory of personality. Reprinted from *Psychoanalytic Studies of the Personality* (1952) with permission of Routledge.

The mother who stimulates longing by overfeeding, hovering anxiously, overdoing a good thing, is experienced and taken in as a painfully *exciting object* and repressed along with a *libidinal ego*. The objects and their egos are joined by their characteristic affects: for the rejecting object constellation, the affects are rage, sadness, and despair; for the exciting object constellation, the affects are unrequited love, anxious neediness, and craving. In the case of those who become perpetual victims, part of the libidinal ego may be fused with the antilibidinal ego, which adds to their suffering, in which they revel.

Fairbairn is in line with Winnicott and Freud and all the theorists of their time in ignoring fathers during the first three years of life. In a modern organization of this set of ideas, we must include both parents. Then we can say that the rejecting or exciting objects are based on experience with both parents. This does not mean that a given parent is necessarily actually treating a child badly. It is simply inevitable that the parents cannot be there every moment and cannot always understand the child correctly, or that they some-times overstimulate the child's needs while trying to satisfy them. There are always some aspects of parenting that the child feels as intolerably bad, and represses the experience as a rejecting or exciting object along with the anti-libidinal and libidinal ego respectively. There are other cases in which the parents are actually bad to various degrees. When they are truly persecutory, the need for splitting is pronounced, and at the extreme in the vulnerable child leads to multiple splits in the self with sharp divisions between them. This aspect of Fairbairn's dynamic formulation is most useful in understand-ing what happens in childhood trauma, and how it is transmitted to the next generation (an aspect that is also being addressed by attachment research, a direct descendent of object relations theory).

The *ideal object*, a good object which remains in consciousness at the centre of the self, is internalized in a less vivid form, being mixed in with the central ego anyway, and carried forward as a general sense of confidence about the world. Fairbairn did not describe a central good object in the first version of the 1944 paper, and he does not locate it in his diagram. So he did not actually have an object for the central ego in that formulation. I'm not sure exactly what year he realized he'd left it out. The ideal object is most clearly described in the hysterical states paper (1954). By then, he had formu-lated it in reference to the narrowing of the range of the good object by the hysteric.

My own diagram (Figure 1.2), which I modified from an early sketch by Alan Cooklin (personal communication), shows the ideal object belonging with the central ego, and the rejecting and exciting objects belonging inside the thoroughly unconscious matrix of the ego. Fairbairn does clearly say that these internal object relationships take the external objects as their models, and become parts of the self that are capable of generating activity and thought, which we see for instance when a patient is taken over by ideas about her mother, and treats her therapist the way her mother treated her. At that

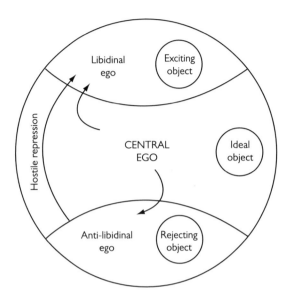

Figure 1.2 Fairbairn's model of psychic organization. The central ego in relation to the ideal object is in conscious interaction with the caretaker. The central ego represses the split off libidinal and antilibidinal aspects of its experience along with corresponding parts of the ego and relevant affects that remain unconscious. The libidinal system is further repressed by the antilibidinal system. Copyright © 1982 David Scharff. Reprinted from *The Sexual Relationship* with permission from Rowman & Littlefield Publishers, Inc.

point, the patient is organized by the internal object, which, however, is always embedded in the larger ego or self. Fairbairn is clear in his original formulation that these objects are parts of the ego. Similarly, the ideal object becomes part of the central ego, but how much of it is conscious and how much unconscious is a matter of debate.

In his paper on hysterical states (1954), Fairbairn describes hysterical patients, who, being unable to stand much seduction or much rejection, try to find an object that does not threaten them either with excitement or rejection. Consequently they have a stripped bare ideal object. Fairbairn describes the ideal object best when describing the pathological type in hysteria, and so he never gives a description of the ordinary good object of the central ego in the healthy state. I prefer to call the ideal object *the good-enough object*, borrowing Winnicott's term, because the term *ideal* carries the negative Kleinian connotation of being overidealized.

It is in describing the exciting object constellation that Fairbairn makes one of his great contributions. Neither Freud nor Klein had explained how, if something is too good, it is a problem. For instance, it is impossible to think about the pathologies of sex without having a concept of the exciting object and why it is libidinally bad. Also clinically useful is his description of the way in which the internal saboteur of the antilibidinal ego in hysteria launches an attack on the exciting object constellation because it is too painful to long for an object that will not give satisfaction. He called this attack *secondary hostile repression*. Hysterics attack and repress the exciting object constellation further so they can remain unaware of their longing because the pangs of desire are more painful than the awareness of anger. For instance, a husband and wife who fight like cats and dogs stay together because their fighting serves to repress their shared longing, so that they are spared the pain of unrequited love.

Fairbairn's model is clinically useful, but it is limited in not specifically allowing for modification due to the influence of relationships over time. In his theory, the more something is repressed, the more fixed the personality appears to become. He is describing only one of the internal dynamics, unable to think about the personality as an open system that influences and is influenced by external experience continually throughout adult life. Yet he does see the parts in movement and in relation to each other. Indeed it is a theory of dynamic internal object relations. That is a major step beyond Freud, and much clearer than Klein, but it does not get us there fully. There are a number of places where he is right on the threshold, but he does not take the next step.

Nevertheless, he makes it easy for us to do so. Henry Dicks (1967) was the first to see how one personality connects with the internal situations of others. By invoking Klein's concept of projective identification in coordination with Fairbairn's theory of endopsychic structure, Dicks could conceptualize how two personalities can be in a state of deep unconscious communication in intimate relationships in adult life. We can now also see how the endopsychic situation is projected in the transference and gives rise to countertransference identifications with projected part objects and part egos. So Fairbairn helped us towards the use of countertransference as the crucial guidance mechanism for the therapist, but I think he did not understand the transference–countertransference dialectic, and Guntrip (1975) skewered him for that.

I have shown the attack from the antilibidinal ego on the exciting object constellation, as Fairbairn described it originally (see Figure 1.2). It captures the basic nature of the endopsychic situation as a dynamic one. I must add that the libidinal ego can attack the antilibidinal constellation as well. I see this in patients who come in looking too good to be true because they attack their own aggression, and push it underground. Usually that means that the aggression goes into their therapists who may feel ready to throttle them for their sanctimoniousness. The multiple projection of parts of ego and object works in all directions. In health, there is dynamic flux back and forth. It is in ill health that it gets fixed and stuck, as Fairbairn shows.

Other contributions in the paper on endopsychic structure (1944)

In the endopsychic structure paper (1944), Fairbairn introduces the concept of dreams as summaries of psychic structure, illustrates his point with the dream of a woman patient, and follows with his diagram of endopsychic structure. This paper is also one of two places where he discusses the Oedipal situation, which he says begins with infantile deprivation and trauma that drive the splitting of the object and the ego to extremes of dissociation. He notes that in psychology, as in drama, the first act is as important as the last act. What Freud picked from the story of Oedipus was the last act of the story – but the first act is one of abandonment and trauma which disrupt the young child's endopsychic development. In Fairbairn's view of the Oedipal conflict, the child invents a situation to account for ambivalence about the mother as a primary object, who is thought to be both good and bad, both accepted and rejected. The child, aware of the mother's intimate partnership with the father, resolves ambivalence about the mother and the parental couple by accepting one parent as the good object, and making the other the bad object; one the exciting object, and one the rejecting object. A good enough mother may be seen as rejecting and the father as exciting. Fathers behave in stimulating ways: they come in and throw their kids up and down, bounce them around a little bit, and then they take off, and the kids forgive them, whereas mothers have a quieter, longer term attitude, equipped to stay there all day and take the flack, soothe and comfort. We now know that these gender differences and stereotypical behaviors may pull for the projection of rejection into the mother and excitement into the father, on the basis of a hard-wired predisposition in the child, but Fairbairn shows that the social construction produced by the infant's endopsychic situation is key.

On the nature of hysterical states

Now I will move through some of the later papers. In the paper on the nature of hysterical states (1954), Fairbairn reminds us that hysteria is the problem that Freud and Janet dealt with, and it led them to theories of dissociation and conversion, and to psychoanalytic technique. Fairbairn reopens the question of repression versus dissociation, which he had first addressed in his MD thesis in 1929, and concludes that repression is a special case of dissociation, the repression of painful contents. The field of psychoanalysis ignored the phenomenon of dissociation for years – dissociated from it as it were – but in the last 25 years it has returned to the forefront because of current interest in the study of trauma.

The dreams that Fairbairn cites as representing the hysterical problem also show the dynamics of personality organization. This is the second place where Fairbairn uses dreams to great advantage, in this case showing that they are not always governed by the pleasure principle and wish fulfillment.

He thinks of dreams as statements both of psychic structure and the formulation of a dynamic problem. He shows that the dreams of hysterical patients are filled with scenes and elements of excitement alternating with rejection that recall the influence of experiences of rapidly alternating excessive excitement and rejection in childhood, which, he believes, cause hysterical organization.

In the paper on hysterical states, Fairbairn's clinical reporting is excellent and he gives us the material we need to understand his theory, and to develop our own ideas about the illustrative cases. He gives his patient Jack's dream of a leopard who sidles around. To me it appears that in the leopard dream Jack is absolutely furious at Fairbairn in the transference. I see it as a dream about transference aggression, but Fairbairn does not write about transference in detail and ignores the transference aspect that I see in that dream.

As an aside, I might mention that Hughes (1989) has informed us that Jack is a pseudonym for Harry Guntrip, Fairbairn's most famous patient and expositor (Guntrip 1961, 1969). In Guntrip's (1975) paper on his analyses with Fairbairn and Winnicott, Guntrip claims that Fairbairn did not understand him as well as his subsequent analyst, Winnicott. I would guess that Fairbairn did not interpret the aggression and the transference as directly as Guntrip would have liked and needed, but then I also think that Guntrip felt he needed a good thrashing. It seems to me that, when he did not get it, he gave it to Fairbairn instead.

In this (1954) paper, Fairbairn goes on to discuss the nature of conversion. Where Freud saw bodily symptoms as representing traumatic memories, Fairbairn sees conversion as the process of substitution of a bodily problem for an emotional one. The patient speaks through a part of the body that resembles the problem to be expressed, and so is used to symbolize it, which brings some psychic relief. Body language is needed because the trauma that produced the problem has occurred before words are acquired or has overwhelmed the capacity for verbal thinking.

Finally, in a nifty turn of thought, Fairbairn claims that Freud's theory of psychosexual development is itself a conversion phenomena, using oral, anal, and phallic zones to speak for emotional development. A child uses these parts of the body to express developmental issues and problems, because they lend themselves to these expressions, not because they are responsible for them. The problem to be represented is how to relate to somebody, and a body zone is the focus of that effort.

The Schreber case

The paper on Schreber (1956) is important: Fairbairn examines Freud's explanation of paranoia and schizophrenia based on drive theory, but also does connect Schreber's mental organization to his experience with his father. According to Fairbairn, Freud's study of contributions to Schreber's homosexuality missed the fact that aggression against the father covers aggression against the mother. Fairbairn says that anality in paranoia represents the use of the excretory function both as a physical and symbolic expression of the projection of bad contents as an attack on the bad objects. He uses this study to say that his understanding of endopsychic structure applies just as much to the study of psychosis as to neurosis. Then he discusses the primal scene, which he does not do often, saying that it is the avoidance of the primal scene in psychosis and paranoia that leads to schizoid withdrawal. Hatred of the primal scene leads to confusional states over an identification with an aggressive mother and a libidinal desire for the father. This confusion is coupled with a denial of the heterosexual primal scene – the sexual aspect of the link between the parental objects – and the confusional state leads to psychosis and paranoia.

On the nature and aims of psychoanalytical treatment

Lastly we arrive at a most important paper on the nature and aims of psychoanalytical treatment (1958). Here, Fairbairn says that it is the relationship with the therapist that is the defining element in therapy. Everything else depends on the centrality of that relationship. Therapy consists of work by the therapist to breach the patient's internally closed system. Resistance is the patient's attempt to keep the system impenetrable to outside influences, and the therapist's job is to breach that inner closed system. Fairbairn sees the organized self as a dynamic open system of the interrelationship of the self and its objects, which are influenced by, determine the nature of, and monitor that external relationship.

Fairbairn's object relations theory, which holds that what is central to development is the need to seek a relationship rather than pleasure, is a fundamental reorientation of analytic theory. The response of analysts in the United States has largely been to ignore Fairbairn. To the extent that he was known, he was not appreciated, because the American analysts stayed loyal to drive/structural theory until about 20 years ago. At that point, they not only converted, but acted as if they had known it all along, and still do not acknowledge Fairbairn's influence on the paradigm shift that has occurred. They are more likely to credit Winnicott and Klein, many of whose ideas purported to stay loyal to drive theory even though object relational. Since their ideas did not amount to consistent theories, they could be taken in more easily as pieces of a collage and pasted on to a drive/structure background.

Differences between Fairbairn and Klein

The disagreements between Fairbairn and Klein can be summarized as follows. Fairbairn says that aggression is a secondary phenomenon. He asked if infants were never frustrated, why would they ever show aggression? On the contrary, Klein said that aggression was innate from the beginning – a position I agree with. Fairbairn says that the introjection of the good object is a secondary phenomenon to make up for the introjection of the bad object. The baby internalizes and represses the bad object to get control of an unsatisfying situation, and then takes in the good object to fortify itself against the internalized bad object. Klein says that taking in the good object under the influence of the life instinct is fundamental from the beginning. Fairbairn is developing his views on introjection to be compatible with his view of aggression as a reactive tendency, and Klein is developing hers to stay true to the death instinct. The main difference between the views of Fairbairn and Klein is one of emphasis. Klein stresses mechanisms of projection: Fairbairn stresses mechanisms of introjection. Each of them is aware that both processes occur and that both of them alter the self. It was Bion (1970) in his paper container/contained who showed that both processes occur in a continuous cycle. We need to credit the influence of introjection and projection as equally crucial mechanisms in the construction of the self.

Fairbairn voiced his disagreement with Klein during the controversial discussions of 1943 (1943b; King and Steiner 1991). The debate concerned whether the best way to think about the structure of the unconscious was to use Klein's idea of unconscious phantasy or Fairbairn's concept of internal ego and object relationships. Fairbairn sent his response to Susan Isaacs's paper on unconscious phantasy, which Dr. Glover read for him, but the Kleinian view remained the dominant one in the political climate of the British Psychoanalytic. To my mind, Klein's idea of unconscious phantasy is a general notion whereas Fairbairn's idea of structure of self and object is a more rigorous theoretical formulation, and for that reason more useful to me.

Conclusion

Fairbairn freed us from the rigid hold that Freudian analysis had on thinking in the first half of the twentieth century, as Freud freed psychology from the hold of nineteenth-century ideas. Both were trapped by their backgrounds, and the culture of their time, but both gave something that opened a new universe to us. It is up to us to continue the evolution. Fairbairn understood that there had been a scientific revolution from the nineteenth through the twentieth century, from the limiting linearity of the physics of thermodynamics to the theory of relativity where matter and energy can be exchanged (Scharff & Birtles 1994). Like matter and energy that are no longer seen as discrete, mental structure and mental contents are in a state of dynamic connectedness. Freud's ideas about psychosexual development are linear, like the principles of thermodynamics, or mechanical physics, whereas Fairbairn's idea of internal object relations is dynamic, like the theory of relativity.

I will conclude with an attempt to put my elaborations of Fairbairn's theory of endopsychic structure in psychopathology on one diagram, as he did in his 1963 synopsis in the *International Journal of Psycho-Analysis*. For his theory to be a general psychology for health as well as for illness, we need to make some modifications. That is what my diagram tries to show (Figure 1.3). Starting at the center of the personality as Fairbairn did, I show the central ego relating to the ideal object. This ideal object (or as I prefer to call it, the good-enough object) is based on a parental object with comfortably arousing (not smothering or overexciting) and limit-setting (not rejecting) qualities. Experience of needs being met has been adequate, not too stimulating, not too withholding, not too severe or overwhelming in either direction, and therefore not in need of repression. This object is in touch with, and may overlap with, the excessively rejecting and excessively exciting aspects of objects. Repressed objects may become more or less rejecting or exciting due to the modifying effects of new experiences in the course of development or in therapy, and so become more or less distinguishable from the good-enough object of the central ego. All these objects are embedded in the self. The intolerably bad, rejecting object results from an experience with a parent who is seen as non-understanding and who sets severe limits on dependency. The exciting object constellation results from a parent who does not set such

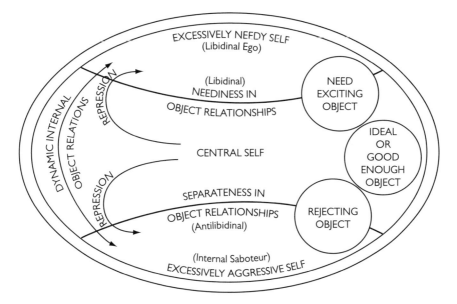

Figure 1.3 Amplification of Fairbairn's model of psychic organization. Neediness and separateness are aspects of the central self. Exciting and rejecting objects partly communicate with the ideal object and are partly repressed. All aspects of self and objects are in dynamic relations. Copyright © 1982 David Scharff. Reprinted from *Refinding the Object and Reclaiming the Self* with permission from Rowman & Littlefield Publishers, Inc.

limits, who is intrusive, and fosters overcloseness and neediness. It is only when the experiences are excessive that they are found to be intolerable, and must be split off, repressed, and organized as an endopsychic structure at the pathological end of the continuum. All of these aspects – ego, object, and the affects that connect them – are subject to internal dynamic shift in all directions. The center of this system is the central self, splitting off and repressing the rejecting and exciting aspects that are painful, but they remain in dynamic relation with each other. One pole (rejecting or exciting) can act against or repress the other. In my view, unconscious internal object relationships can and do repress aspects of the central ego, for instance in the case of the person who seems to have no life and lives in the withdrawn area of the self, so well described by Guntrip (1969).

I recognize that the ego has its mechanisms for maintaining its organization, but instead of talking about the ego and its objects, I prefer to follow Fairbairn's early lead in talking of the organized self. Especially when extending Fairbairn's theory to normal development, I think of an organized self as a structure with more or less integrity, and more or less fluidity of communication between parts. In a healthy individual, the central self is in command, but allows flux. For instance, the healthy woman, on a day when she is possessed by her critical mother may feel that her admittedly successful husband has not tried hard enough. On another day, she may feel beaten down by him as if he were her competitive father. The next day, when she recovers the balance of central self functioning, she feels appreciative of her husband and returns to a sense of well-being. The point is that in pathology the demeanour of the anxious and depressed person is distressingly restricted, and in the manic and borderline person fluctuates wildly, but the demeanour of a healthy person varies in ways that are tolerable to the person, welcome to the family, and enriching to the unconscious communication that underpins intimacy.

In health, our internal structure is not static: it consists of processes that change. Only in pathology do processes get rigidified and behaviors become repetitive. As therapists, we use our knowledge and our own endopsychic structure in interaction with the patients' structure to help them heal their splits, develop a capacity for internal communication between parts of the self, and become flexible in relating to others and open to modifying the self by learning from experience.

References

Bion, W. (1970). *Attention and Interpretation*. London: Tavistock.
Birtles, E. F. and Scharff, D. E. (1994). Introduction to Part I. In *From Instinct to Self: Vol. 2*, pp. 3–5. Northvale, NJ: Jason Aronson.
Dicks, H. V. (1967). *Marital Tensions: Clinical Studies towards a Psychoanalytic Theory of Interaction*. London: Routledge & Kegan Paul.

Fairbairn, W. R. D. (1927). Notes on the religious phantasies of a female patient. In *Psycho-Analytic Studies of the Personality*, pp. 183–196. London, Henley and Boston: Routledge & Kegan Paul, 1952.

—— (1929a). The relationship of dissociation and repression: Considered from the point of view of medical psychology. MD thesis submitted to the University of Edinburgh 30 March 1929. Reprinted in *From Instinct to Self: Vol. 2*, eds E. F. Birtles and D. E. Scharff, pp. 39–79. Northvale, NJ: Jason Aronson, 1994.

—— (1929b). The superego. Reprinted in *Fron Instinct to Self: Vol. 2*, eds E. F. Birtles and D. E. Scharff, pp. 80–114. Northvale, NJ: Jason Aronson, 1994.

—— (1930). The libido theory: the theory of the pleasure principle interpreted in terms of appetite. Reprinted in *From Instinct to Self: Vol. 2*, eds E. F. Birtles and D. E. Scharff, pp. 115–156. Northvale, NJ: Jason Aronson, 1994.

—— (1935). Medico-psychological aspects of the problems of child assault. *Mental Hygiene* April, 13: pp. 1–16. In *From Instinct to Self: Vol. 2*, eds E. F. Birtles and D. E. Scharff, pp. 165–182. Northvale, NJ: Jason Aronson, 1994.

—— (1938a). Prolegomena to a psychology of art. *British Journal of Psychology* 28(3): 288–303. Reprinted in *From Instinct to Self: Vol. 2*, eds E. F. Birtles and D. E. Scharff, pp. 381–396. Northvale, NJ: Jason Aronson, 1994.

—— (1938b). The ultimate basis of aesthetic experience. *British Journal of Psychology* 29(2): 167–181. Reprinted in *From Instinct to Self: Vol. 2*, eds E. F. Birtles and D. E. Scharff, pp. 397–409. Northvale, NJ: Jason Aronson, 1994.

—— (1939a). Is aggression an irreducible factor? *British Journal of Medical Psychology* 18(2): 163–170. Reprinted in *From Instinct to Self: Vol. 2*, eds E. F. Birtles and D. E. Scharff, pp. 264–271. Northvale, NJ: Jason Aronson, 1994.

—— (1939b). The psychological factor in sexual delinquency. *Mental Hygeine* 5(2): 1–8. Reprinted in *From Instinct to Self: Vol. 2*, eds E. F. Birtles and D. E. Scharff, pp. 284–292. Northvale, NJ: Jason Aronson, 1994.

—— (1940). Schizoid factors in the personality. In *Psycho-Analytic Studies of the Personality*, pp. 3–27. London, Henley and Boston: Routledge & Kegan Paul.

—— (1941). A revised psychopathology of the psychoses and neuroses. *International Journal of Psycho-Analysis* 22(2,3): 250–279. In *Psycho-Analytic Studies of the Personality*, pp. 28–58. London, Henley and Boston: Routledge & Kegan Paul.

—— (1943a). The repression and return of bad objects (with special reference to the war neuroses). *British Journal of Medical Psychology* 19(3, 4): 327–341. In *Psycho-Analytic Studies of the Personality*, pp. 59–81. London, Henley and Boston: Routledge & Kegan Paul.

—— (1943b). Phantasy and internal objects. Paper presented by Dr Glover on 17 February 1943 at the British Psycho-Analytical Society in London in reply to Susan Isaac's paper "The Nature and Function of Phantasy". Published in the *Freud–Klein Controversies 1941–1945*, eds P. King and R. Steiner, pp. 358–360. London: Routledge Chapman Hall and the Institute of Psycho-Analysis, 1991.

—— (1944). Endopsychic structure considered in terms of object relationships. *International Journal of Psycho-Analysis* 27: 1270–1293. In *Psycho-Analytic Studies of the Personality*, pp. 82–136. London, Henley and Boston: Routledge & Kegan Paul.

—— (1952). *Psychoanalytic Studies of the Personality*. London, Henley, and Boston: Routledge & Kegan Paul.

—— (1954). Observations on the nature of hysterical states. *British Journal of Medical*

Psychology 27(3): 106–125. In *From Instinct to Self: Vol. 1*, eds D. E. Scharff and E. F. Birtles, pp. 13–40. Northvale, NJ: Jason Aronson, 1994.

—— (1956). Considerations arising out of the Schreber case. *British Journal of Medical Psychology* 29(2): 113–127. In *From Instinct to Self: Vol. 1*, eds D. E. Scharff and E. F. Birtles, pp. 41–60. Northvale, NJ: Jason Aronson, 1994.

—— (1958). On the nature and aims of psychoanalytical-treatment. *International Journal of Psycho-Analysis* 39(5): 374–385. In *From Instinct to Self: Vol. 1*, eds D. E. Scharff and E. F. Birtles, pp. 74–92. Northvale, NJ: Jason Aronson, 1994.

—— (1963). An object relations theory of the personality. *International Journal of Psycho-Analysis* 44: 224–225. In *From Instinct to Self: Vol. 1*, eds D. E. Scharff and E. F. Birtles, pp. 155–156. Northvale, NJ: Jason Aronson, 1994.

Freud, S. (1923). A neurosis of demoniacal possession in the seventeenth century. *Standard Edition* 19: 67–105.

Guntrip, H. (1961). *Personality and Human Interaction*. London: Hogarth.

—— (1969). *Schizoid Phenomena, Object Relations and the Self*. New York: International Universities Press.

—— (1975). My experience of analysis with Fairbairn and Winnicott. *International Review of Psycho-Analysis* 2: 145–156.

Hughes, J. (1989). *Reshaping the Psychoanalytic Domain*. Berkeley and Los Angeles: University of California Press.

Scharff, D. E. and Birtles, E. F. (1994). Introduction to Part 2. In *From Instinct to Self: Vol. 1*, eds. D. E. Scharff and E. F. Birtles, pp. 95–102. Northvale, NJ: Jason Aronson, 1994.

Sutherland, J. D. (1989). *Fairbairn's Journey into the Interior*. London: Free Association.

Winnicott, D. W. (1951). Transitional objects and transitional phenomena. In *Through Paediatrics to Psycho-Analysis*, pp. 229–242. London: Hogarth, 1975.

Chapter 2

The persons-in-relation perspective

Sources and synthesis

Colin Kirkwood

This chapter articulates a synthesis of the contributions of three great twentieth-century Scots: the philosopher John Macmurray (1891–1976), the psychotherapist Ian Suttie (1889–1935) and the psychoanalyst Ronald Fairbairn (1889–1965). I discuss the contributions of Macmurray and Suttie, indicate briefly the significance of Fairbairn's contributions, and identify some key themes of my synthesis, derived from a series of four papers, the first on Macmurray, the second on Suttie, the third on Fairbairn, and the final one a synthesis. Reflecting on my work in progress to date as if it were a football match, I would say that we are about two-thirds of the way through the first half.

The first paper, which discusses the application of the persons-in-relation perspective to counselling, based on John Macmurray's work, was published in the autumn 2003 issue of *Counselling and Psychotherapy Research*. The second paper nearing completion describes the contributions of Ian Suttie, who created in the 1930s an interpersonal and sociocultural psychology which has been unjustly neglected yet has been widely influential. The third paper to be written will be concerned with Ronald Fairbairn's revolutionary account of the interpersonal nature of the basic intrapersonal situation, drawing on his thinking about dissociation and repression, his relationship to the society of his day, and the links between his insights and his own difficulties, as these are explored by his biographer John D. Sutherland. The fourth and final paper will attempt to integrate these intrapersonal, interpersonal and sociocultural dimensions in a new synthesis.

Macmurray, Suttie, and Fairbairn all served in and were affected by World War I. They drew deeply (and in subtly different ways) on Scottish Christian traditions. They benefited from the Scottish educational tradition of training in philosophy which enabled them to challenge Freud's thinking with confidence and authority, without devaluing his contributions. Lest we might imagine that Suttie is the odd man out, the one who has gatecrashed the party, we must note that it was on Suttie's book, *The Origins of Love and Hate* (1935/1988) that John Macmurray based some of his own thinking about persons in relation. Although Fairbairn makes no reference to Suttie in his published work, we know from Sutherland and Guntrip that he was influenced by his writing. Harry Guntrip records that Fairbairn said to him: "Suttie really had something important to say" (Guntrip 1971/1977: 24). Similarly Fairbairn makes no reference to Macmurray in his writings, but we know from his daughter Ellinor Fairbairn Birtles (personal communication) that the men knew each other and may have collaborated, and we know that Harry Guntrip was deeply influenced by both of them and attempted to link their ideas in his own synthesis.

The last 15 years have seen renewed recognition of the contributions of Macmurray, Suttie and Fairbairn. Their works have been republished. There have been critical reassessments of Fairbairn and Macmurray and groundbreaking biographies of Ronald Fairbairn by Jock Sutherland (1989) and of John Macmurray by John Costello (2002). Their perspectives are now influencing thinking and practice worldwide. John Bowlby described Ian Suttie's book as "a robust and lucid statement of a paradigm that now leads the way", adding: "his ideas never died: they have smouldered on, at length to burst into flame" (Bowlby in Suttie 1935/1988: xv).

The contribution of John Macmurray

John Macmurray was a personalist. Personalism is a response to the distortions and hypocrisy of society and religion in the nineteenth and twentieth centuries, a response which does not discard religion but seeks both to rediscover and reinvent its core meaning and revitalize its practice. The key ideas are that human beings are persons, each of whom is uniquely valuable, that the heart of their being lies in their relations with other persons, and that the self-realization of persons-in-community is an end-in-itself which should not be subordinated to other ends. This radical social perspective shares the goals of human liberation and social justice with communism and social democracy, but it holds that these ends cannot be achieved by subordinating the personal to the structural or by worshipping the state. Personalism has its roots in the life of Christ and in aspects of the Jewish tradition, and takes a very specific, relational view of God as we shall see.

Macmurray, like Fairbairn, grew up as an idealistic and committed Christian. The experience of fighting in the trenches in World War I radically reshaped Macmurray's view of religion. He was never tempted to abandon it, but from then on he distinguished between personal Christianity and the spurious Christianity of religious organizations, which he called the national religions of Europe. He did not join a church until he retired in 1959, when he relented and joined the Quakers, perhaps the least institutional form of Christianity.

Macmurray had a successful academic career. He lived a life of commitment, opposing fascism, engaging in dialogue with communism and in the struggle for world friendship and justice through the Christian Left. He affirmed *friendship* as the core value. Macmurray analyses the causes of World War I not primarily in terms of imperial rivalries, but in terms of distortions in values and actions. He highlights pervasive hypocrisy, sentimentality, the substitution of gross materialism for spiritual yearnings, the myth of progress, and the deliberate cultivation of hatred of other nations, "the demonisation of the 'Other' – in order to hide inner contradictions and to enhance a self-image of moral righteousness" (Costello 2002: 168). Against this, he affirms an apparently simple alternative: cultivation of the personal life.

Knowledge, the senses and the emotions

Macmurray describes his philosophical position as grounded in the standpoint of action, or agency. He starts from a rejection of Descartes' *I think, therefore I am*. Macmurray argues that this is a standpoint which isolates the self from others, splits mind from body, the spiritual from the material, and separates thinking from sense experience, feeling and action. Against the egocentric assumption that the self is an isolated individual, he puts forward the view that the self is a person, and that personal existence is *constituted* by our relations with other persons. He substitutes the "You and I" for the solitary "I" (Macmurray 1995c: 11–12).

Against Descartes' disembodied subject, who observes and thinks in isolation, Macmurray proposes the primacy of the self as agent, confronted with other selves, each of whom reflects upon his or her activity. Action is primary. Thinking is vital but secondary, a subordinate activity which serves action. Reason, or rationality – a much wider concept than thinking – begins in sense perception and crucially involves the emotions, which are the sources of our motives and our evaluations. In a memorable phrase, he defines reason as "the capacity to behave consciously in terms of the nature of what is not ourselves" (Macmurray 1935: 19). In this connection, it is worth noting the extent to which Macmurray's thinking about the significance of relationships and emotions anticipates the findings of contemporary neuroscientists like Antonio Damasio (2000). In adopting this standpoint, Macmurray is seeking to overcome the objectification of the other. He writes: "I can isolate myself from you in intention, so that my relation to you becomes impersonal. In this event, I treat you as object, refusing the personal relationship" (Macmurray 1961: 28).

Forms of knowledge

Macmurray argues that the history of philosophy discloses three forms of knowledge:

- knowledge of the inanimate material world, which he links with mathematics, physics, the use of mathematical and mechanical metaphors, and formal logic

- knowledge of the organic world, expressed, for example, in biology, linked with the use of evolutionary and organic metaphors, and dialectical logic
- knowledge of the world of the personal, the highest and most comprehensive form of knowledge being the mutual knowledge of two persons.

Personal knowledge, he argues, subsumes or includes the material and organic forms of knowledge. It does not supplant them, but it does put them literally in their place. They are vital dimensions of the personal, but personal life cannot be reduced to them. Personal knowledge of someone or something is radically different from impersonal knowledge about something or someone. Macmurray makes a sharp distinction between *knowledge of* and *knowledge about*. Intellectual knowledge, which relies on concepts, gives us knowledge about things, not of them. (Macmurray 1935: 43).

To understand what Macmurray means by personal knowledge and *knowledge of*, we need to return to his view of the relationship between knowledge and the activity of sense perception. He holds that it is "through sense-perception [that] I am aware of the Other" (Macmurray, 1957: 106). He takes touch, rather than sight, as the paradigmatic sense perception: "Tactual perception, as the experience of resistance, is the direct and immediate apprehension of the Other-than-myself. The Other is that which resists my will" (Macmurray 1957: 109).

Knowledge of is more than intellectual knowing: it begins with the senses which he calls the gateways of our awareness (Macmurray 1935: 39). To be fully alive we need to increase our capacity to be aware of the world through the senses, cultivating it for its own sake. And we need to cultivate our emotional life. With a nod in the direction of Freud, he acknowledges that the emotions which motivate us are often hidden from our conscious awareness. Nevertheless he believes: "Emotion stands directly behind activity determining its substance and direction" (Macmurray 1935: 26).

Religion, society and the good other

A word about how all this links with religion, society and the good other. Macmurray's reflections on World War I and his commitment to social justice led him to reinvent his Christianity in a new, non-idealist form. He concluded that the institutional churches had abandoned any concern for the material dimension of life: they had become purely spiritual. In place of Christian tradition and doctrine, he puts what he calls the spirit of Christ, the personal, and the core value of friendship-in-community. The following quotations illustrate his view of religion:

Any community of persons, as distinct from a mere society, is a group of

individuals united in a common life . . . its members are in communion
with one another; they constitute a fellowship . . . the self-realisation of
persons in relation.

(Macmurray 1961: 157–158)

Religion is the pressure to live in terms of the reality of persons who
are not ourselves . . . the urge to enter into full mutual relationship
with other persons . . . It is the force which creates friendship, society,
community, cooperation in living.

(Macmurray 1935: 62)

Friendship is the fundamental religious fact in human life.

(Macmurray 1935: 63)

Communion is the keyword of religion.

(Macmurray 1935: 61)

Macmurray's concept of the good other

John Macmurray's mother was a powerful influence in his life, one to whom
he remained deeply attached but from whose emotionally constricting and
fundamentalist qualities he struggled to separate himself. John Costello gives
an amusing account of Macmurray's attempts to answer his mother's
demanding question: "John, where is God in all this?" (Costello, 2002: 320–
321). Where indeed? It is my view that the idea of God as an objective existent
has become superfluous in Macmurray's vision of religion. Macmurray
would not have entirely agreed with me, so perhaps I could put it more
positively, by saying that through his passionate pursuit of the logic of the
personal, he discovered that "God" symbolizes our universal need of, and
love for, the good other.

Macmurray's view of society of his day – the period in the early twentieth
century characterized by the rise of fascism and communism – is that there is
a crisis, and a failure, of contemporary societies, which can be explained by
their disregard of the personal in favour of the functional and the structural.
Another quotation will illustrate this analysis:

The decline of religious influence and of religious practice in our civilisa-
tion . . . betrays, and in turn intensifies, a growing insensitiveness to the
personal aspects of life, and a growing indifference to personal values. If
this influence is removed or ceases to be effective, the awareness of personal issues will tend to be lost, in the pressure of functional preoccupations. . . . The sense of personal dignity as well as personal unworthiness
will atrophy, with the decline in habits of self-examination. . . . Success
will tend to become the criterion of rightness, and there will spread

through society a temper which is extraverted, pragmatic and merely objective, for which all problems are soluble by better organisation.

(Macmurray 1957: 30–31)

In the view of Macmurray's biographer, John Costello, a view which I share, we are experiencing a similar crisis at the start of the twenty-first century, and Macmurray's voice needs to be heard anew.

I want to conclude this summary of Macmurray's ideas by showing how his perspective can help us to understand the significance of counselling and psychotherapy in contemporary British society. This might seem a puzzling link, given the decline in demand for psychoanalytic training and for four or five times a week psychoanalysis, but things look very different if we consider together all the psychological or talking therapies, including counselling. As church membership, religious practice and political collectivism have declined, and individualism and free enterprise have taken hold, we have seen a steady and at times spectacular growth in the demand for counselling and psychotherapy and for training in counselling and the use of the counselling approach.

My hypothesis is that the growth of counselling and psychotherapy is a popular response on the part of clients and therapists to the ravages of predatory individualism, materialism and nihilism, representing a reaching out for help, a search for understanding of self, other and society, a need to be personally known, and embodying a wish to care for and know the other in a direct, personal way. It can be understood as the altruistic giving of oneself to the other, the offer to know the other through a mutual encounter, on the basis of equality of regard. The therapeutic relationship can be seen as a specific form of friendship-in-community. The same case can be elaborated with reference to the significance of counselling and psychotherapy courses as learning groups or learning communities. These can be understood as the intentional creation of opportunities for personal relating which facilitate the growth of friendship-in-community.

The contribution of Ian Suttie

I am deeply indebted to Dorothy Heard for her painstaking excavations and lucid account of Ian Suttie's life and ideas (Heard 1988). Ian D. Suttie was born in Glasgow in 1889, the third child of a family doctor. He graduated in medicine in 1914 and worked as a psychiatrist in Govan before joining the Royal Army Medical Corps. He saw service in France and in what is now Iraq. After working at Gartnavel and hospitals in Perth and Fife, he became a psychotherapist at the Tavistock Clinic in 1928, continuing to work there until his untimely death in 1935. His wife, Jane, was also a psychotherapist there. They shared an interest in the ideas of the Hungarian analyst, Sandor Ferenczi, whose work Jane translated. Ian Suttie was by all accounts a vigorous, kind, brilliant and intellectually combative man who was deeply missed by his colleagues. In his obituary for Suttie, J. R. Rees described his boyish gusto and his passionate advocacy of ideas.

I will offer a summary of Suttie's ideas, followed by close-ups of a selection of his core themes. Essentially, Suttie was engaged in an impassioned – and (sadly) one-sided – argument with Freud, challenging Freud's instinct theory and replacing it with one based on the innate need for companionship and love.

Suttie's key themes

Suttie's only book, *The Origins of Love and Hate* (1935/1988) was written in a great hurry. His themes criss-cross but the author's insight and passion carry the reader along. I have spent several months reading it closely, and have named the key themes in his words as far as possible, organizing them in a sequence in which the one leads easily into the next:

- the innate need for companionship: love, tenderness, interest-rapport, fellowship
- psychic weaning and the development of a social disposition
- play and the development of cultural interests
- self and not-self
- consciousness and social mind
- the emotions, expression and communication
- the taboo on tenderness
- culture and society
- society and the jealousies
- women, children and men
- the critique of Freud
- science and the scientific attitude
- religion as social psychotherapy
- psychopathy as disturbance of the social disposition
- psychotherapy as reconciliation.

In reading this sequence, you may have noticed certain significant features. First, there is an emphasis on interpersonal and sociocultural dimensions throughout. Second, these are seen as closely related to each other; they are not in separate compartments. Third, there is an attempt to develop an overview, a sense of the whole. The jigsaw pieces fit together, and the picture that emerges is coordinated and comprehensive.

The innate need for companionship

Here, I offer a selective summary, starting with the ground-base of Suttie's perspective, the innate need for companionship, embodied in love, tenderness, interest-rapport and fellowship. In positing this innate need for companion-ship, Suttie is rejecting Freud's conception of the infant as a bundle of instincts generating tensions which require discharge, a process in which other persons, if they are needed at all, are only a means to an end. What goes on between people, for Suttie, is more than the satisfaction of appetites. Suttie sees the baby as seeking relationships from the start of life, bringing with it the power and will to love, a love which has a special quality of tenderness, embodied in the devoted, loving ministrations of the mother and the reciprocal emotion of tenderness in the infant. This loving tenderness requires for its satisfaction the awakening of an adequate response of appreciation on the part of the other. Enjoyment, appreciation and company are sought on both sides: this is the interpersonal context in which bodily needs arise and are met. The vital point here is that love is social, not merely sexual, in its biological function. Suttie holds that there is an organic basis to non-sexual love: it creates feelings of satisfaction in the respiratory, circulatory and digestive systems.

This love need is directed towards the nurturing other, usually but not necessarily the mother. The interactions involved are communicative as well as nurturing. The relationship involves mutual giving and getting, and generates a reciprocal sense of security. When this love is thwarted, the first result is anxiety. And when the thwarting persists, it can generate the frustration reaction of aggression.

The development of interest-rapport

The early love relationship, before weaning, is fundamental to everything that comes after. It influences the baby's view of other people, which Suttie calls the *social disposition*. At this early stage, self and other are not discriminated. Babies love their own body, their immediate concerns, their mother's loving attentions and their mother herself. Suttie argues that "the bodily self . . . is the first plaything shared with her" (1935/1988: 37). In the course of these interactions, interest-rapport develops. As the not-self is gradually discriminated, play and fellowship grow. If things go well, the extension of interest from self-and-mother to other persons and physical objects broadens to include, potentially, the whole sociocultural field. The implication of this account is that love generates interest-rapport, which gradually extends beyond the original love relationship. Love does not necessarily cease with the growth of interest-rapport, but the latter can become highly differentiated from the love in which it originated. New interest-rapport relationships with playfellows can now be established without the preliminary establishment of love.

As this picture unfolds, the nature of Suttie's achievement comes into focus. With his concept of the growth and spread of interest-rapport, he replaces Freud's concept of aim-inhibited sublimation of the sexual instinct as the explanation for the development of culture, prepares the ground for the work of Fairbairn, Winnicott and Bowlby, and opens a door for interpersonal and sociocultural perspectives in psychology and psychotherapy.

Just in case the reader is tempted to conclude that Suttie idealizes love, I must emphasize that the account, up to now, is based on relationships going well enough before weaning. They do not always go well enough, as we know. Suttie understands that love is an equivocal as well as a positive factor in human society. This becomes clear in his account of the process of psychic weaning and the development of a social disposition.

The development of a social disposition

The golden age of infant–mother absorption and responsiveness, in which love is unconditional, is brought to an end by weaning, the birth of another baby, cleanliness training, and the need for the working mother to leave her babies. The infant now develops an ambivalent experience of mother, a mixture of love-longing, anxiety and anger, in which love is increasingly experienced as conditional. The child now adopts a life role, a stance towards others and the world which seems preferable both to the child and others: this is what Suttie means by the development of a social disposition.

If the frustration of the love-need is very great, frustrated love converts into anxiety, guilt and finally into hatred. But to hate a loved person, at this early stage, is felt to be intolerable. The child therefore adopts one or more of the following interpersonal strategies:

• keep mother loveable now
• abandon mother as she is now, and replace her with mother as she once was
• seek a good substitute for bad mother (e.g. father)
• engage in love protest: anger, aggression, coercion
• become what is wanted.

These strategies produce certain intrapersonal and interpersonal results. The first can lead to feelings of inferiority or to melancholia. The second can lead to regression, fantasy satisfaction, or turning away from reality. The third can lead to paranoia, feelings of persecution by the bad other. The fourth can lead to the self-important exacting of services from others. And the fifth can lead to a denial of what one really is, and the substitution of a false self. In all of this, Suttie again anticipates Fairbairn and Winnicott.

It is worth emphasizing that Suttie's account of development turns entirely on the actual, ongoing interpersonal situation between the child, the mother or primary caregiver, other loved persons and the whole physical and sociocultural environment.

The emotions as transformations of love

Like Antonio Damasio, Suttie ascribes a crucial role to the emotions, arguing that they are nearly always socially related. In other words, the expression of emotion is a means of communication with others, and is designed to elicit a response. Its function is to keep individuals in rapport with each other: it is essentially social, communicating meaning and maintaining nurturing, playful and cooperative association. The means of emotional communication include the voice, crying, laughter, and all kinds of body language. These elements are apprehended together, not separately.

Suttie sees the emotion of love as primal and pivotal: all the other emotions are interconvertible forms of the urge to love. These transformations of love occur under the stimulus of changing relationships with the loved person, and include the following:

- Love denied turns into hatred.
- Love threatened turns into anxiety.
- Love supplanted turns into jealousy.
- Love rejected turns into despair.
- Loss of the loved person turns love into grief.
- Sympathy for the loved person turns love into pity.
- Love thwarted turns into the quest for power, the quest for admiration, or the quest for possession, resulting in unstable, unbalanced and unilateral relationships.

The taboo on tenderness

The unity of the interpersonal and the sociocultural in Suttie's thinking is demonstrated most clearly in his concept of the taboo on tenderness. For Suttie, tenderness is a primal reality, one modality of love. It is embodied in the activities and feelings involved in the non-sexual fondling relationship between baby and mother, and in the need for companionship with her. Its repression in our culture begins in the process he calls psychic weaning, in which the tender attentions previously enjoyed by the baby are withdrawn. This is experienced by the child as a withdrawal of the mother's love, and also as meaning that the child's love is not welcome to the mother. This thwarting of the child's tender feelings, grief over the loss of the mother and anxiety caused by the change in her attitude, together strike at the root of the child's sense of security and justice. The child is now faced with a number of options: develop companionship with others; fight for its rights; regress; find substitutes; or submit and avoid privation by repression. The last of these options, repression of longings, is the major source of the taboo on tenderness.

But the process of repressing tenderness does not occur in the individual child–mother relationship alone. It has its cultural origin in the stoicism which has pervaded British culture, and British Christianity, for a very long time. Both parents, and the child's older siblings, will already be intolerant of tenderness, to a greater or lesser extent, reflecting the degree of stoicism in their own upbringing. The process is reinforced beyond the family, particularly among men and boys. The taboo on tenderness is expressed by upper-class parents who send their sons away from home to attend private single-sex boarding schools, and by the gang of boys who idealize manliness and repudiate any sign of babyishness and girlishness. Suttie characterizes their state of mind as involving a reaction against the sentiments related to mother and the nursery, and describes these boys as a band of brothers united by a common bereavement.

These attitudes and practices are transmitted from generation to generation. They appear to affect men more than women: in Suttie's view, this is because of women's nurturing role. Although the taboo on tenderness (which he distinguishes from the taboo on sex) has weakened somewhat, it has by no means disappeared. The concept of the taboo on tenderness is, in my view, a powerful tool for understanding societies and cultures deriving historically from English and Scottish roots.

Society and the jealousies

The close interplay of the interpersonal and the sociocultural is highlighted again in Suttie's discussion of society and the jealousies. The starting point lies in his debate with Freud. Suttie poses the question: Is society a spontaneous expression of human nature, or an artefact or force? For Freud – on Suttie's account – society is maintained by the dominance of the male leader over his followers. Social behaviour is the outcome of repression by fear, and the fear involved is the fear of castration. Freud focuses on two jealousies of prime importance in the development of society: men's jealousy of male rivals, and women's penis envy of male partners, and men in general.

For Suttie, on the other hand, love is the mainspring of social life. The jealousies disrupt love and frustrate the need for it. The basic unit of society is the band of brothers and sisters under the same mother. Mother is the first moralizer, encouraging and enforcing mutual tolerance by means of the fear of loss of love. Freud, Suttie argues, only understands the effect of the fear-of-castration factor, not the love factor, in prohibition and inhibition. For Suttie, a physically weaker prohibitor can make a more effective prohibition. Of the two determining factors – fear of punishment and fear of loss of love – fear of loss of love is the more powerful (Table 2.1).

It is impossible to overstate the importance of Suttie's contribution here. At the very least, he supplements Freud's narrow view. At most, he reorients our understanding of society, and socializes psychology. Having said that, I am struck by certain omissions. No mention is made of the jealousy of any child, at any point in the birth sequence, for the talents, qualities or popularity

Table 2.1 Summary of Suttie's account of the jealousies

Jealousy	Characteristics	Suttie's comments
Oedipus complex	The boy wants to get rid of father and get mother for himself. (Suttie acknowledges that Freud later modified his account of the Oedipus complex to incorporate a range of other factors.)	This holds good for patriarchal, guilt-ridden cultures, and in certain family circumstances.
Penis envy	The girl feels incomplete and inferior, and wants her father's or brother's penis for herself.	As above; Suttie adds a further comment on both the Oedipus complex and penis envy. These are neither the earliest, nor the most important, nor the most universal of jealousies.
Cain jealousy	The jealousy felt by the eldest child, of either sex, for the next child, of either sex. (Cain killed his younger brother, Abel, while they were out of sight of their mother.)	The most universal, the earliest and the most powerful jealousy for individual development.
Zeus jealousy	The man/father's jealousy of the woman/mother's childbearing, lactating and nurturing capacities. (Zeus swallowed his pregnant wife, Mitis, in order to bear her child, Pallas, himself.)	The lack of maternal hopes, anticipations and satisfactions may account for male political and economic dominance.
Laios jealousy	The man/father's jealousy of the new child produced by the woman/mother. (Laios was the father of Oedipus, whose mother was Jocasta. Laios abandoned Oedipus on a hillside at birth.)	Suttie comments that this is the aspect of the Oedipus story neglected by Freud, and adds that the advent of the child enriches the woman's love life but to begin with impoverishes that of the man.

of another. Children's jealousy of their parents is also omitted. His list is confined to jealousies within one family grouping, leaving out jealousies between individual members of different families, between families, classes or nations, and jealousies relating to inherited or accumulated differences of wealth, power and social capital. He omits any mention of jealousies, rivalries, comparisons and attractions arising among adults. He fails to distinguish envy from jealousy, using jealousy as a catch-all category. And he fails to discuss adequately the role of fathers in families: it is as if, in his polemic with Freud, he has swung too far towards the opposite extreme.

Having said all this, the general direction of Suttie's analysis is clear and convincing. It opens the way towards a social psychology based on love and its vicissitudes. In terms of psychotherapeutic practice, it shifts the weight of emphasis away from instincts and their representatives, and to some extent also from internal objects and their relations, on to actual inter-personal relationships both past and present. And it challenges us, as theor-ists, practitioners and researchers, to create a new balance and integration of these three factors in psychotherapy.

Psychopathy as disturbance of the social disposition

In his discussion of psychopathy, Suttie distinguishes organic impairment or disease of the brain (which produces symptoms without meaning in terms of social relationships), from psychopathy considered as disturbance in the rela-tionship between an individual and his or her fellows, due to privations, inhibitions and distortions in the person's social or love disposition. Such disturbance generates symptoms which do have meanings, always connected with the individual's social purpose or aim. He calls these symptoms disturbances of rapport, listing them as follows:

- loss of interest in people
- loss of interest in things
- self-depreciation
- over-estimation of self
- anxiety
- despair
- anger/aggression
- regressiveness/return to infantile dependency.

His account of psychopathy stresses the role of emotions. He is particularly insightful with regard to the individual's attempt to "increase its consequence to other people . . . insofar as it feels it has no-one upon whom it can safely depend" (Suttie 1935/1988: 200). Suttie's analysis helps us to understand the process of forming what he calls idealisms, which involve the child in imitat-ing and seeking to emulate envied, outstanding figures in the environment. In a happy phrase for a desperately unhappy development, he describes psych-opathy as "an archaic and . . . inept attempt to improve love relationships" (Suttie 1935/1988: 201). Correspondingly, he sees psychotherapy as an attempt to assist the patient or client on his love quest, and set this upon lines more likely to achieve the desired results.

Psychotherapy as reconciliation

We turn finally to Suttie's conception of psychotherapy. In considering this theme, it is helpful to bear in mind his studies in social anthropology, his interest in the links between psychotherapy and religion, and his view that human psychology is practically always dealing not with the individual alone but with his relations to others.

Psychotherapy is ultimately about reconciliation, and involves the restoration of love-interest-rapport between the self and the social environment. Its aim is to overcome the barriers to loving and feeling oneself loved. Suttie writes: "The ideal attitude [of the therapist] is very like that of Christ . . . serene without being aloof, sympathetic without being disturbed: exactly what the child desires in the parent" (1935/1988: 217). He uses the metaphor of therapist as sacrificial victim (onto whom all hates, anxieties and distrust can be projected), and the therapist as mediator or catalyst, by means of whose genuine engagement the alienated psyche of the client can reintegrate into society, not as an adaptation to a pathological norm, but as a person who is now capable of expressing his hate and his love.

A vital feature of this perspective on therapy is his view of the therapist as a real, ordinary human being, a product of her culture, with her own prejudices and inhibitions, and defended to some degree against her own needs and difficulties by the taboo on tenderness. Suttie is aware, from his own experience, of the anti-therapeutic effect of taking refuge in passivity and objectivity. He attacks those whose accounts of technique idealize passivity, arguing that they represent their relationships with their clients or patients as inhuman, impersonal and purely technical. For Suttie, the role of the psychotherapist is to offer "a true and full companionship of interest . . . [the therapist] shows by his understanding and insight that he too has suffered . . . so there is a fellowship of suffering established" (1935/1988: 211–212).

Suttie refers to the therapist as a man of sorrows. He favours activity and responsiveness on the part of the therapist, and opposes what he calls the fiction of immunity from emotion. Endorsing Ferenczi's argument that it is the physician's love that heals the patient or client, he goes on to clarify precisely what love means in the therapeutic relationship. It is "a feeling-interest responsiveness, not a goal-inhibited sexuality" (Suttie 1935/1988: 212–213). There is no question of the therapist using the relationship to meet his own needs, or engaging in inappropriate self-disclosure. Therapeutic love is an altruistic, non-appetitive love, focussing on the needs and growth of the other. What Suttie is saying is that such a relationship, if it is to be effective, cannot involve self-withholding. The therapist has to be fully present, a real human being communicating genuine emotional responses. A one-sided relationship, as he puts it, cannot be curative.

It is my contention, first, that contemporary psychoanalysis, psychotherapy and counselling have much to learn from Suttie; second that his contribution anticipates much of what has come after, including the work of Fairbairn, Winnicott, Bowlby, Guntrip, Sutherland, the developmental psychologists, our contemporary interest in attunement and attachment, and the more recent contributions of neuroscientists such as Antonio Damasio, who stresses the importance of internal representations of self and other in human relationships, and the vital role of emotions (Damasio 2000).

My third contention is concerned with our human orientation towards living in the twenty-first century. It is analogous to the case so eloquently argued by Alasdair MacIntyre in the opening chapter of his book *After Virtue* (1985) to the effect that, in contemporary culture, the language of morality has been fragmented and nearly destroyed. In the context of modernism and particularly postmodernism, morality, where it exists at all, has been subordinated to situational, structural and technological considerations. The dominant philosophical orientation, if it can be dignified with that name, is a self-centred consumerist hedonism, which celebrates our liberation from the dead weight of the past. Crocodile tears are shed over the failure of the grand narratives of Christianity, Marxism, psychoanalysis and feminism. My contention is that this perspective incorporates a purely negative view of freedom. Against hedonism, I argue that being human involves the challenge of finding a way of life (see Turnbull 1989). This is a challenge that is communal as well as personal, and normative rather than merely descriptive. It asks "How should I live?" and not "What is everybody else doing so that I can do the same?" To struggle for the restoration of such an orientation is not to impose a single religious perspective, but to excavate and piece together an orientation for personal living of what Ian Martin has called the common life in community (Martin 1987). This is the ethical imperative which underlies the attempt to construct a synthesis of the work of Macmurray, Suttie and Fairbairn.

The distinctive contribution of Ronald Fairbairn

The contributions of Ronald Fairbairn are presented more fully in Chapters 1, 3, 6 and 7. Here, I confine myself to answering the question: What distinctive contributions do Fairbairn and his followers make to our understanding of the persons-in-relation perspective? From Macmurray, I have argued, we take the philosophical and religious orientation. From Suttie, we take the creative shift from instincts and their vicissitudes to an understanding of the relations of persons in society, pivoting around love and its vicissitudes. What is missing from the picture they draw, Fairbairn fills in.

In swinging away from Freud's early focus on instincts, Suttie rightly emphasizes real external relationships and sociocultural milieux. But he has relatively little to say about our inner worlds. How do these external relationships affect us inside? Are they once and for all experiences which simply accumulate in our memories like jam sandwiches or plates of porridge, or do they have an impact on us inside in some special way? Suttie's view of psychopathy implies that they do. They help to shape our choice of social disposition. But what exactly is involved, internally, in developing a social disposition? Suttie does not tackle that question in any depth. Fairbairn does.

Fairbairn gives us, for the first time, a convincing account of our inner world conceived primarily in interpersonal terms. He pictures a conscious central ego or I relating to an ego ideal, and a pair of split off repressed parts of the ego, a rejected, persecuted and persecutory part relating to a rejecting or punishing object, and a longing, needy part relating to an exciting or tantalizing object. Added to that, the persecutory part of the ego, also called the internal saboteur, persistently attacks the libidinal pairing. This image of the aggressive and libidinal dynamics of the inner situation, so painstakingly pieced together in "Endopsychic Structure Considered in Terms of Object-Relationships", also applies to his unique understanding of dreams, seen as short films of interpersonal situations representing the drama of internal structure. His view of endopsychic structure also has implications for understanding the transference/countertransference relationship, and it connects with his recasting of the concept of dissociation, of which he sees repression as a special case (Fairbairn 1944; Sandler 1976; Scharff & Birtles 1994).

The careful attention which Fairbairn lavishes on understanding our inner situation has generated new insights on the part of those who have followed him. I am thinking here of Guntrip's dialogue with Fairbairn, leading to his image of the repressed, regressed and withdrawn core of the libidinal ego, holed up in the schizoid citadel, inaccessible to real human contact; of Sutherland's suggestion that the links between the various self–other pairs consist of emotions; and of the Scharffs' application of Fairbairn's model to therapeutic work with couples (Guntrip 1971/1977; Scharff 1994; Scharff and Scharff 1991).

I want to make one final point about Fairbairn's contribution. His own analytic and therapeutic concerns are directed primarily towards understanding the interpersonal nature of the inner world, although he was also aware of the significance of the wider society and culture for inner world configurations: see, for example, his paper "The Effects of a King's Death upon Patients Undergoing Analysis" (Fairbairn 1952). Sutherland's (1989) psychobiography *Fairbairn's Journey into the Interior* portrays Fairbairn in his sociocultural context. Sutherland traces Fairbairn's development of theory in connection to his self-analysis of his difficulties in the context of his family and culture of origin. Fairbairn's personal suffering is the suffering not only of a very private, brilliant, good man: it is also the suffering of a son, husband and father growing up and living out his life in the Scottish and British society of his day. More specifically his psychic suit was made of Edinburgh cloth woven out of threads of intense Christian idealism and professional devotion, episcopalianism with its undertow of Calvinism, sharply contrasting gender roles, kindness and reserve, warmth and distance, science and service. It would be fascinating to know exactly what Ronald Fairbairn had in mind when he said to Harry Guntrip that Suttie really had something important to say. My hunch is that he was thinking not only of Suttie's emphasis on interpersonal relationships and the role of emotions, but also specifically of his concept of the taboo on tenderness – a taboo which applied across much of Scottish society from the death of Burns, throughout the Victorian period and the first two-thirds of the twentieth century, a taboo with which Macmurray, Suttie and Fairbairn all struggled in their different ways.

Towards a synthesis

In this final section I discuss my working toward a synthesis, and I identify some of its principal themes. My aim is to integrate intrapersonal, inter-personal and sociocultural factors in a unified account of the theory and practice of psychotherapy and counselling. The synthesis will be grounded in Macmurray's philosophical, ethical and religious thinking, to which I refer as the persons-in-relation perspective (a term adapted from the title of one of his books). This entails clarifying the distinctions and overlaps of meaning between the terms "personal relations", "object relations", and "persons in relation".

Briefly, *personal relations* is used to refer to the direct relationships between human beings, whether past or present, both descriptively (that is, whatever those relationships happen to be) and normatively (that is, when each person involved is genuinely trying to consider and treat the other as a person rather than as an object).

The term *object relations* is reserved for accounts of the inner worlds of persons conceived in terms of their internalized images or representations of self and other, and the dynamic relationships between and among these self–other representations, whether these are unconscious or conscious, especially but not exclusively where they have become to some degree dissoci-ated, stuck or fixed.

The term *persons in relation* refers to a broader view of human beings in society, in any and every context, seen as persons-in-community whose per-sonhood is constituted by their relationships with other persons. Because this is an essentially normative view, and because not all human relationships are direct, the clarification of the meaning of these three terms leads on to a consideration of the relationships between the personal, the structural and the functional. In the course of this discussion I will draw particularly on Michael Fielding's illuminating application of Macmurray's thinking to the education of children in schools (Fielding 2004). In this connection, it should be noted that Macmurray does not deny the existence or necessity of the functional, but argues that "the personal is *through* the functional" and that "the functional is *for* the personal" (Fielding 2004).

I now turn to some of the implications of these considerations for the theory and practice of psychoanalytic psychotherapy, counselling and groupwork. We should be concerned primarily and pervasively with personal relations, not object relations, in our work with clients, whether the focus of the moment is on external or internal situations or both. Persons are indeed objects, but they are much more than objects. They are subjects who are recipients of their experiences and agents of their actions, who construe and reflect upon those experiences and actions, and who, in their unique experiencing, acting, construing, and reflecting, encounter other persons likewise engaged.

In short, human beings are persons in personal relations with other persons. This is true not only of our external interpersonal relations, but also, in a more complex sense, of our inner worlds, constituted as they are by the internalization of previously external interpersonal relations. I did not take in my father or mother, or my brothers and sister, as objects. They are not bits of fishbone stuck in my psyche: they are significant other persons, however exaggerated, distorted and fixed some of my earliest construing of them may have been. While they are alive, there is a complex interplay of internal personal (object) relations and externally occurring, here-and-now personal relations. When they die, I carry within me the inheritance of an ongoing interplay between myself and their personalities, their lives and relationships, their values and the sociocultural contexts from which they came. This has huge implications for how we should relate to our clients. In this connection, it is heartening to learn from Graham Clarke in Chapter 21 that Ronald Fairbairn wished to call his unique development of object relations theory "personal relations theory" (Clarke 2003).

From the basic assumption that psychotherapeutic work is an intersubjective collaboration between two persons, based on equality of regard, I proceed to my second theme. Persons are constituted not only by interpersonal relations but also by real sociocultural contexts and values which have been internalized and become parts of the self. The challenge of acknowledging the unity, the simultaneity, of the intrapersonal, the interpersonal and the sociocultural is not primarily theoretical. It is a matter of experience and practice. It confronts us when we encounter another person.

When I took in my parents, I did not put their personalities in one box and their significantly different sociocultural backgrounds in another. Nor did I continue relating to them, as I grew up, in a sociocultural vacuum. On the contrary, our relationships were interlaced with direct experiences and representations of post-war austerity, the developing Cold War, the take-off of technology, the eruption of libertarianism, the decline of religion, and so on. That our personalities, our relationships, and our disturbances consist of the interplay of all these factors, and that all of them come into play in the therapeutic relationship, is surely now beyond dispute. This interplay has been clearly demonstrated in the work of feminist psychotherapists like Susie Orbach (1993) in her work with clients whose difficulties revolve around eating and body image, which are partly sociocultural in origin (see, for example, Orbach 1993). It has been demonstrated by Harry Stack Sullivan

(1953) in his account of the painful tensions established in his youthful soul by the different sociocultural backgrounds and expectations of his father and mother (Mullahy 1952). It has been demonstrated by Jock Sutherland in his account of Ronald Fairbairn's personal development, and in his study of John Buchan's "sick heart" (Sutherland 1988, 1989).

This leads to my third theme. In our psychoanalytic and psychodynamic cultures, we are sometimes too narrowly (in a few cases, exclusively) pre-occupied with inner worlds. Without abandoning that focus at all, we need to re-examine our understandings of the relationship of clients' inner worlds to their actual experiences of present and past external relationships, their sociocultural milieux, their value systems and their ways of life.

This leads to the fourth and final theme of the synthesis, which involves questioning our sometimes excessive emphasis on unconscious processes and repression as the sole source and locus of psychological distress. This is not to deny the importance of unconscious processes, but to suggest that society and culture have changed drastically since the days of Freud and Fairbairn. It was possible, in the 1890s and 1940s, to argue convincingly that civilization was based on repression. In the contemporary period, an equally convincing case can be made that our civilization is based on continuous, intentional overstimulation, and on dissociation. Among clients seeking help now, while repression is sometimes a significant factor, many ingrained conflicts and difficulties exist in the domain of conscious awareness and are – very ineffect-ively – coped with by dissociation and the passive tolerance of contradiction. These processes are exacerbated by the fact that most contemporary channels of communication beam out messages implying that people are consumers who should seek, and get, everything they want, whether or not they can afford it, and whether or not it is good for them. The notions of the personal, of personal responsibility, of real freedom in John Macmurray's sense of the term, of the cultivation of the capacity to ponder, to weigh up, to make positive directional choices, and sometimes to say no, have been almost obliterated. For us, as psychoanalytic psychotherapists and counsellors, there is a challenging ethical task: to reaffirm the importance and value of the personal life, and the perspective that society consists primarily of persons in personal relations.

References

Clarke, G. (2003). Personal relations theory: Suttie, Fairbairn, Macmurray and Sutherland. Paper presented at the Legacy of Fairbairn and Sutherland Confer-ence, International Psychotherapy Institute and Scottish Institute of Human Relations, Edinburgh.

Costello, J. E. (2002). *John Macmurray: A Biography*. Edinburgh: Floris Books.

Damasio, A. (2000). *The Feeling of What Happens: Body, Emotion and the Making of Consciousness*. London: Vintage.

Fairbairn, W. R. D. (1944). Endopsychic structure considered in terms of object relationships. *Psychoanalytic Studies of the Personality*, pp. 82–136. London: Routledge and Kegan Paul.

—— (1952). The effects of a king's death upon patients undergoing analysis. In *Psychoanalytic Studies of the Personality*, pp. 223–229. London: Routledge and Kegan Paul.

—— (1986). *Psychoanalytic Studies of the Personality*, pp. 82–136. London: Routledge and Kegan Paul.

Fielding, M. (2004). Philosophy and the end of educational organisation. Paper presented at the Philosophy of Education Society of Great Britain Annual Conference, Oxford.

Guntrip, H. (1971/1977). *Psychoanalytic Theory, Therapy and the Self*. London: Karnac.

Heard, D. (1988). Introduction: historical perspectives, in I. Suttie *The Origins of Love and Hate*. London: Free Association.

Kirkwood, C. (2003). The persons in relation perspective: towards a philosophy for counselling in society. *Counselling and Psychotherapy Research* 3(3): 186–195.

MacIntyre, A. (1985). *After Virtue: A Study in Moral Theory*. London: Duckworth.

Macmurray, J. (1932). *Freedom in the Modern World*. London: Humanities Press, 1992.

—— (1935). *Reason and Emotion*. London: Faber and Faber, 1995b.

—— (1938). *The Clue to History*. London: Student Christian Movement Press.

—— (1957). *The Self as Agent*. London: Faber and Faber, 1995c.

—— (1961). *Persons in Relation*. London: Faber and Faber, 1995a.

Martin, I. (1987). Community education: Towards a theoretical analysis, in G. Allen, J. Bastiani, I. Martin and K. Richards (eds) *Community Education: An Agenda for Educational Reform*. Milton Keynes: Open University Press.

Mullahy, P. (ed.) (1952). *The Contributions of Harry Stack Sullivan: A Symposium on Interpersonal Theory in Psychiatry and Social Science*. New York: Heritage House.

Orbach, S. (1993). *Hunger Strike: The Anorectic's Struggle as a Metaphor for our Age*. London: Penguin.

Sandler, J. (1976). Countertransference and role-responsiveness, *International Review of Psychoanalysis* 3(43): 43–47.

Scharff, D. and Birtles, E. (1994). *From Instinct to Self: Selected Papers of W. R. D. Fairbairn, Vols 1 and 2*. London: Jason Aronson.

Scharff, D. and Scharff, J. (1991). *Object Relations Couple Therapy*. London: Jason Aronson.

Scharff, J. (1994). *The Autonomous Self: The Work of J. D. Sutherland*. London: Jason Aronson.

Sullivan, H. S. (1953). *The Interpersonal Theory of Psychiatry*. New York: Norton.

Sutherland, J. D. (1988). John Buchan's 'sick heart': some psychoanalytic reflections. *Edinburgh Review* 78–79: 83–101.

—— (1989). *Fairbairn's Journey into the Interior*. London: Free Association.

Suttie, I. D. (1935/1988). *The Origins of Love and Hate*. London: Free Association.

Turnbull, R. (1989). Scottish thought in the twentieth century, in C. Beveridge and R. Turnbull (eds) *The Eclipse of Scottish Culture*, pp. 91–111. Edinburgh: Polygon.

Chapter 3

Difference, repetition and continuity

Philosophical reflections on Fairbairn's concept of mature dependence[1]

Ellinor Fairbairn Birtles

Introduction

Fairbairn's neglected concept of mature dependence describes the integrated identity of the human self, and is a vital component of his general psychology. This chapter identifies components of the self, investigates the way the Self is constructed, and illuminates the concept of mature dependence from a philosophical point of view. I draw first on the work of French philosopher Deleuze who examines the way human experience is filed to build an inner world and to form object relations within it. I then draw on Matte Blanco's system of Bi-logic to examine the role of symmetrical and asymmetrical thinking in the establishment of the inner world, to arrive at an enhanced understanding of the concept of mature dependence.

From its outset psychoanalysis concentrated upon the enigma of aberrant, unusual, distressing, and destructive behaviours, the form they took, and the theories about them, which were partially dependent upon the cultural mores and ideas of the time and place in which the analytic theorist and his patients lived. Freud's vital contribution was to demonstrate the activity of the dynamic unconscious, deduce its repression, and develop analytic technique to render it accessible to conscious reflection. Fairbairn's contribution was to develop a general psychology of the human Self, with the basic premise that the purpose of life was to develop individual human potential. Fairbairn himself considered that his theory of object relations, based upon his experience with children, was a viable general psychology.

The fundamental question of the self

What is it – apart from direct genetic inheritance or environmental influence – that forms the personal identity of the individual? In the nineteenth and early twentieth century, philosophers Kant, Hegel, and Marx, psychologists

---

1 Abridged from the original by J. Scharff.

Charcot, Janet, James and Stout, and Freud, himself, did not account for processes involved in the development and evolution of each human individual. What are these principles of development, and how do they work? This question was fundamental to Fairbairn's psychoanalytic thinking. I look to the French philosophers Deleuze and Sartre, the Scottish philosopher Macmurray, and the psychoanalyst Matte Blanco to illuminate Fairbairn's approach to this and related questions.

In the twentieth century, approaches to science and philosophy were marked by detailed examination of minutiae. In psychoanalysis and psychology mental functions were progressively dissected. Living in that culture and influenced by theories of atomic physics prevalent at the time, Fairbairn developed an idea of personality physics, expressed as a system with identifiable parts splitting from other parts and becoming connected to various objects identified by their affective charge (like electrons and protons attracting and repelling by their negative and positive charges).

Where his contemporary Macmurray looks broadly at the conditions of infancy, Fairbairn looks in great detail to see how the experiences of infancy are recorded in endopsychic structure. Macmurray thinks that the infant is "fitted by nature . . . for the conditions" to be encountered. Macurray explains:

> He is in fact "adapted" . . . to being "unadapted", adapted to a complete dependence upon an adult human being. He is born into a love relationship which is inherently personal . . . his very survival depends upon the maintaining of this relationship. . . . The impulse to communicate is his sole adaptation to the world in which he is born.
>
> (Macmurray 1961: 48, 60)

Damasio (1994) reverses Descartes' (1641) famous assertion "I think therefore I am" to "I am therefore I think." Paradoxically both are true, and neither cancels the other out. The "I" of Descartes knows who he is because he is able to contemplate the I who is thinking. In other words, the Self is capable of self-reflection. Damasio's "I" exists as a being because he has the capacity for thought. The problem here is how do "I" know that "I" am a being? How do infants develop the conscious awareness that they have the capacity to think?

The human brain operates on two principles that apply to all mammals, namely the *principle of sameness and the principle of difference*. Mammals and other creatures are capable of differentiation based on an appreciation of sameness and difference. A mother mammal knows her child from the others. We have the ability to recognize where we live and how to reach home. The recognition of similarities and differences in objects and situations is necessary to survival. Plato's concept of *essence* describes the combination of function and construction, for instance, in the commonly given example of "chairness". We recognize any chair as a chair, no matter how or with what it has been constructed. We recognize the construction and function of the object. We have a template in our heads for establishing the essence of any object we can name.

Sameness between objects or situations is identified by a mode of thinking called the *symmetrical mode*, a largely unconscious operational mode, while the comprehension of difference between objects and situations is identified by the *asymmetrical mode*, which operates both consciously and unconsciously (Matte Blanco 1998). Broadly speaking the *symmetrical* mode is concerned with sameness between objects and situations, whereas the asymmetrical mode is concerned with the identification and comprehension of difference between objects and situations. Deleuze (1968) elaborates the *asymmetrical* mode of mental functioning as the identification of *disparateness*, which may be a conscious apprehension of the differing appearances of objects. Difference is not diversity or otherness per se, although it is a distinguishing feature of both diversity and of the other in relation to the subject. Moreover he argues that "difference is not just differentiation from or between two objects or situations" but is "something which distinguishes itself" and is always oppositional in relation to the perceiving subject (p. 28). Deleuze gives the example of a stroke of lightning, which distinguishes itself as a phenomenon, in addition to being distinct and different from the dark sky. This leads him to describe difference as the "state in which determination takes the form of unilateral distinction" (p. 28). What Deleuze stresses is that the next stroke of lightning, seen as separate from the first, has an identity inherently separate from the first.

Appreciation of difference also exists among people. You and I are similar as members of the human race, and we are intrinsically different in terms of individual identity. Deleuze's term for this phenomenon is *univocity*. Thus being is univocal. Being is the state in which I am apprehending the difference between the unique you and the unique me, while understanding that the same state of being is present in you.

I shall now look at repetition, in which the functioning mode is sameness. In his *Treatise of Human Nature*, Hume (1739) makes his famous assertion: "Repetition changes nothing in the object, but does change something in the mind which contemplates it" (quoted in Deleuze 1968: 70). Deleuze asks: "How can repetition change something in the case of the repeated element?" (p. 70). He writes:

> Time is constituted only in the originary synthesis which operates on the repetition of instants. This synthesis contracts the successive instants into one another, thereby constituting the lived or living, present. It is in this present that time is deployed. To it belong both the past and the future; the past in so far as the preceding instants are contained in the contraction; the future because its expectation is anticipated in the same contraction.
> (Deleuze 1968: 70–71)

Repetition occurs over time, which is itself a succession of instants. Successive instants combine and contract within the present, the past, and the future in relation to the passage of time. Deleuze calls this succession of instants by means of contraction a process of *passive synthesis*, not a conscious synthesis: "It is not carried *by* the mind but occurs *in* the mind, which contemplates, prior to memory and all reflections" (p. 71). *Passive synthesis is asymmetrical.* The actual act of contraction occurs in the mind: it is not consciously thought, whereas memory is involved in the process at the conscious level. There has been repetition without change in the object. But there has been a change in the subject who responds automatically and who remembers difference across repetitions. In contrast, *active synthesis* occurs when the mind (through reasoning and its subsequent expression) or the body, is engaged in purposeful activity. Passive synthesis is the automatic habit of living. Active synthesis occurs when the mind is actively involved in the outcome.

It was Hume (1748) who pointed out that experiences passively "contracted or grounded in the imagination remain no less distinct in the memory or the understanding" (p. 71). These images normally take the form of representations in the mind. Elaborating on Hume's idea, Deleuze suggests that memory holds in the mind both the experienced external object and objects that arise from within the mind. Moreover, the fact that external and internal objects are both capable of concrete mental representation means that objects of internal origin can have the force of externally derived objects.

In the *repetition of instants*, separate but identical events are observed. Take, for example, a ticking clock. The tick is differentiated from the tock. The tock is followed by the tick, and the tick by the tock. The tick forms one series and the tock a second series. Each series is held within the moment in which it occurs, but as Deleuze points out, the "present" is fleeting, so the present becomes the past but holds within it the expectation of the future. The "tick" and the "tock" form two separate sets. These sets are enlarged when we hear additional ticks or tocks in the future. Thus it is our expectation that tick will be followed by tock, and this constitutes a working principle in the human mind. This series of events held in time by contraction and passive synthesis is a recognizable entity in our minds. Repetition and difference operate together to consolidate and distinguish the tock from the tick.

Repetition is how we build up our capacities. If we want to play tennis well, we have to practise. Repetition is the means by which we recognize people and things, and by which we develop our sense of continuity. However, when we see somebody after a lapse of time, we notice the difference: "Difference lies between two repetitions" (Deleuze 1968: 76). From one event to another, we may notice a sign that marks the difference. Repetitions can engender a sense of need, which can be identified as a lack of something that needs to be replaced. Deleuze writes: "A scar is the sign not of a past wound but of 'the present fact of having been wounded'. We can say that it is the contemplation of the wound that contracts all the instants which separate us from it into a living present" (Deleuze 1968: 77).

When experience with the mother is unsatisfying, the infant's need is felt as a lack. In Fairbairn's view, this may be the result of the infant's inexperience or the mother's misattunement. Either way, the infant internalizes a sense of lack or dissatisfaction. This leads to the development of unsatisfactory objects which are rejected by the ego because they have been rejecting or exciting of need. These are split from the satisfactory aspects of the objects and repressed. Then the ego splits itself accordingly, in parts attached to the exciting and rejecting aspects of the object to form a *closed system* in the psyche, while the remainder of the infant ego is attached to the satisfying aspects of the maternal object. Closed and accessible systems together form the psyche. The closed system results from the primary infantile experience of being wounded, the behaviour associated with a present sign of the past injury. If the need for splitting is intense, a more reduced part of the psyche remains in realistic contact with the outside world.

In later life when the person identifies an unconscious resonance or repetitive situation within a personal interaction, he or she will be transported back to the initial wounding and will react to the other person in a way that mirrors the child's reaction to caregivers. Fairbairn sees this phenomenon as an active factor in the transference relationship between the analyst and the patient. Analysing this enables the patient to recognize and moderate behaviour in order to mitigate the impact of the original wound. Deleuze (1968) argues that repetition transforms and modifies "imaginary relations within the two series . . . therefore between two presents" (p. 105). Deleuze writes:

> Freud was . . . aware of this, since he did search for a more profound instance than that of repression, even though he conceived of it in similar terms as a so-called "primary repression." . . . We do not repeat because we repress, we repress because we repeat. Moreover . . . we do not disguise because we repress, we disguise by virtue of the determinant centre of repetition. Repetition is no more secondary in relation to a supposed ultimate or originary fixed term than disguise is secondary in relation to repetition.
>
> (Deleuze 1968: 105)

Repetition operates within disguises.

How Fairbairn developed object relations theory

Fairbairn's work with children and adolescents at the Edinburgh University Psychological Clinic from 1927 to 1933 led to the opening of a Child and Juvenile Clinic in 1933, where Fairbairn worked until 1935. He gave a number of papers and lectures on child and adolescent psychology over the years including his ground-breaking paper on child sexual assault in 1935, in which he argues that it is the relationship of the abuser to the child that determines the severity of the after-effects of abuse. When the abuser is a parent upon whom the child relies for emotional security, the effect is most damaging. When that parent physically or sexually abuses a child, the trauma is severe and long-lasting because the dependent child feels fundamentally betrayed and because the child is therefore helpless to do anything about it. Experiencing physical pain usually leads to the action of withdrawal from the noxious stimulus in the present and to the thought of avoiding similar exposure in the future. Even young children can project themselves into possible future situations. But when the dependent child is abused by the person who is supposed to represent security, the child attaches to the pain as well as to the parent who inflicts it, and cannot separate from it. The child would rather imagine that the parent is good and the child bad, than be attached to a parent recognized as bad.

The main task of the parents and caregivers is to protect their children, recognize and affirm their children's growing personal identity, and pay attention to their emotions. The child then becomes a confident person who relates to, and differentiates among, other people or objects. Deleuze notes that emotion is expressed externally in, for example, the face or body, while the associated feelings are an internal mental experience which develops slightly later. William James (1890) says that the bodily expression of tears precedes the feeling of sorrow; and that if we sense danger, we run first, and then we feel fear. Emotion leads to action and action precedes the recognition of emotion. That is to say, emotion and the bodily state are intertwined.

As a result of modern brain scanning and dyeing techniques, neuroscientists have been able to demonstrate this. They can show the effect of sad or joyful feelings on the brain. Stimulation of specific areas of the brain induces specific emotional states. It is possible using scanning techniques to measure neural development in children, and identify the truncation or lack of it in disturbed children. In this way, it is possible to track the effects of adequate and inadequate early care (Schore 1994, 2001).

The self: psychological view

Fairbairn states: "An ego is present from birth. It does not develop out of the id. Libido is a function of the ego" (in Scharff & Birtles 1994: 155). This, of course, does not imply that the ego does not undergo development. The pristine infantile ego is the immanent self. Moreover, the ego is genetically oriented towards objects with whom to relate and have needs met. Thus the ego is inevitably developing within a continuous series of object relationships held in the external and internal environments in which the ego participates. I think that Fairbairn is imprecise in his use of the term ego, for in his theory, the ego, over the course of time experiencing unsatisfying interactions splits into parts that are combined with part objects and their associated affects. Repression of these exciting and rejecting ego/object/affect constellations by the central ego and the rejecting internal object relationship then forms a closed system within the psyche; while the central ego and the ideal object connected by feelings of satisfaction comprise an open system accessible to consciousness. Inner reality consists of conscious and unconscious internal object relationships in dynamic relationship.

Macmurray's theory of human relationships is contemporaneous with Fairbairn's. In *Persons in Relation* (1961) he remarks that "to exist is to endure for a time; and the person, being an agent, generates time as the form of his existence" (p. 107). He argues that "the Self is a person, and that personal existence is constituted by the relation of persons" (p. 12). So without interacting with other persons, we cannot develop a personal identity. We can see how this relates to the operation of repetition and difference in conjunction with that which is other, specifically other human beings.

In *The Self as Agent* (1957), Macmurray is concerned with active involvement in the world and the acquisition of knowledge. He argues: "Knowledge occurs primarily within action and arises from action" (p. xix), and "A self which does not act, does not exist" (p. 100). Macmurray describes the situation further as follows:

> To act and to know that I act are two aspects of one experience; since if I did not know that I was acting I should not be acting. And since to act is to do something, I must know to some extent what I am doing if I am doing it. There cannot be action without knowledge. Yet action is logically prior to knowledge, for there can be no knowledge without an actual activity which supports it; but there can be actual activity without knowledge. Such activity however is not action, but only movement; . . . not a deliberate effort to modify the Other.
>
> (Macmurray 1957: 102–103)

Objects that were established at a preverbal, symmetrical level and kept repressed are inaccessible and unspeakable. If Macmurray is right that knowledge derives from action, the inaccessibility of these objects means that they are not available for current experience, which means that knowledge cannot occur. This inability to process early mental activity in the asymmetrical mode accounts for pathological repetitive actions. We can think of endopsychic structure as a series of repetitions operating in a closed system.

In psychoanalysis, a patient's tendency to operate in the symmetrical mode is evident from the repetitive sameness of interactions between patient and analyst, such as continuing regressed behaviours and inexact interpretations. Becoming conscious of the level of symmetrical thought in the session, the

analyst can intervene in a different way to interrupt the cycle of repetition.
New knowledge will follow this mental activity.

The self: philosophical view

I shall now look at philosophical descriptions of the Self. *The Oxford
Dictionary of Philosophy* (Blackburn 1994) describes the Self as "the elusive
'I' that shows an alarming tendency to disappear when we try to introspect
it". That is not very helpful. In *A Critical Dictionary of Psychoanalysis*,
Rycroft (1968) gives two definitions: "1. When used by itself: indicates an
awareness of its own identity and his role as subject and agent. 2. As part of a
hyphenated word [I take him to mean I-Self]: the subject regarded as the
object of his own activity."

In Fairbairn's early writing during the late 1920s and early 1930s he does
use the term Self to describe the self-identifying human individual. However,
in his later psychoanalytical writings Fairbairn uses the term ego. It is my
view that he does this to prove to the arbiters of the psychoanalytic discipline
that his work is a continuance of, and validation of, Freudian theory.
Furthermore, as one who read Freud's work in the original German, he
picked up the word ego as the translation for Self. However, the Freudian ego
or self is a static hierarchical entity, while Fairbairn's endopsychic structure
comprising a closed and open system has spatially active, dynamic aspects.

Deleuze sees the "I" and the "Self" as two figures of differentiation in a
psychic system and must be seen as psychic species not biological species:

> The I forms the properly psyche of the species, while the Self forms
> the psychic organisation. The I is the quality of the human being as
> species . . . The I therefore appears at the end as the universal form of
> psychic life, just as the Self is the universal matter of that form. The I and
> the Self explicate each other.
>
> (Deleuze 1968: 256–257, 260)

This means that they confirm each other endlessly, but they are differentiated
from each other in an I-Self system, and thus they incorporate difference and
individuating factors. He notes that Sartre (1956) agrees that "the other
became object when I became subject and did not become subject unless I
became object" (Deleuze 1968: 261).

This I-Self system of personal identity is continuously confronted by the
other. Deleuze describes the locus of interaction with the other as a centre for
"enwinding, envelopment or implication", and thus an opportunity for
development of the I-Self system. He writes: "There is no love which does not
begin with the revelation of a possible world as such, unwound in the other
which expresses it." In the case of the mother or caregiver who initiates
this process for the baby: "Words offered by the other confer reality on the

possible." In this way, language exerts its effect *within the internal resonance systems*. "The structure of the other . . . and the corresponding function of language [convey] the tendency towards the interiorisation of difference" (Deleuze 1968: 261).

Deleuze demonstrates that the I-Self system, which is our personal identity, depends upon the interaction between two subject-objects, determined by the position which the one has adopted towards the other, that is to say, their internal orientation and the role which each is playing in activity or contemplative reflection. In short, our understanding and experience of our relationships with other people confirm and enhance our own identity.

Difference, complexity and maturation

Let us look further at difference and at our interactions with the other. Sartre (1956) writes: "The other is the indispensable mediator between myself and me." Through heightened self-awareness "I am as certain of his or her existence as I am of my own existence"; I have an "objective" self, that is a "self for others" (Sartre 1956, quoted in Holmes 1996: 315). In other words, being known and being communicated with are essential to confirm one's Self and its identity. In Fairbairn's terms, the mother and later the wider family are the indispensable mediators between the child and the environment. These mediators are indeed essential. If they often, or continuously, give distorted messages or fail to confirm the validity of the child's feelings, this can lead to inadequate relationships with inadequately differentiated objects. For the individual to attain mature dependence, however, these primary identifications with the other should have been superseded. As Fairbairn puts it: "The abandonment of infantile dependence involves an abandonment of relationships based upon primary identification in favour of relationships with differentiated objects" (1952: 42). He says that mature dependence is characterized predominantly by an attitude of giving (p. 39). Mature dependence is the "capacity on the part of a differentiated individual for co-operative relationships with differentiated objects" (p. 145). Here Fairbairn is describing the achievement of abandoning the comfort of identification with original objects and becoming an identifiable Self with integrity.

Let us now turn to the dependence aspects of the concept of mature dependence. According to Fairbairn, cultural, political and familial interactions determine endopsychic structure. This broad constellation of social interactions becomes our individual identity. This process of interiorization demonstrates our dependence upon other human beings. Dependence continues from infancy when babies are reliant on emotional and physical cues to express their needs, through early childhood when children then have the ability to communicate verbally with others, and on to adulthood. Then language forms our view of the world and limits our mental functioning when constricted by the modes of thought implicit in each individual language. But language also helps to express touch, vision, and experience of the self in action and so it allows us to qualify our ideas of space. Language confirms our individual identity and ensures mental continuity.

Concluding remarks

Each impression or identification is brief and fleeting. It belongs to the past as a memory, to the present as a current experience, and to the future in the form of expectation. We expect recognizable objects to retain their identity into the future when they can be identified again. Similarly when the recognizable object is one of pain, unpleasantness or injury, we will make sure to avoid the repetition of the circumstances, so that the outcome is different. Repetition and difference are held within a time structure. We remember how some impressions are the same, and how others are different, over time. This capacity enables us to learn, to speak, and to communicate. We have a personal history which grows over time, and which we can relate. Because of this capacity for memory, we can recognize ourselves as an I–Self system. We can also recognize others, their names, and their roles in our lives. In other words, under normal conditions, we develop a sense of what it means to have a continuous identity, which fully affirms other personal identities and recognizes that their needs, their desires, are similar to our own, and yet unique to the others. Self and Other have equal rights. When we fully acknowledge this in our interrelationships, we see others not in the roles that they perform for us but as separate I–Selves. Then we can claim to have attained mature dependence.

References

Blackburn, S. (1994). *Oxford Dictionary of Philosophy*. Oxford: Oxford University Press.
Damasio, A. (1994). *Descartes' Error*. New York: Putnam
Deleuze, G. (1968). *Difference and Repetition*, trans. P. Patton (1994). London: Athlone Press.
Descartes, R. (1637). *Meditations on First Philosophy: Second Meditation*, eds and trans. J. Cottingham, R. Stoothoff and D. Murdoch (1985). In *The Philosophical Writings of Descartes*. Cambridge: Cambridge University Press.
Fairbairn, W. R. D. (1951). A synopsis of the author's views regarding the structure of the personality. In *Psychoanalytic Studies of the Personality*, intro. E. Jones. London & Boston: Routledge & Kegan Paul, 1952, and in *Psychoanalytic Studies of the Personality*, intro. D. E. Scharff and E. F. Birtles, pp. 162–179. London and New York: Routledge, 1994.
—— (1952). *Psychoanalytic Studies of the Personality*, intro. E. Jones. London and Boston: Routledge & Kegan Paul. Reprinted, intro. D. E. Scharff and E. F. Birtles. London & New York: Routledge, 1994.
—— (1994). *From Instinct to Self: Selected Papers of W. R. D. Fairbairn. Vol. 1: Clinical*

and Theoretical Papers, eds D. E. Scharff and E. F. Birtles. *Volume 2: Applications and Early Contributions*, eds E. F. Birtles and D. E Scharff. Northvale, NJ: Jason Aronson.

Holmes O. W. (1996). *Perceptions of 'Otherness': Isaac de Pinto, Voltaire, and a Personal Interpretation of Jewish Experience*. Madison, WI and London: University of Wisconsin Press.

Hume, D. (1739). *The Treatise of Human Nature*. Oxford: Oxford University Press, 2000.

—— (1748). An enquiry concerning human understanding. In *The Philosophy of David Hume*, ed. N. Kemp Smith. London: Macmillan, 1941.

James, W. (1890). *The Principles of Psychology*. New York: Dover.

Macmurray, J. (1957). *The Self as Agent*. London: Faber & Faber.

—— (1961). *Persons in Relation*. London: Faber & Faber.

Matte Blanco, I. (1998). *The Unconscious as Infinite Sets: An Essay in Bilogic*, foreword, E. Rayner. London: Karnac (original edition 1968).

Rycroft, C. (1968). *A Critical Dictionary of Psychoanalysis*. London: Penguin.

Sartre, J.-P. (1956). *Being and Nothingness: An Essay on Phenomenological Ontology*, trans. H. E. Barnes. New York: Philosophical Library.

Schore, A. (1994). *Affect Regulation and the Origin of the Self: The Neurobiology of Emotional Development*. Hillsdale, NJ: Lawrence Erlbaum Associates, Inc.

—— (1999). Traumatic attachment and the development of the right brain. Paper presented at the Bowlby conference Minds in the Making, March 2000.

—— (2001). Paper presented at the 7th Annual Bowlby Memorial lecture Minds in the Making. In *Affect Regulation and the Repair of the Self*, pp. 33–57. New York: Norton, 2003.

Chapter 4

Fairbairn in France

Henri Vermorel

Fairbairn in France since 1955

The object relations theory of W. R. D. Fairbairn (1952) was late in being accepted by the British Psychoanalytical Society and, for a long time, remained unrecognized in the United States and Europe. Fairbairn's work has since inspired important trends in psychoanalysis in English-speaking countries, but it remained unknown in France until recent years.

Jacques Lacan (1955) was the first in France to make mention of Fairbairn's works. He had just left the International Psychoanalytical Association (IPA), and was rereading Freud's works as a basis from which to develop his own theory. In his seminar, Lacan referred at length to contemporary psychoanalytic works on object relationships, frequently criticizing them harshly. According to Lacan, the object relationship is speculative compared to the intersubjective relationship, which focuses not on the object to which the "I" relates but on the "I" as subject, an idea taken from Hegel. For Lacan, Need is different from Desire, and the need-based object relationship is different from the "imaginary" relationship between the I and the Other, which involves language as well as unconscious communication.

Though Lacan rather liked Michael Balint, he reproached him for his "two body" psychology, because it contemplates only a dual relationship where the "third" (*le tiers*) is missing (Balint 1965). Lacan was much more caustic in his criticism of Maurice Bouvet (1967), the main French proponent of an object-relationship approach inspired by Freud and Abraham, and one of the brightest psychoanalysts of the Paris Psychoanalytic Society, who sadly died at 49, before realizing his potential. Lacan also heaped reproaches on the Paris Psychoanalytic Society and the International Psychoanalytical Association, both of which he quit in disgust. Incidentally, Lacan also attacked the object representation ideas introduced into American ego psychology, and held a bitter grudge against the International Psychoanalytical Association, which did not give his ideas a warm welcome and refused to reintegrate him.

Lacan's criticism of Fairbairn centered on Fairbairn's (1944) article: "Endopsychic Structure considered in Terms of Object Relations". According to Lacan, when Fairbairn wrote "*Libido* is object seeking", he was guilty of misinterpreting Freud's phrase "*Love* is searching for objects". According to Lacan, Fairbairn confused the "imaginary" object relationship with the "symbolic" intersubjective dimension. For Lacan, the object is hetero-geneous: it is altogether real/imaginary/and symbolic (*réel, imaginaire, et symbolique*), and he objected that Fairbairn did not differentiate these aspects. Lacan thought that the accepted object and the rejected object, in opposition to one another in Fairbairn's endopsychic situation, do not have the same quality. In Fairbairn's system, according to Lacan, the analyst sits as central observing ego, and reconstructs the subject's imaginary world according to his own ego standard, thus neglecting the unconscious dimension.

In his 1956–1957 seminar, Lacan continued his clinical work on object relationships. He stressed that it is the lack of the object that originates desire and the wish to rediscover the lost object. Then he became interested in Winnicott's (1951) work on the transitional object. Winnicott showed that at the beginning there is a coincidence between the hallucination of the mother's breast and the real object, as far as it fulfils the child's need at the right moment. But frustration of the child by the mother imposes a painful delay in which the child learns to make out the difference between reality and illusion. In mentioning the impact of actual frustration, Winnicott went against the psychoanalytic trend, which had reduced actual environmental inadequacies to fantasy frustrations. Lacan made a distinction between frus-tration, which relates to the "imaginary", and deprivation, which relates to the real absence of the object. He did not seem to notice that in stressing the intrapsychic structural response to damage brought about by real inadequacies in the environment, Fairbairn had got ahead of Winnicott. Unlike Fairbairn, Lacan did not pay much attention to the borderline-schizoid states (*les états-limites*) and to the metapsychological revision required after practical experience with them.

Lacan went on building his works on a more and more personal note, diverging from mainstream psychoanalytic theory and technique, while the Lacanian School organized around him split again and again, resulting in the current scattering of the French Lacanian groups. The curse cast by Lacan over the object-relationship concept had long-term repercussions amongst his disciples, and spread even further amongst the French psychoanalysts. For a long time there were hardly any studies on object relationships, Fairbairn remained unknown and none of his texts were published in France.

It was only in 1974, that the first French translation of Fairbairn's famous paper on schizoid states appeared in *Nouvelle Revue de Psychanalyse*, edited by J. B. Pontalis. It is interesting to note that the first comprehensive mention of Fairbairn's theories came from psychoanalysts who, after being close to Lacan, left him to join the Association Psychanalytique de France. Unlike Lacan, Pontalis was interested in Fairbairn's works. Pontalis thought that the endopsychic structure as a closed system, comparable to metaphors about the body, was a viable explanation of the mental workings in non-neurotic states of mind, and gave a way of approaching them from a stance of inquiring "How is it going in there?" instead of "What does that mean?" which is more appropriate in work with neurotic patients. So, Pontalis took up the object-relationship investigation where Lacan had left off, answered his objections from 20 years earlier, and did do Fairbairn justice; although he did not agree that Fairbairn's theory of psychological functioning was valid for pathology other than the schizoid. From 1960, many psychoanalysts such as Racamier, Schweich, Bergeret and Green began to be interested in *les états-limites*, generally without any reference to Fairbairn.

Very conscious of British psychoanalytic writing and of Masud Khan's well-known close relationship with Winnicott, Pontalis welcomed Khan as a member of the editorial board of *Nouvelle Revue de Psychanalyse*. In 1995, Pontalis published a paper, "My Experience of Analysis with Fairbairn and Winnicott", by Harry Guntrip, one of Fairbairn's disciples who had undergone analysis with Fairbairn and subsequently with Winnicott. In this paper in which he described the path of his psychoanalysis with each of them, Guntrip's well-known ambivalence towards Fairbairn was palpable. His rephrasing of Fairbairn's ideas helped make Fairbairn's work more widely known, but Guntrip was sometimes accused of distorting it. Nevertheless Pontalis, Didier Anzieu and Guy Rosolato appreciated Guntrip's text as a precious document, and that brought Fairbairn as well as Winnicott to France. Pontalis's introduction of Winnicott's works in France had a long-lasting impact on French psychoanalysis. Winnicott was extraordinarily successful in France, and his ideas were integrated into French psychological thinking far beyond the analytic circles, in such measure that quite a few psychiatric institutions were named after him. This leads me to question his success in contrast to the lack of appreciation of Fairbairn.

Two other French psychoanalysts, Bela Grunberger and Janine Chasseguet, editors of a psychoanalytic collection at Tchou, published some chapters that were extracts of Fairbairn's ideas under the titles "The Ego Trinity" (1978a); "Libido Searching for Objects" (1978b); "Two Psychological Types: the Schizoid and the Depressive" (1980). These well-chosen extracts gave a good survey of Fairbairn's thought, with accurate commentary. Perhaps it was Grunberger's (1971) interest in narcissism – which for him is a structure chronologically preceding the Oedipus stage – that made him sensitive to Fairbairn's understanding of pre-Oedipal dynamics, even though his own point of view is different. For instance, in contrast to Fairbairn, he gives the anal stage great importance. As for Janine Chasseguet, she uses the object-relations idea to express the subject's investment of energy in objects of love and hate, but she retains the structure of Abraham's developmental stages.

Fairbairn's article "Considerations Arising out of the Schreber Case" (1956) appeared in *Le Cas Schreber*, an anthology of papers on Schreber's paranoia, translated from English into French, and published in 1979 by Eduardo Prado de Oliveira in the Bibliothèque de Psychanalyse, run by Jean Laplanche at PUF Publishing.

Didier Anzieu (1996) paid tribute to Fairbairn as the first to outline the paradoxical transferential mechanism in psychosis and other pathologies. He found in Fairbairn a first intuition of this phenomenon, which Fairbairn described as the persistent tie to the bad object, in which the child, misunderstood or ill-treated by the environment, cannot acknowledge that his sufferings originated with his parents, and prefers to internalize this evil and perceive himself as bad, thus sparing the environment he depends on. Bernard Brusset's (1988) book *Psychanalyse du Lien, la Relation d'Objet* is a well-documented study on various object-relations concepts. For the first time in France, Fairbairn's theories were clearly explained and thoroughly discussed, but in the book's preface André Green (1988) expressed caution about accepting the value of object-relations theory.

Not many analysts in France have shown a true interest in Fairbairn's works. Only in the last ten years of the twentieth century did Fairbairn's works become more widely accessible to French readers. In 1987, Fairbairn's paper "Observations on the Nature of Hysterical States", introduced by Henri Vermorel, appeared in the *Revue Française de Psychanalyse*. Of special note is the publication by the tenacious, competent Edouard Korenfeld (1988–2005) of Fairbairn's collected works as *Editions du Monde Interne*. In 1998, a first volume *Etudes Psychanalytiques de la Personnalité* appeared, well translated by Pierre Lecointe, with a preface by Henri Vermorel, and an afterword by James Innes-Smith, Fairbairn's former analysand. In 1999, the second volume *Structure Endopsychique et Relation d'Objet* was published (third volume 2005). These publications were a turning point in the dissemination of Fairbairn's ideas. Knowledge of his work increased, and therefore he was more often quoted. In 2001, the first French psychology doctoral thesis devoted to Fairbairn's work was submitted at Paris VII University, by Sabine Vuaillat, under Jacques André's leadership. It is an extremely well-informed and serious study, in which Fairbairn's work is sympathetically set out, put in context, examined as to its origins, and thoroughly discussed from a French psychoanalytical point of view in which drive theory keeps its place. (See Chapter 11 for a shortened version of this thesis.)

Current evaluations of Fairbairn's contributions

The publication of *Sexualité infantile et attachement* (André and Laplanche 2000) gave importance to the ideas of the British Independent Group; to Balint's (1937) paper "Early Developmental States of the Ego: Primary Object Love", to Bowlby's (1969–1980) theory on attachment, and Fairbairn's (1952) ideas on object-relations theory. The book gathered chapters by Jean Laplanche, Pierre Fedida, Jacques André and others, all APF members, who continued the debate that emanated from a Daniel Widlöcher (2000) article on the respective positions of drives and object relationships. This volume gave a good account of the current French position that ascribes a major place to drive and infantile sexuality, while also linking them to object relationships.

The question remains why Fairbairn's ideas have taken such a long time to be welcomed in France. The reasons are certainly complex. I have several hypotheses. Fairbairn was unknown for a long time in his own country, Edinburgh being far from London, the heart of British psychoanalytic activity, and the British Psychoanalytical Society was not open to the innovative thinking of the Scottish psychoanalyst during his lifetime. I believe that may explain why Fairbairn became known beyond Scotland only during the late 1950s, in the last ten years of his life. In France, psychoanalysis had a new start after World War II, when it was greatly influenced by psychoanalysis in England, which had become the psychoanalytical international centre. French psychoanalysts could only reluctantly welcome Fairbairn's works because he wished object-relations theory to take the place of drive theory, which was given great importance in France; and because Lacan's hatred of object relations had a long-lasting effect, even amongst those who were not Lacan's disciples. Nevertheless, from the 1960s French psychoanalysis developed from within and matured in its capacity to accept foreign approaches to psychoanalytic theory and practice, welcoming Winnicott's ideas and to a lesser extent Bion's, both of whom had been active during the war years at the time of the controversial discussions concerning the opposition between the theoretical positions of Anna Freud and Melanie Klein, and their followers (King and Steiner 1991).

Why has Fairbairn, himself a member of the Independent Group of the British Psychoanalytic Society, been overshadowed? Being in Scotland and uncomfortable travelling, he was geographically removed from the centre where the discussions took place, and he was chronologically stuck between Freud's first and second generation disciples. Jones in England was ten years older than Fairbairn, and the Winnicott/Bion generation was ten years younger. More importantly, the extraordinary success of Winnicott's works in France certainly overshadowed Fairbairn's fame. Analysts in France knew of Fairbairn's ideas but did not recognize them as such, since they came via Winnicott who played on the same ground as Fairbairn, having been inspired by nearly all his themes.

Among the themes common to Winnicott and Fairbairn, first place goes to the importance of the family circle at the beginning of the baby's life. Winnicott's (1945) emphasis on the mother's holding and handling of her infant in a psychosomatic partnership is at odds with Melanie Klein's focus on the endogenous source of frustration. For Winnicott, a baby does not exist without a mother. She must be "good enough" for her baby to be able to grow. Injury caused by lack of care in the baby's environment leaves its mark throughout life and, without being remembered as such, is lived again in analysis, as a "fear of breakdown" being about to happen. Unlike Fairbairn, Winnicott gives his own version of drives and in particular "life strength", to which "primary creativity" is tied. Winnicott conceived of analysis as a meeting place in which to play rather than to interpret, and in which to experience the transference. Like Fairbairn, he is opposed to Melanie Klein's idea of an endogenous death drive. Winnicott's concept of "transitionality" incontestably proceeded from Fairbairn's idea of an object relations transitional stage between infantile and mature dependency. Winnicott elaborated on Fairbairn's ideas creatively, giving them a personal shape of less severity; for instance, expressing his understanding of human experience in user-friendly terms such as "living creatively" and "feeling real". The "self" to which Winnicott gives such great importance, is related to Fairbairn's primary unsplit ego, a primary ego of the narcissistic core.

Winnicott seldom mentions Fairbairn's works. Only at the end of his life, in a few lines in *Lettres Vives* (1989), did he recognize in retrospect his debt towards Fairbairn. Winnicott had been particularly critical of Melanie Klein's concept of envy. Might his attack on envy have a personal echo? For in one of his last letters he confessed that it was difficult for him to take into account and to discuss others' writings; quite remarkable for a man known for his equanimity and maturity. Could it be that the same sort of envy prevented him from mentioning earlier what he owed to several of his contemporaries, and especially to Fairbairn?

More the media psychoanalyst than Fairbairn ever was, Winnicott developed some of Fairbairn's intuitions in a creative and original way so that Winnicott's concepts of "false self" (1960), "primitive anxiety" (1945) and "fear of breakdown" (1963) are now familiar to French psychoanalysts, who, however, are generally quite unaware that the starting point for these ideas is in Fairbairn.

On the other hand, French psychoanalysis has taken into account the contributions of infant observation and attachment research stemming from the work of Bowlby, another member of the Independent group. These findings have demonstrated the importance of attachment and underlined the lifelong influence of the first stages of psychic functioning, all of which come together to confirm Fairbairn's initial intuitions.

The stakes for a debate

Fairbairn criticized Freudian theory because it was a drive theory. Even if we think his criticism excessive, we might admit that his contributions put a new light on the construction of the sexual drives themselves by reminding us that the sexual drives need strongly built self-preservation drives if they are to achieve their full dimension. Unlike Fairbairn, Benno Rosenberg (1991) gave drives an essential place. Yet when Rosenberg considered erogenous masochism as a "life guard" (*gardien de la vie*), suggesting that it involves a mixture of life and death drives and depends on a self-preservation role, his view ran in parallel with Fairbairn's. In Rosenberg's view, the equilibrium of life and death drives derives from a prior sufficiency of gratification of the child's needs at the beginning of life, and so prevents the destructiveness otherwise found in hysteria, moral masochism, borderline states, perversions and psychosis. Fairbairn also contradicted Freud's (1914) idea of primary narcissism, primary self-eroticism, and an original symbiotic stage. In this objection, he has been joined by Michel Fain who describes a narcissism that is mainly secondary, and Jean Laplanche (1987) who refutes primary self-eroticism and narcissism.

Jean Laplanche (1987), who did not show great fondness for Fairbairn's theories, nevertheless subsumed them when he described the "object-source of the drive" (*l'objet-source de la pulsion*) and that of "generalized seduction" (*séduction généralisée*), in which "enigmatic messages" (*messages énigmatiques*) sent by the parents are, from the beginning of life, the source of the intrusion of sexuality into the baby's psychic life. Narcissistic seduction injects sexuality into the first intersubjective experience.

Fairbairn (1941) criticized Freudian theory on the grounds that it located the source of the drives in the erogenous zones and considered them to be zones of lesser resistance. Fairbairn (1954) studied the genesis of the hysterical symptom of conversion in which a function of the body is altered under the influence of psychic conflicts transferred onto the body. He suggested that localization of a conversion symptom is preceded by an earlier stage of "somatic compliance", a mechanism that had always remained obscure to Freud. Somatic compliance goes along with an excess of the mother's investment in the child's body and of the functions of the orifices. In this perspective, the building up of the erogenous zones results from parental overinvestment. But these are pathological somatic conversions involving bodily zones overinvested in the mother–child primitive relationship. Fairbairn argued that symptoms of anal fixation are breakdown products, a regression to drive behaviour because object relationship had been inadequate, and not evidence of primary anal sexuality.

In my view, erogenous zones are planned in mankind for a precise physiological function and psychic mechanisms are modelled on physiological ones metaphoricaly. If I take into account not only the way the child behaves libidinally towards the object but also the mother's way of teaching her child control of the anal sphincter, as Fairbairn did, I do not see why the anal erogenous zone could not become a privileged zone, the function of which has its equal in the psyche. My perspective restores the concept of "anality" that was so discredited by Fairbairn.

And what about desire, fantasy and infantile sexuality which, along with drive, are all rejected by Fairbairn who stresses need and the search for the object as the primary motivation, and who wants to replace drive theory by object relationships theory? Indeed, Freudian drive theory is not devoid of inadequacies and deficiencies, but evicting it, purely and simply, as Fairbairn does for the benefit of an object relationships theory is not itself free from contradiction or deadlock. I suggest it would be more in accordance with current psychoanalytical knowledge to try to join together these two opposite poles of analytical theory. Little by little, Fairbairn excludes drives and desire from his vocabulary, which is a major deficiency of his system. Yet libido, in the form of attachment that supports the search for the object, calls for an appropriate operational and environmental response. Indeed, when we conceive of the building of sexual and death drives on the self-preservation drives, we are no longer in a strictly instinctual field, but already in a psychic order which transcends the purely innate. That which is innate and that which is acquired are in a state of mutual influence that ethologists call "interactional epigenesis".

Piera Aulagnier (1975) said that the mother is the interpreter (*porte-parole*) of the human order. She worms her way into answering the infant's search. With her own unconscious directly connected with the child's psyche, she conveys her heritage and culture to the next generation. Culture is grafted through narrative, preverbal communication expressed in the mother's care of her infant, and in the sexuality of the union between the mother and her newborn. However intimate this union may be, it is nevertheless not a pure dyad because the father is always present in the mother's desire. When she finds once again her desire as a woman, she breaks the narcissistic union with the baby. Only because of her momentous deinvestment can the presence of "the third" (*le tiers*) appear. That third was later acknowledged as the paternal object (Michel Fain and Denise Braunschweig 1975). Writing in the same vein, Bion (1963) said that when the mother is taking care of the baby, she addresses her "rêverie" to the father. In contrast, neither Fairbairn nor Winnicott showed much interest in the role of the father in the life of the pre-Oedipal child.

From 1905, Freud described the mother as "the first object" of the infant's drives, but he later overshadowed the role of the original mother in his theory building. In 1938, he added that the mother is also "the first seductress" who, through care and feeding, contributes to building her child's psyche. Paul-Claude Racamier (1992) developed the concept of the "narcissistic seduction" through which the mother's sublimated eros plays its part in the creation of the child's narcissism, contributes to setting up the erogenous zones, and making the mother a sexual object. Following Freud, who thought that the sexual drive leans on the self-preservation drive, Laplanche and Pontalis (1967) elaborated the concept of "leaning on", which makes it possible to connect infantile sexuality to fantasy – a link that Fairbairn had a tendency to put out of his theory. This fantasy ensues from the desire for hallucinatory satisfaction, which is built up by repeated experiences of need satisfaction, and therefore creates the sexual object, which is linked to auto-erotism.

This new object – the mother as both a total object and a sexual object – introduces the logic of infantile sexuality, radically different from the logic of the needs. In Freud's polymorphous perverse child, auto-erotic object relationship is not of the same nature as that of breast object relationship described by Fairbairn. The two levels of functioning coexist, and it is necessary not to reduce this complex reality to a single principle. Infantile (psychic) sexuality is the start of human desire, long before the genital sexual maturity of adolescence. Psychic desire must meet up with physical genitality, and here is a potential for many difficulties to arise as desire and genitality combine in action.

Conclusion

Even if we cannot accept Fairbairn's excessive criticism of drive theory, we must agree that his conception of the impact on psychic structure of the maternal response to infantile dependency put a new light on the construction of the drives, especially on the drive for self-preservation. We must acknowledge that Fairbairn's work on love becoming dangerous and destructive and on the tie to the bad object led the way to the study of paradoxical process, later described by the Palo Alto School, and developed in French psychoanalysis by Paul-Claude Racamier, Didier Anzieu and René Roussillon (1992) who found that flaws in self-preservation generate a reversal of behaviours.

Fairbairn led the way for understanding borderline states and other pathologies in which the early frustration of need causes a destructive quality in the personality. When the self-preservative drives are not supported by the environment, they cannot play their part and the balance is tipped towards destruction. Neurotic conditions result from misadventures of desire and fantasy and for them therapy is a search for meaning, but the borderline states result from flaws of self-preservation that interfere with the capacity for symbolization. These patients are no longer trying to satisfy their desires, because they are concerned only with the survival of their psychic life, and this situation therefore calls for different strategies.

All the history of neglect of Fairbairn's work in France does not in anyway detract from the current level of interest; through its innovative radical quality, it has found a place in the history of psychoanalysis. Its appearance on the French stage led us to rethink the drive/object relations debate in depth. So we must acknowledge Fairbairn as the first to underline the essential part played by the environment in the genesis of the psyche, showing that lack of attention to the child's needs is the root of the most serious injuries. When the mother is not good enough at tuning in to her infant, the early frustration of need creates a destructive aspect in the infant's evolving personality and later gives rise to serious emotional illness. The ideas of Fairbairn, extended by those of Winnicott, gives analysts in France another way of conceptualizing the endopsychic situation of those who fall outside the neurotic category, and more importantly a way of asking them "How is it in there?" and then helping them to a healthier adjustment to their trauma.

References

André, J. & Laplanche J. (eds) (2000). *Sexualité infantile et attachement*. Paris: PUF.

Anzieu, D. (1996). *Créer. Détruire*. Paris: Dunod.

Aulagnier, P. (1975). *La Violence de l'Interprétation: du Pictogramme à l'Énoncé*. Paris: PUF.

Balint, M. (1965). Early developmental states of the ego: primary object love. In M. Balint *Primary Love and Psychoanalytic Technique*, pp. 74–90. London: Tavistock.

Bion, W. R. (1963). *Aux Sources de l'Expérience*. Paris: PUF, 1979.

Bouvet, M. (1967). *Oeuvres Psychanalytiques I. La Relation d'Objet*. Paris: Payot.

Bowlby, J. (1965–1980). *Attachment and Loss: Vols 1–3*. New York: Basic Books.

Brusset, B. (1988). *Psychoanalyse du Lien, la Relation d'Objet*. Paris: Centurion.

Fain, M. and Braunschweig, D. (1975). *La Nuit, le Jour*. Paris: PUF.

Fairbairn, W. R. D. (1941). A revised psychopathology of psychoses and psycho-neuroses. *International Journal of Psycho-Analysis* 22 (2, 3): 250–279.

—— (1952). *Psychoanalytic Studies of the Personality*. London: Tavistock.

—— (1954). Observations on the nature of hysterical states. *British Journal of Medical Psychology* 27(3): 106–125.

—— (1956). Considerations arising out of the Schreber case. In E. P. de Olivera (ed.) *Le Cas Schreber*. Paris: PUF.

—— (1987). Observations on the nature of hysterical states. Intro. H. Vermorel. *Revue Française Psychanalyse* 66: 571–603.

—— (1988). *Collected Works of Ronald Fairbairn. Vol. 1: Etudes Psychanalytiques de la Personnalité*, trans P. Lecointe. Paris: Editions du Monde Interne.

—— (1999). *Collected Works of Ronald Fairbairn. Vol. 2: Structure Endopsychique et Relation d'Object*, trans. P. Lecointe. Paris: Editions du Monde Interne.

—— (2005). *Collected Works of Ronald Fairbairn. Vol. 3* trans. P. Lecointe, Paris: Editions du Monde Interne.

Freud, S. (1905). Three essays on the theory of sexuality. *Standard Edition* 7: 135–243.

—— (1914). On narcissism. Trans. *La Vie Sexuelle*. Paris: PUF, 1969.

—— (1938). Le clivage du moi dans le processus de défense. *Résultats, Idées, Problèmes, 2*. Paris: PUF.

Green, A. (1988). Preface. In B. Brusset *Psychoanalyse du Lien, la Relation d'Objet*. Paris: Centurion.

Grunberger, B. (1971). *Narcissism: Psychoanalytic Essays*. Madison CT: International Universities Press.

Grunberger, H. and Chasseguet-Smirgel, J. (1978a). The ego trinity. In *Les Grandes Découvertes de la Psychanalyse*. Paris: Tchou.

—— (1978b). Libido searching for objects. In *Les Grandes Découvertes de la Psychanalyse*. Paris: Tchou.

—— (1980). Two psychological types: the schizoïde and the depressive. In *Les Grandes Découvertes de la Psychanalyse*. Paris: Tchou.

Guntrip, H. (1977). My analysis with Fairbairn and Winnicott. *Nouvelle Revue de Psychanalyse* 15: 5–27.

King, P. and Steiner, R. (1991). *The Freud–Klein Controversies 1941–1945.* London: Routledge.

Lacan, J. (1955). L'analyse objectivée. Critique de Fairbairn. *Le Séminaire, Livre II.* Paris: Seuil, 1978.

Laplanche, J. (1987). *Nouveaux Fondements pour la Psychanalyse.* Paris: PUF.

Laplanche, J. and Pontalis, J.-B. (1967). *Vocabulaire de la psychanalyse.* Paris: PUF.

Pontalis, J.-B. (1974). A propos de Fairbairn. Le psychisme comme double métaphore du corps. *Nouvelle Revue de Psychanalyse* 10: 56–59.

Racamier, P.-C. (1992). *Le Génie des Origines.* Paris: Payot.

Rosenberg, B. (1991). Masochisme mortifère et masochisme gardien de la vie. *Monographies de la Revue Française Psychanalyse.* Paris: PUF.

Roussillon, R. (1992). *Paradoxes et Situations-limites de la Psychanalyse.* Paris: PUF.

Vuaillat, S. (2001). L'œuvre de Fairbairn, sources, description et fonction de sa théorie psychanalytique de la relation d'objet. Doctoral thesis. Paris VII University.

Widlöcher, D. (2000). *Sexualité Infantile et Attachement.* Paris: PUF.

Winnicott, D. W. (1945). Primitive emotional development. In *Through Paediatrics to Psycho-Analysis*, pp. 145–156. London: Hogarth: 1975.

—— (1951). Transitional objects and transitional phenomena. In *Through Paediatrics to Psycho-Analysis*, pp. 229–242. London: Hogarth, 1975.

—— (1960). Ego distortion in terms of true and false self. In *The Maturational Processes and the Facilitating Environment*, pp. 140–152. London: Hogarth, 1965.

—— Fear of breakdown. In C. Winnicott, R. Shepherd and M. Davis (eds) *Psychoanalytic Explorations*, pp. 87–95. Cambridge MA: Harvard University Press.

—— (1989). *Lettres Vives.* Paris: NRF Gallimard.

Chapter 5

Fairbairn in Germany

Rainer Rehberger

History of the introduction of object relations theory in Germany

Among the first psychoanalysts who supported German colleagues in their efforts to establish the new German Psychoanalytical Association (DPV) after World War II and the Shoah were Michael and Enid Balint. They had been contacted by Alexander and Margarete Mitscherlich back in the 1950s. Before long, Balint and his books were well known in Germany. It took some years, however, before the theories of other representatives of the British school of psychoanalysis were adopted in western Germany. In 1962 a collection of Melanie Klein's papers was published in Germany for the first time. The first translation of Winnicott came out in 1969. Several years later *Attachment*, the first part of John Bowlby's trilogy, became available in a German translation. Peter Kutter, Frankfurt, edited a reader with several papers on object relations theories in 1982, including Balint, Winnicott, Bowlby, Sutherland, Grunberger, Modell, Guntrip and others. This book contained the first German translation of a paper by Fairbairn, "Object Relationships and Dynamic Structure".

In the late 1970s Gerald von Minden, a psychoanalyst from Munich, was the first German author – as far as I know – to reflect Fairbairn's thinking. He became familiar with progress in psychoanalysis from his sojourns in the United States and Great Britain, where he probably met John D. Sutherland. Von Minden had already been acquainted with the concept of "ego splitting" in Germany. He said that reference to ego splitting in Müller-Braunschweig's 1970 paper "On the Genesis of Ego Disturbances" (*Zur Genese der Ich-Störungen*) was typical of German psychoanalysis in the early 1970s, but there was no link made to the work of Fairbairn or Melanie Klein.

Gerald von Minden published his paper "Disturbances in Ego Structure and the Theory of Object Relations" in 1978 (*Der strukturell Ich-gestörte Patient und die Theorie der Objektbeziehungen*). He gave an impressive introduction to the thinking of British psychoanalysis. Above all he presented Fairbairn's concept of the schizoid personality, his basic assumptions about the early development of the child, his concept of object-seeking libido, and his theories of dynamic ego structures and the basic endopsychic situation. He also discussed and compared the contributions of Melanie Klein and Winnicott with object relations theory as formulated by Otto Kernberg.

In 1988 von Minden published *The Fragmented Person* (*Der Bruchstück-Mensch*), in which he described the problems of modern narcissistic people in a technocratic world. To preface his remarks, he discussed the development of psychoanalytic theories during the 1960s and 1970s in Great Britain and the United States, including Kernberg and Kohut on ego structure, and explored their connections to the theories developed by Fairbairn many years earlier.

In his effort to understand the reasons for certain disturbances, particularly of patients with borderline symptoms, von Minden used the concept of the schizoid personality and the theory of dynamic ego structures developed by Fairbairn. For von Minden, the central task of analysis is the attempt to integrate the split off parts of the ego into the central ego. In the most important clinical part of his book von Minden explores the problem of anxiety being induced within the analyst by his patient's regression as well as by his own. However, von Minden did not attract a sufficient number of interested readers to enlarge the reception of Fairbairn's ideas in Germany.

Gerd Heising, co-worker and one of the successors of Horst-Eberhard Richter at the Psychosomatic Clinic at the University Clinics in Giessen, chose a rather different approach to Fairbairn's thinking. His views have been summarized by Hensel, Rost and Vorspohl in the preface of a recently published reader, *The Attraction of the "Bad Object"*. In the introductory part of this book Heising, drawing on object relational concepts of the British school in a typically idiosyncratic manner, conceived of his own theoretical model. On the one hand, like Fairbairn, he stressed the splitting of the object leading to an exciting and rejecting libidinal object. On the other hand, like Winnicott, he focused on the caring, non-exciting maternal object described by Winnicott. Heising traced these concepts back to Freud's writings about sexuality and the choice of partners. Strongly criticizing the neglect of the important role of sexuality in post-Freudian developments of psychoanalytic thinking, Heising combined the central place which sexuality occupies in Freud's drive theory with vital elements of the theories of Klein, Fairbairn, Guntrip and Winnicott. Heising was fascinated by the function of the exciting and rejecting object in sexuality. He formulated his theory of "Freud's sexual object-psychology". However, Heising's clinical papers on the importance of sexuality revealed his eclectic use of concepts of the various British theorists and his neglect of any deeper discussion of their thinking.

Inspired to study Fairbairn by Heising, Bernhard Hensel, Patricia Williamson and Ellen Kindschuh-van Roje (Giessen) set out to translate several chapters of Fairbairn's *Psychoanalytic Studies of the Personality* in the early 1990s, and used this material in training seminars at the Giessen Institute of Psychoanalysis.

My own path to Fairbairn and object relations theory

I have to go back to the time of my personal analysis with Dr A, which started 30 years ago. For me, interruptions of my regular sessions due to holidays and so on were accompanied by painful reactions. In particular I remember the Easter break during the first years of analysis, when I had planned to drive to Baden-Baden to visit an exhibition of European symbolists. Day after day passed, I felt depressed and was not able to make the trip to the city 150 kilometres away. Finally, on the last day of my holidays, I drove there and saw the exhibition. Of all the interesting paintings one remained in my memory. The "Isle of Death" by Arnold Boecklin, a romantic painter from Switzerland.

For my analyst – to whom I owe a lot in becoming an analyst myself – one of the main reasons for my condition was guilt due to the envy and hate activated in my transference to him. He thought that I hated him for causing the separation, repressed my hate and suffered consciously as a result of my unconscious self-punishment for my hateful feelings. This was back in the 1970s.

As a young psychotherapist then working as a resident at the Department of Psychotherapy and Psychosomatics at the University Clinics, Frankfurt/Germany, I met many patients suffering in a comparable manner while separated from me during therapy. I found it impossible to give a satisfactory explanation for such a regular phenomenon with the concepts I had learned at the Freud Institute, namely repressed drive conflicts and guilt resulting from Oedipal constellations. During this era, German analysts had not made the linkage of clinical symptoms to mourning and depression caused by separation during treatment interruptions. I started to make a systematic collection of the clinical pictures I saw before and after such breaks. I observed a pattern of missing sessions to enact the loss, as well as repression of pain, fear and anger, and denial of loss.

During the IPA congress in Rome in 1989 I discovered Guntrip's *Schizoid Phenomena, Object Relations and the Self* in the congress bookshop, a book that made a deep impression on me. It was the first time I ever heard of Fairbairn. Shortly after returning home I ordered Fairbairn's book. Reading it was a difficult task for me, but I appreciated Fairbairn's putting the need for object relations at the core of his theory, pointing to separation anxiety as the first anxiety in early development, and giving the need for connection a central role in affective life. I had found what I was seeking for the last ten years when I had been struggling to explain separation anxiety and all the phenomena connected with it in therapy.

These experiences of analysis, clinical experience, the chance discovery of

Guntrip's book, and my laborious reading of Fairbairn in English were key moments in my clinical and theoretical journey, recorded in my 1999 book *Verlassenheitspanik und Trennungsangst* (*Panic of Abandonment and Separation Anxiety*).

I have tried to deepen my understanding of Fairbairn's thinking, step by step, and to share at least the basic concepts with younger colleagues in training at the Sigmund Freud Institute in Frankfurt. I have worked with the concept of the libido seeking the object and the multiplicity of subsidiary egos alternately influencing the central ego. I have found it illuminating to integrate the dynamic ego structures of the libidinal ego, antilibidinal ego, and central ego, on the one hand, with the positive, negative and unobjectionable transferences Freud described in 1912. In contrast to Fairbairn's central, libidinal and antilibidinal egos, the traditional view of the ego and the id does not accommodate the positive, the negative and the unobjectionable transference within a functional topography.

Thanks to Elisabeth Vorspohl I had the opportunity to recommend publication of Fairbairn's work to Klett-Cotta, Stuttgart, in 1993. For several years Elisabeth Vorspohl had been trying to get several distinguished publishers interested in Fairbairn's work, but the flourishing enthusiasm about reading Kleinian ideas did not yet reach beyond a well-defined circle of explicitly Kleinian authors. It was Gerd Heising – after reading my 1995 paper about the remarkable neglect of Fairbairn in Germany – who told me about Bernhard Hensel's efforts to translate Fairbairn.

One year after Hensel and I met on the occasion of my first workshop on Fairbairn at the Conference of the German Psychoanalytical Association (DPV) in 1996, we jointly began to popularize Fairbairn's thinking among German analysts at the DPV. But we were not successful in finding a publisher. Then in 1999, David Scharff was invited to some German psychoanalytical institutes to give lectures about object relations theory. He got to know the *Psychosozial* publisher, Hans Jürgen Wirth of Giessen, who decided to give us the chance to publish Fairbairn in German.

In 2000, Bernhard Hensel and I edited Fairbairn, with Ellinor Fairbairn Birtles and David Scharff as experienced advisors, Elisabeth Vorspohl as translator, and supported by financial aid from the Society for Propagation of Psychoanalytical Literature from Other Languages (*Förderverein zur Verbreitung fremdsprachiger psychoanalytischer Literatur*).

Elisabeth Vorspohl was our first choice as translator. She had been interested in a German Fairbairn edition for a long time. She had already translated Kleinians and Independents as well as Anna Freudians, so she was thoroughly familiar with the different British schools of theory. We had a fruitful collaboration accompanied by sometimes controversial discussions. With these collaborators, my joint project with Bernhard Hensel was successful at last, and the book sells well, indicating increasing interest in Fairbairn in Germany.

Problems in adopting new ideas after World War II and the Shoah

For a generation after World War II, psychoanalysts in western Germany remained closed off from the changes that challenged psychoanalysis in other countries. Obviously this isolation was due to the history of psychoanalysis in the time of national socialism and during the post-war era. German psycho-analysts were entangled, compromised, and heavily traumatized by the deprivation, banishment, persecution, and murder of their Jewish colleagues and their families, the banishment of Sigmund Freud and his family, and the murder of Freud's sisters.

They had to come to terms with the past as they reached for international acknowledgement again. Struggling with this, the German Psychoanalytical Society split into two societies. This enabled those who stayed with the German Psychoanalytical Association and who cherished the illusion of a non-contaminated history to feel secure and self-righteous, and maintain their association with the International Psychoanalytical Association. Presumably this splitting and denial served to ward off shame and guilt by association, and defended against actual guilt that psychoanalysts carried as Germans, possibly former national socialists, or as children of former national socialists.

Within the DPV it took 29 years until there could be discussion about the participation of psychoanalysis in the developments of German history. Those who, acknowledged by the International Psychoanalytical Associ-ation, held on to the original theories of Freud felt themselves to be on the right side, compared with the colleagues who were not. Many psychoanalysts denied the ongoing worldwide developments within Freud's psychoanalysis. The generational change in the 1980s went hand in hand with a strengthening of contacts with psychoanalysts outside Germany, especially Jewish analysts, for consultation and supervision. Only then when they faced their guilt and made reparation and links, did German psychoanalysts become more receptive to new developments in the field.

It seems to be no coincidence that many psychoanalytical institutes in Germany took no official notice of the importance of Kleinian theories before the 1990s. The reason for this neglect was, of course, Melanie Klein's rivalry with Anna Freud. At the same time, British object relations theory may have been difficult for German psychoanalysts to adopt because of the entirely new approach to concepts like relating and aggression. Fairbairn's thinking provided both a challenge and an opportunity for German psychoanalysts. It made it imperative to see one's own destructiveness in the context of experi-ences in one's own family and society, and to examine it in the light of introjection and splitting. No longer could destructiveness be attributed to biological fate in the form of innate drives. Indeed, the implications of an object relations approach to German history in general, and in particular to the history of German psychoanalysis and its institutions, are, at times, disturbing.

Fairbairn in Germany now

Last but not least I would like to summarize the special 2002 "Fairbairn Today" conference in Seefelden-Lake of Constance. The DPV invested in spreading knowledge of object relations theory by distributing 2000 flyers announcing the conference and 35 participants attended from all over Germany and from Sweden.

T. Borgegärd of Uppsala presented his reflections on Fairbairn, connecting his life history and his theory. B. Hensel of Giessen compared and contrasted important concepts of Klein and Fairbairn. He pointed to agreement in regard to the concepts of early development and the features of schizoid personality, and disagreement in regard to the importance of drive theory, experience in relationships, and the origin of inner objects. For Klein, inner objects derive from unconscious fantasies, while for Fairbairn, they depend on introjection of actual experiences with external objects, split off and repressed by the central ego.

S. Wollnik-Krusche and P. Potthoff from Köln and Ratingen reported on their clinical experiences in the treatment of traumatized patients. They stressed the important role of dissociation as a vertical defence, compared with repression as a horizontal one. What has been dissociated remains unintegrated with other parts of the self and gains access to consciousness through enactments. I emphasized the relevance of Fairbairn's concept of dynamic ego structures for understanding Racker's concept of concordant and complementary transferences. A clinical vignette illustrated the transmission of hate and violence through three generations. A woman analysand's experience at the hands of an oppressive and violent grandmother led the analysand to control her own son by outbreaks of anger and hate. Only when the son resisted maternal control and so broke his mother's antilibidinal ego identification with the antilibidinal object, did the analytical field open and permit access to memories of the suffering the woman had gone through under the extreme control exercised by her grandmother. Finally, U. Rupprecht-Schampera of Tübingen demonstrated her use of Fairbairn's dynamic ego structures to understand the development of children who experienced good and bad relationships to their primary objects. She combined Winnicott's concept of true and false self with Fairbairn's endopsychic structure, and demonstrated depressive and schizoid developments in either case.

Summary

Fairbairn showed up in the thinking of German authors – von Minden, Kutter, Heising in the 1980s. The discovery of Fairbairn in Guntrip's "Schizoid Phenomena, Object-Relations and the Self" concluded my search for a sufficient theoretical explanation of conscious or repressed separation anxiety before and after separations in psychotherapy and psychoanalysis. German psychoanalysts after World War II and the Shoah were too much in denial to be open to new developments in psychoanalysis. In the 1990s, the integration of Fairbairn into the training at the Sigmund-Freud-Institut in Frankfurt am Main and at conferences of the DPV, the object relations lecture tour of Germany by David Scharff, the collaboration of the translator Elisabeth Vorspuhl, the publishing by Hans Jurgen Wirth, and the editing by Hensel and Rehberger were principal efforts to popularize Fairbairn's thinking in Germany. A short summary of the special 2002 "Fairbairn Today" conference in Seefelden-Lake of Constance brings the story up to date.

References

Heising, G., Hensel, B.F., Rost, W.-D. *et al.* (2002). Zur Attraktivität des "bösen Objekts". In E. Vorspohl (ed.) *Anwendungen der Objektbeziehungstheorie in der Giessener Schule.* Giessen: Psychosozial-Verlag.

Hensel, B. E. (1997). Die Bedeutung von Absenz und Präsenz des Objekts für das Spaltungskonzept von Fairbairn. In H. Peters and T. Rollwagen (eds) *Denken in der Gegenwart des Anderen. Tagungsband der Arbeitstagung der DPV.*

Hensel, B. E. and R. Rehberger (1999). Äußere und innere Lebenstatsachen in der Übertragung und im psychoanalytischen Prozess. In U. Ostendorf and H. Peters (eds) *Lebenstatsachen und Psychoanalytischer Prozeß. Tagungsband der Arbeitstagung der DPV.*

Klein, M. (1962). *Das Seelenleben des Kleinkindes.* Stuttgart: Klett-Cotta.

Kutter, R. (ed.) (1982). *Psychologie der zwischenmenschlichen Beziehungen.* Darmstadt: Wissenschaftliche Buchgesellschaft.

Mahler, M. S. (1979). *Symbiose und Individuation. Bd. 1. Psychosen im fn Kindesalter.* Stuttgart: Klett-Cotta.

von Minden, G. (1978). Der strukturell Ich-gestörte Patient und die Theorie der Objektbeziehungen. In *Zeitschrift für Psychosomatische Medizin und Psychoanalyse.* Göttingen: Verlag für medizinische Psychologie im Verlag Vandenhoek & Ruprecht.

—— (1988). Der Bruchstück-Mensch. Psychoanalyse des früh–gestört neurotischen Menschen der technokratischen Gesellschaft. München-Basel: Reinhardt.

Mitchell, S. A. (1981). The origin and nature of the "object" in the theories of Klein and Fairbairn. *Contemporary Psychoanalysis* 17(3): 374–398.

—— (1988). *Relational Concepts in Psychoanalysis – An Integration.* Cambridge, MA: Harvard University Press

Müller-Braunschweig, H. (1970). Zur Genese der Ich-Störungen. *Psyche* 42: 657–677.

Racker, H. (1959). *Übertragung und Gegenübertragung: Studien zur psychoanalytischen Technik.* München, Basel: Ernst Reinhard, 1978.

Rehberger, R. (1995). *Die Begegnung mit D.W. Fairbairn. Gedanken zu seiner Rezeption und seiner bemerkenswerten Unbekanntheit.* DPV Information Nr. 18.

—— (1999). *Verlassenheitspanik und Trennungsangst.* Stuttgart: Klett-Cotta.

Rehberger, R. and Hensel, B. E. (2000). Fragen des Ichs – die dynamischen Ich-Strukturen als ein heute allgemein anerkannter Theorieansatz. In *Tagungsband der DPV in München 2000.*

Chapter 6

An object relations view of sexuality based on Fairbairn's theory

Bernhard F. Hensel

Introduction

Fairbairn (1940, 1941, 1943) himself did not investigate sexual phenomena in detail, but his concepts apply to the understanding of love and sexuality and give a new perspective on sexual manifestations. Critics of Fairbairn have misunderstood his theory as desexualized, but I find that it enables me to explore sexual phenomena in consistently object relational terms which transcend a purely drive-psychological perspective. In Fairbairn's view, sexuality is determined by the character of the internal object relations rather than by fixations of libido, as Freud thought. In contrast to Balint and Winnicott, Fairbairn believes that object relationships are relevant not only to infantile dependency but to all stages of development, and are applicable to all sexual phenomena. Fairbairn sees sexuality as a channel by which an object relationship can be established and expressed. Sexual activity is an element of the stage of mature dependency, in which the self perceives the external object as a whole person, values giving over taking, and shows love to the good, loved object via sexuality. For Fairbairn, it is not sexual discharge that is decisive, but the reaching of the object. The ideal of maturity is reached when genital sexuality and object constancy are integrated. This ideal is challenged by various sexual activities, which constitute efforts to save a less good internal object relation and make it seem good.

It is obvious that from the beginning of life, physical contact – which is embedded in a relationship – plays an important role. The bodily experience of the infant creates a potential space in which an object relationship forms. The contentedly sucking infant may perceive the relationship as affectionately accepting and nurturingly exciting, in which case the infant experiences pleasure. The needy, biting, vomiting infant may perceive it as passively or actively rejecting, and experiences pain and dissatisfaction.

The central ego need not split off and repress affectionate tactile interactions with the ideal object or accepted object, but may keep them in consciousness, there to retain access to them in later life in the form of the experience of goodness and tenderness and the capacity for concern, cross-identification, and object constancy. Excessively strong frustrations, in contrast, have to be split off and repressed under the pressure of an early relationship with a bad object. The antilibidinal ego contains affects of anger and hate directed against the rejecting object and gives rise to the mental agency responsible for rejection, alienation and hate in adult sexual inter-action. The libidinal ego contains extremely strong longings for love which have not been gratified when the exciting object has been disappointing. In later life, the exciting object relationship fuels sexual desire, extreme hunger for love, hypersexuality, and a desire for heavenly fusion. Internal conflict among contradictory object relationships or, in a more mature form, feelings of ambivalence about contradictory aspects of the object, enter into sexuality and must be dealt with by defence mechanisms that do not always support sexual aims.

The internal object relationship, constructed from processes of internaliza-tion, expulsion and intrusion, can express itself with the external object in corresponding ways, as the person excites, triumphs over, devaluates, sup-presses, surrenders to, confides in, relaxes with, devours, gets devoured by, becomes excited by, or alienated from, the object. These various modes of relating enable the individual to overcome schizoid narcissistic isolation, enter the stage of transition, and establish direct experience of being in rela-tionship in external reality where the conflict of ambivalence between loving and hating can be indirectly dealt with. But in external reality these longings are met by exciting and rejecting objects that trigger and activate the internal dilemma. Feeling sexual excitement and desire for the other always carries that risk since people are unconsciously dominated by their internal object relations to a greater or lesser extent. The process of building an intimate relationship occurs in an area of risk from facing issues of surrender and dependency, and cannot proceed at all if the personality remains in a closed system where the other cannot be given importance. The personal internal balance governing this process determines the achievement of healthy sexual-ity, varying realizations of the sexual phenomena associated with the risk of surrender and dependency, or manifestations of polymorphous-perverse sexuality.

Stephen Mitchell (1988) described sexuality in interaction with a respon-sive other as the most intense way to experience oneself as alive and valid-ated. The "true self" can reveal itself and be confirmed, or at least can be presented to the object, thereby becoming visible in an indirect way. In sexual relationships, partners re-enact dimensions of early object relationships and enact hopes for an actual solution. David Scharff (1982) also holds this view of sexuality. For Fairbairn object relationships are by definition masochistic in nature, because from the beginning the child is absolutely dependent on his primary relationship.

Specific forms of sexuality

Masturbation

To begin with I want to consider masturbation, developmentally the first form of practised sexuality. In masturbation, an object is fantasized which is not available for the time being, and may remain generally unavailable if the masturbating individual is always or temporarily alone. The masturbating individual discovers and stimulates a part of the body such as penis or clitoris, thereby creating excitement and physiological aliveness without being dependent on another person in external reality. So the feeling of risk and, in a broader sense, of surrender to a real outer object can be avoided. Omnipotent control is maintained, a gratification that is central to the individual who is prone to obsessive masturbation. At least temporarily, feelings of loneliness, emptiness, schizoid isolation, internal restlessness, and the anxiety of being abandoned can be overcome or alleviated by fantasies of the object and the excitement that results from this imagery.

During masturbation, self-doubts and feelings of inferiority can be brushed aside. Questions that arise in the interpersonal situation can be ignored, such as "Am I loveable? Is my body in good shape (height, general appearance, face, nose, legs, breast, hips, penis, etc.)? Does the other reject me? Am I being exploited (physically, sexually, or on a material or intellectual level, etc.)? Will I be disappointed? Will I find myself abandoned? Am I the one to give all without ever getting what I really want? Am I loved for who I am or for my body? Can I be and remain myself, or will I be forced to give myself up if I am open to another person's needs?" All these uncertainties and realistic difficulties can be avoided in masturbation.

The self-sufficiency afforded by masturbation enables individuals to conjure up relationships in fantasies peopled by their internal object relations – as far as these are allowed to reach consciousness – and to overcome their loneliness at least partly and temporarily. Those fantasies of, and wishes for, a relationship can be reinforced by pictures, films or other devices, and they can be enacted in a direct or voyeuristic way so that a self-sufficient world of fantasized exciting and rejecting object relationships is created. A relationship with both good and bad objects (loving, hateful, exciting, rejecting, sadistic, masochistic, voyeuristic, exhibitionistic and fetishistic) can be imagined in fantasy corresponding to an internal object relationship. This way, surrender to an external object in reality and anxieties about losing a sense of identity in the presence of the other can be avoided, but at the heavy price of failing to establish a good, real, mutually confirming interaction, which is an integral part of sexual interaction in most instances. Quite frequently masturbatory enactments of an internal object relationship do not appear to be linked with the personality on a conscious level, so that it takes a long time in analysis until those split off aspects of the personality can be integrated. This is illustrated by the following case vignette.

Case example

A man of about 40 years asked for a consultation because of depressive feelings, hypochondriacal anxieties, a feeling of loneliness and panic attacks – especially in small rooms – headaches, and tension in his back. He had already consulted a number of physicians. He talked to me so rapidly that I had difficulty following him. He sounded like machine-gun fire. At first I experienced this as an aggressive way of talking. I realized later on that he was talking as though his life depended on it, as though he was afraid that he would not be convincing, and that I would not believe or accept him. After some time of analysis he revealed that he had extremely disturbing masturbatory fantasies.

Here I want to add that my patient was the second son, born ten months later, and had always been in the shadow of the favourite, the firstborn son who was to inherit the parents' medium-size business. As a boy, he appeared to have played only a small role in his family. He thought that his mother, who spent all her time at work, was rather aloof and emotionally unavailable. As a member of a Christian sect, she set strict moral standards, and used to threaten him with punishment when he refused to attend church service. He could not remember that she ever hugged him. He himself was attached to his grandfather, a well-known scientist who used to denigrate my patient's father for being only a craftsman. His father was no more available to my patient than his mother, because he openly favoured his firstborn, practical-minded son and made him a partner in the family business. As a boy, my patient felt like a lost and lonely outsider. He loved to sit by a small pond near home for hours, contemplating the landscape, or to take long solitary walks, lost in thought. This made him feel relaxed and calm. When he quarrelled with his mother, she incited her husband to punish him in the evening. Quite often, without a chance to justify himself, he was hit with a leather belt by his father. His father also denigrated him because of his small stature, calling him "shortie" or "midget". He was jealous of his perfect brother. One time when his brother had a bike accident, my patient just rode away pretending that he had not noticed.

During his elementary and middle school years, my patient was a poor student. Then inspired by one teacher who made a deep impression on him, he started to concentrate, passed his entrance exams, and studied economics at university. He encountered difficulty with his thesis because he felt devalued by his supervisor, but he graduated, and got a job at a bank in the audit department, so that now he was in control of others.

In the early phase of analysis I got an impression of his loneliness. On the couch, he sank into his schizoid world that provided a space in which, though being alone, he felt ahead of me just as he had felt ahead of his parents. More or less incidentally I learned that he still lived in his parents' neighbourhood in one of the family's houses. Manifesting what Fairbairn called the moral defence, he still tried to please them by acting as their financial adviser and paying excessive rent. He had maintained the loyalty of a small boy for his rejecting parents. He told me that he could not leave them because he loves living in the countryside, which is after all where he feels at home, but he also stressed how much he despised his father for what he called his punitive proceedings.

I found myself bored in the initial phase of his analysis because of his constant talk about poorly functioning computer software. Any attempt to address our relationship was strictly resisted. In his view, ours was a clear business relationship, its only function being to get him analysed. Analysis was important for him; he never missed sessions, was never late, and paid my fees promptly. Nevertheless he appeared to expect nothing from me. He seemed to assume that he had to do all the work himself. His withdrawal from me was intense.

Just as he had felt in the past, I now felt useless, helpless and rejected, corresponding to his internal libidinal ego. My comments along this line were rejected as extravagant psychoanalytic constructions. His contempt for my remarks extended to the whole treatment and challenged its viability. In the transference his antilibidinal objects were activated as he conveyed to me how he had always felt rejected and devalued by his father and mother. His withdrawal was an attempt to protect himself and me against his split off, disintegrated internal objects.

In one repetitive dream of war, he dreamed of watching the battles anxiously from a safe place of shelter. In a more daring dream, he saw a man enter his garden, and feeling frightened, he took a small pistol and shot at the man, who was wearing a uniform and holding a gun. When his little pistol was useless, he was stricken with terror. We analysed this dream as an expression of his relationship with me as a dangerous father who enters his ground, gets closer to him, and makes him feel that his pistol (genital) is useless in asserting himself against me/his father. He agreed that he felt inferior to me, and added that he feared that I would overwhelm and manipulate him. However, he managed to try to match me and indicated his potency by dropping some tips for risk-free stock transactions. In this way he not only demonstrated the power he possessed on his own territory, and his superiority to me in the world of finance, but also, in being generous with his tips, he showed that he could experience me as a libidinal object and our relationship as a libidinal one, insofar as we were mutually able to give.

After this work, he had to struggle with deep feelings of guilt and shame to reveal what he regarded as his true problem, the size of his penis. My didactic comments – that satisfying sexual experience does not depend on the size of the penis – were futile, of course. I understood that he was devaluing his own body – an antilibidinal identification with his denigrating parents – and that he had not been able to integrate his genitals in his body schema. In my view this was also an expression of his precarious male identity. He told me that as an adolescent he used to have sexual intercourse on the quiet with a girl who lived in his village, but because she was so small minded he had been ashamed to date her officially. He never dared to approach really attractive women, because he felt that they were only interested in real men with large penises.

Following the phase in which I was experienced as his antilibidinal father in the transference, he told me a longer dream in which he was walking through the long corridors of a large house. He was feeling tense, and there were a lot of screaming children, shut inside "relaxing rooms". After a while, he entered an elegantly decorated room, where a seductive, sexy woman with black stockings and suspenders was sitting. A strong, vigorous-looking man approached her while he watched. When they started to touch each other, he went over to them and the woman sucked his penis, while the other man penetrated her from behind.

I was not quite sure whether he was relating a daydream, a masturbatory fantasy, or a dream proper, but I dealt with his account as a dream because he had presented it as such. I remembered that his parents had often sent him out of the room when he was a child, and that they ignored his screaming and raging, sometimes shutting him in his nursery. I commented that he seemed to banish his desires and needs until he forgot them altogether, but with this dream he seemed to have entered a new internal space. He agreed. Then he remembered that in watching pornographic films he preferred fellatio scenes. The woman in his dream was very erotic – in reality he would never dare to make advances to her. He rejected aggressive forms of sexuality, but got excited at the same time. I commented that maybe I was the other man whom he allied with to come close to the desired woman. Accompanied by an aggressive man standing for his father he felt free to let his penis be caressed and excited by an affectionate woman, while the other man also represented the aggressive, antilibidinal aspects of his self that he defends against.

He reacted to my interpretation with surprise, scepticism, and then withdrawal. Eventually, he was able to reveal his masturbatory fantasy, which he found extremely embarrassing because this fantasy was inconsistent with all his principles. He imagined an athletic, muscular man whose big penis penetrated women so thoroughly that they screamed with lust and pain, which in turn satisfied him. That man was in complete control so that the women agreed with everything he wanted, including coitus from behind. He despised violence and aggression and was ashamed to discover such impulses in himself. We clarified that the athletic man also represented a part of himself which he tried to ward off because he wanted to remain a clean, decent son, and then he was able to be open to continuing the discussion. After a while I offered him the interpretation that his aggressive fantasies allowed him a sexually exciting version of the early traumatic situation in which he had been at his parents' mercy. It is the woman, representing unconsciously his own female, helpless part that is maltreated, not himself. He returned to the dream about raging and screaming children who are shut up. I said that they expressed his repressed feelings of surrender and helplessness in childhood.

Following this phase of analysis, he started to dress in a more fashionable way, bought a motorbike, and exercised in a fitness studio. He was able to meet an attractive woman who was on business from another European country. She was exciting to him, he was able to approach her, and found that she was interested in him. However, he suffered from a panic attack when she took him to her hotel room. Because she was able to manage the situation in an easy way, he was able to have intercourse with her when they met again, and their relationship progressed. Because of their regular separations due to distance, their relationship provided the distance he needed so that the exciting object was also a rejecting object, a necessary compromise at this stage of his treatment.

Now I would like to turn to theoretical considerations again. A pervasive inability to masturbate indicates great difficulties in carrying out activities independently from mother, father or partner, and in connecting to the internal object relationships. It suggests that the body is not experienced as a source of life, and that there is massive difficulty in experiencing oneself as separate from others. In those who cannot masturbate, the antilibidinal ego is so strong that it persecutes the libidinal ego (even when they are focused on their own body) and does not allow for excitement and longing for love. Another possibility to be considered is inability of the central ego to tolerate the aggression of the antilibidinal ego in the form of aggressive masturbatory fantasies, which are then defended against and cannot become integrated.

Sublimated masochism

The sublimated form of masochism (moral masochism) and the attractiveness of the bad object can readily be explained by the moral defence that Fairbairn (1943) described, as an alternative to the death instinct to which Freud attributed masochism. Mildly masochistic tendencies are an inherent part of object relationships in general because these are internally associated with a more or less complete surrender to another person – mother in infancy, spouse or partner in later life, and so on. In Fairbairn's view, pronounced masochistic tendencies are common to both phobia and hysteria, whereas sadistic features prevail in obsessional neurosis and paranoia. Sadism may serve as a defence against a masochistic relationship, earlier experiences of passivity, helplessness, and impotent dependency being warded off by activity of the antilibidinal ego leading to an attitude of omnipotence, control, and sadistic suppression of the other.

I think of the attractiveness of a harsh object at a deeper level in terms of

Fairbairn's moral defence (Heising *et al.* 2000). Under the pressure to improve one's internal state, the rejecting object is fused with the ideal object. That is, an unconditional bad internal object is turned into a conditional bad internal object, which is searched for in external reality. Children continue to hold on to their internal objects and hope for a corresponding internal change. This situation gives rise to the hope that under specific conditions in future they will be granted the love of the rejecting object which they actually deserve now. Longings for a harsh but fair tyrant, or calls for increasingly rigorous and severe laws, can be seen in this perspective. However, such an attitude is accompanied by the hope that later on they (in identification with the object) be allowed to display such severe but fair behaviour.

These dynamics apply equally to the sexual attractiveness of a conditional bad object, which must own rejecting and exciting attributes and must be internally linked up with the ideal object. This internal constellation defends against the aggressiveness of the antilibidinal ego. Those people who seem doomed always to love the ones who are the most difficult to reach, hope to master their feelings of inferiority and emptiness by associating with the idealized exciting object. The state of longing and suffering for such an idealized but ultimately unrealizable object enables them to experience a degree of liveliness and intensity. This accounts for the intensity of unrequited love and phenomena like movie star worship. Readiness to sacrifice oneself for a partner with exciting and rejecting attributes holds the promise to obtain access to a paradise, which not infrequently turns out to be a painful, disappointing experience.

Erogenous masochism

The erogenous (sexual) masochist is excited by submission to a harsh, rejecting (conditional bad) object. Here an internal relationship, corresponding to the moral defence on the neurotic level, is enacted in actual sexual behaviour, making the internal conflict totally concrete. The masochist surrenders to a conditional bad object, in hopes of changing it into a good one. Not infrequently a feeling of pride arises when the masochistic enactment is over, because the individual has been able to master the corresponding ritual and the physical pain which represents mental pain. Masochists have faced their conditional malice or badness and have got their just desserts. In the last analysis, masochists try to change a bad sadist into a good loving object. They express their love by trustful surrender to a harsh antilibidinal object. Unconsciously the suffering of pain gives proof of the especially deep longings for love and care as well as of the specialness of the love relation. The sense of uniqueness and intensity allows for the enactment of imagined intimacy or, rather, the expression of ardent longings for emotional resonance. If, however, this hope is frustrated in spite of all sufferings, the feelings of isolation and loneliness are especially strong, and a severe risk of a schizoid withdrawal arises. For the masochist, physical pain is of special importance, because it transforms antilibidinal internal relationship into bodily experience. Physical pain helps repress psychical pain and binds it psychosomatically creating a concrete experience in the here-and-now to establish a barrier against previous traumatic experience. Moreover, the concrete pain creates a feeling of liveliness which greatly helps in overcoming feelings of isolation.

In contrast, sadists have connected aspects of the antilibidinal ego to the central ego, and this enables them to live out their anger and hate. Via projective identification, they attribute their inner weakness and lack of self-confidence to others, to masochists. In this way the antilibidinal ego's hate of the loving, libidinal object can be enacted interpersonally. In most instances the alleviation of feelings of guilt as well as the rationalization of the situation require that the object has been made to feel guilty of an unconscious crime – equated with conditional badness – which often forms part of the ritual. In anal sadism, a secret place is found, a forbidden space, which is inaccessible for anybody else and becomes the place of truth and of the true meeting without mask and hiding. The aim is to reach a rejecting object located in a person who will show love as soon as pain reveals the true face, formerly hidden behind the mask. So the previous surrender to the primary object, being overwhelmed by it, and retreating in schizoid withdrawal and deceit, all are magically reversed.

Fetishism

Freud (1927) described fetishism as an effort to manage castration anxiety. The woman with a fetish may unconsciously imagine herself to be in possession of a penis. From the object relations perspective, this situation is caused by schizoid conflict dealt with by fetishism. Fairbairn pointed out: "It is the great tragedy of the schizoid individual that his love seems to destroy; and it is because his love seems so destructive that he experiences such difficulty in directing libido towards objects in outer reality. He becomes afraid to love; and therefore he erects barriers between his objects and himself" (1941: 50). In my view, the fetish represents the exciting, intensely loved object, but in a materialized, displaced, and alienated form that prevents it from being emotionally experienced in a direct way that could threaten the self with surrender. Only on the condition that this defence is securely maintained is the ardently desired libidinal object allowed to reach consciousness. Then sexual excitement can be experienced without interference from conflicts over early deprivation and hopeless, destructive love, and rejection. After all, the fetishistic element seems to be merely an accessory, which cannot be destroyed by the excitement. In this way, the schizoid conflict is also defended against, and the self is safe. Love and intense desire cannot threaten the fetish with destruction. Therefore, the fetish represents the indestructibility of the loved libidinal object. This very element is the precondition for desire and deep excitement. Fetishistic tendencies enter into love relations frequently without reaching pathological proportions. In my view, they serve as an important means to manage universal schizoid conflict and are, therefore, not particularly alarming.

Mild forms of fetishism are often encountered: for example, preferences for long legs, large or small breasts, a certain shape of bottom, colour and structure of the skin, stature, general appearance, and so on. These fetishistic components contribute to object choice. They become pathological when they are obligatory, a necessary condition for excitement with a partner. When a person is exclusively fixated on a fetish, there remains no important part – or no part at all – for a real person to play. Black silk stockings and garter belt, varnish, or leather clothing fetishes create an alternative to the partner's skin as the surface for contact. Sexual excitement may be connected only with anonymous items such as a stolen umbrella or with odorous items such as stockings smelling of foot perspiration or worn panties. In those who have a fetish, the central ego is poorly developed, while the libidinal ego is so extremely strong that the libidinal object has to be safeguarded by massive barriers so that it does not have to connect with a real object – with the result that excitement is experienced only with an alienated, fetishistic libidinal object during activities that are extremely pressing in nature. The extraordinarily strong antilibidinal ego is the reason that most fetishists condemn and hate themselves for their activities.

Case vignette

These dynamics are illustrated in a case in which a particular scenario brought punishment by the police directly into the enactment. The patient experienced most intense pleasure when he slowly opened an umbrella which he had previously stolen from a department store. His earlier experiences of dehumanizing, humiliating and devaluing maltreatment had given rise to a state in which the hope to reach and be emotionally open to a partner could only be attached to a thing, in this case the unfurling of an umbrella. In short, in fetishism, excitement cannot be associated with any real person and any relationship is viewed as enormously threatening and alienating from the self.

Male and female differences in fetishism

Fetishism is much more significant for men than for women. This is presumably due to the social consequences of biological gender difference. Because in male development there is no shift from the primary object to the sexual object, problems in the early mother relationship will affect the sexual object choice. Given a marked schizoid conflict, the sexual object must become especially alienated in order to show the least similarity to mother. In contrast, in female development, there is a shift from mother to a male object.

Due to this change, the schizoid conflict loses some of its dramatic power, because the girl's father assumes the role of the other who by means of splitting can become idealized. This development is more important for women than it is for men. Fetishistic elements, however, are also meaningful to women. A certain hair colour, chest hair, athletic stature, choice of car, ownership of property, or professional status may be the precondition for idealization of a sexual partner.

The difference in the appearance and functioning of the male and female sexual organs is a determining factor in the person's need for a fetish. To a high degree, masculine self-confidence is dependent on sexual excitement, accompanied by the erection of the penis. The erection is clearly visible and cannot be faked. The man either has an erection or not. Fetishistic elements that create excitement guarantee erectile potency. In the subjective male experience in general, sexual confirmation and mutual gratification are heavily dependent on penile erection, and the man is under pressure to have a sustained erection. Women are under a more diffuse pressure with regard to their body shape and appearance. They seek confirmation and affection in response to how they look, going to great lengths to improve bodily features. In extreme cases, the woman's body may turn into the bad object, which has to be improved at all costs and corrected by plastic surgery. She is driven to remove bad parts in a concrete way as a precondition of finding – or keeping – a love object. In the emotional sphere, women are much more able than men to perceive their sexual experience on a continuum.

Because of the invisibility of their primary sexual organs, the degree of excitement in women remains a secret for anyone but themselves. They can lubricate without a subsequent orgasm. They are also able to keep their partner at a distance by the technique of playing roles (Fairbairn 1940) in order to avoid intolerable surrender. She delegates surrendering to excitement to the man, who is thereby forced to perform and prove himself by doing so. However, the price the woman has to pay is all too often the feeling of having been used or exploited.

Finally, in order to be able to penetrate the vagina with his penis the man must have successfully integrated an aggressively penetrating sexuality. The man with a schizoid conflict who worries about destroying the object with love, and the man with a depressive conflict who fears that his aggression will destroy the object, may try to secure the vulnerable object by using fetishistic elements to get distance from his sexual attack.

Conclusion

I apply Fairbairn's theory and terminology to clinical sexual phenomena to achieve a deeper understanding of the dynamics of sexuality and to make possible more efficient work on transference and countertransference. I think of sexuality as a feature of the transitional stage, good and bad objects contributing to the excitement. Fairbairn's concepts enable us to understand masochism as a bridge to an object relationship with the conditional good object discovered in the transference. Through the use of fetishism or fetishistic elements, a person with intimacy conflicts is able to maintain a relationship to the exciting object, separate it from the original object, and find excitement and interaction in fantasy or reality. I propose that paraphilia and perverse sexual elements can be seen as an expression of a preferable internalized relationship rather than as a manifestation of erotized hate. In this way sexuality provides contact with a real or fantasized object which unconsciously promises to improve or reverse the early situation and change the passive position of the past into an active one.

References

Fairbairn, W. R. D. (1940). Schizoid factors in the personality. In *Psychoanalytic Studies of the Personality*, pp. 3–27. London: Routledge & Kegan Paul, 1952. *Das Selbst und die inneren Objektbeziehungen*. Giessen: Psychosozial-Verlag, 2000.

—— (1941). A revised psychopathology of the psychoses and neuroses. In *Psychoanalytic Studies of the Personality*, pp. 28–58. London: Routledge & Kegan Paul, 1952. *Das Selbst und die inneren Objektbeziehungen*. Giessen: Psychosozial-Verlag, 2000.

—— (1943). The repression and the return of bad objects (with special reference to the 'war neuroses'). In *Psychoanalytic Studies of the Personality*, pp. 59–81. London: Routledge & Kegan Paul, 1952. *Das Selbst und die inneren Objektbeziehungen*. Giessen: Psychosozial-Verlag, 2000.

Freud, S. (1927). *Fetischismus. GW* Bd IX.

Heising, G., Hensel, B. F. and Rost, W. D. (2000). *Zur Attraktivität des bösen Objekts*. Giessen: Psychosozial-Verlag.

Mitchell, S. A. (1988). *Relational Concepts in Psychoanalysis – An Integration*. Cambridge, MA and London: Harvard University Press.

Scharff, D. E. (1982). *The Sexual Relationship*. London: Routledge. Reprinted paperback, Northvale, NJ and London: Jason Aronson, 1998.

Chapter 7

Satisfactory, exciting, and rejecting objects in health and sex

Jill Savege Scharff

Fairbairn's (1952) *Psychoanalytic Studies of the Personality*, the foundation of all object relations theory, describes internal psychic structure as a system of parts based on aspects of early experience with important figures. Fairbairn conceives of infants' experience of their mothers as inevitably disappointing compared to the enjoyment of automatic attention to needs before birth. He thinks that infants take in their experience with their mother (their object of desire and attachment) to learn from it and to control the unpleasant aspects of it. They keep in consciousness whatever feels good, and split off and repress the aspects of it that are unsatisfactory. At this point in consciousness the infant has a good object in the central area of the self. In the unconscious, objects that caused frustration are sorted into two categories: those that caused feelings of abandonment and provoked rage; and those that excited feelings of longing and craving in response to frustration.

As soon as experience is overwhelming, infants protect themselves from the pain of relating to their objects by this process of introjection, splitting and repression. At birth the ego is whole, and as soon as infants are exposed to the vicissitudes of infantile dependency, the ego splits in association with the split off and repressed parts of the object, and it represses itself along with the affects that connect to the objects. But these repressed areas are always seeking reconnection to the center. The organism aims for integration, but the need for defense pushes against that. The repressed internal object relationships press for expression and reveal themselves through behavior directed at the people to whom the person is closest.

In various chapters we have shown how internal object relationships take form outside the self in intimate relationships. Here we will concentrate on their expression in sexual dysfunction. First we need to link Fairbairn's system of the endopsychic situation with the explanatory and connective power of Klein's (1946) concept of unconscious projective identification.

Bringing her formidable intuition to understanding the infant's unconscious phantasies concerning the mother, her breast, and her relationship to the infant's father, Klein detected an unconscious process of communication and defense called projective identification, through which the infant gets rid of an aggressive part of the self that is terrified of being annihilated, locates it in the mother's breast, and then experiences her as the source of the anxiety. The infant then takes in a bad object and identifies with it; a part of the ego becomes like the internalized object. Fortunately the infant also gets rid of loving, lively aspects of the self to keep them from being annihilated and locates them in the breast too. This action colors the mother in positive tones and taking in that object leads to a warm view of the self as acceptable. The loving and transformative capacity of the actual mother was not in focus until Bion (1962, 1967) described her reverie as an instrument of containment for detoxifying affective experience and giving it back to the infant in a manageable form.

Dicks (1967) was the one to show how Klein's concept of projective identification linking mother and infant also applied to the functioning of the marital bond and provided a way of explaining the patterns of interaction of an intimate couple. But it was Fairbairn's idea of the construction of the individual personality as a system of parts of ego, object and affect that gave psychoanalysis the change in stance that made it relevant to understanding families and couples and the role of sexuality in relationships. In particular, Fairbairn's (1954) description of the exciting object relational constellation led, for the first time, to an understanding of the role of excessive excitement in relationship to the too good object. The exciting object plays a crucial role in sexual difficulty when failed longing for such an object leads many couples to turn away from, or attack, their own sexuality (Scharff 1982; Scharff and Scharff 1991).

Individuals' internal object-relations sets are expressed in the way that they treat and are treated – by their loved ones. An intimate partner may identify with either the ego or the object pole of the internal object relationship. So a husband may treat his wife as a forbidding mother and turn away from her; or he may act like his own forbidding mother, causing his wife to feel as he did when he was a frightened child. A couple connects on the basis of conscious appreciation of compatibility, friendship, and sexual attraction. But the long-term nature of the couple relationship is determined by the degree and nature of fit between the repressed internal object relationships. Dicks (1967) thought that the couple created a joint personality greater than the sum of its parts. In this joint personality, the individual finds lost parts of the self in the partner and treats the partner according to how that part of the self was treated, whether it was cherished or attacked.

As the couple moves into a sexual relationship, the physical state of sexual arousal in association with the emotional state of falling in love reduces the boundaries between the partners. At these moments of vulnerability there is even more likelihood of finding lost parts of the self in the other with whom one is joined. In the sexual situation, the projection of good and bad parts of the self occurs into the sexual body parts of self or partner. Scharff refers to "the erotic zone as a projection screen" (1982: 6). Penis and vagina, breast, anus and body hair become the locus for split off and condensed conflicts with parent figures and intimate partners. Broader issues of competition, envy, shame, fear of being hurt, wishes to hurt, and so on are reduced to a physical sensation or function in the relatively small space of the genitalia and secondary sexual characteristics.

A sexual dysfunction is a condensation of a personal internal problem projected onto the body screen of the genitalia. Symptoms of sexual dysfunction illustrate Fairbairn's point that conversion phenomena occur when bodily problems are constituted as substitutes for emotional problems. As we have said, the mechanism through which this is accomplished is projective identification into the body. In this way, the psyche rids itself of unacceptable and irresolvable emotional issues by relocating them in the body. Sometimes a problematic sexual relationship reflects the nature of the intimate relationship. For instance, in the example of the warring partners who never feel sexually aroused, the deadness of their love is reflected in parallel by the non-responsiveness of their sexual organs. Sometimes the split off projection runs in opposition to the general nature of their relationship. This is illustrated by the case of partners who get along really well, love each other, and work well as parents, but simply cannot have good sex with one another.

The symptoms of sexual dysfunction take many forms from the occasional to the deeply ingrained. For instance, a husband returns from a hard day at the office where he felt rejected by his supervisor. He wants to relax with his wife, but he still feels irritable. He makes love to her with some ambivalence: he wants to be with her, but he is tired and jangled and the whole world still seems unfriendly. She wants to respond, but she reads his mood as one of irritation with her. He moves too quickly. Her clitoris feels irritable. The sensation is unpleasant, and she withdraws. He loses his erection. She feels undesirable. He feels rejected at home as well as at the office. Feeling rejected at work, he expects more rejection, and his behavior provokes the outcome that he fears. This is one bad day in their sexual life, and, if they ordinarily have a good sexual relationship, they will get over it.

However, if his rejection at work stimulates an intense resonance with a rejecting parent who did not welcome his loving advances, and if his wife has a history of feeling excited and let down by men, and before that by a mother who offered pleasure but disappeared, the likelihood of this event becoming part of a larger pattern is greater. This is even more likely if they have a history of many such failures. By the time the couple seeks therapy, a negative mutual response pattern is ingrained, reflecting the activation of rejecting and persecuting internal objects in a state of dynamic relation inside the self, and displayed between the self and the other in the couple relationship.

Erectile dysfunction

Andy and Diane, married for 15 years, love each other and enjoy their children, but they do not have satisfactory sex. Sex is not as important to him as it is to her, and he did not realize until recently how upset she is about the lack of sex in their relationship. Both of them are being treated for long-standing depression. Their individual psychiatrists referred them for sex therapy.

Andy is thin, anxious, compulsive, and highly disciplined. He works long hours in his own business and frets over his customers. Diane is overweight, laid back, and less ambitious than he is. They rarely have sex because he does not make time for it, frequently rejects her advances, and often loses his erection. Diane tries to accommodate Andy's sexual anxiety by not pressuring him for sex and by agreeing to be on top so he can lie there in the passive position he says he needs. But she feels unhappy and unloved. She wants to feel that she is number one with Andy, but he would rather be at work, with the children, or with his family, than be alone with her. For him sex is fraught with anxiety because he cannot count on his erection. She thinks that he does not get an erection because he finds her ugly, which he denies. He can stimulate her to orgasm, which is her preferred way of climaxing, but he knows that she wants intercourse as well, and he feels pathetic that he cannot give her that pleasure reliably. In the main, however, he feels unhappy because she is unhappy.

Diane comes from a chaotic, dysfunctional family with an alcoholic father and a mother who lived in a sweet pink world of denial. Her parents gave their children lots of freedom to go out and play, and most of her siblings are now quite disorganized. She visits her family, but does not expect Andy to put up with their craziness.

Andy's parents supervised his studying, his food intake, and his bowel movements. They were anxious but did not talk about their worries. They showed no affection, but once a week he heard giggling from their bedroom. His mother would call him to the bed, and he would jump on his father and that would end the giggling. Andy likes to visit many members of his family, and expects Diane to come with him, but he does not really connect with them or with her when he is there.

In couple therapy sessions, Andy and Diane expressed their distress and revealed some longings and fantasies that they had not told each other before. Andy said he felt guilty about having fantasies of making love to supermodels, because he thought that he should be thinking about the woman he is with, and he loves Diane regardless of her weight. In contrast, Diane feels that it is normal to have fantasies of other men, and so when these enter her mind during sex she is not perturbed. Sex happens so rarely, however, that she has dealt with her frustration by shutting off sexual feeling.

This balance was upset recently when she happened to meet an ex-boyfriend and was surprised to feel sexual excitement since she had concluded that her sexual feelings were no longer there. That experience showed her how much is missing from her life with Andy. She said that she has no intention of leaving Andy even though this ex-boyfriend still wants to be with her, but she feels miserable in the intimate aspect of her marriage. Diane was crying as she told this. Andy seemed not to notice her anguish.

In the next session, Andy reported a dream. He was with a girl from his high school class, a girl that all the boys had crushes on. He was amazed at how sexually aroused he felt in her company in the dream, when in reality he always felt frozen near her. She asked him to marry her, and he said he would rather be with Diane. I said that, like Diane's experience with her ex-boyfriend, this dream seemed to speak of his wish to find a lost part of himself, experience passion, and bring it into the marriage.

Diane was not ready to let go of the idea that her passion was connected to her ex-boyfriend. Sure, she would rather be with Andy, but she emphasized again how excited she had felt for days by being with this man. Andy retaliated by saying that he had never told Diane this, but he married her because, being fat, she was unlikely to be attractive to some other man who would take her away. Diane was devastated to hear that he objected to her weight when he had always said he loved her and her appearance had nothing to do with his sexual anxiety, and she did not believe that other men would find her unappealing, because she had the proof of her ex-boyfriend's interest in her.

Couple therapy was devoted to recovering from the assault of Diane's excitement about her ex-boyfriend and Andy's criticism of her weight and then arriving at renewed commitment to make time for each other. Diane decided not to control her weight, which Andy said he could live with, but she began to care about her grooming, and her appearance became more attractive.

The couple agreed to begin sex therapy, which consists of a series of pleasuring exercises (called sensate focus exercises) to be done in the privacy of the couple's bedroom, and then reviewed in the next therapy session. The assignments proceed from non-sexual touching to sexual touching, then intromission, and finally intercourse, proceeding in gradations that build in a secure base and desensitize the phobic partners. The first exercise is to explore the partner's body front and back avoiding the woman's breasts and genitals of both. The purpose is to reflect on the experience of touching and being touched; it is not to try to give the other pleasure.

At the next therapy session Andy said that it was not tedious to do the exercise as he had expected. He reported how much pleasure he had from touching Diane's belly. Her skin reminded him of a baby's. He loved how soft and cushiony she felt. He enjoyed "poking around" and found it fascinating to observe the ripple effect. Diane was smiling to hear what he was saying about her. It was nice to hear that he liked her body when she thought of herself as pendulous, asymmetrical, out of proportion, and unattractive. It was marvelous to him to enjoy her body so completely, and he thought it was because he did not have to worry about getting an erection.

Although Diane had no sexual dysfunction, she had much more difficulty with the sensate focus. When she was touching Andy she felt bored, just thinking of things to do that he would like. Her hands looked like spiders moving over him. When she said that, suddenly Andy remembered that when he was touching her abdomen he had noticed her navel and then thought about his own navel and how harshly his mother always reminded him to get the disgusting accretions out of his navel, as if he didn't always shower properly.

Diane was furious. She said that he would rather think about his mother than about her, and really he wanted her to be his mother. In fact, his saying that he was thinking about his mother made her feel that to him she *is* his mother. Andy replied that that was the furthest thing from his mind. He had felt relaxed, sexual, and totally with her as his wife. He was reassuring her, but the moment of reverie was ruined, as if Andy's mother had poked her finger into the middle of the session and found the lint.

Andy and Diane have a marriage that works well at the level of their central egos, but only because their rejecting and exciting object relationships are strongly repressed. Diane's exciting object is active in terms of enjoying sexual feeling and finding Andy attractive, but her rejecting object attacks her exciting object by keeping herself unattractive to him and to herself. Andy's exciting object is deeply repressed and surfaces in the form of totally unattainable ideals of perfection – supermodels who he knows would reject him. (Incidentally his mother was tall and thin, but he rejects any idea that she is the prototype for the supermodel fantasy.) When he successfully released his exciting object to reconnect with the central ego and express itself in relation to Diane's belly, he was interrupted by a memory of an admonishing rejecting object. Then Diane's rejecting object – seen as a self-image of spider hands and felt as hatred of being seen as a mother – joined in hatred of his mother and of her mother, and the pleasure of the sexual moment recollected in the session was ruined. The memory of the need to poke into the navel to get rid of nasty accretions is also a forewarning from the rejecting object of the dangers of putting the penis in the vagina. No wonder Andy prefers to lie passively beneath Diane so that it appears as if *she* is the one entering *him*, and therefore he could not be guilty either of poking around in her vagina or contemplating his navel, unconsciously connected to his mother and to masturbation fantasies.

Dyspareunia

Michelle and Lenny are young, and they do have sex. They enjoy foreplay, but engage in intercourse cautiously because Lenny does not want to cause Michelle the pain she feels on penetration. He is not put off by her physical discomfort in sex or by her disparaging comments about his misplaced devotion to her. Lenny is certain that he loves Michelle and is attracted to her no matter how she looks, no matter how critical or rejecting she is of him. They keep up a lively, amusing banter about the dead-end of their relationship, or as Lenny put it "sounding like a jazz band playing at a New Orleans funeral." Michelle is highly verbal, runs rings around him, and is so aggressive in stating her wish to break up with him, that it is hard to understand why he is with her. She hates herself so much, it is hard for her to believe he loves her and her body. He is steadfast and loyal, and immune to her complaints. He has eyes only for her, but she would rather be with an assertive man like her brother.

As a boy, Lenny was his mother's adored only son, and brother to sisters whom he was taught to protect. He said, "My father did not bring the masculine element into the family." Michelle's parents were an idealistic couple, but they got divorced, and she said little about her father. As a girl, Michelle envied her younger brother who was so special to her mother. This love has filled him with confidence that she does not have. As Michelle said, "I'm missing that little part. There's a part of me that constantly finds holes in herself." Later she added, "For a girl who had penis envy as a child, I hate them now. I see sex as a man sticking it to a woman."

Michelle and Lenny have been together four years. He treats her like a queen, and they have a lively interaction, but they are unable to marry. Michelle says she wants to break up because she is afraid of being bored. She says that she is afraid of Lenny's passivity, but the unconscious meaning is that she is afraid of literally being bored, being penetrated physically and being entered emotionally at the deepest level of intimate communication. The basic fear is that he and she will both find nothing there.

Michelle has identified with a rejecting object based on her experience of her mother turning away from her in excitement at the birth of Michelle's brother. She also identifies with that excitement, and functions as an exciting object for Lenny, stimulating his desire and frustrating his longing for an ongoing relationship. She has projected into Lenny the repudiated object that she feels herself to be and at the same time sees him as the desirable object like her brother. She stays with him and tries to get rid of him. She envies his success and his confidence and attacks him for it. She appreciates his patience with her sexual difficulty, but her body language says that she wants him to keep out. She has projected her rage into his penis as a representative of the phallic, confident brother she envied. Her vagina is the repository for the pain, emptiness, and sense of something lacking that she has felt for years as a girl in the shadow of a phallic brother.

The bodily locus of object relationships

Sex therapy assignments isolate the body parts that carry the negative exciting and rejecting aspects of internal object relationships, and show how sexual parts of the body convey emotional experience. Physical symptoms located by conversion, that is, by projective identification into one's own body, and expressed in bodily interaction with a partner symbolize unconscious conflict as succinctly as do dreams and the play of children. The analytic sex therapist asks for the couple's associations to the physical experiences and finds the latent content, in a process similar to that of analyzing a dream.

Analytic sex therapy aims to reverse the conversion phenomena of internal object relations projected into the body. Sexual symptoms are experienced and discussed, then reconnected to their source in troublesome internal objects. Then, sex can return to its normal function of giving and receiving love in a psychosomatic partnership that recalls the early experience of the child with giving, loving parents, and at the same time in a state of adult sexual arousal that is free of parental influence. Adult sexual interaction restores the image of good parents as a good couple in the internal world, and this image supports the person to join in a couple relationship as someone who cares and accepts being cared for with someone who is not a representative of a forbidden Oedipal object. At the same time, sex replays the struggle to overcome the image of the rejecting or withholding parent who seems not to care. Sex encompasses tolerating, forgiving, and repairing bad objects. Sex is also a way of building new objects out of good experience that, because of its physical and emotional intensity, reaches deep into the internal world. Paradoxically, it is the failed internal object shown in moments of breakdown with the partner that provides the impetus to come together in a healing way. Good enough sex is part of the self's ongoing effort to make things whole, to allow each partner to feel loved while giving love, and to ward off the threat of loneliness and the destruction of intimacy.

This approach to sexuality corresponds to Fairbairn and Sutherland's emphasis on the lifelong process of integration of the self and of the need to love and be loved, to find expression for all aspects of the self in all spheres of relating, and most of all to find meaning in existence.

References

Bion, W. R. (1962). *Learning from Experience*. New York: Basic Books.
—— (1967). *Second Thoughts*. London: Heinemann; reprinted Karnac 1984.
Dicks, H. (1967). *Marital Tensions*. London: Routledge & Kegan Paul.
Fairbairn, W. R. D. (1952). *Psychoanalytic Studies of the Personality*. London: Tavistock.
—— (1954). Observations on the nature of hysterical states. *British Journal of Medical Psychology* 27: 105–125. In *From Instinct to Self: Vol 1*, eds D. E. Scharff and E. F. Birtles, pp. 13–40. Northvale, NJ: Jason Aronson, 1994.
Klein, M. (1946). Notes on some schizoid mechanisms. In *Envy and Gratitude and Other Works 1946–1963*, pp. 1–24. New York: Delacorte Press, 1975.

Scharff, D. (1982). *The Sexual Relationship*. London: Routledge & Kegan Paul; reprinted Jason Aronson, 1998.

Scharff, D. and Scharff, J. S. (1991). *Object Relations Couple Therapy*. Northvale, NJ: Jason Aronson.

Scharff, J. S. (ed.) (1994). *The Autonomous Self: The Work of John D. Sutherland*. Northvale, NJ: Jason Aronson.

Chapter 8

From Fairbairn to a new systematization of psychopathology

The intuitive position and the alienated and oscillating structures

Ricardo Juan Rey

From Fairbairn and beyond Fairbairn

In 1941, William Ronald Fairbairn had the extraordinary courage to refute the drive theory of Freud and the theory of the erotic zones of Abraham. If he were alive, he would surely give us strong support for applying his ideas widely, and going beyond them. I will show how I build on crucial aspects of Fairbairn's contribution to arrive at a new system of psychopathology.

I take as my starting point the paper "Synopsis of the Development of the Author's Views regarding the Structure of the Personality" in which Fairbairn (1951) described the endopsychic situation, which develops as the pristine ego copes with inevitably somewhat frustrating experience by the defensive techniques of splitting and repression of the object and the ego. I relate the concept of the endopsychic situation to Klein's description of the paranoid-schizoid position, in which the ego's relation to its objects is characterized by splitting and projection of the bad object. Fairbairn emphasized that at birth the object is pre-ambivalent, and in 1951 suggested the existence of a previous phase of object internalization. He said that the first phase of internalization of the object is the taking in of the pre-ambivalent object in the early oral phase:

> Ambivalence must be regarded as a state first arising in the original unsplit ego in relation to the *internalized* pre-ambivalent object; and the motive determining the internalization of the pre-ambivalent object in the first instance will be provided by the fact that this object presents itself as in some measure unsatisfying as well as in some measure satisfying. The establishment of ambivalence once this has been accomplished, leads to an inner situation in which the unsplit ego is confronted with an *internalized ambivalent object.*
>
> (Fairbairn 1951: 178)

The intuitive position

Inspired by these thoughts, I postulate the existence of another position that is universal and involves specific erogenous zones. I call this *the intuitive position*, distinct from, and preceding, *the paranoid-schizoid and depressive positions*. This concept sheds new light on some normal and psychopathological conditions that are difficult to explain if we do not take it into account, and introduces intuition as a new element in the structuring of the mind.

After birth, the baby finds a mother different from the one of intrauterine life. The baby's mental apparatus must be put to work in order to recognize continuity between the intrauterine mother and the mother of the newborn. I do not agree with Bion that the infant has an inborn preconception of the breast. I think that the infant finds in the external world reminders of the fetal one.

The fetus responds to the mother's voice and, although it sounds different outside the womb, its melody is familiar and recognizable. Skin contact with the mother and with bath water reminds the baby of contact with the amniotic fluid and the uterine wall. Changing blood sugar levels following feeding at breast or bottle remind the infant of similar sensations in utero after the mother had eaten her meal. Inborn behavior, like that found in animals by Lorenz (1974), directs mother–infant interactions, including the especially important visual communication between mother and child. With this endowment and with continuity of experience, the infant comes equipped with an intuitive internal world.

The crucial issue about the intuitive position is that the infant searches constantly and permanently for contact with the mother to have an experience as if there is no separation between baby and mother. The intuitive position is expressed in bodily changes: a decrease in motility, a fixed look of intense concentration, superficial imperceptible respirations, all signs of the feverish mental work involved in looking for reminders of the old object in the somewhat different, now somewhat frustrating, object.

Each time the mother is experienced as frustrating, the baby searches for experience in which the mother as she was before birth is still recognizable. If this effort is satisfactory, the baby can maintain contact with the new version of the mother. This is the baby's subjective way of ordering the world. *The present is explained as a slight modification of the past.* The intuitive position is a link between the pristine unsplit ego at birth and selected aspects of the maternal object, which match the original. Like a computer reading a bar code, the baby registers the specifics of the post-birth maternal object in order to establish continuity between fetal and infant reality. I call the establishment of this *the link of fascination*.

In the realm of the mind, the intuitive position produces convergence of what Bion (1965) described as K, L and H links. The L link is the tendency to establish a permanent libidinal union. The H link makes the new object a hostile object that cannot be accommodated to historical objects. The K link is the mental work of urgently trying to understand the new object.

In the realm of the body, the intuitive position connects with an erogenous zone located in the respiratory tract and in the skin. It is experienced as changes in breathing and longings to be touched and held, or aversive reactions.

In the realm of relationships, according to Pierre Marty, the infant has a "primordial desire to reach the object, and to mix and fuse with it. The patient has great intuition, and works to efface the real distance between the subject and the object" (1958). Marty referred to this as the *allergic object relationship*. This conceptualization is helpful in understanding allergic diseases – which I think are related to the problem of identifying what is the same as me, and what is strange to me. Once the intuitive position is established, autistic regressions may occur if the self can not tolerate sudden changes in the object that are not compatible with going on building the intuitive link. The infant's inability to establish an intuitive position because of environmental failure produces autistic illness.

The concept of the intuitive position is relevant to the understanding of mystical and religious experience; mystical delirium and other psychotic manifestations; and the perception of beauty and truth, in addition to somatic diseases such as asthma, allergies, and skin diseases; and the profound withdrawal of autism.

The building of reality

In his 1943 paper Fairbairn brilliantly explained how the unsatisfactory aspect of the object is introjected and how the schizoid endopsychic situation arises (later adapted by Klein as the paranoid-schizoid position). He described the splitting of the mind into three parts: the libidinal ego, the antilibidinal ego, and the central ego, each one of them with an affective link to a part object – the exciting object, the rejecting object, and the ideal object. Reading these papers, it seems to me that the splitting occurs in order to maintain contact with the external object. The ideal object is only one intrapsychic version of the external object. Yet, with increasing tolerance to successive disappointments induced by the real object, there is a progressive approximation between the external object and the ideal object.

Fairbairn did not take into account this progressive approximation between the real and the ideal object mediated by the maternal link, as the mother confronts the baby with increasing amounts of reality and the baby engages in serious mental work to cope with the changing versions of her, and integrate them as aspects of a whole object.

Winnicott (1963), however, did deal with a similar construction when he wrote about object relating. He said that the initiation of object relating is complex. It cannot take place except by the environmental provision of object presenting done in such a way that the baby creates the object. The baby develops a vague expectation that has its origin in an unformulated need. The adaptive mother presents an object or a manipulation that meets the baby's needs. In this way the baby comes to feel confident in being able to create objects and to create the actual world. The mother gives the baby a brief period in which omnipotence is a matter of experience:

> In health, when the infant achieves fusion, the frustrating aspect of the object's behaviour has value in educating the infant in respect of the existence of a not-me world. Adaptation failures have value *in so far as the infant can hate the object*, that is to say, can retain the idea of the object as potentially satisfying while recognizing its failure to behave satisfactorily.
>
> (Winnicott 1963: 181)

The part of the mind that is able to confront and assimilate reality develops in direct relation to the mother's ability to notice the unsatisfactory aspects of the baby, tolerate them, and value their being contained by others who are equally meaningful to the baby, such as the father. Only then can the baby introject the ability to tolerate others as different from him or her.

The alienated structure

Lack of capacity to develop an ideal ego in contact with the ideal object modified by successive contributions of the real object, produces pathologic splitting. My term for this situation is *the alienated structure*.

What type of link is established then? We believe that these mothers demand the child as a necessary participant in a plot built in her fantasy in relation to old conflicts between the mother and her parents. The satisfactory object acquires instead the characteristics of a seductive object that produces cumulative trauma, as described by Khan (1979). I think that cumulative trauma is produced when the child is confronted again with not being recognized and loved as an individual. As Fairbairn (1940) stated in his paper "Schizoid Factors in the Personality," these children are not loved for themselves, and a feeling of futility dominates their existence. In place of an ideal object, the libidinal ego despoils its own exciting object, and forms a rigid closed structure, a claustrum in which libidinal investment comes at the cost of real life in the real world, and gives rise to the need for a false self. The description by Masud Khan of these patients is of great interest:

> The relation between the mother and the son is of one of idolization. The mother cathects and invests something very special in the child but not as a whole person. The child gradually becomes an accomplice in maintaining this special created object. They are astonishingly empathic to their

mothers' moods and they seem to resign prematurely from offering anything from their side. The ideal is two persons that leave their identity
and their state of separation, to work in connivance, and in service to
ecstasy and autoerotic intimacy. The conduct of these mothers is both
traumatizing and seductive.

(Khan 1979: 12–13)

I consider that these children are seduced to fulfill their mothers' requirements, a transgenerational transmission of trauma. Child and mother are
"orphans of the real" (Grotstein 2000: 261).

Fairbairn's papers on hysterical patients and on the nature and aims of
psychoanalytical treatment point to the profound needs of these traumatized
patients and how the analyst can help them. He arrived at his revolutionary
concept that it is the participation of the analyst as a real person that mobil-
izes the cure. He wrote: "The analyst has to effect breaches of the closed
system which constitutes the patient's inner world and thus to make this
world accessible to the influence of outer reality." The patient after analysis
can live "in an open system in which the inner and outer reality are brought
into relation" (Fairbairn 1958: 84).

The alienated structure is not a universal but a psychopathological one. It is
useful in explaining paraphilia, hysteria, paranoia, anorexia nervosa, and
psychosis. In the case of paraphilia and hysteria, the patient maintains spor-
adic contact with external reality by acting out in crises. In paranoia, external
links are felt to be dangerous in general, and in anorexia nervosa, the threat
resides particularly in food. In psychosis, the patient has lost all contact with
the real world and lives in a projective, hallucinatory, and delirious world.

The oscillating structure

I do not accept that manic-depressive illness has been explained satisfactorily
by the Kleinian depressive position. I consider that illness to be a particular
resolution of the alienated position. I call it *the oscillating structure*. Here is
how I arrived at this idea. Manic-depressive patients try to compensate for
claustrophobic aspects of the ideal object. They feel anger when they get in
touch with the indifference or rejection of the insufficiently containing primary object, and deal with it by immediately trying to build an alternative
claustrum with another object. If successful in this endeavour, they experience a manic feeling of triumph, but its duration is limited, as guilt about the
fate of the primary object produces depressive illness.

Using the work of Fairbairn as his inspiration, Harry Guntrip said it his
own way: "Depression in the classic sense is set up by the failure of a certain
type of defence against a powerful underlying compulsion to seek safety in a
regressive withdrawal from object relations" (Guntrip 1961, personal communication). The rejection of the primary containing object produces the

danger that the lost object can be followed by loss of the ego, resulting in a state of severe depersonalization. This is what sets in motion a frantic triumphant search for an alternative claustrum. Guntrip went on to explain:

> The manic state . . . is a desperate attempt to force the whole psyche out of a state of *devitalized passivity* . . . and regression. The harder the struggle to defeat the passive regressed ego, the more incapable of relaxation and rest the patient becomes. . . . When the battle becomes a losing one it may well happen that euphoria turns into aggression and violent sexuality. The pathological forms of sexual and aggressive impulse are aspects of the struggle . . . to defeat regression and the flight from life on the part of a person who feels that at the deepest mental level he hardly has an ego at all to be active with. There are also other "active" capacities which can be used for this purpose . . . thinking, overworking, the hectic social round.
>
> (Guntrip 1962: 154)

I believe that the oscillating structure is useful to explain depressive illness, manic-depressive illness, the addictions, obsessive-compulsive symptoms and obsessional neurosis.

From the depressive position to the objective position

The establishment of a real and complete object allows for the construction of a normal Oedipus complex, and is the main feature of the depressive position described by Melanie Klein. Fairbairn's genius lay in his description of the Oedipal situation as an end product of infantile security, rather than the cause of psychoneurosis. I believe that to reach the establishment of the depressive position, growth of the central ego is required, with the support of an adequate external object.

The establishment of the depressive position is the first step towards what I call the *objective position*. This position is characterized by tolerance of dissent and difference, and recognition of others as different and separate. About the mental registration of that which is foreign the Argentine analyst Isidoro Berenstein states:

> The reality principle is not to find an object that is the same as the object of the mind, but to meet a foreign object, and in that way a new significance is recorded. The patient has to give the other a place as foreign, not to get mad. Registration of the foreign is threatening because with the emergence of the new link, something old is no longer there. The world will be different, the old world is a lost world and the subject is no longer what he was.
>
> (Berenstein 2001: 174)

The last stage of development in the objective position is *the transcendent position* described by Grotstein (2001). Patients who arrive at the transcendent position accept that external reality is indifferent to their projections, a point that can only be reached by some of them. Grotstein described an ideal patient who had opened his claustrum, spared the satisfying object, and reintrojected the paranoid ego (corresponding to Fairbairn's term, the internal saboteur) and reached a new steady state without splitting.

Erikson (1950) considered the last vital step of the lifecycle to be the achievement of wisdom. I think he was referring to the ability to embrace the perspective of the objective position. The French philosopher François Jullien (2001) made a similar point, holding that the wise person has no ideas, because to have an idea is to establish a point of view, and the wise person faces the world without projecting into it any preconceived point of view. The attainment of the objective position is severely impeded in perverse, hysterical and manic-depressive patients unless the analyst first dismantles the alienated structure or the oscillating structure, and moves the patient into the depressive position.

Conclusion

My ideas on mental growth and pathology expand on various key contributions of Fairbairn – introjection of the bad object, establishment of the endopsychic situation, prior introjection of an ambivalent object, futility as a result of not feeling loved, the importance of the contact with the analyst as a real person so as to break the closed system of the alienated position, and the extraordinary concept of the Oedipus as a final consequence and not as an initial explanatory cause of neurosis. Expanding on these valuable contributions, I propose that normal mental development has three positions – the intuitive, the paranoid-schizoid, and the objective position – and that psychopathological mental development is produced by autistic, alienated, or oscillating structures, which need to be analyzed if development is to proceed. These ideas are the findings of my work in progress on a new system of mental development and psychopathology.

References

Berenstein, I. (2001). Transference: a new fact and/or repetition, individual or joint production. In *The Subject and the Other*, pp.167–193. Buenos Aires: Paidos.

Bion, W. R. (1965). *Transformations*. Bath: Pitman.

Erikson, E. (1950). *Childhood and Society*. New York: Norton.

Fairbairn, W. R. D. (1940). Schizoid factors in the personality. In *Psychoanalytic Studies of the Personality*, pp. 3–27. London: Routledge & Kegan Paul.

—— (1943). The repression and the return of the bad objects. In *Psychoanalytic Studies of the Personality*, pp. 59–81. London: Tavistock, 1952.

—— (1951). Synopsis of the development of the author's views regarding the structure of the personality. In *Psychoanalytic Studies of the Personality*, pp. 162–180. London: Tavistock, 1952.

—— (1952). A revised psychopathology of the psychoses and psychoneurosis. In *Psychoanalytic Studies of the Personality*, pp. 28–59. London: Tavistock, 1952.

—— (1958). On the nature and aims of psychoanalytical treatment. In *From Instinct to Self: Selected Papers of W. R. D. Fairbairn Vol. 2*, eds E. F. Birtles and D. E. Scharff, pp. 74–92. Northvale, NJ: Jason Aronson, 1994.

Grotstein, J. S (2000). Why Oedipus and not Christ? In *Who is the Dreamer Who Dreams the Dream?* pp. 255–279. London: Analytic Press.

—— (2001). Bion's transformations, the concept of the "transcendent position". In *Who is the Dreamer Who Dreams the Dream?* Hillsdale, NJ: Analytic Press.

Guntrip, H. (1962). The clinical diagnostic framework: The manic-depressive problem in the light of the schizoid process. In *Schizoid Phenomena, Object Relations and the Self*, pp. 116–130. Edinburgh: H. Guntrip Foundation.

Jullien, F. (2001). *Un sabio no tiene ideas*. Madrid: Siruela.

Khan, M. R. (1979). *Alienation in Perversions*. London: Hogarth Press and Institute of Psychoanalysis.

Lorenz, K. (1974). *On Aggression*. Mexico City: Fondo de Cultura Economica de Mexico, pp. 48–56.

Marty, P. (1958). The allergic object relationship. *International Journal of Psycho-Analysis* 39, 2: 98–103.

Winnicott, D. W. (1963). Communicating and not communicating leading to a study of certain opposites. In *The Maturational Processes and the Facilitating Environment*, pp. 179–192. New York: International Universities Press, 1965.

Chapter 9

How current are Fairbairn's ideas on hysteria?

Ute Rupprecht-Schampera

Since the 1980s, I have been developing a clinical theory on hysteria, which allows all clinical forms of hysteria – male and female hysteria, neurotic and borderline hysteria, and hysterical conversion – to be fitted into a common psychodynamic model (Rupprecht-Schampera 1995). I had found the classical explanatory model unsatisfactory for the confusing defensive operations of my hysterical patients and I knew that Fairbairn was in fundamental disagreement with Freud's instinct theory and that he stressed the object-seeking motivation of the child. In my first publication, I referred to Fairbairn merely as a witness.

It was not until later when I had read Fairbairn thoroughly that I realized that, in describing the central defensive organization in hysteria, I had partly arrived at the same conclusions Fairbairn had already made 40 years earlier. However, due to the independent development of my principles of explanation, differences from Fairbairn's concepts also came to light. In this chapter, I will show where I validate Fairbairn's formulations on hysteria and where I cannot confirm his specific ideas from the point of view of the theory that I developed. However, Fairbairn's basic theoretical lines of understanding are still enormously useful and productive for the development of a modern theory of neuroses. I will first give a brief description of my hysteria model as a basis for discussion and compare my ideas with Fairbairn's.

A common model for all hysterias

I understand hysteria as a particular attempt at separation, but one that has failed and leads only to a specific form of pseudo-separation. Furthermore, I think of the need for early triangulation as a decisive factor in hysteria. I understand the forced search for triangulation as the central organizing principle in all hysterical manifestations. My central consideration is that the child, who will later show hysterical development, suffers from having a father who is experienced as insufficiently available in his triangular function during the early mother–child relationship, which is filled with fear, depression, or hate. In search of a solution for separation, the child will defensively use the modalities of Oedipal triangulation in order to achieve pre-Oedipal (early) triangulation and thus establish a (pseudo-) separation from the mother. This is how pre-genital and genital phenomena connect in hysteria.

Female hysteria

If the child is a girl, she uses the Oedipalized, erotized mode of approach – not necessarily regarded as a later mode, simply another developmental mode (Stern 1985) – in order to win over the father, who has formerly been experienced as uninterested or psychologically absent. This is how she might finally be able to introduce him as a protective figure into her difficult relationship with the mother.

However, a double conflict arises from this defensive solution: The child gets entangled too early in Oedipal instinctual conflicts, while still searching for the solution to pre-Oedipal conflicts. The outcome may be benign, but more often, within a progressively sexualized solution, severely traumatizing relational experiences can occur and result in emotional upsets, severe anxiety, and conflicts over guilt and hate. The girl has possibly won over the father as an Oedipal, incestuous object with all the associated satisfactions and grandiose fantasies, but is let down as before when he fails once again in his function as the helpful but intrusive third object.

If the girl is thus able to mobilize her father's interest and no further traumatic experiences occur, only a mild or benign hysteric personality may result. However, if the sexualized approach of the father results in more difficult experiences which cause severe disillusionment or retraumatization, further defensive operations will be necessary – repression, disavowal, dissociation, and infantile withdrawal. As these defenses back up the sexualized defensive solution, the well-known pronounced hysterical personality results. Repression serves to keep memories of the eroticized, perhaps incestuous events, and the feelings of guilt, shame, rage, and hate, out of the realms of consciousness. Disavowal is necessary to abolish disillusionment with the Oedipal father and to guarantee his idealization, which has to be secured as an eventual guarantor of separation from the early mother.

With the help of these layers of defense, a self-container-phantasy is established, which I have called the "pseudo-Oedipal myth": On the surface it resembles the normal Oedipus conflict and can be confused with it, because the father is seen as the longed for idealized Oedipal figure and the mother as the rival, who will not let the daughter reach the father, but actually it is different because in the hysterical patient, the Oedipal parent was "to be had", and the state of non-separation from the early mother persists.

Male hysteria

To defuse or overcome his originally highly conflict-prone or hopeless relationship to his mother, the boy may try an Oedipalized defensive solution and
erotize the relationship with her. However, the seductive courting relationship
takes place with the very object that was threatening, and so the threatening
quality of the exciting Oedipal object never vanishes. And if, on this level, a
second layer of traumatization should occur, it will be more devastating, as it
comes again from the same object. So, the male hysteric's situation is quite
different from that of the hysteric girl, who by turning towards the father in
an Oedipal way uses a third object in the form of a real person which she can
– at least in fantasy – introduce into the scene with the mother. In contrast,
the boy can only find a "third object" in his own sexualized, idealized phallus
to take the place of the absent father. This is why the hysterical solution for
the male is always more difficult and threatening from the start than for the
female.

Hysterics of both sexes try to overcome their unresolved conflictual relationship with the early mother by seductiveness, demands for attention, and
the expression of exaggerated emotions towards the Oedipal parent of the
opposite sex, but this also brings them back to enormous feelings of Oedipal
guilt, which they try to avoid by regression to functioning as if innocent and
helpless. But this secondary defensive move throws them back into a lack of
separation. New attempts at separation by forced flight to the Oedipal object
are elicited, and thus a neurotic cycle is completed.

The function of physical symptoms in hysteria

My concept of separation and early triangulation sheds light on the functional, interactive meaning of conversion. However unpleasant a physical
symptom may be for the patient, paradoxically it is useful to him, as it dis-
tracts the patient and analyst away from the inner world of dangerous and
uncontrollable relational feelings and on to body feelings, which are one-
person-feelings, and can be unconsciously manipulated at any time, uninfluenced
by the external world. By using physical symptoms, hysterics demonstrate
that relating to their own self is safer than dealing with real people. They stay
immune from the impact of relational experiences that could be emotionally
injurious.

Although physical symptoms are multiply determined and have to be carefully analyzed at different levels, they are often surprisingly quickly solved by
interpretation if their triangular function is understood. I assume that conversion symptoms arise from the collapse of organized psychical triangular
constellations of a higher structural level involving real people or fantasies.
The body is then being used as a replacement for the early third object. This
definition of conversion is compatible with Rangell (1959).

I see hysteria as a progressive, sexualized, defensive way out of deficient or traumatic separation and triangulation experiences, and I see it as a neurotic form of resolution for a central human developmental conflict.

Discussion of Fairbairn's hypotheses on hysteria

Fairbairn's hypotheses about the psychodynamics of hysteria appear in "A Revised Psychopathology of the Psychoses and Psychoneuroses" (1941) and in "Endopsychic Structure considered in Terms of Object-Relationships" (1944), as well as in "The Nature of Hysterical States" (1954).

As early as 1941, Fairbairn developed the remarkable view that the individual goes through a *transitional stage* in the movement from early childhood dependence to various forms of mature dependence from which the different neurotic defensive techniques – paranoid, obsessive-compulsive, phobic, and hysterical – arise. However, his first psychodynamic formulations for the four defensive techniques hardly differed from his formulation of the basic conflict of the transitional phase itself, and thus did not add much to a new understanding of the neurotic styles. But in 1944, for hysteria in particular, a remarkably differentiated psychodynamic hypothesis appeared. Fairbairn wrote:

> I have yet to analyze the hysteric, male or female, who does not turn out to be an inveterate breast-seeker at heart. I venture to suggest that the deep analysis of a positive Oedipus situation may be regarded as taking place at three main levels. At the first level the picture is dominated by the Oedipus situation itself. At the next level it is dominated by ambivalence towards the heterosexual parent; at the deepest level it is dominated by ambivalence towards the mother.
>
> (Fairbairn 1944: 124)

Fairbairn's (1944) view is now much more specific about the layers of defense, and recalls my idea of the *pseudo-Oedipal myth*, an Oedipal level defense against the mother of attachment, which also covers up the traumas encountered in connection with the sexualized defensive solution. In his paper on hysteria, Fairbairn asserted that hysterical conversion as a defense technique represents "the substitution of a bodily state for a personal problem," and that "so long as successful repression can be maintained, there is no occasion for resort to the defence of hysterical conversion" (1954/1994: 29). This corresponds to my thoughts completely, and anticipates Rangell's (1959) definition of conversion.

Writing about the sexuality of the hysteric, Fairbairn said:

> It is characteristic for genital sexuality to have been prematurely excited . . . doubtless related to the intervention of their fathers as rejecting

figures at critical moments . . . of intense need. However . . . the experience of rejection in the presence of excitement due to the stirring of urgent need constitutes a traumatic situation of the highest order for the child.

(Fairbairn 1954: 26)

Fairbairn's conclusions concerning the role of premature sexualization, possibly including trauma, in the etiology of hysteria are similar to mine. On the topic of rejection by the father, however, Fairbairn is ambiguous. From case studies in the 1954 paper (for example, Olivia or Morris) Fairbairn appears to think that the father's rejection of the child's Oedipal approach is the trauma. But his definition allows the unspoken idea that there are other "urgent needs," which the father rebuffs. Fairbairn was a clear thinker, so an ambiguous formulation that allows different readings could mean that he was unsure about the causative psychological factors and deliberately left the matter open.

My introduction of the concept of the search for triangulation helps to solve the problem. In my concept, the father has been experienced as a *rejecting object* refusing to satisfy the original need for early triangulation. But as the Oedipal parent, he has also responded to the child in ways that intensified the excited, sexualized search for triangulation. Thus, traumatization results from over-excitation at the Oedipal level, and not from rejection of the sexualized approach.

If the parent of the opposite sex is openly or even aggressively rejecting, this will not result in hysteria but will give rise to other defensive solutions, such as fearful clinging to the primary object and phobic disavowal of the need for the third object, or sexualization of a homosexual object choice, or withdrawal to auto-eroticism or inanimate sexual objects, such as in fetishism or paraphilia. But these are not hysterias, however, even if they show phenomenologically similar traits such as acting out and affective instability. From my point of view, only those defensive formations, which – at least on the surface – demonstrate a positive Oedipal sexualization and idealization of the parent of the opposite sex, can be called hysteria. Fairbairn described the Oedipus situation as follows:

It is in the . . . child's relationship with his mother that the differentiation of the endopsychic structure is accomplished and that repression originates; and . . . only after these developments . . . the child meet(s) the particular difficulties . . . [of] the classical Oedipus situation . . . The Oedipus situation is one . . . in which the child identifies one parent (usually of the opposite sex) predominantly with the exciting object, and the other parent (usually of similar sex) predominantly with the rejecting object.

(Fairbairn 1954: 28)

I agree that hysterical conflict does not have its roots solely in the Oedipal triangle, but in pre-Oedipal issues that influence the psychic processing of the Oedipal phase. Also, I am convinced that the exciting object is projected onto the parent of the opposite sex, in the normal course of Oedipal development. This recalls my emphasis on the idealization of the Oedipal parent of the opposite sex as a necessary condition for the development of hysteria. But does the male hysteric also project the early maternal exciting object onto the Oedipal mother, as the female does in relation to the idealized father? What do both sexes do with the paternal exciting object? Fairbairn seems to solve these theoretical problems when he states: "Thus, in my view, the triangular situation which provides the original conflict of the child is not one constituted by three persons (the child, his mother and his father) but one constituted essentially by the central ego, the exciting object and the rejecting object" (1954: 28). Here, he stresses that the triangular conflict situation of the hysteric is not to be found in the personal area, but in a conflict between the split off ego structures. His central definition of hysteria given right at the beginning also applies: "So far as the hysteric is concerned . . . the exciting object is excessively exciting and the rejecting object is excessively rejecting" (p. 18).

I am addressing the same theoretical problem of where the triggering triangular conflict occurs. I approach this by introducing the search for early triangulation and by conceptualizing the use of the Oedipal triangulation as its substitute. In the 1954 paper, Fairbairn executed the leap to the structural level and was then forced to locate the triangular conflict between the split off structures of introjected objects. He correctly assumed that the structure of the split off ego is the same basic structure for all personality types and pathologies, and attributed hysteria to the excessive intensity of these split off bad introjects. However, given the relative intensification of circumstances already present in neurotics, the hysteric could appear to be little more than a super-neurotic.

Fairbairn noticed that some of his cases given to illustrate his definition of hysteria actually contradict it. He pointed out that projection of the exciting object into the parent of the opposite sex does not apply in the case vignettes of Olivia and Morris. For them, the parent of the opposite sex is linked with the rejecting introject. Could it be that Louise, Olivia and Morris are not hysterics? If they are not hysterics, they are not required to have projected the exciting object into the parent of the opposite sex. By my definition, several of Fairbairn's cases in his hysteria paper are not hysterics. Granted they have histories of over-excitement and rejection, but no idealization of the parent of the opposite sex, and their mass of symptoms with heavy acting out are characteristic of borderline and phobic patients. These dramatic cases – Louise, Olivia and Morris – do not fit my definition of hysteria. Apart from the case of Jean, whom I agree is a hysteric but also a borderline, these are the cases presented in the first part of the paper, whereas the cases presented in the second part – Ivy, Jack, and Gertrude – certainly do fit my criteria for the classification of hysteria.

How does this come about, and what does it mean? Fairbairn's hysteria paper actually consists of two parts, and two correspondingly different explanatory hypotheses. In the first part of the paper, Fairbairn defines hysteria completely in terms of *ego-structures in the endopsychic situation relating to introjected bad objects*, whereas in the second part he derives hypotheses from the use of the body and sexuality, and so are concerned with *the relation of the subject to his real objects*.

Fairbairn's cases that I regard as borderline with different defensive techniques, and not as hysteric, are all presented to underline the *structural* definition, whereas the patients who, by my definition, are also clearly hysterics are given to support the *relational* definitions of hysteria. Also, all the hypotheses which my work confirms originate from the second part. So it seems that Fairbairn presented patients that he thought of as acting out hysterics, and they did indeed fit his structural definition, but I suggest that they were in fact borderline. Could it be that his structural formula does not define hysteria apart from other neurotic conditions, but that his formulations on the use of the body and of sexuality do?

This confusion can be disentangled. Fairbairn said that "the development of hysterical symptoms depends upon the *simultaneous* [my emphasis] experience of excitement . . . and frustration or rejection . . . all in the setting of object relationships" (1954: 23). Fairbairn's cases fit this definition, but he does not define further which parent excites or rejects, when, how, or in what respect. His definition uses general criteria applicable to borderline patients, independent of their respective defensive technique. By his definition, borderlines could pass for "super-neurotics." In my view, Fairbairn's structural definition covers a central trait of the borderline condition, including the claustro-agoraphobic syndrome of the borderline patient described by Henri Rey in illustration of Guntrip's ideas (1979). I might even suggest that Fairbairn has developed a concept of the claustro-agoraphobic conflict in this paper on hysteria.

My conclusions are that Fairbairn's basic assumptions concerning endopsychic structure and the transitional phase as the situation in which neurotic defensive techniques develop are to the point; his global structural definition remains valid for borderline conditions but not for hysteria; and he was not successful at giving a specific structural definition of the hysterical technique, although his relational definition remains valid for hysteria.

References

Fairbairn, W.R.D. (1941). A revised psychopathology of the psychoses and psychoneuroses. In *Psychoanalytic Studies of the Personality*, pp. 28–58. London: Routledge, 1952/1990.

—— (1944). Endopsychic structure considered in terms of object-relationships. In *Psychoanalytic Studies of the Personality*, pp. 82–136. London: Routledge, 1952/1990.

—— (1954). The nature of hysterical states. In *From Instinct to Self: Vol. I*, eds. D. E. Scharff and E. F. Birtles, pp. 13–42. Northvale, NJ: Jason Aronson, 1994.

Rangell, L. (1959). The nature of conversion. *Journal of the American Psychoanalytic Association* 7: 632–663.

Rey, H. (1979). Schizoid phenomena in the borderline. In *Advances in the Psychotherapy of the Borderline Patient*, eds. J. LeBoit and A. Capponi, pp. 449–484. New York: Jason Aronson.

Rupprecht-Schampera, U. (1995). The concept of 'early triangulation' as a key to a unified model of hysteria. *International Journal of Psycho-Analysis* 76: 457–473.

Stern, D. (1985). *The Interpersonal World of the Infant*. New York: Basic Books.

Chapter 10

The real relationship with the analyst as a new object

Peter Potthoff

Introduction

A woman client complains bitterly for years, "I didn't have a real family. Something is missing, and it cannot be replaced. What you offer me is all right, but it isn't what I really need." She plainly tells me what she expects, "You should, above all else, accept me the way I am, do not criticize anything about me, and be constantly available." Inevitably she finds me disappointing, insufficiently involved and at the same time too demanding and intrusive. "I pay you for it," she reminds me, "but we don't really have a relationship." She has trouble recognizing the reality of her relationship to me, and she is unable to establish and maintain meaningful relationships with her family and others, or even to sustain good contact with herself. Her parents had fought bitterly throughout her childhood and divorced when she entered puberty. Lacking a real family, she is captive to her powerful internal family. She draws me into the internal object world into which she has pulled back, and makes me over as a replica of a disinterested, and yet overwhelmingly intrusive, primary object. The notion that I could possibly have anything else of value to offer her other than this appears highly doubtful to her.

Fairbairn's theory of personality and treatment

To understand this woman's situation of entanglement with her pathogenic internal objects and lack of connection in the there-and-now, I call on Fairbairn's (1944) structural theory of the basic endopsychic situation. He holds that the early relationship to the primary object is conserved in split off and repressed libidinal and antilibidinal self-object parts, leaving the central part of the ego emptied out, a schizoid void. The personality is in a state of psychic retreat. This explains why the external relationships seem either superficial or hollow when repression has to be severe, or intensely irritating or seductive when internalized relationships to exciting and rejecting objects dominate. Accordingly, the prominent symptom is frustration and emptiness in relationships, or lack of relationships, accompanied by feelings of futility and of an inner void (which is often mistakenly called depression). Identification with a devaluing, rejecting object induces an acute problem of poor self-esteem. In postmodern narcissistic disturbances, this *psychic retreat* is in juxtaposition to a normal self that can be conceptualized in terms of Freud's structural theory.

Fairbairn (1958) distinguishes between one part of the analytic relationship, which he attributes to the transference, and another part, which he attributes to the real relationship, which offers a new experience of the object as a vehicle for development. The working through of the split off and repressed object-units in the transference, together with the new object experience, facilitates a resynthesis of the personality.

The new object

Freud (1912a, 1912b, 1914) distinguished positive and negative object-libidinal transferences from the so-called unobjectionable transference, which he thought operated as "the motor" of therapy and required no further analysis. His standard technique emphasized the analyst's abstinence and neutrality, both essential in preventing any contamination of the unfolding transference. Freud thought that any deviation from the correct neutral stance called for further analysis of the analyst's infantile conflicts. He did not recognize that the personality of even the most mature analyst inevitably has an effect on the expression of the transference. Research on countertransference (Heimann 1950; Racker 1957) centred on the significant contribution made by the personality and conflicts of the analyst. Alexander and French's (1946, 1950) concept of the analyst's role in offering a corrective emotional experience condoned the analyst's manipulation of the transference and deliberate role playing, which discredited the therapeutic value of a corrective emotional experience in analysis for decades. The analyst is both the object of the transference and an object differing from the transference object. Psychoanalytic literature has explicitly dealt mainly with the problems inherent within the transference. Yet, the topic of the new object surfaces implicitly in many schools of analytic thought.

Loewald (1960) described the *therapeutic relationship* in terms of a parent–child relationship operating as an open system. Greenson (1965, 1969, 1972) described the *working contract* as a pragmatic, rational relationship, relatively free from transference. Already in the 1930s, Ferenczi (1933) and Balint (1932) introduced the concept of the *new beginning* to connote a completely different kind of relationship between analyst and patient. Their related idea of therapeutic regression as a necessary precursor to new development is echoed in Winnicott's concept of *transitional space*. Bollas (1986) envisioned the analyst as a *transformational object*. Contemporary Kleinian analysis includes the intersubjective dimension of Bion's (1970) model of the *container/contained*. Daniel Stern *et al.* (1998) presented a process model, which described the continual unfolding of the transference relationship on the intersubjective level, where *moments of meeting* between analyst and patient emerge from the usual context of the transference and countertransference. Here, the analyst reveals himself selectively, answers personally, and responds genuinely, thus allowing the relationship to reach new levels of connection and mutuality.

My thesis

I would now like to distinguish between two aspects of the therapeutic relationship. The first is the transference level on which old object relational patterns are repeated. The second is the level of new object experience, which has many dimensions, all of which reflect the quest of the patient for a new experience together with and assisted by the analyst.

The psychoanalytic setting offers a responsive *facilitating environment* and a *collaborative approach to creating a new type of relationship*, adapted to the needs of each patient, thanks to the analyst's affective attunement. The analyst's abstinence, acceptance, empathy and availability for personal encounter enable the patient to experience the object in an entirely new way. The *working alliance* is an area of mutual reflection on the transference level at which old object relations patterns are repeated, and on the level of new relationship. The concept of the *real relationship* cannot fully convey the transformational element of new object experience. These new experiences are increasingly made possible as the transference progressively unfolds and dissolves. Conversely, the patient who experiences the analyst as being different from the transference-object and who becomes more secure in the new relationship can, to a certain extent, afford to experience the analyst more fully on the transference level. In my view, *both elements of the therapeutic relationship are closely related to each other and influence each other*.

Fairbairn perceives the defences in the analytic situation as being directed towards the analyst rather than towards drives and traumatic memories. They are directed against the establishment of transference and aim to prevent the experience of the analyst as a new object. In many cases new experience of the object seems to occur in a rather matter-of-fact way, passing almost unnoticed and meriting no particular attention. However, in certain cases, more explicit new object experience is essential for the analytic process. This is particularly the case when strong bonds to pathologic inner objects are vigorously maintained and as a result relatively few normal structures have been developed.

Case vignette

A 28-year-old woman consulted me because of her repeated failure to establish a mutually satisfying relationship with any man. With a man, she repeated a pattern of attraction and repulsion, revealing a sado-masochistic tie to an exciting–rejecting primary object. Without a man, she felt depressed and lonely, which she dealt with by drinking and watching television excessively.

As a child, she had enjoyed a close relationship with her mother. It was, however, so close that it excluded bonds to others. Her father usually lay in front of the TV in his bedroom, instead of interacting in the family room or helping to put the children to bed. When she was 6 years old her mother abruptly withdrew from her, and from that moment she appeared alternately disinterested or intrusive and critical toward her daughter. The child withdrew into herself, refused to participate in family meals, and took up drinking while still living at home. This was accepted without comment by her parents. Later on, she easily established herself as the head of a large research laboratory with a minimum of effort, which, however, she could not recognize as an achievement. The job suited her. It gave her a great deal of independence and required little or no contact with clients.

Introjects based on experience with her father and mother are compressed into one massive rejecting object which is associated with an equally enlarged antilibidinal ego. This structure suppresses her libidinal potential while her central ego maintains a fragile, constantly threatened connection to the world. In the failed relationships to her boyfriends she refound the traumatizing concretization of the exciting and rejecting object in the outside world.

The first years of the analysis were dominated by her conflict with the setting and with establishing a meaningful relationship to me. Despite agreeing to four weekly sessions, she came for only two or three sessions, usually considerably late, whereupon she proceeded to carry on endless discussions about the rules, which she criticized as one-sided and disrespectful of her individuality. An unusually tall, attractive woman, she could have looked stunning, but she dressed in old, uncomfortable clothes, and she exuded an extremely unpleasant body odour.

I felt constantly attacked, rejected and uncertain about whether she would continue the analysis at all. I suffered what she had probably suffered as a child when her attempts to establish contact were rebuffed by her parents. She was projecting aspects of the libidinal ego onto me, while she remained an unattainable exciting object. Sometimes this constellation was reversed, in which case she persistently tried to push me into the position of the rejecting antilibidinal object to whom she felt strongly attached, and yet whose influence she feared and tried to curtail, she herself taking the position of the antilibidinal ego. Her longing for me was intense. She expressed it indirectly in a wishful fantasy of joining my family during the summer holidays.

After some time in analysis, she began to enjoy a satisfying relationship with a partner and her depression and drinking disappeared. She now insisted on reducing the frequency of the sessions to twice a week, otherwise she would leave the analysis. Had I accepted her suggestion, I would have supported that side of her which was convinced that our relationship was unimportant to me. At the same time she probably would have been extremely disappointed that I had not realized this, as she secretly hoped that I would not acquiesce to her appeal to weaken the analysis. I told her that replacing a session of analysis with time with her boyfriend would not solve the problem, and I said that her commitment to analysis did indeed matter to me. I told her that I would continue the analysis only on the basis of four weekly sessions and would agree to a reduction of frequency only in preparation for termination of the treatment, as I was not willing to be relegated the menial role of her valet. The patient was visibly taken aback and impressed. We renegotiated the analysis on the basis of four weekly sessions.

Somewhat later, the situation escalated. Ostensibly the discussion centred on the treatment contract. She insisted that I alone was responsible for the many hours that she cancelled on short notice justifiably, she believed, because of her feeling that the situation between us was basically bad. She turned a deaf ear to everything I said to her. Once again, the analysis seemed doomed. For many hours I asked myself what I had failed to understand and why I was unable to contain and detoxify her aggression. It seemed that any longer accepting and enduring this behaviour passively was an admission that I was indeed the bad mother, and that her reproaches were fully justified.

In one tense hour I told her, in a clearly irritated tone of voice, that I was not willing to continue like this; her way of using the hours seemed pointless. I understood that she wanted me to feel what it had been like for her to live with a constantly nagging mother, but this was exactly the situation that she perpetuated. She said she knew that; that was why she was here, and she was simply telling me her associations! I said that I wanted to understand why she continued to repeat this pattern, instead of getting beyond it. After this hour I feared that I had caused irreparable damage. Even though I had made it clear that she had pushed me to the limit, I had also conveyed my confidence in her ability to be more constructive. She was quite affected by this.

Having reflected on how she had managed to poison and destroy relationships in the past through her constant nagging, she arrived at the next session ready to discuss this with me. She stopped projecting so much, and became aware of her contribution to the way her relationships evolved. Over and over, she expressed regret about the way she had treated me. It had been extremely important to her to reach me and to elicit a response in me in which I clearly told her how I felt. I presented myself as an object for her use in this moment of meeting. In so doing, my authentic subjectivity responded effectively to the challenge of her invitation to engage in a depersonalizing, deindividualizing relational experience.

In a later phase, the relationship between us seemed to disintegrate again. She failed to keep several appointments. When she did attend, she appeared remote, and questioned the analysis in general. After a while I told her that she seemed not to be talking to me as a person at all. Clearly affected by this, she spoke about her belief that everyone was interchangeable. She told me that she was convinced that I did not care about her at all.

Months later, she needed me as an ally – a third paternal object – to protect her from a difficult, rather mad, considerably older man who tried to keep her in the position of his baby-woman. She had the choice of defying him and risk being thrown out, or being completely submissive. She said that as I had not been forthcoming with any advice on partnership matters before, she did not expect any useful comments from me now. I said that she saw me as being weak like her father, and that she therefore could not expect anything of value from me. Because of this she was only willing to give me half a chance. She said that she had never actually taken any man seriously! Speaking from the vantage point of the third position, I said that she had not really considered her position as a woman, and that she concentrated solely on her partner. This was an entirely new perspective for her, which provided relief. She realized that by catering to the needs of her boyfriend (representing her bond to the exciting–rejecting maternal object), she prevented herself from taking care of her own needs. Now for the first time she was able to successfully set boundaries between herself and a man.

The feeling of general futility played an enormous role in the existence of this woman. Other than following her scientific interests and attaining success in her career, she refused everything else that she deemed absolutely inessential for survival, such as books, personal grooming, and even basic hygiene. After a year it became possible to mention her unpleasant body odour. I asked if she might feel more comfortable if she bathed, wore shoes that fitted, and if so, her comfort might become something of value for her. She was surprised. At first, she experienced my suggestion that we mutually reflect upon this as extraordinary. She compared me to a computer, which was fed data and spat out results. For a long time she had no ideas of her own, but at the same time did not want to do what everyone else was doing. Only after a long, increasingly vital relationship to me had been established was she able to change her relationship to herself.

Conclusion

I have tried to show how new object experiencing can be important for the course of an analysis. My patient needed me, at certain points, as a personal and distinctly new object, whose subjectivity set limits on her basic, omnipotent attitude. Accepting these limitations, she could also deal with her intruding inner objects more fully in the transference. As her bond with the rejecting inner objects began to loosen, an increasingly libidinal cathexis became possible, first towards the analyst, and then towards herself and the world in general. With this kind of change, a reintegration of split off egos and a resynthesis of the personality became possible.

The therapeutic setting facilitated her reliving the experience of lack of continuity in her life and her attacks on the setting showed clearly the activation of the dominant antilibidinal part object relationship. The libidinal part object experience came into view only in later stages of the analysis when the luring-exciting qualities of her objects came under scrutiny. Active participation in the therapeutic relationship beyond a prescribed kind of abstinence was crucial at certain key moments. I entered into dialogue with her as a separate person with my own subjectivity, explicitly rejecting the designated role of indifferent or intrusive object. My stance must, however, be distinguished from blind acting out in the countertransference. I invited her to reflect with me, which created a search for meaning and purpose, a new beginning.

It is crucial that the focus is simultaneously directed at the transference and the previously non-existent reflective object experience. To a certain extent, this woman fashioned a new father for herself. In the case of patients who are plagued with problems similar to these, it is necessary for the analyst not only to analyse the transference thoroughly but also to present himself as a new object. With a disturbed patient like this woman, the analyst must actively grasp and support the patient's budding attempts to develop a new object relationship.

References

Alexander, F. (1950). Analysis of the therapeutic factors in psychoanalytic treatment. *Psychoanalytic Quarterly* 19: 482.

Alexander, F., French, T. *et al.* (1946). The principle of flexibility. Interruptions and termination of treatment. In *Psychoanalytic Therapy, Principles and Application*, pp. 35–49. New York: Ronald Press.

Balint, M. (1932). Character analysis and new beginning. In *Primary Love and Psychoanalytic Technique*, pp. 151–164. London: Hogarth.

Bion, W. R. (1970). *Attention and Interpretation*. London: Karnac.

Bollas, C. H. (1986). *The Shadow of the Object – Psychoanalysis of the Unthought Known*. London: Free Associations.

Fairbairn, W. R. D. (1944). Endopsychic structure considered in terms of object relationship. In *Psychoanalytic Studies of the Personality*, pp. 82–135. London: Routledge and Kegan Paul, 1952.

—— (1958). The nature and aims of psycho-analytical treatment. *International Journal of Psycho-Analysis* 39: 374–385.

Ferenczi, S. (1933). Confusion of tongues between adults and the child. In *Final Contributions to the Problems and Methods of Psychoanalysis*, pp. 156–167. London: Hogarth, 1955.

Freud, S. (1912a). The dynamics of transference. *Standard Edition* 12: 97–108.

—— (1912b). Recommendations to physicians practicing psychoanalysis. *Standard Edition* 12: 111–120.

—— (1914). Remembering, repeating, and working through. *Standard Edition* 12: 147–156.

Greenson, R. R. (1965). The working alliance and the transference neurosis. *Psycho-analytic Quarterly* 34: 155–181.

—— (1972). Beyond transference and interpretation. *International Journal of Psycho-Analysis* 53: 213–217.

Greenson, R. R. and Wexler, M. (1969). The non-transference relationship in the psychoanalytic situation. *International Journal of Psycho-Analysis* 50: 27–39.

Heimann, P. (1950). On countertransference. *International Journal of Psycho-Analysis* 31: 81–84.

Loewald, H. W. (1960). On the therapeutic action of psychoanalysis. *International Journal of Psycho-Analysis* 41: 16–33.

Racker, H. (1957). The meanings and uses of countertransference. *Psychoanalytic Quarterly* 26: 303–357.

Stern, D., Sander L. W., Nahum, J. P., Harrison, A. M., Lyons-Ruth, K., Morgan, A. C., Bruschweiler-Stern, N. and Tronick, E. Z. (1998). Non-interpretative mechanisms in psychoanalytic therapy. The 'something more' than interpretation. *International Journal of Psycho-Analysis* 79: 903–921.

Winnicott, D. W. (1965). *The Maturational Process and the Facilitating Environment*. London: Hogarth.

—— (1971). *Playing and Reality*. London: Penguin.

Chapter 11

Fairbairn's object relations theory

Explaining the refusal to cathect the analyst

Sabine Vuaillat

Fairbairn's work was unknown in France until recently. In Chapter 4, however, Vermorel shows that French analysts have now been taking interest in it. The eminent French analyst Widlöcher quoted Fairbairn in his paper on the links between the child's love directed to real persons and sexual fantasies linked to the child's autoerotic activities, in which he proposed that the child reviving the sucking experience by hallucination begins to construct for himself a fantasy that he will be able to recreate and transform at will. He wrote: "that which we call object relationship describes the structure of this phantasm" (Widlöcher 2000: 32). Like the child who revives the sucking experience and creates an object relationship, Fairbairn relived the technical difficulties that had confronted him in many analyses, slowly elaborated the features of resistance in these analyses, and came up with object relations theory. In this chapter I will present some observations on the genesis of Fairbairn's ideas and his raison d'être.

Linear development of Fairbairn's work

I distinguish three main periods in Fairbairn's work: the first period beginning in 1927 and ending in 1939; the second from 1939 to 1944; and the third from 1944 to 1952. In his 1927 paper, Fairbairn interpreted the patient's fantasies totally at the Oedipal level. Reading it now, we can detect another deeper level, which Fairbairn was to examine more deeply in the 1940s. His final work articulated both levels.

Fairbairn's early period: Clinical papers and appearance of destructiveness 1927–1938

Many of the early papers described clinical situations: the religious fantasy of a patient (1927), a patient with a genital abnormality (1931), the nervous child (1932), the child's imagination (1934), and the effect of a king's death upon patients undergoing analysis (1936). Other papers questioned Freudian metapsychology – the ego and the id (1929a), libido theory (1930), dissociation

and repression (1929b) – and psychoanalysis applied to the study of communism (1935 and 1937), and art (1938a).

I will focus on Fairbairn's early period with references to his papers on
communism (1935 and 1937), and art (1938a). Fairbairn regarded communist
ideology and its legislative applications in the USSR as an attempt to deal
with the Oedipus complex by abolishing the Oedipus situation. Later, he
reflected on the infantile roots of dependence on dictators. He thought that
dictators take advantage of dependent individuals, who are not able to overcome infantile frustrations, by manipulating their love and hate. I would add
that totalitarian states are in control through direct contact with the individual's emotions without making room for a "third person" who can keep a
distance from emotions. This strikes me, because what Fairbairn pointed out
subtly about this social process in the 1930s seemed to be forgotten by him in
the 1940s. For instance, in 1944 he wrote about how endopsychic structure
channels aggression and libido, without recognizing the importance of the
Oedipus complex.

Fairbairn often quoted Melanie Klein's 1935 paper "A Contribution to the
Psychogenesis of Manic-Depressive States", which had a big impact on him.
In that paper, Klein deals extensively with destructive phantasies. This notion
had a great impact on Fairbairn. In his 1938 papers he underlined the influence of destructive phantasies and phantasies of restitution in works of art,
which are external to the artist or to the perceiver, but nevertheless speak of
intimacy. Fairbairn was suggesting that the internal object which is destroyed
on a fantasy level may be repaired in a work of art. The appearance of these
themes on destructiveness and the abolition of the Oedipus complex in the
papers on art and communism show that Fairbairn's thinking about object
relations was in process a few years before he gave birth to a fully developed
theory, the beginnings of which were evident from 1940.

Fairbairn's second period: The beginning of the original theory 1938–1944

In 1938 the second period of Fairbairn's work began, a period called "the
creative step" by Sutherland. In this second period, Fairbairn reacted to the
notion of destructiveness in a different way from Klein. He wrote a paper on
schizoid personalities (1940) characterized by attitudes of omnipotence, isolation and detachment, and a preoccupation with inner reality. He concluded
that schizoid personalities cannot give love because of never having felt loved
as real, unique individuals. They take more than they give. At the oral level
sucking the breast signifies emptying it, but at the relational level, loving the
mother signifies destroying her.

In 1941 Fairbairn described obsessional, phobic, hysterical, and paranoid
techniques for differentiating the self from the object during the long transition
from infantile dependency to mature dependency, specifically by accepting or

rejecting the object and locating it inside or outside the self. Schizoid person-alities are in conflict over whether to take in or destroy the breast, to let the object exist or not inside the psyche. With this, Fairbairn began to create a new metapsychology that totally revised Freud's libido theory. Gradually the object relationship became central in Fairbairn's thinking. He called his the-ory object relations theory because it is organized by the central idea that libido is primarily object seeking, not pleasure seeking.

In 1943, in both papers on the war neuroses he described libido seeking a repressed bad object, a dynamic that operates as a resistance in analysis (1943a, 1943b). After seeking and internalizing bad objects, the child internalizes good ones and no longer feels that the world is full of destruc-tion. The good objects fill the role of the benign superego. The patient often utilizes the superego, through a sense of guilt, in order to keep the bad object repressed. Fairbairn named that the moral defence. Libido is the primary dynamic aspect of the psychic structures, and aggression is secondary to inevitable frustration experienced at the hands of the mother.

In 1944, Fairbairn proposed the concept of *endopsychic structure*, consist-ing of a complex world of parts of the ego related to internal objects that are formed from elements of the mother that are overly frustrating and overly exiting of need. These elements become split off from the whole experience of the object and repressed along with corresponding split off parts of the ego. I want to emphasize the importance of the ego from which everything derives: the original ego splits off and represses the antilibidinal ego, also called the internal saboteur, and the libidinal ego, which, according to Fairbairn corres-ponds to the Freudian id. In Fairbairn's theory there is no id, and the role of the Oedipus complex becomes secondary to the pre-Oedipal arrangement of the internal objects. He wrote: "A sufficient deep analysis of the Oedipus situation invariably reveals that this situation is built up around the figures of an internal exciting mother and an internal rejecting mother" (1944: 124). A "poor second" (1941: 40), the father is only later acknowledged by the child, and experience with him is subjected to the same process of internalization and splitting off into exciting and rejecting objects (1944). The child seeks to convert this complex situation of being confronted with two exciting and two rejecting objects by equating one parental object with the exciting objects and the other with the rejecting objects, thus avoiding recognition of the parents as an exciting couple and minimizing the impact of the primal scene. The primal scene was only alluded to in his 1944 paper. When he mentioned the effect of the biological sex of the child, Fairbairn emphasized the jealousy between the child and one of the parents, and did not go further to describe the child's experience of the primal scene.

The third phase: Consolidation and new issues

Between 1944 and 1952, many texts again took up object relations theory without significant changes. In other words Fairbairn's theory appeared to come to a standstill. Sutherland (1989) puts together all the texts between 1944 and 1963 as a group concerned with consolidation and recognition. This grouping obscures the difference in Fairbairn's writing of 1944 to 1952, and 1952 to 1963. It is often forgotten that Fairbairn's later papers actually reshape his theory. 1952 to 1963 should be considered as a third period in Fairbairn's work when his theoretical stance softens and new issues reappear, including a consideration of the technical consequences of his theory, an application that he pursues only from the middle of the 1950s.

In his 1954 paper "Observation on the Nature of Hysterical States" Fairbairn began by summarizing his conception of the endopsychic structure, but in the rest of the paper he took up new issues: how the hysterical states are linked to the failures of object relationships, so that libido is diverted into bodily systems, and parts of the body become the repository of traumatic experience when the personal relationships are disturbed. I notice that in this text greater attention to the father and sexuality appears, if not explicitly at least implicitly. In his paper on the Schreber case, Fairbairn (1958a) focused his attention on object relations theory, but introduced the question of the primal scene and his patients' resistance to it. He noted that President Schreber imagined, in the fantasies underlying his illness, all forms of procreation excepting the genital one.

In the paper "On the Nature and Aims of Psychoanalytical Treatment", Fairbairn (1958b) developed the idea of the "closed system" that patients set up during analysis. This closed system consists of a specific object relationship that is constantly repeated in the internal world: for example, Fairbairn's patient, Ivy, tries to maintain her internal world as a closed system characterized by her wish to destroy herself, and so she can only hate him for interfering with her death circuit. From these three periods we have distinguished, an internal process in Fairbairn's theory can now be specified.

The internal process of Fairbairn's theory and his main themes

The early texts foreshadow the later theory. Fairbairn's thesis submitted in 1929, in which he studied dissociation (especially as Janet had conceived of it), announces his interest in the mental mechanism he would later call "splitting". In the early papers, he referred frequently to persecutors, but mentioned them only as external persecutors such as dictators and sexual offenders. He presented the child as an innocent, infected by the adults' badness so that the external persecutors become internal ones. Fairbairn became preoccupied with the idea of the internal persecutor, and I link this with the "internal saboteur" he would go on to propose in 1944. By 1954 he would write that, instead of the superego as a single entity proposed by Freud, three components of the ego function together: the ego ideal, the antilibidinal ego, and the rejecting object.

A final important theme concerns libido, discussed in the paper written in 1930, but not published until 1994. Fairbairn used Drever's theory to address an issue which he could not express in analytic terms as yet. He found it difficult to articulate the difference between appetitive tendencies (pleasure seeking) and reactive tendencies (responding to the external environment) as if he did not yet appreciate the psychical apparatus as capable of fantasy. Fairbairn's object relations theory would have to link the impulse's source to the object so as to admit fantasies of an object relationship. When such fantasies are felt to be persecutory, they give rise to a persecuting internal object relationship that is acted out in the transference. I will come back to this in a moment.

From the end of the 1930s, undoubtedly influenced by Klein, Fairbairn was exploring the issue of destructiveness. In his texts on art, he wondered about the internal or external object being destroyed in fantasy and repaired in works of art, and in the text about the effect of the king's death upon patients, he asked to what extent the death of an external object influences the internal world of a patient.

In 1940 Fairbairn's attention was caught by the difficulty shown by schizoid patients who cannot accept the link to the other and cannot easily express emotion, because they feel that their love can be immensely destructive. Similarly the schizoid patients' links to the analyst are vulnerable because they are afraid that their transference love will be destructive. Fairbairn, however, did not formulate clearly the question, "Can the object threatened by destruction become the analyst in the transference?" This 1940 paper focused on early relationships between mother and child. In my view, the mental mechanisms of the psyche, at this archaic level, are modelled on bodily functions – taking in, spitting out, and so on. In the 1941 paper, Fairbairn put forward a model of a psyche which indeed functions as a body, taking in, expelling, and so surviving the destructive effect of the object, but remaining unable to elaborate on the experience. The dynamic of the psyche functioning like the body opens the way to the patient's acquisition of interiority. In relation to an analyst, Fairbairn (for the moment) thought that the psyche becomes animated and so can grow, without being able to change the structure of what appears.

The object may be destroyed by love (1940), internalized or externalized (1941), repressed but released by the impact of war (1943), rejecting or frustrating (1944) and transformed in analysis. The object comes alive, structured by fantasy, denying the still intolerable elements. He said that libido and object cannot be separated. Immersed in his concept of internal object relationships formed during infantile dependency, Fairbairn (1944) denied that the Oedipus complex is an explanatory concept, and he subordinated the pleasure principle to the object's existence. He maintained that the ego is the initial structure out of which all else ensues, and that there is no id. Granted the risk of disintegration may emerge, but one function of the endopsychic structure proposed by Fairbairn is to channel this dangerous energy within object relationships.

Fairbairn displayed an internal moving world before our very eyes, created in his imagination of the patient's experience from the patient's apparent refusal of relationship to him in analysis. It is only later, with a second thrust, that his theory presents the analyst less as an observer and more as an actor. It is as if he tried to get out of the patient's fantasy of a therapeutic relationship in which the analyst-spectator and the patient-ego are the same reflection in the mirror of an observer banishing emotion and commitment to the analytic relationship.

Beginning in 1954, Fairbairn questioned the scientific validity of psychoanalysis, as if that might be the tool to get him out from under the patient's fantasy. The analyst-observer came alive, and the importance of the relationship between patient and analyst increased. Fairbairn pondered the need for breaching the patient's closed system when the patient has steadfastly refused the analyst's interpretations. Some more Oedipal themes appear, concerning the primal scene and clinical examples in which the father is more present. The relationship between analyst and patient became the main theme of his last significant paper (1958b).

The analyst's stance

In the first period Fairbairn had set up some themes regarding, for instance, internal destructiveness and the internal persecutor, before being caught by the technical difficulty set by the patient who takes a stand against the analyst. What can we do when the destruction reaches the transference link itself?

My hypothesis is that Fairbairn's work is an attempt to revive these patients who suffer from a "de-emotionalization of the object-relationship" (1940: 14). He aims at recreating an interiority, a fantasy world which seems absent or, at the very least, hidden from the analyst. Fairbairn's work attempts to deconstruct the patient's resistance. That could disintegrate the whole psyche, but Fairbairn does not allow for the occurrence of a breakdown.

Fairbairn's theory invites thinking about the object relationship particularly when it tends towards an exclusive internal dyadic relation, confounded by a relationship to the mother that does not allow room for a third person, namely the father – or even a space between the two, or the possibility of an absence – as seen in those patients whose fantasy is that the analyst is with them between sessions. Then the internal situation becomes stifling and totalitarian. Accepting this exclusive, dyadic object relationship, and then analysing it so as not to get stuck in it may open the path to better understanding of this fantasy and the closed system of the internal object relationship, and to revival of the deadened psyche. Fairbairn's theory allows us to continue to think and analyse in spite of patients' destructiveness.

Conclusion

Fairbairn's theory considers the conditions in which analysis is possible, particularly when the connection between analyst and patient is lacking, because the patient feels that the analyst is imminently dangerous. It is not easy to accept being viewed as a prison guard, Nazi, or torturer. At these times, interpretation of the threat that the analyst poses seems ineffective, or interpretation may intensify the patient's feeling of being persecuted, in which case the analyst becomes the persecutor without realizing it. With Fairbairn's theory as a support, the analyst can accept such a relationship in which analyst and patient observe each other, with the analyst avoiding too much interpretation of persecutory fantasy so as not to become too much of a persecutor. What is needed is an interpretation of the dyadic nature of the relationship with no space for creative thinking to develop. Becoming conscious of this transference relationship permits us to better understand the patient's feeling, tolerate deadness and projective identifications, and eventually interpret the claustrophobic, dyadic relationship in which there is hardly enough space for thinking creatively. Slowly the space will open and then interpretations about persecutory feelings become possible, and the patient's interior life revives and moves forward.

References

Fairbairn, W. R. D. (1927). Notes on the religious fantasy of a female patient. *Psychoanalytic Studies of the Personality*, pp. 183–196. London: Routledge, 1952.

—— (1929a). Is the superego repressed? In *From Instinct to Self: Vol. 2*, eds E. F. Birtles and D. E. Scharff, pp. 101–114. Northvale, NJ: Jason Aronson, 1994.

—— (1929b). The relationship of dissociation and repression considered from the point of view of medical psychology. In *From Instinct to Self: Vol. 2*, eds E. F. Birtles and D. E. Scharff, pp. 13–79. Northvale, NJ: Jason Aronson, 1994.

—— (1930). The libido theory and the theory of the pleasure principle interpreted in terms of appetite. In *From Instinct to Self: Vol. 2*, eds E. F. Birtles and D. E. Scharff, pp.115–156. Northvale, NJ: Jason Aronson, 1994.

—— (1931). Features in the analysis of a patient with a physical genital abnormality. *Psychoanalytic Studies of the Personality*, pp. 197–222. London: Routledge, 1952.

—— (1932). The nervous child. In *From Instinct to Self: Vol. 2*, eds E. F. Birtles and D. E. Scharff, pp. 183–194. Northvale, NJ: Jason Aronson, 1994.

—— (1934). The place of imagination in the psychology of the child. In *From Instinct to Self: Vol. 2*, eds E. F. Birtles and D. E. Scharff, pp. 195–209. Northvale, NJ: Jason Aronson, 1994.

—— (1935). The sociological significance of communism considered in the light of psycho-analysis. *Psychoanalytic Studies of the Personality*, pp. 233–246. London: Routledge & Kegan Paul, 1952.

—— (1936). The effect of a king's death upon patients under analysis. *Psychoanalytic Studies of the Personality*, pp. 223–229. London: Routledge & Kegan Paul, 1952.

—— (1937). Communism as an anthropological phenomenon, *Edinburgh Medical Journal* 44, 7: 433–447.

—— (1938a). Prolegomena to a psychology of art. In *From Instinct to Self: Vol. 2*, eds E. F. Birtles and D. E. Scharff, pp. 381–396. Northvale, NJ: Jason Aronson, 1994.

—— (1938b). The ultimate basis of aesthetic experience. In *From Instinct to Self: Vol. 2*, eds E. F. Birtles and D. E. Scharff, pp. 397–409. Northvale, NJ: Jason Aronson, 1994.

—— (1940) Schizoid factors in the personality. *Psychoanalytic Studies of the Personality*, pp. 3–27. London: Routledge & Kegan Paul, 1952.

—— (1941) A revised psychopathology of the psychoses and psychoneuroses. *Psychoanalytic Studies of the Personality*, pp. 28–58. London: Routledge & Kegan Paul, 1952.

—— (1943a). The war neuroses: their nature and significance. *Psychoanalytic Studies of the Personality*, pp. 256–288. London: Routledge & Kegan Paul, 1952.

—— (1943b). The repression and return of bad objects (with special reference to the war neuroses). *Psychoanalytic Studies of the Personality*, pp. 59–81. London: Routledge & Kegan Paul, 1952.

—— (1944). Endopsychic structure considered in terms of object-relationships. *Psychoanalytic Studies of the Personality*, pp. 82–136. London: Routledge & Kegan Paul, 1952.

—— (1952). *Psychoanalytic Studies of the Personality*. London: Routledge, 1996.

—— (1954). Observations on the nature of hysterical states. In *From Instinct to Self: Vol. 1*, eds D. E. Scharff and E. F. Birtles, pp. 13–40. Northvale, NJ: Jason Aronson, 1994.

—— (1958a) Considerations arising out of the Schreber case. *British Journal of Medical Psychology* 29, 2: 113–127. Reprinted in *From Instinct to Self: Vol. 1*, eds D. E. Scharff and E. F. Birtles, pp. 41–60. Northvale, NJ: Jason Aronson.

—— (1958b) On the nature and aims of psychoanalytical treatment. In *From Instinct to Self: Vol. 1*, eds D. E. Scharff and E. F. Birtles, pp. 155–156. Northvale, NJ: Jason Aronson, 1994.

Klein, M. (1935). A contribution to the psychogenesis of manic-depressive states. *International Journal of Psycho-Analysis* 16: 145–174 and in *Love, Guilt and Reparation and Other Works 1921–1945*, pp. 262–289. London: Hogarth, 1975.

Sutherland, J. D. (1989). *Fairbairn's Journey to the Interior*. London: Free Association.

Widlöcher, D. (2000). Amour primaire et sexualité infantile: un débat de toujours. In *Sexualité Infantile et Attachement*, pp. 1–55. Paris: PUF.

Chapter 12

Dissociation and repression in trauma

Sabine Wollnik

The topics of dissociation and trauma fascinated Fairbairn. Using the psycho-economic and object-theoretical models recommended by Bohleber (2000), I will show how Fairbairn connects the clinical phenomena of dissociation to the effects of trauma on the self-and-object structures. I shall describe the extent to which the clinical phenomenon of dissociation finds its place in Fairbairn's theory of the endopsychic situation.

Definitions of trauma and dissociation

Trauma means overwhelming, fragmenting stress. Fischer and Riedesser (1998: 79) defined traumatic experience as "a vital discrepancy between the experience of threatening factors and the individual's coping abilities, which involve feelings of helplessness and vulnerability, resulting in a permanent destabilization of the understanding of the self and of the world".

Dissociation literally means splitting. Scheidt (2000: 146) wrote that in dissociation "different mental processes, such as thinking, feeling, identity, and memory, which are normally connected, are separated from each other". This results in a splitting of consciousness, and the integrative function of the self gets lost – permanently in pathology, temporarily in hypnotic inductions, trances, and the creative processes of artists. There seems to be a wide spectrum of dissociation from normal to pathological states. The concept of dissociation has not yet been clearly defined and remains controversial among analysts (Krause 1999).

In the nineteenth century, there was great interest in dissociative phenomena. More than a century ago, Janet (1904) developed the classic concepts of dissociation to describe the mental mechanisms of the hysterical state. Fischer and Riedesser (1998) summarized Janet's explanation that dissociation is the result of an excessive demand made upon consciousness to cope with traumatic, overwhelming experiences. When memories of the traumatic experience cannot be adequately dealt with, they are split off from consciousness, dissociated, only to surface later on in life as emotionally experienced states, physical states, ideas, flashbacks, or the compulsion to repeat.

Dissociation and repression: Freud

Freud distanced himself from Janet's concept, replacing the passive concept of dissociation with an active concept of repression of the conflicting drives by the ego: "Psychoanalysis also assumes the existence of dissociation and the unconscious, but places them in a different relationship to one another" (Freud 1909: 96). Freud abandoned the concept of dissociation to a great extent and replaced it with the concept of repression in order to protect his newly developed drive theory and its emphasis on the unconscious. Nevertheless, he continued to describe traumatic phenomena in his works. Toward the end of his life, in his last great work "Moses and Monotheism" (1938), Freud wrote about the trauma of early childhood. He mentioned two results of these early traumatic experiences: the fixation on the trauma, and the compulsion to repeat. He wrote:

> All of these phenomena . . . indicate . . . an existence independent of the organization of the other psychic processes that are adapted to the real outside world . . . they are not at all or not sufficiently influenced by the outside world . . . They exist as a state within a state and at the same time remain an inaccessible, uncooperative party, which is capable of over-whelming the so-called normal and forcing it into serving its own aims. When this happens, a peculiar psychic inner reality dominates over the reality of the outside world, thus opening the way for psychosis.
>
> (Freud 1938: 181)

The "memory traces of the early experiences" remain intact within the individual, but "only in a peculiar psychological state" (p. 201). From time to time, parts surface in conscious thought, "but they still remain isolated, like foreign bodies disconnected to the rest" (p. 201). For Freud, the phenomenon of dissociation creates "a state within a state" (p. 181). Freud's descriptions are quite compatible with contemporary ideas on traumatization and its effects.

Dissociation and repression: Fairbairn

In 1929 in his doctoral thesis, Fairbairn examined the relationship between dissociation and repression. He reviewed the ideas of Freud and Janet. He was particularly intrigued by Janet's concept of disintegration of the ego, but he disputed the assertion that dissociation was a passive process: "Janet's explanation of dissociation as the result of a failure of mental synthesis shows that he conceived it as a passive process" (Fairbairn 1929: 52). Fairbairn defined dissociation as an active psychic process. Within this context, he understood repression to be a special form of dissociation. In dissociation, mental *contents* are kept unconscious, whereas repression keeps the mental *structures* unconscious in order to avoid a conflict with the "organised self". By this argument, he attempted to distinguish between the phenomena of repression and dissociation without discarding dissociation, as Freud had done after establishing drive theory.

In the 1940s, Fairbairn developed his theory of dynamic self-and-object structures and invoked the concepts of dissociation and splitting. In 1954 he wrote:

> Further consideration reveals that the process of dissociation, as conceived by Janet, carries with it the implication of a split in the personality, variable in its extent and often multiple . . . in my opinion, there is no fundamental distinction between the process of hysterical dissociation, to which Janet drew attention, and that splitting of the ego, which is now recognized as a characteristic feature of schizoid states . . . repressing and splitting of the ego represent simply two aspects of the same fundamental process.
>
> (Fairbairn 1954: 14–15)

According to Fairbairn, the structures which are created by splitting and repression incorporate the dissociated contents.

In his book *Unformulated Experience: From Dissociation to Imagination in Psychoanalysis*, Stern (1997) offered a broad definition of dissociation, regarding dissociative phenomena not exclusively as the result of trauma but as ubiquitous phenomena. Whereas repression excludes already processed psychic experiences from consciousness, dissociation prevents unprocessed experiences from entering consciousness. Dissociation hinders both interpretations and verbalizations of these experiences. The well-known defence mechanisms are inadequate for this lack of structure, which can then neither be forgotten nor changed, because symbolic development and language conceptualization have not taken place, and so they are not properly embedded within a narrative structure. The patient remains unaware of the experience and the experience remains unarticulated.

Further developments

In the nineteenth century, dissociation was viewed primarily as a result of traumatization. Contemporary opinion increasingly considers dissociation to be an ubiquitous phenomenon.

Neurobiological advances: Memory research

In his paper "Trauma and Memory", Krause (1999) proposed that different perceptions are differently stored in separate memory areas. Little children reacting to trauma are usually too shocked to choose between running away or attacking the perceived source of danger, and so they dissociate in order to avoid being overwhelmed. Verbal semantic processing has been interrupted and therefore normal memory processing is prevented. Those events which cannot be voluntarily recalled can become accessible in situations that call forth similar affects, states of excitement, or physical sensations, and so trigger memory.

Information processing takes place in various areas corresponding to the specific modalities in which the perceptions have occurred. Perceptions that occur within the context of actions are organized motorically as action components, and are usually not semantically registered (Krause 1999). These singular partial-memory systems have little access to one another, which means that a certain amount of dissociation exists already at the level of perception and at the level of processing. According to Krause, in addition to these partial systems, there are two overarching memory systems: a language system and an episodic memory system. The episodic memory system "coordinates the actor's intention with the object's reactions perceived within a scene" (p. 42). It is both idiosyncratic and autobiographic. The single episodes which are stored there organize our expectations.

Flashbacks

Huber (2001) investigated a dissociative phenomenon in a neurobiological experiment, and tracked the activity of different brain areas during flashbacks. He discovered that the hyperactivity of the closed circuits induces a bonding of attention to the intrinsic event and prevents attention from being focused on the outside world. This leads to disturbances in memory and difficulties in coherent recall for traumatic content in verbal memory.

The emotional unconscious: De Masi

De Masi (2000) developed the concept of the *emotional unconscious* derived from his assimilation of recent neuro-scientific knowledge:

> According to the neurobiologists . . . an unconscious or implicit memory definitely does exist, or rather a number of memories of unconsciously stored experiences, each operating within different subsystems. However, neurobiological research bears out some of the data of psychoanalysis, confirming as it does that the emotions have an unconscious life, separate from the higher processing systems . . . The unconscious of the neurosciences coincides with *that of which the subject is unaware* and not with the repressed.
>
> (De Masi 2000: 7)

De Masi suspects that the emotional unconscious is disturbed as a result of traumatization and psychosis. His idea of an emotional unconscious is complementary to the structural unconscious as described, for example, by Freud or Melanie Klein.

Grotstein (2002) differentiated between Freud's concepts, which describe the neurotic area, and those that describe, as he puts it, a third area of the psyche: Fairbairn's endopsychic structures, Rosenfeld's pathological organizations and internal gang or Mafia, Steiner's psychic retreats, and Winnicott's areas of pathological fantasizing. In short, dissociation means a split in consciousness and cannot be grasped within the usual theoretical concepts of the unconscious.

Clinical example

Mr P left his wife and 2-year-old son and entered a sexually exciting relationship. By the time he had turned to me for analysis (which proceeded four times a week), this relationship had already proven itself hollow and flat. Mr P was desperate and suicidal. Although he had left the marriage of his own accord, he acted as if he had been deserted. He lived in a state of almost unbearable misery, which he did not understand. He was driven, and yet hardly able to get his work done. He felt as if there were no escape from the terrible affect; death alone seemed to offer him relief from his misery. He was completely overwhelmed in both his mental state and his family situation. However, at the same time he was able to meet the demands of everyday life and work, although sometimes with difficulty. His affect felt overwhelming, yet some ego structures functioned autonomously. I thought that the affect states that brought Mr P to analysis might correspond to flashback phenomena. Mr P was focused on the inner goings on and could not connect them with what was happening in the outer world. All we knew was that when his son became 2 years old, this had evoked a scene of being abandoned. Those involved did not understand this as the triggering of an enactment, nor did I at the beginning.

Haunted by a trauma in his past, Mr P was in despair without recognizing its source. He conveyed his profound despair to me non-verbally via projective identification. We named and worked through the almost unbearable conditions of nameless dread and despair. We talked about his very irritating body sensations, such as an unbearably sore throat, and tight feelings in his legs and arms. He felt as if his throat were wrapped in cotton gauze, as if his skin were peeling off in strips, and as if his legs and arms were tightly bound. I said that I thought that this was a somatic memory of traumatic early experience.

During a visit to his mother's home, he asked his mother for help to understand his distress. She told him of an early trauma of abandonment. I learned that at 2 years of age Mr P had been hospitalized because of diphtheria and was kept there by himself for four weeks, during which time he had no visitors, which was common practice then. When he returned home, his younger sister, who had been born during his absence, was lying on his mother's lap. Mr P then contracted scarlet fever and was again isolated for weeks, this time at home. His relationship to his mother seems to have been irreparable from that time on. Adding to his trauma, when he was 11 years old his father died after exactly two years of illness. The working through of this in the analysis effected a significant relief, and he was able to return to his wife and child.

Discussion

Dissociated affective content, as described by Freud, dominated the beginning of Mr P's analysis but this was not the sole expression of his problem. It was apparent from the beginning that the dissociated material was embedded in specific enactments of self-and-object relational structure: the rejecting object, in that he had rejected his wife and child, and the exciting object, in that he had entered a sexually exciting relationship. Scenes oscillating between rejection and excitement were delivered into the analytic situation, in which the trigger and the content both represented abandonment, for instance, in the transference symptom of lateness.

Mr P always arrived somewhat late. Waiting for the hour induced in him the complex of feelings associated with the early trauma of abandonment and revealed the self-and-object relationship pattern. He rejected me by coming late to the hour, and spent the time driving fast to his session fantasizing an exciting encounter in the transference with me.

Dissociation means that there is a split in consciousness, and this cannot be grasped within the concept of the unconscious. Phenomena appear in consciousness which do not correspond with the structural unconscious according to Freud or Melanie Klein. These are unfinished processes from different psychic regions. Other laws apply here and other theoretical concepts are necessary. Freud recognized this, and spoke of a "state within a state". De Masi described the emotional unconscious as an area of activity of implicit memory systems laid down in response to trauma. The material which has been stored in a dissociated condition finds access to the conscious in varying degrees and can then cause structure to develop. The impact of trauma can, under certain circumstances, leave traces in a dissociative area (which corresponds to De Masi's disturbed emotional unconscious) and vertical splitting of the ego creates the typical post-traumatic ego structure.

Dissociation probably occurs at the moment of perception *before* psychic processing occurs, in contrast to repression, in which the ego wards off conflict-related material *after* it has already been dealt with psychically and translated into a narrative. Repression is a horizontal defence mechanism, pertaining to the hierarchical organization of psychic structure in contrast to splitting, which is a vertical defence mechanism within the ego.

Dissociation, fantasy development and real relationships lead via mutual influence to an internalized self-and-object world. In the case of a traumatization having to do with rejection by a frustrating object, self-and-object relationships organize themselves around rejection-sensitive, somato-sensory complexes in the emotional unconscious. Typical of traumatic situations, as the primary object fails to intervene in a helpful manner, the rejecting object appears to play a key role. Dissociated material is not easily made conscious but is expressed in imagery, body sensations, and dreams. In relation to new experiences and fantasies, dissociated material reappears and influences self-and-object relationships in an essential way. Fairbairn's theory succeeds in grasping the long-term effects of trauma, its reflection in the emotional unconscious, and its embodiment in the internalized self-and-object structures.

References

Birtles, E. F. and Scharff, D. E. (eds) (1994). *From Instinct to Self: Vol 2*, Northvale, NJ: Jason Aronson.

Bohleber, W. (2000). Die Entwicklung der Traumatheorie in der Psychoanalyse. *Psyche* 54: 797–839.

De Masi, F. (2000). The unconscious and psychosis: some considerations on the psychoanalytic theory of psychosis. *International Journal of Psycho-Analysis* 81: 1–20.

Fairbairn, W. R. D. (1929). Dissociation and repression. Doctoral Thesis. In *From Instinct to Self: Vol 2*, eds E. F. Birtles and D. E. Scharff, pp. 13–79. Northvale, NJ: Jason Aronson.

—— (1952). *Psychoanalytic Studies of the Personality*. London: Tavistock.

—— (1954). Observations on the nature of hysterical states. In *From Instinct to Self: Vol. 1*, eds D. E. Scharff and E. F. Birtles, pp. 13–40. Northvale, NJ: Jason Aronson, 1994.

—— (2000). *Das Selbst und die inneren Objektbeziehungen*, eds B. Hensel and R. Rehberger, trans. E. Vorspohl. Gießen: Psychosozial-Verlag.

Fischer, G. and Riedesser, P. (1998). *Lehrbuch der Psychotraumatologie*. München, Basel: Reinhardt.

Freud, S. (1909). Die psychogene Sehstörung in psychoanalytischer Auffassung. *GW* VIII: 93–102.

—— (1938). Der Mann Moses und die monotheistische Religion. *GW* XVI: 101–246.

Grotstein, J. S. (2002). Endopsychic structures, psychic retreats, and 'fantasying': the pathological 'third area' of the psyche. In F. Pereira and D. E. Scharff (eds) *Fairbairn and Relational Theory*, pp. 145–182. London: Karnac.

Huber, M. (2001). Aktivierung thalamocorticaler Funktionsschleifen während posttraumatischer Flashbacks. In W. Bohleber and S. Drews (eds) *Die Gegenwart der Psychoanalyse – die Psychoanalyse der Gegenwart*, pp. 190–196. Stuttgart: Klett-Cotta.

Krause, R. (1999). Trauma und Erinnerung. *Persönlichkeitsstörungen* 3: 36–44.

Scharff, D. E. and Fairbairn Birtles, E. F. (eds) (1998). *From Instinct to Self: Vol. 1*. Northvale, NJ: Jason Aronson.

Scheidt, C. E. (2000). Konversion und Dissoziation – alternative oder komplementäre Konzepte der Hysterie? *Persönlichkeitsstörungen* 4: 146–153.

Stern, D. B. (1997). *Unformulated Experience: From Dissociation to Imagination in Psychoanalysis*. Hillsdale, NJ: Analytic Press.

Chapter 13

Fairbairn's theory, borderline pathology, and schizoid conflict

Rubén Mario Basili and Isabel Sharpin de Basili

> The devil you know is better than the devil you don't know, and better than no devil at all.
>
> (Scottish proverb)

Introduction

We will focus on a universal conflict that we call *engulfment–abandonment*. Founded on Fairbairn's object relations model of endopsychic structure, the concept of engulfment–abandonment is useful to address clinical, theoretical and technical issues, metapsychological aspects, and psychosexual development (Basili 1988, 1990a, 1990b, 1992, 1993, 1994, 1995, 1996; Basili and Etchegaray 1995; Basili and Montero 1999; Basili *et al.* 2001, 2002a, 2002b; Basili and Sharpin de Basili 2002a, 2002b; Basili and Donnoli 2003). We hold that dissociation activates splitting in separation anxiety, defensive functioning, schizoid phenomenon, abandonment conflicts, paranoia, and hypochondriac personality traits. We think of the ego as an endopsychic structure with a self capable of dissociating, self-repressing, and entering into conflict within itself. We postulate that engulfment–abandonment conflict occurs in precocious oral phases and acts as a common pathway for differentiation–non-differentiation, separation–individuation, and attachment–detachment. We propose Fairbairn's psychoevolutional scheme from infantile dependence, to transitional techniques, and then on to mature dependence as a universal model for psychoanalysis. We propose using *the object situation* (referring to the number and quality of internal object relationships) to explain neurosis, psychosis, and the borderline conditions, and acute schizo-affective psychosis. We propose the use of the term *bivalence–ambivalence* as a marker for structural intrapsychic change. We will give detailed clinical examples of serious pathology to illustrate the importance of interpreting schizoid conflict in terms of Fairbairn's model of object relationship, session after session, for the analysis of dissociation, dependence, separation anxiety, aggression, guilt, ambivalence, transitional phenomena, and outer reality.

Fairbairn (1958) defined schizoid conflict by referring to a number of parameters: anxiety, defense, mental contents, objects, and a characteristic object relationship. Implicit in Fairbairn's view is a fundamental conflict over acceptance and abandonment, particularly evident in the transference in serious pathology. To be loved is to be not abandoned by the accepted object, which in treatment is located in the analyst (Basili 1990a, 1990b). We believe that the unconscious conflict over acceptance versus abandonment is important in normal and pathological development, and we propose an evolutionary psychopathological model based on Fairbairn's ideas. We will use clinical material to illustrate the analysis of dissociation, dependence, separation anxiety and abandonment anxiety, aggression, guilt, ambivalence, transitional phenomena, and issues of identity and external reality (Skolnick and Scharff 1998). Conflict is a go-between that links internal and external objects, and transference and countertransference. The universality of the schizoid conflict is seen in the myth of Medusa and the fable of the porcupine (Basili *et al.* 2002b).

Schizoid conflict

Taking Fairbairn's work as our starting place, we note that Fairbairn (1963) regarded separation anxiety as the earliest and most primary form of anguish. Schizoid conflict is characterized by separation anxiety, abandonment (Gunderson 1996, 2001) and engulfment (Mahler 1972a, 1972b; Masterson 1976, 1981). Others have referred to conflict over approach avoidance (Masterson 1976; Basili 1990a, 1990b; McWilliams 1994; Morgan 1968). Taking our cue from Greenberg and Mitchell (1983) who described "fear of approach because of engulfment, or fear because of abandonment" (1983: 162) we have coined the term *engulfment–abandonment* to refer to this area of self pathology found in serious cases.

According to *Fairbairn* (1970), the endopsychic situation develops when the object and the relationship with the object are internalized and dissociated from the central ego, split from its main core, and repressed as internal object relationships, also called units of object relationship (Hamilton 1989, 1995), and building blocks of mental structure (Kernberg 1979; Blum 1983; Koenigsberg *et al.* 2000). We think of the ego as an endopsychic structure with self energy capable of dissociating and repressing parts of itself, and entering into conflict within itself. This is the underpinning of intrasystemic unconscious conflict, which is always pathological in borderline personality organization. This construct is fundamental to our ideas of borderline personality organization and psychosis. Internal objects and the parts of the ego that are attached to them are projected into the external world, and the conflict is then externalized, and detectable in interaction with the analyst.

Schizoid conflict plays its part in the oral stage, acting normally and pathologically, as a final common pathway in the developmental challenges listed by various authors: undifferentiation–differentiation (Eagle 1988; Celani 1993, 1999); approach–avoidance (Gunderson 2001); engulfment–abandonment (Masterson 2000); separation–individuation (Mahler 1972a, 1972b); and attachment–detachment (Fonagy 2001; Fonagy and Target 2003). We add another challenge that we call identification–disidentification. In the early mother–child relationship when the child is 2 to 3 years of age, the schizoid conflict is integrated through the achievement of object constancy, a critical evolutional period in the development of subsequent borderline pathology (Basili 1990a, 1990b; Basili *et al.* 2001).

Schizoid conflict and transitional phenomena

Borderline patients have difficulty in being close to the analyst because of engulfment–abandonment fear. They have to maintain an ideal pre-Oedipal distance from the object. Here we turn to Fairbairn's ideas on transitional phenomena. "Fairbairn put the term transitional into psychoanalysis and used the term in many places" (Winnicott 1981: 313). To treat the borderline patient we have to provide a transitional space for relating. We may suggest a day hospital as a transitional object for those who are psychotic (Winnicott 1981; Hughes 1990; Grotstein and Rinsley 1994).

For others, the analyst serves as a transitional object, like the mother and also not her, which protects the patient from separation and abandonment anxieties. Extrapolating from Fairbairn (1970), we suggest that a transitional object is normal in development. Without it, the partial object of the schizoid position (good breast–bad breast) can lead to schizophrenia, and the whole object (good mother–bad mother) of the depressive position can lead to manic depressive psychosis, paranoia, and schizo-affective disorder.

Infantile dependence

In borderline pathology, we postulate that the transitional object is a whole accepted–rejected object treated as oral, anal, urethral-phallic mental contents, typical of the way the child handles objects in Fairbairn's transitional stage. In normal development, there is a relationship to a part object at first, and later to a whole object, marked by a movement from the use of splitting mechanisms to the capacity for ambivalence. Schizoid phenomena become integrated with the move to mature dependence.

To summarize, we propose that schizoid conflict is a universal conflict, which updates and re-edits itself in the Oedipal phase of development, and throughout the entire lifecycle, when situations of loss of the object and separation shape normality and pathology.

Fairbairn underlines the importance of schizoid phenomena in the analysis of neurosis, especially hysteria (Fairbairn 1954; Birtles & Scharff 1994; Scharff & Birtles 1994). Schizoid conflict is the "final common pathway" that determines the form of pathology stemming from problems in infantile dependence (with which we connect psychosis), through stage of transition (with which we connect borderline personality organization), to mature dependence (with which we connect neurosis).

From birth, the central ego is present and capable of conducting a relationship with the object. Libido is a function of the ego. The ego, and consequently libido, is fundamentally object seeking (Fairbairn 1963). Frustration of object seeking originates and then reactivates schizoid conflict. At birth the ego may tend to fuse with the object or it may tend to separate from the object. This tendency defines both poles of the self (Kernberg 1987, 1995), and the oscillations of approach–avoidance; engulfment–abandonment; separation–individuation; attachment–detachment; and identification–disidentification. If we start with the idea of fusion of self and object, then we look to schizoid conflict as a way of achieving self-object differentiation.

We propose that the concept of a part of the ego fused with the object matches Freud's idea of primary narcissism, and that of the part which relates with the object matches secondary narcissism. We understand development as a bidirectional shift between two vectors of equal and opposite directions. There are cycles of *progression and regression* in the pre-Oedipal phase, associated with eventual normality and pathology, depending on the degree of resolution of schizoid conflict.

Schizoid conflict, object, object relationship, drive

To avoid separation anxiety that results from the frustration of being kept from the object, the subject dissociates from and represses two part objects: one good (satisfactory) and one bad (unsatisfactory). Schizoid conflict results from this splitting mechanism, and the object relationships that it gives rise to organize affects and drive and liberate energy (Kernberg 1988; Rubens 1984; Spezzano 1993).

Loss and object loss occur throughout development and throughout analysis. According to Fairbairn, pathology unfolds from relationships with internalized bad objects. Relationships with bad objects are better than no object relationship at all (Guntrip 1971a, 1971b), because the bad object and the relationship with it protect against separation and abandonment anxieties (Freud 1923a; Fairbairn 1970; Grotstein 1993).

We think of psychopathology as a psychological manoeuvre, a technique to recover and maintain relationship with a lost object and avoid anxieties of separation or abandonment.

The object situation in terms of number and quality

We think that:

- the ego relates to only one, partial object in the primary oral phase of infantile dependence, and that this gives rise to schizophrenia
- the ego relates to two whole objects in the secondary oral phase of infantile dependence, and that this gives rise to manic-depressive psychosis, paranoia, and schizoaffective disorder
- the ego relates to two whole objects in the transitional stage and that this gives rise to borderline pathology
- the ego relates to three whole objects in mature dependence, and if there is a problem this gives rise to neurosis.

Relationship of the whole object type is never fully achieved, because the positive and negative Oedipus of the phallic phase can never be completely resolved and schizoid phenomena cannot be fully integrated because of failure to deal fully with frustration (Basili *et al.* 2002a). More important than the object, however, is the relationship with the object (Baranger 1976; Pereira and Scharff 2002), and whether losses and frustration are dealt with through splitting or ambivalence (Basili *et al.* 2002a). The development of ambivalence must always be evaluated in psychoanalytic treatment as a guide to the maturation of object relationships (Kernberg 1988; Rubens 1984; Spezzano 1993). The Oedipus conflict plays out with three good and three bad part objects, and later with three whole objects, at which point the child is capable of feeling ambivalence concerning the primary scene.

Bivalency

We differ with Fairbairn (1970) and with Abraham (1924, 1961, 1980) regarding their idea that there is a preambivalent phase during the primary oral phase of infantile dependence. We think that the ego is capable of bivalent affect from the very start and faces the conflict over investing or not investing in the object. This must be analysed within all object relationships in all psychoanalytic sessions. This bivalency may be simultaneous or alternating. In *simultaneous bivalency*, two antithetical affects are projected towards two different objects (a whole object gets split into two differentiated part objects), as occurs in manic-depressive psychosis (whole object holds relationship with partial object); paranoia and schizo-affective disorder (good breast–bad breast); and in borderline pathology (accepted mother–rejected mother). In *alternating bivalency*, two antithetical affects are projected at different times upon the same object as in schizophrenia and schizotypal personalities where all reality testing is lost (a part object relates to a partial object relationship). In schizophrenia, all that is good and all that is bad is projected on the single object alternately.

Schizoid conflict, infantile dependence, mature dependence

Loss or experience of object loss can occur during any developmental phase, and tends to produce reactions that, if severe, lead to typical pathology later. *Loss in the primary oral phase* (*one partial* object in *partial object relationship* with *good or bad breast*) is associated with dissociation and projection, and produces psychosis. Delirium and hallucination appear in the attempt to recover the object and the object relationship so as to protect the subject against separation anxieties.

Loss in the second oral phase (*two whole* objects relating, in a *partial object relationship*, with the *good mother–bad mother*). All that is good and all that is bad is projected simultaneously over two whole objects and this leads to bipolar illness with mania and depression, and eventually paranoid ideas. The hope is to recover the lost object in this way and protect against separation and abandonment anxieties. When the good and bad objects are both lost (especially the bad one because it protects from separation anxieties) paranoid delirium appears in an attempt to recover it.

The object situation of borderline organization is similar to that of manic depressive psychosis (Silver and Rosenbluth 1992; Rolla 2000) except that the dissociative level is played out later, and the internalized bad object has been dissociated and repressed as an *exciting* (*libidinal*) *object* and a *frustrating* (*antilibidinal*) *object* (Fairbairn 1963). Impulsive borderline patients with pre-Oedipal perversions show schizoid conflict with high abandonment anxiety (Kernberg 1994a; Rosen 1996; Basili and Hamra 1998).

Clinical case

Charles, a 45-year-old man fulfills the criteria for borderline and schizo-affective psychosis. He gets depressed and shows akinetic mutism with waxy flexibility. His diagnosis is catatonic schizo-affective psychosis (Basili *et al.* 2001; Basili and Donnoli 2003).

The schizo-affective aspect

Charles behaved in ways that reveal his schizoid conflict. When he achieved something important, he tended to fight and lose it. He put his property assets in his wife and children's names, and later counted every cent he gave them. He built an airport, then caused a fire there by his carelessness, and made mistakes when drawing up his insurance policy. When in my office, he tended to become confused, and then experienced my office as alternately friendly and unfriendly. He had a fantasy of dwelling and not dwelling in an unoccupied body, showing ambivalence about his body image. Charles dissociated the bad object into two parts: (1) the accepted one, protecting him against the anxieties of abandonment, externalized onto the analyst; (2) the rejected one projected into his body image (internal object), and later into an external object (the analyst). He attempted to maintain an object relationship with me through aggressive discharge.

The psychotic aspect

In the course of outpatient treatment, Charles, who had not been psychotic previously, became catatonic. I interpreted his catatonic condition as an attempt to maintain a relationship with me as a transitional object. It allowed him to keep an optimal pre-Oedipal distance, avoiding separation and engulfment anxieties. I also thought of it as a straightjacket that prevented him from attacking me and yet was an attack on the treatment setting of analysis. When coming out of the catatonic condition, but still mute, he waited for me in the hall, smiled as I came closer, and still smiling, punched me. Greeting me with a smile, he projected the accepted object onto the analyst and, punching me, located the rejecting object in his body, and vice versa. I felt his love and his hate. Like him, I felt confused and paralyzed.

We think of Charles's catatonic reaction as an exception to the rule. Charles improved after the psychotic episode as soon as he became capable of ambivalence about closeness to the analyst, at which point he became pre-occupied with themes of incest and parricide. Psychopathic and paranoid transferences changed into depressive transferences (Kernberg 1992). His themes of incest were interpreted as a defence against abandonment, and his thoughts of parricide as a defence against engulfment. Dreams (Sharpin de Basili 1989) and childhood memories appeared and were interpreted as an improvement in the psychoanalytic process. Feelings of emptiness, futility, and inability to experience pleasure disappeared after that.

Characteristics of borderline pathology

Patients with borderline psychopathology are intolerant of aloneness and ambivalence (Gunderson 1996; Basili et al. 2002a). They cannot connect good and bad representations of self and object, and so they hold contradictory images of self and object, which causes identity diffusion (Erikson 1969). Ambivalence activates schizoid conflict and splitting with (primitive) dissociation, projection, and negation. Borderline patients show a high degree of ambivalence and aggression, and a hypersensitivity to ambivalence and aggression (Rinsley 1989). These are acquired in the object relationship and should be interpreted as secondary to frustration.

At the point of maximum ambivalence, borderline patients act out in analysis. It is critical to the success of the analysis that the analyst should tolerate this. They may become psychotic, like Charles (Basili *et al.* 2002a), or they may abandon the treatment. On the other hand, they may learn from experience under maximum affective tension, experiencing ambivalence about the analyst in the transference. Ambivalence indicates the attempt to connect with the whole object.

Conclusion

Fairbairn's model is fundamental for the analysis of dissociation, separation and abandonment anxiety, aggression, and dependency. Borderline pathology is a pathology of dissociation (Kernberg 1989, 1994b), and of abandonment (Gunderson 2001). We add the importance of aggression secondary to frustration of dependent longings and wishes to relate. Fairbairn's concept of schizoid conflict helps us to understand fusion and differentiation; separation and individuation. A clinical indicator of schizoid conflict is the development of ambivalence (Basili *et al.* 2002a). Fairbairn's object model relationship is indispensible in the analysis of borderline pathology. We think of borderline pathology as a gruelling, unsuccessful attempt at resolving schizoid conflict where the relationship with the accepted object in the transitional stage is fundamentally flawed, and so the borderline structure develops as a clinical manoeuvre to maintain a relationship with the bad object in order to protect the self from separation anxiety.

References

Abraham, K. (1924). Breve estudio del desarrollo de la libido a la luz de los trastornos mentales. In *Contribuciones a la Teoría de la Libido*. Buenos Aires: Hormé, 1994.
—— (1961). *Estudios sobre Psiquiatría y Psicoanálisis*. Buenos Aires: Paidós.
—— (1980). *Psicoanálisis Clínico*. Buenos Aires: Paidós.
Baranger, W. (1976). *Posición y Objeto en la Obra de Melanie Klein*. Buenos Aires: Kargieman.
Basili, R. M. (1988). Teoría de la angustia en psicopatología. Presentado en el concurso para profesor titular de la materia Psicopatología en la Facultad de Psicología de la Universidad Nacional de Buenos Aires.
—— (1990a). Utilidad del diagnóstico psicoanalítico en el tratamiento de las personalidades narcisistas graves. Nuestra experiencia clínica. *Revista de Psicoanálisis* 47(1): 153–176. Premio Céles Cárcamo, Asociación Psicoanalítica Argentina (APA).
—— (1990b). Desarrollos en las Escuelas Psicoanalíticas Británicas sobre las personalidades narcisistas graves. Nuestra experiencia. *Revista de Psicoanálisis* 47(1): 1087–1112.
—— (1992). Psicopatología malheriana contemporánea de los cuadros limítrofes y desamparo, trauma psíquico y defecto yoico. In B. Lerner (ed.) *Pacientes Limítrofes. Diagnóstico y Tratamiento*, pp. 35–46. Buenos Aires: Lugar.
—— (1993). *Estudio Psicoanalítico de las Catatonías*. Departamento de Psicosis de la Asociación Psicoanalítica Argentina (APA).

—— (1994). *La imagen del cuerpo en la psicosis*. Departamento de Psicosis de la Asociación Psicoanalítica Argentina (APA).

—— (1995). La interpretación psicoanalítica de las intervenciones psiquiátricas en el proceso analítico de los pacientes borderline. 2° Congreso Internacional de Psiquiatría, Asociación Argentina de Psiquiatría (AAP).

—— (1996). Interpretación psicoanalítica de las intervenciones psiquiátricas en el proceso psicoanalítico de los pacientes fronterizos. *Trabajos Distinguidos en Psiquiatría* 1(2): 200–213. Premio al Mejor Trabajo Anual AAP.

Basili, R. M. and Donnoli, V. (2003). Borderline y catatonía. Interdisciplina. *La Escucha Psicoanalítica en Psiquiatría*, 4: 31–48.

Basili, R. M. and Etchegaray, E. (1995). Escuela Inglesa. In G. Vidal, R. Alarcón and F. Lolas Stepke (eds), *Enciclopedia Iberoamericana de Psiquiatría, vol. 3*, pp. 1249–1252. Bogota: Médica Panamericana.

Basili, R. M. and Hamra, E. D. (1998). La masturbación anal en pacientes graves. *Revista de Psicoanálisis* 4(3): 509–529. Leído en el XL Congreso Psicoanalítico Internacional (IPA), Barcelona.

Basili, R. M. and Montero, G. J. (1999). ¿Psicoanálisis o psicoterapia psicoanalítica?: Parámetros psicoanalíticos en el tratamiento de los trastornos narcisistas graves. *Revista del XXVII Congreso Interno y XXXVII Symposium de APA*, pp. 141–148.

Basili, R. M. and Sharpin de Basili, I. (2002a). Las actuaciones (en especial en pacientes graves en análisis). Presentado al Premio Bleger, Asociación Psicoanalítica Argentina (APA).

—— (2002b). Un ejemplo mitológico abordable 'pre'-, y edípicamente: La cabeza de Medusa de Freud a la luz del conflicto de ambivalencia. Presentado en el XXIV Congreso Latinoamericano de Psicoanálisis, Montevideo, Uruguay.

Basili, R. M., Hamra, E. D. and Sharpin de Basili, I. (2001). Un aporte del psicoanálisis a la psiquiatría y a la medicina legal: las psicosis esquizoafectivas agudas, *Revista de Psicoanálisis* 8: 333–371.

—— (2002a). Eros y Tánatos en conflicto de diambivalencia: Su trabajo y desarrollo en la relación de objeto. Aplicabilidad en pacientes graves, *Revista de Psicoanálisis*, 60(2): 395–425.

Basili, R. M., Hamra, E. D., Montero, G. J. and Sharpin de Basili, I. (2002b). Conceptualización y tipificación psicoanalíticas de los trastornos narcisistas (en sentido estricto). *Revista de Psicoanálisis* 59(3): 581–613.

Birtles, E. F. and Scharff, D. E. (eds) (1994). *From Instinct to Self: Vol. 2*. Northvale, NJ: Jason Aronson.

Blum, H. (ed.) (1983). *Diez Años de Psicoanálisis en los Estados Unidos*. Madrid: Alianza.

Celani, D. (1993). *The Treatment of the Borderline Patient: Applying Fairbairn's Objects Relations Theory in the Clinical Setting*. Madison, CO: International Universities Press.

—— (1999). Applying Fairbairn's object relations theory to the dynamics of the battered woman. *American Journal of Psychotherapy* 53(1): 60–73.

Eagle, M. N. (1988). *Desarrollos Contemporáneos Recientes en Psicoanálisis. Una Evaluación Crítica*. Buenos Aires: Paidós.

Erikson, E. H. (1969). El problema de la identidad del Yo. *Revista Uruguaya de Psicoanálisis* 5(2–3): 267–338.

Fairbairn, W. R. D. (1954). Observations on the nature of hysterical states. *British Journal of Medical Psychology* 27(3): 106–125.

—— (1958). On the nature and aims of psycho-analytical treatment. *International Journal of Psycho-Analysis* 39: 374–385.

—— (1963). Synopsis of an object-relations theory of personality. *International Journal of Psycho-Analysis* 44: 224–225.

—— (1970). *Estudio Psicoanalítico de la Personalidad*, 3rd edn. Buenos Aires: Horne.

Fonagy, P. (2001). *Attachment Theory and Psychoanalysis*. New York: Other Press.

Fonagy, P. and Target, M. (2003). *Psychoanalytic Theories. Perspectives from Developmental Psychopathology*. London and Philadelphia: Whurr.

Freud, S. (1923a). *El yo y el ello. Vol. XVIII*. Buenos Aires: Amorrurtu.

Greenberg, J. R. and Mitchell, S. A. (1983). *Object Relations in Psychoanalytic Theory*. Cambridge, MA: Harvard University Press.

Grotstein, J. (1993). A reappraisal of W. R. D. Fairbairn. *Bulletin of the Menninger Clinic* 57(4): 421–449.

Grotstein, J. and Rinsley, D. (1994). *Fairbairn and the Origins of Object Relations*. New York: Guilford Press.

Gunderson, J. (1996). The borderline patient's intolerance of aloneness insecure attachments and therapist availability. *American Journal of Psychiatry* 153(6): 752–758.

—— (2001). *Borderline Personality Disorder. A Clinical Guide*. Washington, DC: American Psychiatric Publishing.

Guntrip, H. (1971a). *Estructura de la Personalidad e Interacción Humana*. Buenos Aires: Paidós.

—— (1971b). *El Self en la Teoría y la Terapia Psicoanalítica*. Buenos Aires: Amorrortu.

Hamilton, N. (1989). A critical review of object relations theory. *American Journal of Psychiatry* 146(12): 1552–1560.

—— (1995). Object relations units and the ego. *Bulletin of the Menninger Clinic* 59(4): 416–426.

Hughes, J. (1990). *Researching the Psycho-Analytic Domain. The Work of Melanie Klein, W. R. D. Fairbairn, and D.W. Winnicott*. Berkeley, Los Angeles, London: University of California Press.

Kernberg, O. (1979). *Desórdenes Fronterizos y Narcisismo Patológico*. Buenos Aires: Paidós

—— (1987). *Trastornos Graves de la Personalidad*. México City: Manual Moderno.

—— (1988). Object relations theory in clinical practice. *Psychoanalytic Quarterly* 57: 481–504.

—— (1989). The narcissistic personality disorder and the differential diagnosis of antisocial behavior. *Psychiatric Clinic of North America* 12: 553–570.

—— (1992) Psychopathic paranoid and depressive transferences. *International Journal of Psychoanalysis* 73: 21.

—— (1994a). *La Agresión en las Perversiones y en los Desórdenes de la Personalidad*. Buenos Aires: Paidós.

—— (1994b). Aggression, trauma, and hatred in the treatment of borderline patients. *Psychiatric Clinics of North America* 17(4): 701–714.

—— (1995). Personal comunication to Dr R. M. Basili, White Plains, Cornell University, USA.

Koenigsberg, H., Kernberg, O., Stone, M., Appelbaum, A., Yeomans, F. and Diamond, D. (2000). *Borderline Patients: Extending the Limits of Treatability*. New York: Basic Books.

McWilliams, N. (1994). *Psychoanalytic Diagnosis Understanding Personality Structure in the Clinical Process*. New York: Guilford Press.

Mahler, M. (1972a). *Simbiosis humana: Las vicisitudes de la individuación*. México City: Mortis.

—— (1972b). On the first three subphases of the separation–individuation process. *International Journal of Psychoanalysis* 53: 333–338.

Masterson, J. (1976). *Psychotherapy of the Borderline Adult: A Developmental Approach*. New York: Brunner and Mazel.

—— (1981). *The Narcissistic and Borderline Disorder and Integrated Developmental Approach*. New York: Brunner and Mazel.

—— (2000). Disorders of the Self: Differential Diagnosis and Treatment. American Psychiatric Association, 52nd Institute on Psychiatric Services, 25–29 October, Philadelphia Marriot Hotel.

Morgan, J. J. (1968). Personal comunication to Dr R. M. Basili.

Pereira, F. and Scharff, D.E. (eds) (2002). *Fairbairn and Relational Theory*. London: Karnac.

Rinsley, D. (1989). *Developmental Pathogenesis and Treatment of Borderline and Narcissistic Personalities*. Northvale, NJ: Jason Aronson.

Rolla, E. (2000). *Organizaciones de Personalidad*. Buenos Aires: Lumen.

Rosen, I. (1996). *Sexual Deviation*. Oxford: Oxford University Press.

Rubens, R. L. (1984). The meaning of structure in Fairbairn. *International Review of Psychoanalysis* 11:429–440.

Scharff, D. and Birtles, F. E. (eds) (1994). *From Instinct to Self: Vol. 1*. Northvale, NJ: Jason Aronson.

Sharpin de Basili, I. (1989). Utilidad de la Teoría Psicoanalítica de Ángel Garma en la interpretación de los sueños de pacientes con personalidades narcisistas graves. Monografía presentada en la Asociación Psicoanalítica Argentina.

Silver, D. and Rosenbluth, M. (eds) (1992). *Handbook of Borderline Disorders*. Connecticut: Madison.

Skolnick, N. and Scharff, D. (1998). *Fairbairn Then & Now*. Hillsdale, NJ: Analytic Press.

Spezzano, C.H. (1993). *Affect in Psychoanalysis. A Clinical Synthesis*. Hillsdale, NJ: Analytic Press.

Winnicott, D. (1981). *Escritos de Pediatría y Psicoanálisis. 1931–1956*. Barcelona: Laia.

Chapter 14

"Disorder and early sorrow"

An integration of the motivational system of aversion and Fairbairn's endopsychic structure in child treatment

Theresa Aiello

> Ellie is not too pleased with her looks – a sign that already she troubles
> about such things. Snapper, four years old, is self-critical too, though more
> in the moral sphere. He suffers from remorse for his attacks of rage and
> considers himself a tremendous sinner. He is quite certain that heaven is
> not for such as he; he is sure to go to the "bad place" when he dies, and no
> persuasions will convince him to the contrary, as that God sees the heart
> and gladly makes allowances.
>
> (Thomas Mann, *Disorder and Early Sorrow*, 1989)

On one of his last trips to America, John Sutherland, Fairbairn's biographer
and principal disciple (1989), said that he thought that had Fairbairn lived he
would have been very interested in self psychology. He added that he had
been informed that Fairbairn's work was talked about in Kohut's Institute
(Grotstein and Rinsley 1994). He cited a passage in Kohut's *The Analysis Of
The Self* where he refers to "dangerous repressive potential in the narcissistic
personality referred to as *schizoid personality*" [Kohut's italics] (Kohut 1971,
cited in Sutherland 1994b: 4). He went on to say that Fairbairn had been very
interested in systems of motivation throughout his life.

Motivational systems inaugurated by Lichtenberg *et al.* (1992) is a contemporary self psychology theory of the psyche culled from current infant
research and used as a theory of technique. Unlike object relations theory,
which emphasizes the need to analyze and elucidate the negative transference
by exploring aggression, contemporary self psychology emphasizes the need
to develop an idealized self object transference and addresses the negative
transference under the rubric of repetitive transference.

Children who have experienced excessive abuse frequently enter treatment
with a negative transference, being immediately critical and overtly hostile to
the therapist, or expressing it only later when they experience the therapist as
safe and familiar. Fairbairn's endopsychic structure allows us to examine the
nature of a child's attachment and affiliation in light of what is felt to be bad.
I believe that Fairbairn's endopsychic structure and motivational systems

theory have much in common to add to considerations of technique in child treatment. In the end, more than theory, technique makes or breaks successful treatment. Technique embodies the relational experience of treatment, as I hope to show presently in my discussion of the therapy of two children whom I will call Ellie and Snapper.

Fairbairn's endopsychic structure

Fairbairn's endopsychic situation is the structure that results from and supports an object-seeking ego (1944). In his vision of psychic structure, the ego is tripartite: each section of the ego is attached to a bad exciting, bad rejecting, or ideal object. When a child feels unloved or has been traumatized, and has therefore taken in a rejecting object, the ego splits and represses a powerful antilibidinal ego.

Fairbairn suggests that experience and motivation are shaped from the earliest period of life throughout adulthood by a motivational quest for, and maintaining of contact with, others (Greenberg and Mitchell 1983). When the child experiences early deprivation and abuse in relationships, the child internalizes bad objects and subsequently seeks them out through projection, or through choosing similar types that replicate the early bad object ties which are familiar and often function as a tease. Fairbairn describes the "obstinate attachment" as a way of replicating and even commemorating early dysfunctional relationships because they are so familiar (Fairbairn 1943: 177). The need to repeat them maintains hope that this time the subject will win love (which had previously been denied) from a person similar to the early caregiver.

Striving for contact is the primary motivation in Fairbairn's system. Aggression is an expression of failed, unsatisfying object relations. Aggression is not therefore primary for Fairbairn as a motivating factor, but it is a major focus of work in the clinical context (Greenberg and Mitchell 1983). Fairbairn believed that internalized bad objects must be released from the unconscious – a theory of analysis that he himself called a kind of exorcism. While emphasizing that the negative transference is fundamental to object relations theory, Fairbairn also thought that "bad objects can only be safely released . . . if the analyst has become established as a good object for the patient" (1943: 113).

Fairbairn identifies the schizoid personality as embodying the experience of alienation (Grotstein and Rinsley 1994). Grotstein and Rinsley pointed out that the schizoid process can be witnessed in infant research. In situations of unsuccessful bonding or misattunement, the infant becomes detached and withdrawn, and then gives up (Murray 1991, in Grotstein and Rinsley 1994; Trevarthan 1991, in Grotstein and Rinsley 1994). Symington (1993) described this turning away as a spurning of the life-saving object (the narcissistic option) and connected it to a disavowed spontaneous, jealous, or resentful part of the child that was not given a chance to speak. Fairbairn thought that early maladaptive or non-existent attachment leads to an early fixed schizoid belief that love kills, is bad and dangerous, and that it is safer to withdraw (the schizoid option). Pathology for Fairbairn rests in the failure "of the capacity to love and be considered a person in his own right" (Grotstein and Rinsley 1994: 12).

The technique of motivational systems contained in the model scene

Motivational systems theory posits five basic needs and innate responses that develop into motivational systems through *lived experience* (Lichtenberg *et al.* 1992). On the basis of these systems, Lichtenberg *et al.* developed a theory of technique (1992: 3).

Lichtenberg describes the "disturbed regulation" of the motivational systems as the result of "disturbances and deficiencies in mirroring, alter ego or idealizing experiences," that is fragmentation products. He posits:

> Disturbances of eating, sleeping, eliminating breathing are primary defects in lived experiences. These represent failures between caregiver and child; similarly all of the motivational systems relate to this type of disruption.
>
> (Lichtenberg 1989: 296)

In terms of technique these emphatic ruptures and their corresponding motivational factors are in need of empathic mirroring in the treatment experience. These empathic issues can be encapsulated in the *model scene*. The model scene is the co-construction by patient and analyst of just such disruptions that can be perceived as significant past distressing scenarios or memories of the patient. These can be analyzed in terms of their importance as recurring themes in the life of the patient.

In child treatment, where dialogue is frequently sparse, the model scene may be enacted in play or in interactions between child and therapist as will be illustrated in the two cases presented further on in this chapter.

The five motivational systems are psychological entities built around fundamental needs, each observable in the neonatal period (Lichtenberg *et al.* 1992: 1). They are:

- the need for psychic regulation of physiological requirements
- the need for attachment and later affiliation
- the need for exploration and assertion
- the need to react aversively through antagonism or withdrawal (or both)
- the need for sensual enjoyment and sexual excitement.

During infancy each system of these needs develops into mutual interaction with caregivers: a functional or dysfunctional motivational system. The systems may be arranged in hierarchies at different developmental phases throughout the lifecycle. At any time one system or another may gain in priority, reflected in unconscious and conscious preferences. Based on lived experiences, motivations may have or lack vitality, depending upon the interaction of the infant with caregivers. Model scenes are co-constructed by patient and analyst to encapsulate compelling developmental experiences that act as an emblem or metaphor for "significant past problematic experiences" (1992: 1–9). Because children are still so much in formation it is often difficult to capture coherent model scenes. Children do, however, participate quite vigorously in this endeavor through enactments that are largely symbolic (via play or fantasy or by sheer interpersonal interaction).

In the two cases I will describe, the therapist has to bear most of the labor in attempting to isolate commemorative events or identify repetitive themes. Both of these children demonstrated aversion as a primary motivational system at the point of referral. Both are what Corrigan and Gordan call *mind-object children* (1993); children who are precocious but wish to be self-sufficient to the point of refusing normal childhood dependency on the way to narcissistic or schizoid-like options.

Snapper – "a fully digitalized child"

Snapper was referred to treatment at age 8 because of his distress due to his parents' separation. His parents, both extremely good-looking, elegant people were caught up in so much rage at each other that their only child was overlooked. He seemed lost and terrified. His father moved out but lived nearby, seeing his son every day, bringing him to school in the mornings and spending weekends with him. Snapper's father did not find an apartment but chose to live in the back of his store, which curiously sells beautiful home furnishings to wealthy and famous customers. His mother remained at home and for a long time confided her worries to her son. She made good use of her own treatment for her worries, and was motivated to get help for her child. Snapper is a very beautiful, always stylishly dressed boy. He has friends but like his father, is extremely attached to every new digital or computerized solo game. Nevertheless, I noted that in therapy he chose interactive games like cards and pick-up sticks.

After our first session I acknowledged that I couldn't make his parents get back together. He was so disappointed in me that he said he would not speak to me again. I suggested that maybe he could tell me about himself so that we could free him from his worrying about his parents. He smiled and said "Maybe," and proceeded to initiate an adversarial style of relating that lasted fully a year and a half. In every game he blocked my moves, cheated me out of turns, did not answer even benign questions, and ended every session looking very satisfied and pronouncing, "This was a good session!"

Whenever I asked "Am I ever going to figure out this game?" and "Do I ever get a turn?" he would smile and say, "Keep playing." One pivotal moment in the treatment occurred several months into our work when I said that it made sense that the games should be harder for me: as a grown-up, I should have tougher rules. He agreed. His mother told me the next week that he had complained to her that he shouldn't have to worry about his parents. He told her that he was "just a little boy" and that "it's not fair."

In a session with his father, he complained tearfully that he wanted his father to have a real home, not in the store. Motivated (incorrectly) by a wish to smooth things over, I said, "I live where I work too. Is that hard for you?" He answered, "You live in a real home." The first year of treatment Snapper refused birthday or Christmas presents, which I offered him, as I routinely do as part of my child therapy technique. By the second year he asked for a small appointment/address book he had seen in a neighborhood store, a tiny book with a picture on the cover of two country mailboxes leaning on each other. As we became closer and more able to communicate, he began to feel safer, making critical remarks of me but often in a playful way.

For instance, one day in the waiting room where his friend was meeting him, he boldly asked me in front of his friend what kind of car I drive, and pressed for an answer. I told him that he'd probably be very disappointed that I drive a '91 Honda Civic. He slapped his head in disgust. The next week I acknowledged his embarrassment at my answer, and he told me that he'd thought about what I needed. He had chosen for me a car called the Navigator programmed so that I would never lose my way because I would be staying under a satellite for guidance. Another day, as I stirred cocoa for him, he embarked on a series of criticisms of the environment I provided. "Theresa, have you ever thought of living in a nice modern apartment? This place is full of old things. That stove looks like someone died in it. This cup is stained. I got a splinter from the table – I knew this would happen someday." The therapy home that he cherished and craved had become a bad exciting object, and I was now stained like my coffee cups (which were in fact new). This period of treatment initiated a caroling of my name, "Theresa," over and over, as if controlling me as an object for his use at his beck and call. He continued to cheat at cards, tried to pick the lock of my front door with a hairpin, even looking me up on the computer. He also spied on his mother, fearing that she or his father might find a new lover. He threatened to run away if this should happen, but agreed that he would call me or come to my office first.

The model scene

1   A father selling beautiful furniture without a home.
2   A child with beautiful objects without substance desperately craving relatedness and nurture.

Ellie/Spike – the boy/girl wizard

Ellie was referred at age 8 for encopresis. She had temper tantrums and episodes of stealing. She looked and dressed like a boy, had only boys as friends, and expressed open contempt for girls. Her birth mother in China had abandoned her at the age of two months, and she spent the next three months in an orphanage. Then she was adopted by Caucasian-American parents who appear to be warm, concerned, and fairly liberal in attitude. They noticed that she had severe rashes over her buttocks (probably due to lying in feces and urine too long). From what I understand of orphanage conditions in China, it is probable that she was given the bottle propped in her mouth without much opportunity to regulate her feeding intake and with little other interaction.

Model scene

Cumulative trauma during her pre-adoption life when the motivational system of physiological regulation was primary: this is not so much a model scene as a thematic, traumatic experience. Ellie's loss of her mother at 2 months, neglect at the orphanage, abandonment issues, and inability to sustain minimal infantile self-regulation led to the rageful, arrogant child that she occasionally becomes. Early memory of the familiar environment encoded in the five senses – sounds of her language of origin, the smell and tastes of foods, the sight of familiar Chinese faces – recorded losses that could not be completely compensated for by loving parents.

Ellie loves therapy. She likes to play at being the "boy–girl wizard named Spike." She makes me play a witch ("you're smart and good at the trans-formations"), but one who is old and failing in her powers. She vanquishes me at every turn and wants no comfort. She says that "Spike doesn't love because you can be hurt if you get too close." She tells me that Spike changes into a girl only if someone threatens him with castration. It has been clear to Spike and me that she would not have been rejected by her birth mother, and therefore would not have been adopted, if she were a boy.

Initially in treatment, Ellie made clay models of feces-like shapes. She then moved on to make models of penises. I explored the possibility of sexual abuse with her and she denied this convincingly. She did at one point make a model of a phallus and attempted (laughingly) to affix it to my forehead. I told her that I didn't need a penis, that my brain was my source of power, and that she had brains too. She grinned at me and said that she didn't need a penis, wouldn't want one anyway.

Reminiscent of having to lie in feces at the orphanage, Ellie kept her stool in her underwear. She also liked to keep things in her pockets. I offered her a plate of pretty colored rocks and stones. She was entranced. We agreed that in every session she would take one for her pocket. She volunteered that she could use them to try to control her defecating in her pants, and her stealing. She could squeeze the rocks hard in her pockets if she were angry. (Tustin has described the autistic child's love of hard objects as a need for boundary-giving substances in an out of contact situation.) She knew that she would get more rocks without having to steal them. I believe that in the period of time she spent in the orphanage, abandoned by her mother, the literal presence of feces were experienced as company. This would explain her need for the com-panionship of things in her pockets. After nearly two years of treatment the encopresis was essentially cured.

No longer always the old witch, I now sometimes play the bad or good queen. The bad queen tries to steal Spike's powers. The good queen is his friend, "not his mother, because he's an orphan. He survives all by him-self." In one session, the good queen must counsel his friend, a little wolf. I tell the wolf to guard Spike at all times, protect him while he sleeps, and warn him of danger. The wolf bows and says, "Yes, my Lady," and then begins to kiss my face over and over. Spike says, "He's kissing you," a brief moment in which Spike accepts dependent longings – and expresses love directly.

Conclusion

For "Snapper," the therapy relationship itself is a tease in that it takes the form of home – the thing Snapper desires most. For Ellie/Spike, early scenes of abandonment have become encoded as fear of attachment. For both chil-dren, the system of aversion enters into intimacy. In Fairbairn's terms, the schizoid part of the child withdraws and acts negatively because of thinking that love kills. The intersection of motivational systems and Fairbairn's object relations is in the model scene where bad exciting/rejecting objects come together with the dominant motivational system.

References

Corrigan, E. and Gordan, P. (eds) (1993). *The Mind Object: Precocity and Pathology of Self-Sufficiency*. Northvale, NJ: Jason Aronson.

Fairbairn, W. R. D. (1943). The repression and the return of bad objects (with special reference to the "war neuroses"). In *Psychoanalytic Studies of the Personality*, pp. 59–81. London and New York: Routledge, 1952.

—— (1944). Endopsychic structure considered in terms of object relationships. In *Psychoanalytic Studies of the Personality*, pp. 82–136. London and New York: Routledge, 1994.

—— (1952). Theoretical and experimental aspects of psychoanalysis. *British Journal of Medical Psychology* 25(2,3): 122–127.

Greenberg, J. R. and Mitchell, S. (1983). *Object Relations in Psychoanalytic Theory*. Cambridge, MA: Harvard University Press.

Grotstein, D. and Rinsley, D. (eds) (1994). *Fairbairn and the Origins of Object Relations*. London and New York: Guilford Press.

Kohut, (1971) *The Analysis of the Self*. New York: International Universities Press.

Lichtenberg, J. (1989). *Psychoanalysis and Motivation*. Hillsdale, NJ: Analytic Press.

Lichtenberg, J., Lachmann, F. and Fosshage, J. (1992). *Self and Motivational Systems: Towards a Theory of Psychoanalytic Technique*. Hillsdale, NJ: Analytic Press.

Mann, T. (1989). Disorder and early sorrow. In *Death in Venice and Seven Other Stories*, pp. 179–213. New York: Vintage International Press/Random House.

Mitchell, S. (1994). The origin and nature of the object in the theories of Klein and Fairbairn. In J. Grotstein and D. Rinsley (eds) *Fairbairn and the Origins of Object Relations*, pp. 66–87. London and New York: Guilford Press.

Robbins, M. (1994). A Fairbairnian object relations perspective on self psychology. In J. Grotstein and D. Rinsley (eds) *Fairbairn and the Origins of Object Relations*, pp. 302–317. London and New York: Guilford Press.

Sutherland, J. (1989). *Fairbairn's Journey to the Interior*. London: Free Association.

—— (1994a). The autonomous self. In J. Scharff (ed.) *The Autonomous Self: The Work of John D. Sutherland*, pp. 303–330. Northvale, NJ: Jason Aronson.

—— (1994b). Fairbairn's achievement. In *Fairbairn's Journey to the Interior*, pp. 162–177. Reprinted in J. Grotstein and D. Rinsley (eds) *Fairbairn and the Origins of Object Relations*, pp 17–33. London and New York: Guilford Press.

Symington, N. (1993). *Narcissism: A New Theory*. London: Karnac.

Chapter 15

Fairbairn on trauma

Individual therapy of a sexually abused child

Hope Cooper

I will present clinical material to illustrate the effects of childhood sexual abuse, a contemporary topic to which Fairbairn drew attention as early as the 1930s. The clinical material comes from the opening phase of individual therapy with a child I will call Tiffany, a 5-year-old girl who had been sexually abused in her earlier years. I will discuss my countertransference and its implications for understanding the nature of work with sexual trauma.

Between 1931 and 1935 at the Edinburgh University Clinic for Children and Juveniles where he treated many physically and sexually abused children, Ronald Fairbairn explored the problems that result from victimization. At the end of that time, he wrote "Medico-Psychological Aspects of Child Assault," a paper remarkable for its time as it shows an advanced understanding of child development and sensitivity to the impact of early trauma. While it received attention in the child care community, it went largely unnoticed in the child analytic literature. In this paper, Fairbairn (1935) reconsiders the pathology of the perpetrators, recommends types of treatment, and discusses the impact of abuse on pathology, especially in causing hysterical neurosis. He makes a point of disputing the then commonly held notion that the victim should be encouraged to forget the experience completely. He argues that the emotional experience must be worked through because excessive repression leaves the trauma unresolved and sure to produce pathology. I find myself in agreement with his recommendations for a helpful therapeutic stance:

> An unobtrusive effort should be made to provide the child with an opportunity to ventilate the memory of the traumatic incident, and to work off its emotional reactions in an atmosphere which is free both of sentimentality and moral indignation.
>
> (Fairbairn 1935: 174)

Sentimentality and moral indignation were, however, strikingly present in my countertransference to Tiffany. I will use clinical material from her treatment to examine this ego-dystonic countertransference, and consider how Fairbairn's ideas apply today. I will highlight the absence or presence of guilt in the child's internal world as seen both in the play, the transference, and the countertransference. In the course of this work, I came to understand dissociation as a projective identification, an affective representation of the tie to the bad object.

Clinical example

The consultation: collateral visit with the aunt

Tiffany began weekly psychotherapy with me shortly after her fifth birthday and just before she entered primary school. She and her 3-year-old brother lived with their paternal aunt and her husband. Tiffany's aunt told me of an intergenerational transmission of trauma – in particular, incest and sexual abuse. Tiffany's mother had been sexually abused by her father and at 14 had become pregnant by him. She gave birth to a boy, Bobby, who lived with this man who was both his father and grandfather, until he was 9, when it was discovered that the father/grandfather was sexually abusing him. Tiffany's mother had become able to leave home and marry, leaving Bobby behind, but she remained psychologically disturbed and suffered severe postpartum depression when Tiffany was born. Two years later she gave birth to Tiffany's brother, which precipitated a more severe depressive reaction so that she was often entirely unable to look after the children's basic needs. Tiffany was left to look after herself and her brother much of the time.

When Tiffany was 3, her father found Bobby, then 9, in her bed under the covers, on top of Tiffany as if they were having intercourse. This is the only incident that was discovered. When Tiffany's father told his sister what he had seen, she called child protective services. The children were removed from the parents' home, and placed with the father's sister and her husband. The children have remained with their aunt and uncle and have formed a good relationship with them. Ultimately, Tiffany's father left her mother, and now he resides with his children in his sister's home. Tiffany's mother visits only rarely. When she does, she brings Bobby, who is 12, with her. The extent of the sexual abuse remains unclear because it was not witnessed, but Tiffany's aunt thinks it likely that both Tiffany and her baby brother were victims of ongoing sexual abuse by Bobby.

Tiffany's aunt was appropriately concerned about the impact of the trauma and abuse. She said that Tiffany's behavior ranged from outright defiance to passive resistance. She described Tiffany as being easily frustrated and quickly enraged with a poor capacity to manage transitions, and a tendency to decompensate in the face of change. Aunt was therefore very concerned about Tiffany beginning kindergarten. She reported that Tiffany was at times protective and almost motherly with her brother and at other times her jealousy brought out a violent response. She said that Tiffany was obsessed with food and painfully afraid that there was never going to be enough. She told me that Tiffany was a "Daddy's girl"; she idealized her father but was stand-offish and disinterested around her mother.

The first session with Tiffany

When I first saw Tiffany in the waiting room I was immediately struck by how small she was and how much younger than 5 she looked. Aunt introduced her to me and she smiled. Aunt asked Tiffany if she'd like her to go into my consulting room with her, and Tiffany said, "No." Without any apparent anxiety she left her aunt's side and came into my consulting room. I, on the other hand, felt some anxiety about her apparent trust of me, a complete stranger.

In the consulting room, Tiffany went immediately to the table with markers and paper. She said the single word, "Color!" almost like a 2 year old. She began to draw. I asked if she knew my name and who I was. She smiled and merely said, "No." I told her my name, and said a little about what she and I would work on together. When I finished talking, she simply smiled.

I immediately felt that her smile was both engaging and seductive. I wondered if she really didn't know my name – surely her Aunt had told her – and wondered what she was getting at in pretending that she did not. Simultaneously there was a sense of presumed familiarity. She came in as if she knew me. I was left with the feeling that we had somehow skipped some steps in the get-to-know-you process.

Tiffany played in the dollhouse for most of the session. She was clearly able to make use of symbolic play. She spoke in baby talk, and most of the conversation with the dolls had to do with looking at what was in the babies' diapers and watching the older dolls use the toilet. About halfway through the session, she turned to me and asked, "Do you want to see my pee-pee?" Before I had a chance to respond, Tiffany pulled up her skirt and pushed her underwear to the side, showing me her genitals. She exclaimed excitedly, "Pee pee!" I was a bit too dazed to know what to say. I had missed an opportunity to tell her that she didn't need to show me – she could tell me.

In the first month of treatment

I continued to feel that I was missing opportunities to be therapeutic. I struggled to make interpretations, and most of my thoughts came in the aftermath of sessions. This made me feel guilty and insecure. I thought maybe I wasn't the best therapist for her and that I didn't have enough experience with sexual abuse. I later wondered whether this sense of "better not say anything" – and the guilt that I felt about having missed a chance to intervene – represented a re-enactment of the family's not knowing about the abuse.

Only one month into the treatment Tiffany told me about the time that she remembered being attacked by Bobby. This brought up a powerful feeling in the countertransference of disgust and horror, which made it even more difficult for me to think in her presence. Sometimes when I was with Tiffany I had images of this monstrous little boy assaulting her, and I then felt a visceral revulsion.

A session at one month

Tiffany is dressing a doll. She tells me that Daddy lives with her but Mommy just visits. Then she says, "Mommy has a brother. He's scary."

I'm confused and wonder who she means. I know that Bobby visits when Mother does. I think about how in a perverse way Bobby *is* Mother's brother and I wonder about the unconscious communication in the family. So I ask, "Do you mean Bobby?"

Tiffany looks up at me and says, "Yes! He's scary. He's always trying to touch me and one time he pulled my pants down. Aunt won't let him touch me now."

Trying to get my bearings, I say, "How scary! It's good to have Aunt protecting you." I pause and wonder how much to probe and cannot stop myself from asking, "Was it only once?"

Tiffany says very seriously, "One time he pulled my pants down."

I ask, "Did he touch you?"

She answers, "He touches me." She pauses and then seems to correct herself. "He tries to touch me. I run away. He's scary. I scream."

I say, "It's a good thing to scream when he does that."

Tiffany says, "Yes."

I feel overwhelmed by revulsion and guilt – revolted by the idea of her being abused and guilty about asking all these questions in what feels like a voyeuristic way.

A session at three months into treatment

Material from three months into treatment shows that it is still hard for me to contain my own anxiety around the abuse. I have great difficulty knowing when we are in a fantasy mode, and when I should move into reality, and how to manage their intersecting.

Tiffany comes into the room and takes out a baby doll. She says she wants to take it home with her. I say that we need the toys to stay in the room so we can play with them to do our work. Tiffany looks angry and yells, "NO!"

She then sits at the table to draw and says, "You're a butthead!" She makes a drawing (Figure 15.1). When she finishes, she giggles, and asks me to write on it, "*This is a BUTT.*" Cutting it out, she asks, "Do people ever have blood in their poop?"

Looking at the drawing makes me extremely anxious. I ask, "Do you ever have blood in your poop?"

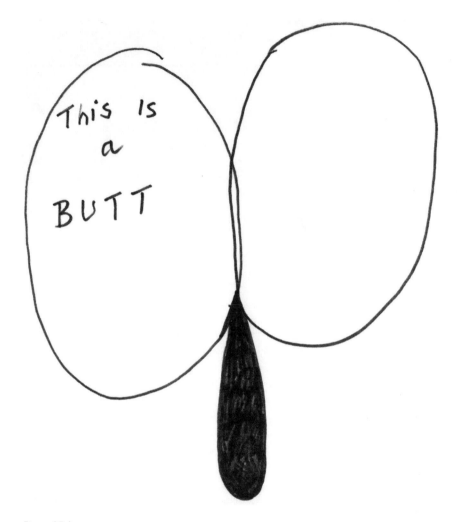

Figure 15.1

"Yes," she says, "I look in the toilet and see it."

I ask if she tells her aunt when that happens.

"NO!" Tiffany was alarmed by the thought.

I ask why she doesn't tell anyone.

Tiffany says, "Aunt would say I have to go into time out."

I ask, "You think she would think you'd done something bad?"

Tiffany says, "Yes!"

I say, "Do you think there's blood in your poop because you've done something bad?"

Tiffany thinks a moment and then says, "No. How does blood get in your poop?"

I say, "It could be a number of things. A doctor might need to check you out to be sure – but it could be because your butt has been hurt."

Tiffany says, "No."

She is quiet for a while and then says, "I don't want to just talk about butts!" Then she tells me she's going to make a purse. At the end of the session she tells me defiantly that she is taking her purse home!

I had a difficult time maintaining an analytic stance. Looking at the picture as she and I talked, I vacillated between thinking of her drawing as a representation of her anger at me in the transference – pooping on me because I would not let her take the baby doll home – to wondering whether she had been anally penetrated. Were the questions about blood arising from unconscious phantasy, or from the physical effects of straining, or from abuse? My anxiety always went to the worst possible place.

In nearly every session Tiffany made a purse which she decorated carefully and colorfully, and she stubbornly insisted on taking the purse home. I told her that our work needed to stay in the playroom so that we could think about it together as the weeks went by, but she always took the purse with her. Being unable to contain the purse play in the therapeutic space induced in me a sense of inadequacy and guilt for failing to understand whatever it symbolized. I came to the idea that if the purse represented her genitals, then her need to make a purse with me, and then take home what we had made together, was her way of looking after her genitals with my help.

I often thought of Fairbairn's statement:

> The usual effect of an assault on a child is not only to stimulate sexual impulses but to activate guilt . . . So far as repression takes place, both the sexual propensities and the guilt are simultaneously repressed in a state of emotional tension, with the result that, though the conflict disappears from consciousness, it continues unabated in the depths of the mind.
>
> (Fairbairn 1935: 173–174)

This led me to wonder how much Tiffany had repressed. It helped me to formulate what I was feeling and how it reflected Tiffany's experience projected into me in the transference. I resonated with her sense of guilt whenever I had to set a limit. I guessed that sexual abuse began when she was in the anal period developmentally, and if so, her play showed me both the protection of the female genitals and the analization of the sexual assault.

A repetitive countertransference of dissociation

Into the sixth month of treatment, I noticed that I felt less present. It wasn't that I was bored. It's that I felt lulled – not into sleep but into a state of mindlessness. I couldn't remember what my thoughts were when I drifted into that state and I couldn't track any unconscious projections. It worried me that I seemed so unable to stay in the moment. Was the material in the play causing me to dissociate to avoid difficult affect or was it my way of managing it? As I paid more attention to this state of mind that being with Tiffany induced, I began to see her communication of dissociative affect as a link to the traumatic experience of the abuse. This led me to consider whether communications of affect might convey not only the link to the bad object but also the link to the parts of the self that have been contaminated. With these questions in mind, I'll now present material from a recent session with an eye toward tracing the affective states in the countertransference.

A session at ten months

Tiffany gives me a big smile when I greet her in the waiting room. She hops off her chair and takes my hand as we go to the stairs. At the bottom of the stairs Tiffany turns and whispers to me, "I'm going to be 6 on Friday!"

I say, "Two days! That's exciting!"

Tiffany grins and starts to crawl up the stairs but her crawl turns into a run, and she's on her feet again. I say something about her feeling like a big girl when she turns 6.

In the playroom Tiffany goes straight to the dollhouse. She takes out the bed for the little girl and starts to set up the bedroom. She's busy with this for a moment, and then asks, "Does anyone that comes here steal?"

I ask what she's thinking.

She says, "Stealing is bad."

I say that people who come here might feel like stealing. They might feel they have to steal in order to get what they want.

She's quiet, and then commands, "You make me a purse."

I say, "Can you help me? Give me some ideas of what you want?"

"No! You make it! And make it pretty with flowers and hearts and butterflies! Make it pretty!" (Her tone is a combination of desperate and angry.)

Tiffany suddenly jumps up and says she has to pee. She runs out of the room, and is back shortly. She comes over to me, and looks at what I've done. She adds a butterfly and some hearts and corrects the way I've done the handle. Then she tells me to do some more hearts and flowers and butterflies.

She then lies down in front of the dollhouse, and sets up more of the rooms. She burps, and then says, "Adults burp too."

I say, "You mean adults and children do lots of the same things?"

"They pee and poop too!" Tiffany giggles.

I say, "Adults burp, pee, and poop – just like kids?"

"Yeah!" She's very excited by this idea.

Tiffany gets up and tries to climb on top of the table. I go over to get her down, saying it isn't safe. She gets mad at me when I put her down. She goes back to the dollhouse.

"You stink," she says.

"I stink when I don't let you do what you want."

"Yeah, and you're dirty. You're stinky and dirty!"

I say, "And you have to come here to be with this stinky, dirty person."

Tiffany laughs and says, "Smelly too. You smell."

Tiffany gets up and rummages through the toy bins. She brings over the three princesses and the prince. She says, "I'm a princess."

I ask what a princess is.

She says, "A princess gets the prince."

Tiffany says she wants to draw the princess (Figure 15.2). She tries to trace the princess but that doesn't work well, and she scribbles it out. She looks up at me and says, "I'm going to draw your butt!" She giggles. She tells me that I have lots and lots of poop coming out of my butt. She says this several times, giggling somewhat hysterically. Tiffany goes on, "I am clean and smell nice. I make things clean."

I say, "You mean I'm the smelly one with all the poop inside, and you're the nice, clean one?"

"Yes," she laughs. She's quiet a moment, and then whispers in my ear, "I have a prince – Andrew." (Andrew is the boy she chases in school.)

I ask what she and her prince do.

She says, "We kiss. But it's okay. Because he's my brother."

Figure 15.2

Discussion of the shifts in my affective states through this session

In the waiting room I am always hit with a wave of sentimentality when Tiffany smiles in her sweet way at me and then takes my hand to go up the stairs. She makes me feel "special." Is it possible that this affect of "*special-ness*," projected into me, contains the defense against the horror of the abuse – the horror is turned into a feeling of being sweet and special – that is, the sentimentality itself is a defense against and a tie to the bad object?

When Tiffany brought up the question of stealing, I felt a shift into *excitement*. She then ran to the bathroom to pee. Was she evacuating the excitement? When she returned, and I was drawing, she was quiet. Meanwhile, I drifted into that blank state where I had no thoughts at all; the feeling of excitement led to *dissociation*. After a bit we moved into the discussion of pee and poop and my being stinky and dirty while she is clean. We had moved back into the *excitement* – indeed, it had something of a manic quality to it. I was to carry the dirty, smelly parts of her self. By projecting those feelings into me she was free to feel an excitement about them. Simultaneously, I felt some *guilt* – as if I were doing something bad to her. The excited discussion about the smells relieved me of the guilt. And then her drawing induced even more *excitement*. Then came the story about her being a princess – the little girl who is a princess and has her prince. Her statement that it was okay for them to kiss because he was her brother made me feel an instantaneous *revulsion*. The images of her abuse forced themselves into my mind. I could not wait for the session to end. She left me with the picture. Eventually I was able to put the session out of my mind. In summary, the movement of affect in session was as follows:

*   sentimentality
*   excitement
*   dissociation
*   excitement/guilt
*   disgust
*   dissociation.

Conclusion

I propose that sentimentality and dissociation are affective movements away from the traumatic experience but nonetheless represent the tie to the abusive object. Excitement links up with the exciting/persecuting part of the bad object. Guilt and disgust highlight the contaminated part of the self tied to the abusive object and link it to the healthy part of the self that rejects the abusive object. When sexual abuse has occurred early in life without narrative memory, the best clue to the child's experience comes from the therapist's recognition of affect states in the countertransference. Fairbairn's willingness to explore the dynamics of sexual abuse early in his career undoubtedly affected the eventual development of his object relations theory of psychic structure, and accounts for its relevance to thinking about and working with abused children.

References

Fairbairn, W. R. D. (1935). Medico-psychological aspects of child assault. *Mental Hygiene* 13: 1–16. In *From Instinct to Self: Vol. 2*, eds E. F. Birtles and D. E. Scharff, pp. 165–182. Northvale, NJ: Jason Aronson, 1994.

Chapter 16

The Nemesis within

Women, relationship addiction, and the moral defence

Carol Tosone

The goddess Nemesis, feared by Zeus and all gods for her ability to destroy and devour, has come to symbolize victorious retribution. She signifies the universal fear that too much happiness leads to hubris which must be punished. When applied to the realm of psychoanalytic inquiry and the psychology of women, it is fitting that Nemesis is personified as a woman. Each woman has a Nemesis within, a part of herself which potentially contains the seeds for her own self-demise. Many factors are involved in determining whether that seed will germinate, and her self-defeating behavior and accompanying affective and cognitive states may become manifest in a common gender specific path, such as eating disorders, depression, somatization, victimization, and a tenacious attachment to an abusive or unavailable partner, also referred to as relationship addiction. This chapter will address this last, and perhaps the most prevalent, self-destructive manifestation in women through a discussion and application of Fairbairn's (1943) *moral defence*.

The widening scope of addictions

The term "addiction" is frequently employed in the mental health lexicon, yet it is not the official term used in the *International Statistical Classification of Diseases and Related Health Problems, Tenth Revision (ICD-10)* or in the *Diagnostic and Statistical Manual of Mental Disorders, Fourth Edition, Text Revision (DSM-IV-TR)*. Initially applied to the abuse of alcohol and other substances, its use has broadened to include addiction to eating (Yeary and Heck 1989), gambling (Lesieur and Blume 1991; Davis 2002), spending (Barbanel 1996), sexual compulsivity (Goodman 1998), and relationships (Peele 1976, 1988).

Common to all these addictions is the use of something outside oneself, be it a substance or an object substitute, to manage intolerable affects and to serve in lieu of a substantive relationship with another. The self-medication hypothesis, first articulated by Khantzian (1985), emphasized that addicts gravitate toward a substance which will fill their psychological void. The addict's inability to regulate affective states originates in childhood and reflects the child's lack of internalization of parental care, manifesting in later life as a profound difficulty regulating self-esteem and self-care (Khantzian 1995, 1997). Similarly, Dodes (1996) observed that addictions serve as a self-destructive attempt to control one's internal affective experience. Loss of control and autonomy is a significant source of shame and guilt, and may contribute to the addict's denial of the severity of the problem.

Relationship addiction in women

Akin to other types of addiction, relationship addiction to an abusive or unavailable partner can be as injurious as substance abuse, but the addictive element is a compulsive need to connect with and remain attached to a particular person. Women in the throes of relationship addiction use their connection to such partners to modulate their internal affective states and, when separated from these partners, often report overwhelming feelings of despair, emptiness, and helplessness, as well as an inability to be sated. Concomitant to these emotions, many women express shame about the self-destructive nature of their behavior. They often avoid therapeutic help which would illuminate the extensiveness of the problem and possibly lead to the dissolution of the relationship, or, in the parlance of Fairbairn, exorcise internalized bad objects.

In his seminal work on the issue, Stanton Peele (1976) identifies relationship addiction as existing when the nature of one's attachment to another person lessens one's ability to attend to other personal needs in the environment. Characterized by an exclusive, inward focus, outside relationships are perceived as threatening to the primary bond and are often terminated in an effort to maintain a sense of security in the addictive relationship. Despite the ensuing isolation, the addictive relationship endures and is often mistaken for love.

Relationship addictions have been categorized broadly as either attraction or attachment types. Diamond (1988, 1991) contends that women demonstrate a proclivity toward attachment-type addictions, whereas men are prone to addictions of the attraction type. That is, the man's emphasis is on romance and attraction, and he may have difficulty committing to one relationship. By contrast, a woman may attach readily to one person, but have difficulty leaving the relationship should it deteriorate. Her commitment may be to an emotionally or physically abusive lover, or to one that is essentially unavailable, such as Tuch (2000) describes in the single woman–married man syndrome.

Popularized in the lay press as a largely women's phenomenon, numerous self-help titles have appeared on the topic, most notably *Women Who Love Too Much* (Norwood 1985); *Men Who Hate Women and the Women Who Love Them* (Forward and Torres 1986); *Is It Love or Addiction?* (Schaeffer 1987); and *Women, Sex, and Addiction* (Kasl 1990). As a trendy social idea, relationship addiction has received substantial attention, but, as a clinical construct, it has been conspicuously absent in the professional literature. In particular, the psychoanalytic scholarship devoted to the topic of women in addictive relationships is sparse and, when discussed, often comes under the rubric of masochism (Benjamin 1988; Tuch 2000). Authors vary their terminology depending on the nature of their readership, whether it be the lay public or a professional audience. Therefore, this chapter will attempt to bridge these two bodies of literature by applying psychoanalytic theories in general, and Fairbairn's concept of the moral defence in particular, to the understanding of relationship addiction in women.

The moral defence and the development of relationship addiction in women

Multiple psychoanalytic perspectives, including classical, feminist, attachment, and relational theories, can be aptly applied to the understanding of relationship addiction in women. While each offers important insights into the childhood antecedents of the disorder, it is Fairbairn's work which provides, I believe, the most profound understanding of the woman's motivation to protect this perceived vital connection. In his elaboration of an object relations theory of the personality, Fairbairn (1941, 1943) postulated that infants were object seeking from birth, and that aggression arises in response to frustration and deprivation, especially when the sense of security is disturbed in the mother–infant relationship. To be loved by one's parents and to have that love accepted by them is the child's greatest need. In the absence of such assurances, separation anxiety is pronounced and infantile dependence is maintained. Fairbairn suggests that frustration of such need is the greatest trauma a child can experience, one which leads to a defensive, unconscious internalization of the object with its exciting and frustrating aspects, an inevitable occurrence in childhood. As a result, internalized bad objects are present, to a greater or lesser extent, "in the minds of all of us at the deeper levels" (Fairbairn 1943: 65).

Consequently, the *moral defence* refers to the child's unconscious efforts to maintain good object relations with the frustrating yet needed internalized bad objects, by internalizing the burden of badness that resides in the external parental objects. In becoming bad, the child purges the object of its badness, and, if successful, experiences outer security at the price of inner insecurity. Or, in Fairbairn's often quoted words, "it is better to be a sinner in a world ruled by God than to live in a world ruled by the Devil" (1943: 66–67). The key aim of the moral defence is to convert the original situation of a child surrounded by external parental bad objects into a new situation where the child perceives external objects as good and the child as bad.

Having worked for years as a social work educator and clinician, I can attest to the validity and timeless quality of Fairbairn's keen observations on defensive internalization, particularly for children in the foster care system, and for victims of domestic violence and sexual abuse. My clinical experience supports the view that women, in general, have a greater propensity for internalization and so are more susceptible to the moral defence. Women involved in abusive relationships often justify their emotional pain and self-sacrificing behavior as being in the service of love. The justifications "I can't leave him because I love him" and "He can't help himself. He doesn't mean to hurt me" are commonly uttered to well-intentioned family and friends and in the privacy of the clinician's office. If the woman were involved with an unavailable or married man she might instead add, "If he could be with me now, he would. He can't, but I know he really loves me." She frequently attributes the rejecting response of her partner to her own behavior.

Emotions identified as love become the raison d'être for the relationship. Yet the same words which depict this type of love – dependent, destructive, excessive, and obsessive – can also be employed to describe addiction. In such relationships the woman often consciously believes that her emotional and physical survival is dependent on the love object, without which her existence would be meaningless. Her subjective experience is echoed in literature, music, and movies that depict the painful nature of dependent, romantic love. Such words and images from popular culture suggest the regressive longings of a helpless infant for its powerful mother, as well as a young child's need to elicit affection from a rejecting parent as symbolized by the absent or cruel lover.

In sharp contrast to addictive love, mature object love features secure attachments and no preoccupation with abandonment. Mature, loving women are capable of, and comfortable with, mutual dependency. According to Sternberg (1986, 1988), they are capable of maintaining the three ingredients essential to mature love relationships: intimacy, passion, and commitment. Like women in addictive relationships, these women tend to idealize their partners, but their idealization takes place in the context of an integrated, whole-object relationship, with the concomitant capacity for experiencing tenderness, guilt, and reparative trends. Their idealization is distinct from that of women in addictive relationships who idealize the love object at their own expense. Women capable of mature object love demonstrate a capacity for idealization which exalts the body as well as the total person and value system of the love object. Their capacity for passion and mature idealization, coupled with their ability to integrate love and aggression, with love as the dominant feature, constitutes an advanced developmental level of functioning (Kernberg 1974, 1995).

Women in addictive relationships are considered developmentally arrested "on the way to object constancy" (Mahler *et al.* 1975). Many were raised in chronically unpredictable home environments where their mothers were inconsistent in their displays of affection; the children were alternately rewarded and punished for the same behavior. As a result, these children

were not highly exploratory and became preoccupied with issues of abandonment. These trends continued throughout childhood, adolescence and
into adulthood.

These women tend to present in treatment with masochistic character
organization and are often drawn to challenging, unavailable, or abusive
people (Tosone 1998, 1999). Out of their tenacious longing for an idealized
partner, such women often project these qualities onto potential partners who
are not desirable. They readily fall in love out of a need for attachment. The
masochistic woman is sexually attracted to an idealized partner who initially
provides a whirlwind romance; later the partner may reject or abuse her. In
essence, the exciting and rejecting bad objects are personified by the lover.

Glickauf-Hughs and Wells (1995), applying Fairbairn's ideas to work with
couples, emphasized the reciprocal nature of the female masochistic–male
narcissistic dyad. They noted their interlocking dynamics: Narcissists have
a propensity for projecting unwanted parts of themselves onto others, while
masochists tend to internalize aspects of others that are not part of themselves. Women in addictive relationships are vulnerable to the unrealistic
promises which narcissists make early in the relationship, thereby enacting
their fantasies about ideal love and the ideal partner. That is, by attributing
the partner's negative characteristics to herself, the woman is free to view the
partner as ideal, much as a child needs to view a parent. Masochistic women
generally seek relationships where they are nurtured and gratified as a child
would be by a parent, yet they tend to become caretakers in the relationship
by treating others as they wish to be treated themselves. Submission and
caretaking assures them a sense of interpersonal control and security.

Additional theoretical contributions to the understanding of relationship addiction in women
Classical, attachment, feminist, and relational perspectives

Noteworthy in the discussion of theorists to follow is the extent to which each
emphasizes internalization as a key aspect of the development of masochism
in women. Writing subsequent to and often independent of Fairbairn's ideas
on defensive internalization, each expresses ideas which are largely compatible with his theoretical formulations. Writing from a classical perspective,
Lax (1977) for instance posits that as early as the oral and anal phases, the
infant girl experiences her mother as unloving and depriving. Regardless of
what she does, she does not feel accepted as good enough by her mother.
Since she needs to believe in the goodness of her mother on whom she
depends so heavily, she internalizes the sense of badness and blames herself
for the poor treatment she receives. In a similar vein, Bernstein (1983) maintains that this early mother–daughter dynamic has relevance in the discussion
of why women in physically abusive relationships seem to possess a greater
tolerance for physical pain. These women acquiesce to and identify with a

cruel, sadistic love object who, on an unconscious level, is reminiscent of the original love object, the mother. Through repetition compulsion, these women attempt to resolve elements in their early maternal relationship, the goal being a more satisfying outcome than occurred originally.

From the viewpoint of attachment theory, Hazan and Shaver (1987), Walker (1977), and Dutton and Painter (1993) have built on the work of Bowlby. Hazan and Shaver (1987) would categorize women in addictive relationships as anxious/ambivalent lovers given their tremendous fear of abandonment and craving for intimacy. While their relationships are of a highly dependent nature, they are repeatedly drawn to unavailable or inconsistent partners who frustrate their need and desire for security. Dutton and Painter (1993) developed traumatic bonding theory to address the finding that powerful emotional attachments are strengthened by intermittent good and bad treatment. Under threatening conditions, such as physical or emotional abuse, the attachment system is activated. In essence, the abuse serves to enhance the strength of the bond as the abused woman seeks greater proximity to her lover. Earlier, Walker (1977) coined the phrase "battered women syndrome" to describe the cyclical pattern of domestic violence. Essentially, the woman becomes "hooked" on the relationship as her partner's intermittent abuse produces a deeper, emotional connection, which interferes with her leaving – and remaining out of – the relationship.

From a relational perspective, Benjamin (1988) proposes that the masochistic woman submits to and adores the man in an effort to gain access to his power. The narcissistic male, controlling the woman by her own submission, loses the sense of recognition and connection he seeks. Benjamin notes that when a woman accepts her own object status and denial of self, she is re-enacting an early identification with her mother, a replication of the maternal attitude of self-alienation. In addition to the mother's contribution, Benjamin describes "ideal love" as a form of masochism that is rooted in the female child's relationship to her father. He serves as a representative of and link to the outside world, and by his example, he provides a model for freedom and self-realization. Should the girl's identificatory love for her father be thwarted in childhood, it can lead to a solidification of her identification with her mother, resulting in self-debasement.

The feminist perspective (Van Den Bergh 1991) also considers the subjugation and object status of women, but emphasis is on the imbalance of power between the genders in a patriarchal society. In regard to women in addictive relationships, feminist ideology has explanatory power primarily on the sociopolitical and interpersonal levels. On the macro level, the feminist perspective concludes that economic factors, such as wage differentials, employability, and need to care for dependants, as well as how men and women are acculturated into their respective gender-stereotyped roles of power and passivity can account for some women's tendencies to remain in addictive relationships. Much has been written in the feminist literature specific to the topic of domestic violence (Caplan 1993; Walker 1977; Westlund 1999). Caplan (1993), in particular, observes that women in addictive relationships do not enjoy pain per se, but rather pain is seen as a necessary evil to maintain ties to the desired symbolic love object. The woman's bond is not to the abuse, but rather to the partner's warmer, affectionate side which reflects her healthy need to be loved. Caplan (1993) and other feminist authors, such as Miller (1976), Chodorow (1978) and Gilligan (1982) underscore women's relational developmental needs. They consider the establishment and maintenance of close relationships as the guiding principle in women's lives. Their ideas have direct relevance for women in addictive relationships who are generally more attuned to their partner's needs than their own. Pain, whether emotional or physical, becomes the obligatory cost to preserve the bond.

Feminist, classical, attachment, and relational paradigms are valuable clinical tools in understanding the etiology of relationship addiction and informing the course of treatment. These paradigms underscore the import of internalization as a feature in women's development and defensive responses. The following case example will illustrate clinical features of relationship addiction.

Case illustration and discussion

When Janine arrived for her first appointment, she was disheveled and hastily clad in her neighbor's large clothes that hid her petite frame. As would become her custom in treatment, she began the session with an apology. On this day she apologized for her appearance, drawing attention to her right arm resting in a sling. She spent much of the previous evening in the emergency room awaiting treatment for her sprained arm, an injury sustained when her husband pushed her during an argument. Following the hospital visit she sought refuge in her neighbor's home where she planned to remain until her husband, Tom, came to his senses.

Janine spent the initial session and many subsequent ones analyzing and apologizing for his irrational and sometimes explosive behavior. She knew the intimate details of his unmet childhood needs, but none of her own. She focused her discussion on their courtship, a time when Tom was loving, generous, and nurturing of her career as a realtor. Janine convinced herself that, without Tom, life was meaningless. Only he fully knew her and could satisfy her hungry longing for love. His outbursts, she concluded, were primarily her fault. Janine initially sought treatment to understand him better and to make herself a more responsive partner.

Janine and Tom had a well-established pattern, one consistent with the clinical observations of Walker (1977) and Dutton and Painter (1993). Janine and her husband would get into a heated argument, generally over his excessive drinking or her inadequate housekeeping, followed by his berating and sometimes hitting her. She would leave briefly, but find the separation intolerable. Each time she would return convinced that she could not live without him and be more determined to make the relationship work. To do so, she had to neglect other meaningful relationships and her career, two areas that were increasingly being compromised.

During the assessment and early treatment phase, Janine exhibited the classic features of relationship addiction: obsessive longing for and idealization of the symbolic love object; impairment in other areas of functioning due to the preoccupation with the relationship; and lack of control over her affective state. Much of our discussion centered on her feelings of panic and dread at the prospect of living without her husband. When apart, unbearable feelings of emptiness and loneliness consumed her, especially on those occasions when he left home. Her subjective state was suggestive of an infant unable to self-soothe in her mother's absence, as if there was no certainty in the mother's return. Her preoccupation with abandonment was pronounced as she had difficulty eating, sleeping, and functioning in her daily life. This experience is evocative of an early psychosomatic memory of object loss. When reunited with her husband, however, she enjoyed a blissful symbiotic union where words were superfluous in communicating mutual love and understanding.

As treatment continued, we spoke at length about her fear of being able to survive alone, not only emotionally but financially. At age 35, she was already an established and successful realtor, but she maintained the self-image of a helpless child and "people pleaser." She described herself as a self-proclaimed "codependent," a term she learned in Al-Anon when she was previously married to an abusive alcoholic. She left her first husband to marry Tom as he was nicer and drank less often. While Tom did not drink as heavily, he was easily hurt and prone to narcissistic rages that sometimes escalated to physical force.

As we addressed her desire to attune herself to his unmet needs, I observed the disparity between her keen awareness of his desires and lack of her own. While she had an intellectual understanding of how she was repeating the past in the present, she spoke about her childhood without emotion. That is, Janine knew she was negatively impacted by her depressed, dependent mother and her critical, alcoholic father, but her emotional energy was centered on her relationship with Tom. According to Janine, her parents were elderly and frail, and they were not the cause of her current problems. The goals of alleviating her depression and desire to have a healthier marriage provided the only impetus for Janine to explore her harrowing past.

Early memories first described as "no big deal," became laden with emotion in the late phase of treatment. Her earliest memory at age 5, for instance, involved her father smashing a pizza in her face because she would not eat. Janine had just returned elated from her first piano recital and when she would not heed her father's angry insistence that she eat, he held her head back and forced the pizza in her mouth. She recalled tearfully her feelings of anger and humiliation at his abusive behavior. Janine also wondered out loud as to her mother's whereabouts on that day. It was rare when she could recall her mother's consistent availability and protection, especially those times when her father would have angry outbursts. While he was rarely physically abusive, he was prone to angry outbursts, especially while drunk.

Janine's early memories about her mother proved equally illuminating. At age 7 she stood outside of church with her mother trying to stifle her urge to say a curse word. At the time, Janine rebuked herself for being "a very bad girl." In recalling this memory, Janine mentioned that her mother nearly died when giving birth to her (due to a severe hemorrhage). Her mother was cautioned by the physician not to have other children as it might be life threatening. From childhood on, Janine was constantly aware of her mother's frailty and felt guilty whenever she was angry with her.

Janine's frequent violent dreams, however, were filled with gruesome murders of her mother, father, and Tom. There were many murderers in her dreams but she was never the agent. Treatment addressed her bitter disappointments with these important love objects and her fear that her anger would devastate them. As she gradually came to appreciate the depth of her anger and pain, she began to understand her fear of being alone. She came to realize that she invested more in the care of others than in her own self-development. The prospect of being alone reminded her of her helpless state as a child.

Janine has taken important steps in the therapeutic process. She has a better grasp on the unconscious elements involved in her addictive relationship, as well as the larger familial and societal issues about women's traditional role as nurturer. Correspondingly, she understands that her marital relationship represents an addiction, not mature love. Janine has become more self-protective in the marital relationship and remains committed to the relationship as her husband has sought professional help for himself.

Conclusion

Janine's situation is illustrative of Fairbairn's moral defence in operation. In essence, she developed the template for relationship addiction in her early childhood and was drawn to an intermittently responsive partner whom she needed to idealize, and so she attributed the partner's negative attributes to herself. Like countless women in her situation, she experienced in her love relationship an obsessive longing, punctuated by short bursts of intense gratification and longer periods of yearning, frustration, and abuse. For women in such relationships, the initial exciting object is transformed into a rejecting one, but it is difficult for the woman to accept that the previously caring person is now critical and rejecting. The partner is perceived to have all the necessary narcissistic supplies and the woman desperately tries to get the partner to respond favorably. Her tenacious belief that the partner can provide what she needs is reinforced by the intermittent positive attention which leaves her feeling that her partner's love is potentially available. It is only when the original pains and frustrations of childhood are exposed that the internal demons Fairbairn so eloquently described can be exorcised.

References

Barbanel, L. (1996). *Sex, Money and Power: Smart Ways to Resolve Money Conflicts and Keep Them from Sabotaging your Closest Relationships*. New York: Macmillan.
Benjamin, J. (1988). *The Bonds of Love*. New York: Pantheon Books.
—— (1995). *Like Subjects, Love Objects: Essays on Recognition and Sexual Difference*. New Haven, CT: Yale University Press.
Bernstein, D. (1983). *Female Identity Conflict in Clinical Practice*. Northvale, NJ: Jason Aronson.
Caplan, P. (1993). *The Myth of Women's Masochism*. Toronto: University of Toronto Press.
Chodorow, N. (1978). *The Reproduction of Mothering: Psychoanalysis and the Sociology of Gender*. Berkeley, CA: University of California Press.
Davis, D. (2002). The queen of diamonds: women and compulsive gambling. In S. L. A. Straussner and S. Brown (eds) *The Handbook of Addiction Treatment for Women*, pp. 99–126. San Francisco: Jossey-Bass.
Diamond, J. (1988). *Looking for Love in All the Wrong Places: Overcoming Romantic and Sexual Addictions*. New York: G.P. Putnam's Sons.
—— (1991). Looking for love in all the wrong places. In N. Van Den Bergh (ed.), *Feminist Perspectives on Addictions*, pp. 167–180. New York: Springer.
Dodes, L. (1996). Compulsion and addiction. *Journal of the American Psychoanalytic Association* 44: 815–835.
Dutton, D. and Painter, S. (1993). Emotional attachments in abusive relationships: a test of traumatic bonding theory. *Violence and Victims* 8(2): 105–120.
Fairbairn, W.R.D. (1941). A revised psychopathology of the psychoses and psychoneuroses. In W.R.D. Fairbairn (1981) *Psychoanalytic Studies of the Personality*, pp. 28–58. London: Routledge & Kegan Paul.
—— (1943). The repression and the return of bad objects. In W. R. D. Fairbairn *Psychoanalytic Studies of the Personality*, pp. 58–81. London: Routledge & Kegan Paul, 1952.
—— (1954). *An Object Relations Theory of the Personality*. New York: Basic Books.
Forward, S. and Torres, J. (1986). *Men Who Hate Women and the Women Who Love Them*. New York: Bantam.
Gilligan, C. (1982). *In a Different Voice*. Cambridge, MA: Harvard University Press.
Glickauf-Hughes, C. and Wells, M. (1995). *Treatment of the Masochistic Personality: An Interactional Object Relations Approach to Psychotherapy*. Northvale, NJ: Jason Aronson.
Goodman, A.G. (1998). *Sexual Addiction: An Integrated Approach*. Madison, WI: International Universities Press.
Hazan, C. and Shaver, P. (1987). Romantic love conceptualized as an attachment process. *Journal of Personality & Social Psychology* 52: 511–524.

Kasl, C.D. (1990). *Women, Sex and Addiction*. New York: Harper & Row.

Kernberg, O. (1974). Mature love: prerequisites and characteristics. *Journal of the American Psychoanalytic Association* 22: 743–768.

—— (1995). *Love Relations: Normality and Pathology*. New Haven, CT: Yale University Press.

Khantzian, E. (1985). The self-medication hypothesis of addictive disorders. *American Journal of Psychiatry* 142: 1259–1264.

—— (1995). Self-regulation vulnerabilities in substance abusers: treatment implications. In S. Dowling (ed.) *The Psychology and Treatment of Addictive Behavior*, pp. 17–42. Madison, CT: International Universities Press.

—— (1997). The self-medication hypothesis of substance use disorders: a reconsideration and recent applications. *Harvard Review of Psychiatry* 4: 231–244.

Lax, R. (1977). The role of internalization in the development of certain aspects of female masochism: ego psychological considerations. *International Journal of Psychoanalysis* 58: 289–300.

Lesieur, H.R. and Blume, S. (1991). When Lady Luck loses: women and compulsive gambling. In N. Van Den Bergh (ed.) *Feminist Perspectives on Addictions*, pp. 181–197. New York: Springer.

Mahler, M., Pine, F. and Bergman, A. (1975). *The Psychological Birth of the Human Infant*. New York: Basic Books.

Miller, J. (1976). *Toward a New Psychology of Women*. Boston, MA: Beacon Press.

Norwood, R. (1985). *Women Who Love Too Much*. New York: Pocket Books.

Peele, S. (1976). *Love and Addiction*. New York: New American Library.

—— (1988). Fools for love: the romantic ideal, psychological theory, and addictive love. In R. Sternberg and M. Barne (eds) *The Psychology of Love*, pp. 159–188. New Haven, CT: Yale University Press.

Schaeffer, B. (1987). *Is it Love or is it Addiction?* New York: MJF Books.

Sternberg, R. (1986). A triangular theory of love. *Psychological Review* 97: 119–135.

Sternberg, R. (1988). Triangulating love. In R. Sternberg and M. Barnes (eds) *The Psychology of Love*. New Haven, CT: Yale University Press.

Tosone, C. (1998). Revisiting the 'myth' of feminine masochism. *Clinical Social Work Journal* 26(4): 413–426.

—— (1999). Illusion, disillusion, and reality in romantic love. In C. Tosone and T. Aiello (eds) *Love and Attachment: Contemporary Issues and Treatment Considerations*, pp. 3–24. Northvale, NJ: Jason Aronson.

Tuch, R. (2000). *The Single Woman–Married Man Syndrome*. Northvale, NJ: Jason Aronson.

Van Den Bergh, N. (1991). Having bitten the apple: a feminist perspective on addictions. In N. Van Den Bergh (ed.) *Feminist Perspectives on Addictions*, pp. 3–30. New York: Springer.

Walker, L. (1977). *The Battered Woman*. New York: Harper & Row.

Westlund, A. (1999). Pre-modern and modern power: Foucault and the case of domestic violence. *Journal of Women in Culture & Society* 24(4): 1045–1066.

Yeary, J. R. and Heck. C. L. (1989). Dual diagnosis: eating disorders and psychoactive substance dependence. *Journal of Psychoactive Drugs* 21: 239–249.

Chapter 17

Aggression in the couple relationship

Fairbairn's object relations theory and Hendrix's Imago relationship therapy

Stephen Plumlee

A friend recalled going alone to a restaurant. The hostess approached him and asked, "Are you one?" At first he thought the answer obvious; after a few seconds he recognized that the question bore cause for reflection. Is one ever really only one?

Awareness of the complexity of the internal relational system of each individual and, consequently, of every external relationship as well, is the legacy of psychoanalytic object relations thinking. The process of self-definition is amply demonstrated by Fairbairn and Sutherland, and by Harville Hendrix, who developed the Imago system of working with couples: a method of doing couples therapy recognized in North America, but still not well known in other parts of the world. The theories of Fairbairn and Hendrix are both based on the premise that the human organism defines itself in terms of its relationships.

According to Fairbairn (1952b, 1954), the yearning for connection is universal; when love is withheld from infants or given in ways that threaten to consume them, they feel rage and aggressively try to force a good connection or repudiate it. In so doing, according to Fairbairn's object relations theory, infants create psychic structures filled with rage and aggression, which seek expression in adult relationships. In terms of Hendrix's Imago relationship theory (1988, 1996), as adults of marriageable age, they follow the resulting internal expectations into relationships that replicate the early defective ones, with concomitant anger and aggression. Imago therapy deals not with individual personality structures but with the effect of developmentally induced expectations on relationships. Rage and aggression in adult intimate partnerships result from defective relationships in earlier developmental phases. I will describe effective tools used in Imago therapy for resolving those emotions and behaviors: the mirror, verbalization, and the container mode of communication, all of which require therapists to look deeply into their own rage and aggression so as to work toward resolution.

Imago

The term imago has been employed variously in psychoanalytic literature. Freud (1930) first used it to refer to the internal representation of a powerful gratifying, frustrating, or threatening person in the life experience of the infant and young child (Sutherland 1994a). Infants develop these inner figures such as a mother imago and a father imago, which stand for those who have satisfied or frustrated their yearnings for sucking and nurture. Unless those imagoes are remedied, they will determine the infants' expectations of all the people who might meet their needs.

Melanie Klein (1929) said that the painful affects of annihilatory anxiety and intense aggression stemming from the death instinct lead to developing persecutory imagoes. Pleasurable experience under the influence of the life instinct leads to good breast-mother imagoes. When the affect within the relationship is too disturbing and inner objects become too frightening or too enviably good, the feared object is controlled by being split into parts and projected outside the self.

Fairbairn (1952a) moves from Klein's perspective on libido and aggression deriving from instincts expressed as biological needs requiring gratification. The first psychoanalyst to identify libido as the desire for relationship, Fairbairn thought that libido was a primary yearning for relationship, and that aggression resulted from frustration of that wish (Sutherland 1994b). The imagoes of good mother and good father express experiences of receiving warmth, closeness, and connection, and imagoes of bad mother and bad father result when they are withheld (Fairbairn) or spoiled by the child's aggression (Klein).

The term imago derives primarily from Carl Jung. Jung (1975) saw the imago as a generic template, a composite of the multitude of experiences that the infant has with mother and father and other significant figures. The child combines that variety of memories into one imago that represents expectations of all subsequent figures expected to provide care or nurturance. It is from the Jungian use of the term imago that Hendrix drew his inspiration. In the Hendrix model of Imago relationship therapy (1988) intimate partners create from their early experiences with significant caregivers a vast internal set of beliefs and expectations about all future intimate figures. To the extent that infantile experiences with caregivers were painful and even threatening, and therefore had to be repressed or suppressed, they remain unconscious in the imago. The largely unconscious quality of the imago makes it both a predictor of the partner to be selected, as well as a driver in the selection process. The subject is always trolling for an object whose behaviors and appearances fit the unconscious model. Thus the imago tells its subject not only what concatenation of qualities to look for, but is also the "search engine" that discriminates which object to select.

There has never been an attempt from within the Imago therapy movement to map the development of psychic structures within the individual, as does Fairbairn, for example, with the concepts of central self, libidinal self, and antilibidinal self. The focus in Imago theory has been rather to describe the development of psychic processes within the unitary self. Nevertheless a major attraction of the Imago model has been its compatibility with the object relations mode of conceptualizing the person and with a religious view of the person in relation to God. For me its applicability to the Eastern Orthodox Christian tripartite experience of God and of the human person is particularly appealing. These two perspectives have profoundly enriched my understanding of the psychic person as definitively a relational being, externally with other persons, and internally with the substructures of the psyche.

Theory within the Imago therapy tradition has centered on the developmental stages of childhood and early adulthood, conceptualizing the related characterological patterns as reactions to wounding from deficiencies in parenting. These wounds excite fears, which in turn elicit typical adaptations or defensive maneuvers. All patterns reactive to content in the imago are based on fear of one kind or another – fear of abandonment by a withholding parental figure, fear of being consumed by a needy parent who does not provide adequate care, fear of being used, fear of being shamed. In any case, the traditional patterns of fight or flight (attacking or fleeing the frightening object), and seduction (mating with the object perceived to be threatening) are all seen to devolve ultimately from fear of loss of being, death.

Aggression from the Imago perspective

Theories of anger that highlight social learning seem most compatible with the Imago vision. Angry and aggressive impulses always develop in a social context. Every person is a product of a relationship, and rage and aggressiveness are experienced in a relational context (Shelly 2002). Anger and aggression are the results of the individual's relational and social journey. When any aspect of the unitary self has been suppressed, derided, or denied, the reaction is self-hatred and aggression towards oneself. As a defense against the threat of loss of being in death, the rage is turned outward toward the perceived threatening, powerful object.

The connective space between intimate partners is often contaminated when one dislikes the other because of differences from aspects of the self that are valued, and because of similarities to aspects of the self that are hated. When the connective space is a void, the self uses aggression to protect itself from loss of connection and annihilation, even when the behavior aims to hurt or destroy the other (Shelly 2002). It is as if each partner believes that aggression is the only way to achieve visibility in the eyes of the other, to wriggle out from being absorbed in the other, and to sustain being in relationship. The central question for me as a couple therapist is how to deal with rage and aggression without actually provoking more of it.

Fairbairn on aggression

Fairbairn's thinking on aggression is predicated on the idea of a personality developed from reaction to defective parenting practices (1954). Coming along a different route, Hendrix arrived later at the idea of a person defined by the quality of developmental relationships (1988). However, Fairbairn and Hendrix do not meet at quite the same crossroad. In Hendrix's writing, the person can only be perceived and identified in the context of a relationship. In Fairbairn's writing, the person is derived from reactions to the quality of parenting received (1952a). Thus Fairbairn offers a more psychoanalytic view in proposing that the person actively creates the self by splitting off subparts of libidinal self and antilibidinal self from the pristine central self. The libidinal self demands fulfillment of libidinal yearnings for connection, and so protects and sustains itself in the relational matrix. The antilibidinal self suppresses its yearnings and plays at self-sufficiency to preserve a feeling of acceptance in the relationship. In object relations theory, the person is constructed in relationship, and indeed defined by ongoing relationship, but the therapeutic focus is on the relationship among the internal selves. The person living in schizoid isolation can still work at therapeutic healing among intrapsychic structures.

Fairbairn (1952b) sees aggression as forcible control over the object, by expulsion or retention. He believes that it develops in the late oral stage, when the object thought to be bad may be bitten to destroy it. This late oral phase presents a profound problem for the self: How can the self love the needed and desired object without destroying it through hate? The yearning for love with the object (libido) and simultaneous hate (aggression) for the same object creates ambivalence once the person has the capacity to differentiate the hated object (bad mother) and the loved object (good mother) as aspects of the same person. In Fairbairn's scheme, libido and aggression may be ambivalently present in attitude toward the same object. The libidinal self yearns for the good object, cathexis, connection, and genital gratification, and is enraged at the frustration of these desires. The antilibidinal self seeks to reject its dependence on the object by denial of its craving for connection. It labels the object bad and attempts to repudiate it psychically and to eliminate it by destructive biting. The antilibidinal self is enraged at having to give up connection and intimacy, as well as the inefficacy of its efforts to crush its dependence on the object. When rage takes over as a means of overcoming the dysphoria of fear, in a flash all rational and realistic ego functions of the central self and the powerful yearnings of the libidinal self disappear. When epinephrine floods the brain and provokes heightened fear of rejection, abandonment, or annihilation, and norepinephrine release follows immediately, these physiological changes arouse intense urges to attack and destroy (Lidz 1983).

Fairbairn addresses the processes of introjection, projection, and rageful aggression, both passive and active, which occur when the triadic self displaces its representations onto others in later life. He does not, however, speak of the system of selecting a partner for those purposes, based on both the libidinal yearning and the destructive rage excited by the imagoes, as does Hendrix who raises the questions of how one gets to the relational home freighted with craving and hate. However, Fairbairn does provide understanding of the intrapsychic structures in their drama of love and destruction.

Remediation

The therapeutic process of healing lies in recreating the aggressive relationship, based in unconscious fearful reactions to imago stimuli, as a healing one. That movement requires building a state of trust, safety, empathy, and visibility to the partner. How is the therapist going to help the couple achieve that posture? What therapeutic process can remedy the dreary, exhausting, and destructive cycles of couples who designate the object of love as the anamnestic bad object, project their self-hatred onto their partners, and aggressively attack their partners and themselves. I will describe three areas of therapeutic process that I have found effective: *mirroring*, *naming the affect*, and *container mode of communication*.

Mirroring

The first approach is of an individual nature, although often used to advantage in a couples' therapy setting. It consists in effecting the return of the bad objects from the unconscious and promoting the dissolution of the cathexis to them (Fairbairn 1952a). This aim can be attained in several ways. One of the most effective is to mirror to the person the attributions and physical behaviors directed at the partner and reveal their contradictory nature. That moment provides a precious opportunity for the therapist to interpret the person's two-sided yearning for, and sadistic attack on, the object. In this way, each member of the couple appreciates both sides of their ambivalence toward each other, and learns to accept it and transform it without projecting it onto the partner.

Reflective listening or mirroring has become a popular tool in many therapies, and can be effective when therapists judiciously paraphrase, put into their own words what they have heard, and integrate their impressions. However, if the therapist literally simply repeats what the patients have said they think and feel, and the partners learn merely to echo what one another has said, the process insidiously becomes trivialized, the patients feel repudiated, they turn aggression onto the therapist, and capsize the therapy. The therapist may not have received the message explicitly, but simply realizes one day that the therapeutic relationship has entered a downward spiral and is impervious to attempts at reversal.

Naming the affect

Therapists having difficulty with the intense, fragmenting expression of hate and rage in a fragile, borderline or psychotic patient may find it helpful to interrupt the outpouring of affect and ask for names of the feelings and thoughts. This has a calming effect. Although this approach is clearly a non-analytic relationship therapy, I think of its effectiveness in terms of object relations theory. I believe it is helpful because it enables the patient's own central ego strengths.

Container mode of communication

The container dialogue is useful because it allows for a full range of affect without overwhelming either partner, provided it is done under the firm direction of the therapist functioning as a coach (Hendrix 1996). I find that patients often feel safe, valued, and attended to by firm interventions from the therapist instead of feeling abandoned to their own floundering and shame-producing excesses. The container dialogue is performed with the partners seated facing each other; the therapist centered on them. One partner, the sender of the communication, tells of an annoying or distressing action taken by the other; the other partner, the receiver of the communication, listens and paraphrases it. The therapist helps the listener to create a psychic armor against being personally wounded and encourages the sender to unfold the full depth of anger gradually, with the approval of the fortified receiver and the assistance of the therapist. When the rage peaks, the sender experiences an implosion of hurt and fear, often with tears and other physical expressions of distress. The therapist coaches the sender to connect the present affective moment to feelings in early childhood relationships and encourages the receiver to respond with warmth and acceptance, soothing sounds, and perhaps physical touch. When the sender is emotionally spent, the receiver behaves in ways that are empathic and reassuring, in preparation for a change in the receiver's behavior that will be healing to the wounds identified from the sender's early relationship. The final – and essential – last stage is that the sender initiates high-energy play that the two engage in together. I have found that the container dialogue can be remarkably healing by promoting differentiation between the partners, safe interaction between two more distinct persons, and a stronger libidinal communication.

Techniques aside, my stance as traveling companion with an individual or couple in a therapeutic process demands that I look courageously into my own structures of self-hatred, self-protection, and aggression toward the other, as well as my own libidinal yearnings for connection. It would be wise to remember that the unique character of the analytic method is that its means of investigation is the investigator himself, using his own personal life experience as it has been expanded by his or her education.

Summary

Every human being is a person in relationship. I find it helpful to think of the wounds and distortions of character as deriving from relational expectations embedded in imago memories. For me, however, imago memories are useful only when I seat them in a psychoanalytic understanding of the internal structures of the personality warring with each other and protecting the self. Fairbairn's concept of the triadic self, protecting its viability within the self and managing its external relationships, enables me to conceptualize the dilemma of the partners in couple therapy with me and design the most appropriate, respectful and caring therapeutic intervention for them and their relationship.

My initial anecdote holds true at the end of the day. One is never only one, and knowledge of one's own interactive parts makes for reconciliation and integration.

References

Fairbairn, W. R. D. (1952a). Repression and return of bad objects. *Psychoanalytic Studies of the Personality*, pp. 59–81. London: Tavistock.
—— (1952b). *Psychoanalytic Studies of the Personality*. London: Tavistock.
—— (1954). *An Object Relations Theory of the Personality*. New York: Basic Books.
Freud, S. (1930). Civilization and its discontents. *Standard Edition* 21: 64–145.
Hendrix, H. (1988). *Getting the Love You Want*. New York: Henry Holt.
—— (1996). *Getting the Love You Want: A Couples Workshop Manual*, rev. edn. Winter Park, FL: Institute for Imago Relationship therapy.
Jung, C. (1975). *Archetypes and the Collective Unconscious*. In *The Collected Works of C. G. Jung*, Vol. 1. London: Routledge.
Klein, M. (1929). Personification in the play of childern. In *Love, Guilt and Reparation and Other Works 1921–1945*, pp. 199–209. London: Hogarth, 1975.
Lidz, T. (1983). *The Person*. New York: Basic Books.
Shelly, E. (2002). Reflecting on anger/aggression regarding the use of the container exercise. Presented at the annual conference of the Association for Imago Relationship therapy, Chicago, October 25–27.
Sutherland, J. D. (1994a). Object relations theory and the conceptual model of psychoanalysis. In *The Autonomous Self: The Work of John D. Sutherland*, ed. J. S. Scharff, pp. 3–24. Northvale, NJ: Jason Aronson.
—— (1994b). Fairbairn's contribution. In *The Autonomous Self: The Work of John D. Sutherland*, ed. J. S. Scharff, pp. 53–59. Northvale, NJ: Jason Aronson.

Chapter 18

Theories of art and theory as art

Torbjörn Borgegård

Introduction

Every psychological theory bears the signature of its creator. It is not possible to understand a theory without considering the person who constructed it. For instance, Freud, Jung, Reich and Rank developed metapsychological constructions which are by and large a reflection of their personal lives and experiences, and their theories were designed to deal with personal motives. The personal and the subjective generally play such a large part in theoretical formulations that they must be taken into account. The same holds true for studying the construction of a work of art. Indeed, the maker of psychoanalytic theory may fruitfully be compared with the artist: both pursue an intensely personal project. To explore the construction of a theory, it is helpful to use the psycho-biographical approach of Atwood and Stolorow (1993) which applies a hermeneutic method (Ricoeur 1974) to analyzing theoretical texts and relating biographical material to theoretical statements. When the theory maker's work of art is one that expounds on the creation of art, a unique opportunity for study presents itself. Ronald Fairbairn provides such an opportunity.

In this chapter, I apply a psycho-biographical method to Fairbairn's theories with reference to his published work on the creating of art (Fairbairn 1938a) and the experience of art (Fairbairn 1938b) collected by Birtles and Scharff (1994). I believe that these two articles provide a key to all Fairbairn's theory building. I do not focus on his opinions about art from a history-of-art perspective but on his views on creativity and on the psychological meaning of the art product. I draw parallels between the creation of art and the creative work of formulating psychological theories, and view Fairbairn's productions in the light of his personal situation.

The arguments against such an adventure are many. You can argue that the subjective is merely a style, a surface that does not affect the core of the theory, or an interference that disqualifies the whole theory project. You can object that the subjective element in the constructing of theories is the personal colour that really should have been taken away. You can argue that, if theories are to be generally applicable, then the personal elements are like countertransference in classical psychoanalysis – something that should have been eliminated through personal analysis. On the contrary, my view takes its starting point in accepting the inevitability of the subjective element.

Art theory

In his 1938a article, Fairbairn focuses on the artist. He sees the artist's work as a creative act and an expression of lust and joy. He thinks that art derives both from work and play. He writes:

> So far as artistic activity is concerned, we must regard it as falling into the "play" class in proportion as the artist seeks the pleasures of artistic creation; but it must be regarded as falling into the "work" class in proportion as the artist harnesses his art to some ulterior motive such as making a living, gaining social prestige, or propagating a cause.
>
> (Fairbairn 1938a: 383)

Defined as playing, producing art means creating something for fun. From this standpoint Fairbairn states that everything that has come about in this way is art. And therefore there is no difference among artists – the little child is as much an artist as Michaelangelo. Fairbairn distances himself from what he calls a puritanical attitude that all art which does not aim at the salvation of the soul is sinful, mad, and without legitimacy.

Fairbairn finds a striking analogy between dreamwork and artwork. He finds support in Freud's (1900) opinion that dreams are an outlet for suppressed wishes in the dreamer. He sees the condensation of unconscious material as one way to reduce psychic tension, both when the result is the manifest dream and when the condensation work results in a piece of art. The quality in the piece of art is proportional to the pressure from the unconscious fantasies in combination with the strength of repression. When unconscious fantasies can be seen too clearly they result in bad art – as in crude surrealism where even symbolization is too overt. But it is not only libidinal wishes that are worked through. Even destructive forces add to the creation of art.

The child's striving for compensation and restitution is a means of dealing with destruction (Klein 1929). In the balancing of the destructive and libidinal impulses directed towards the love object, the restitutional principle appears and leads development in the direction of truth, goodness, and beauty, and sometimes also religion. Fairbairn states that this principle plays a large part in the creation of art. Fairbairn puts forward the idea that, in the light of Freud's later developed structural theory (Freud 1923), dreamwork must be seen as an ego function that modifies both id impulses and demands from the superego in a positive way. For art, it is important that the piece is so constructed that it can be presented in a form that escapes the censorship of the ego ideal or the superego. It must not be so close to unconscious symbolic content that it escapes condensation. Good art appears when there is the right balance between these forces. This is a common motive in children's creative work. When the child draws Mom or Dad the picture is a work of repair that balances destructive and loving forces. Fairbairn states that the quality of the child's artistic creativity improves after the development of the superego, and that creating art is to be compared to a moral act. That is true even for that kind of art creation in which the purpose is to limit inner tensions, find relief, and have fun. Incidentally, Fairbairn's psychology of art papers were written before he refined his idea of the superego as a function carried out by a constellation of the ideal object, the antilibidinal ego, and the rejecting object. Later he might have located the development of the moral sense in a different way.

Aesthetic experience

When Fairbairn discusses the aesthetic experience (1938b) he distances himself from the definitions of art that combine art with beauty. In his view, anything that is made for fun is art, and the artistic product "represents a tribute of restitution paid by the artist's ego to his superego, provides a means of surmounting the difficulties inherent in prevalent conceptions in aesthetics" (p. 398). Art is evoked as a development of the discovery of the object, and the discovery itself constitutes the creative act. Art is developed from the fulfilment of the artist's wishes. The found object finds its place right in the personal needs of the artist, sometimes as through a sudden discovery. Artists have a well-developed ability to find objects in their surroundings or in their inner world and give them good form. If this found object that the artist offers as art corresponds with an unconscious object carried within the viewer, then the viewer resonates with the art, and the artist is successful. Perhaps the viewer likes the piece of art, finds it beautiful, useful, or instructive, or hates it. An emotional connection has been made. Good art also includes an element of surprise. It makes room for a sudden discovery. If the artist is not successful it may be because it does not have the right balance. If the piece is oversymbolized the artist has not submitted to the demands of his superego, and then the contents of his unconscious are shown too explicitly. The content has no artistic quality regardless of the technical brilliance. If it is undersymbolized, the superego of the artist has been too severe, and then the artist has nothing to tell the viewer, and the work is sterile.

Time-related elements

Fairbairn's texts were naturally influenced by the times in which he lived. He took artistic examples from the 1936 London exhibition of surrealistic art, which he visited in the fall of 1937, and from Read's book *Art and Society* (Read 1936). Fairbairn was greatly interested in art and he often visited art galleries (Sutherland 1989). But he did not particularly like surrealistic art even if it was technically superb, because he felt that it was oversymbolized, presenting unconscious material without working it through. In spite of that limitation, it provided good material for illustrating Fairbairn's reasoning.

Fairbairn wrote his articles on art (1938a, 1938b) during his "pre-Fairbairnian" period. He used Freudian terminology, but he also referred to Klein's opinions about the destructiveness inherent in children (Klein 1929), and thereby showed her influence on him. The articles on art were written before Fairbairn's main theory developing period (which according to Sutherland 1989 happened in the period 1940 to 1957), but they were forerunners of what was to come nevertheless.

In his paper, (1938a), Fairbairn uses simple technical language close to Freudian terms like the "pleasure principle," and everyday words like "fun." Fairbairn qualifies his use of the word "fun" to include the relief felt when inner tension is released, which widens the concept and leaves space for that artistic creativity that is motivated not only by giving joy but also by expressing inner pressure. Fairbairn argues that Freud's model of dreamwork must be altered. For Fairbairn, dreamwork is not only a negatively censoring work as Freud suggested, but it is also a positive striving from the ego in relation to the superego. In his doctoral thesis, Fairbairn (1929a) sees the superego as the most important part in Freud's structural theory, and it becomes one of the foundations for his own theoretical work (1929b). Fairbairn acknowledges the id only in connection with the superego's censuring of id impulses in dreamwork. He thinks of libido as a set of impulses which embodies the life principle and expresses itself by self-preservation, sex, and love (1930). Destructive impulses represent a denial of the life principle. Even if the aim of the repression is to preserve the ego from the consequences brought about by these destructive tendencies, the close connection between destructive and libidinal strivings in early childhood lead to a significant repression of libido.

Sutherland (1989) treated Fairbairn's two articles on art as immature works. He was especially critical about Fairbairn's idea that art is anything made for fun, a statement that he found unscientific. He did not connect the content of the papers on art to the themes of Fairbairn's life at their time of writing. Yet he gathered and published the information that lets me put these papers in their context. Sutherland described Fairbairn's personal situation at the time when these articles were conceived as one full of difficulties. Fairbairn had been deprived of his position as a teacher in the Mental Philosophy Department at the University of Edinburgh for ideological reasons. The professors in authority in psychology and psychiatry did not want to encourage psychoanalytic thinking, especially not if it was influenced by Klein. Sutherland also described Fairbairn's marriage as one that was under strain from his wife's objections to the direction of his work and his heavy workload. Encouragement to continue came from the warm reception his articles met with in psychoanalytical circles, including the Scottish branch of the British Psychological Society and the British Psychoanalytical Society in London. (They were also sent to Freud.) I propose that it was the psychoanalytical work that gave Fairbairn joy in life and relief from the strain in his marriage in spite of the family difficulties caused by his devotion to psychoanalysis. His lone pursuit of psychoanalytic practice, theory building, and presenting papers is reminiscent of the loneliness of the artist who creates his isolation in order to seek later public recognition (Read 1931, quoted in Fairbairn 1938a).

Why is it so annoying to Sutherland and to some of us that Fairbairn insisted that doing art is doing something for fun? That Fairbairn did not include these articles in the book *Psychoanalytic Studies of the Personality* (1952) could possibly be because he too was not content with them scientifically, as Sutherland suggested (1989). Another interpretation could be that Fairbairn was interested at that time in presenting his theoretical additions to psychoanalysis and therefore restricted himself to clinical examples and metapsychology. Seen in that light, the articles on art would appear too personal and too revealing of himself. Another more likely explanation would be that these articles do not depict the view on the personality that Fairbairn had developed since writing the papers. Looking back in 1952, they could well be regarded as theoretically immature or, as I might prefer to say, premature, not come to term. In my view, Fairbairn's articles on art and his doctoral thesis are middle stations along the way to his eventual theory of the personality.

Personal references

The sympathy Fairbairn feels for the joy in artistic creativity points to a wish to be open to lust and to create freely, far from the tyrannical superego of the Calvinist tradition and its sermons full of sin consciousness. Fairbairn's father Thomas insisted that the family worship twice on Sundays in Morningside on the south side of Edinburgh in a little church devoid of artistic adornment, far from vanity and the beauties of this world where all fun is equivalent to sin (Sutherland 1989; N. Fairbairn 1983, personal communication). Thomas Fairbairn was a practical but rather compulsive man who had shown strong resistance to higher education for his only son, but his wife Cecilia had her way on that topic (Sutherland 1989; N. Fairbairn 1983, personal communication). When his father died, Fairbairn left the Church of Scotland and joined the Anglican Church, the church of his mother. His father and mother were both strongly moralistic, the mother being described as particularly punitive when it came to sexual curiosity (Sutherland 1989). The tyrannical superego appeared years later in the form of the anti-psychoanalytical department at the University of Edinburgh and in his wife's displeasure at Fairbairn's taking pleasure in writing about psychoanalysis.

According to Fairbairn, artistic work cannot reach a particularly high artistic level unless the superego has developed sufficiently to contain the unconscious material to be expressed, but not so much as to defuse its energy. Fairbairn carries an inner force to create, and in psychoanalytic writing he finds an area within which he can express himself. He takes parts of his inner world and submits them to the rigours of the superego until they meet outer scientific and clinical demands. Out of this play and this labour, he constructs a theoretical model for psychic structures. This work may be described as his own piece of art which he works on, summarizes, and reworks during his clinically active years many times (Fairbairn 1944, 1951, 1963a, 1963b in Scharff and Birtles 1994). Over and over, it is the same picture he paints with small alterations, just as an artist repeats the same theme with small but interesting alterations.

Fairbairn's theory as art

I consider Fairbairn's theory a piece of art, but does it meet Fairbairn's own definition of art? Fairbairn (1938b) works with two concepts – the found object and the object of restitution. By the found object Fairbairn means something significant that the artist finds in outer and inner reality – for instance, a theme, a form – as a starting point for creation. During artistic work that meets the demands of the artist's superego, the found object will be changed into the object of restitution.

Fairbairn's work of art is his analysis of the structure of the personality. Freud's (1923) "The Ego and the Id" is Fairbairn's first found object. Other found objects are clinical experience, intellectual ambition to develop psychoanalysis, and the distinction between dissociation and repression – the theme of his doctoral thesis – all of them to be worked upon by the artist/ theoretician Fairbairn until the result is accepted. But if these found objects and the transformations he makes of them are not in accordance with the inner conditions of his patients, his readers, and his own intellect, they will be only temporary guests in the inner world. The artistic technique he uses is analysis of the structure of the personality. The concept of the endopsychic situation is the piece of art. The abstract expression in the final form of theory is the compromise that his inner world accepts.

Discussion

It is in the metapsychological aspects of a theory of the personality that one finds the theoretician as a person (Atwood and Stolorow 1993). Fairbairn's metapsychological theses circle around the importance of unsatisfying experience in the structuring of the personality, the unreliability of the parental objects, and the inner strategies the child uses for defence against outer reality. In his art, Fairbairn provides a form in which to express his inner world. The piece of art must meet the demands of the superego. In his theoretical model, the superego has been split into object and ego structures clearly related to the self and the parents. In this way, the personal dilemma appears in its nakedness. His task is to write so that it is acceptable to his mother and father and to his internalized mother and father. Fairbairn's abstract structure of the personality meets these demands.

As I understand it from the vantage of his 1938a paper, in which he takes off from the found objects of Freud and the internal objects of Klein, Fairbairn makes it legitimate to build a theory, properly positioned between the repressed object and the demands of the superego. It occurs to me that, having used Freud and Klein as his parental figures, he now has to create something for himself, even if Freud and Klein would not be totally satisfied. His task is to withstand the parental persons, and understand how to take care of his own ideas. He shows that one has to do this for oneself and use content from one's own inner life. That he understands this internalizing process is his creation, his personal creativity. The articles of 1938 mark the beginning of Fairbairn's new ideas. By 1963, Fairbairn's theory is fully articulated in his own terms, and like fine art, it stimulates, instructs, provokes debate, and stands the test of time.

References

Atwood, G. E. and Stolorow, R. D. (1993). *Faces in a Cloud: Intersubjectivity in Personality Theory*. Northvale, NJ: Jason Aronson.

Birtles, E. F. and Scharff D. E. (eds) (1994). *From Instinct to Self: Vol 2*. Northvale, NJ: Jason Aronson.

Fairbairn, W. R. D. (1929a). The relationship of dissociation and repression: Considered from the point of view of medical psychology. In *From Instinct to Self: Vol 2*, eds E. F. Birtles and D. E. Scharff, pp. 13–79. Northvale, NJ: Jason Aronson, 1994.

——— (1929b). The superego. In *From Instinct to Self: Vol 2*, eds E. F. Birtles and D. E. Scharff, pp. 80–114. Northvale, NJ: Jason Aronson, 1994.

——— (1930). Libido theory re-evaluated. In *From Instinct to Self: Vol 2*, eds E. F. Birtles'and D. E. Scharff, pp. 115–156. Northvale, NJ: Jason Aronson, 1994.

——— (1938a). Prolegomena to a psychology of art. *British Journal of Psychology* 28(3): 288–303. Reprinted in *From Instinct to Self: Vol 2*, eds E. F. Birtles and D. E. Scharff, pp. 381–396. Northvale, NJ: Jason Aronson, 1994.

——— (1938b). The ultimate basis of aesthetic experience. *British Journal of Psychology* 29(2):167–181. Reprinted in *From Instinct to Self: Vol 2*, eds E. F. Birtles and D. E. Scharff, pp. 397–409. Northvale, NJ: Jason Aronson, 1994.

——— (1944). Endopsychic structure considered in terms of object-relations. *International Journal of Psycho-Analysis* 25(1–2): 17–93.

——— (1951). A synopsis of the development of the author's views regarding the structure of the personality. *Psychoanalytic Studies of the Personality*, pp. 162–179. London: Routledge & Kegan Paul.

—— (1952). *Psychoanalytic Studies of the Personality*. London: Routledge & Kegan Paul.

—— (1963a). Synopsis of an object-relations theory of the personality. *International Journal of Psycho-Analysis* 44: 224–225.

—— (1963b). Autobiographical note. In *From Instinct to Self: Vol 1*, eds D. E. Scharff and E. F. Birtles, pp. 462–464. Northvale, NJ: Jason Aronson, 1994.

Freud, S (1900). The Interpretation of Dreams. *Standard Edition* 4: 1–338 and 5: 339–721.

—— (1923). The ego and the id. *Standard Edition* 19: 3–63.

Klein, M. (1929). Infantile anxiety – situation reflected in a work of art and in the creative impulse. *International Journal of Psycho-Analysis* 10: 436–443.

—— (1950). *Contributions to Psycho-Analysis 1921–1945*. London: Hogarth Press.

Read, H. (1931). *The Meaning of Art*. London: Faber and Faber.

—— (1936). *Art and Society*. London: Faber and Faber.

Ricoeur, P. (1974). *The Conflict of Interpretations: Essays in Hermeneutics*. Evanston, IL: Northwestern University Press.

Scharff, D. E. and Birtles, E. F. (eds) (1994). *From Instinct to Self: Vol 1*. Northvale, NJ: Jason Aronson.

Sutherland, J. D. (1989). *Fairbairn's Journey into the Interior*. London: Free Association.

Part II

Sutherland and Fairbairn

Introduction to Part 2
Jill Savege Scharff

John D. Sutherland's work inspired me to become a psychoanalyst, group therapist, and community psychotherapist. I had the great privilege of working for "Jock" as his registrar and senior registrar in Community Psychiatry in Edinburgh in the early 1970s. As a psychotherapy trainee, I attended his supervision groups at the Royal Edinburgh Hospital and his first training course called "The Person in The Caring Contract" at the newly established Scottish Institute of Human Relations which he co-founded. I learned most of what I know from him. So it is a great pleasure to introduce the man and his ideas.

Part II begins with a remarkable chapter: "The Self and Personal (Object) Relations" written by John D. Sutherland himself. As far as I know, it has not been published as a paper, and indeed it is marked restricted for discussion by the members of his circle. But Jock gave a copy to one of them, Mike Field, and he gave it to me to consider it for publication. Dated February 1978, this paper may be grouped with "The Psychodynamic Image of Man" (1979) and "The Autonomous Self" (1980) which are in Sutherland's collected works (Scharff 1994). With typical modesty, Jock writes: "This 'paper' represents working notes, my gropings in a very complex area. Naturally I have derived much from the writings of others though I would not claim to have understood all that they are saying. My interest in this topic during the last 15 years has been very much related to trying to understand the problems that have not responded to analysis – both to my own work and that of others." He tells the seminar members for whom this paper was intended that he hopes to revise these working notes and "make substantial amendments in the light of discussion on the unclarities, confusions and contradictions that they must contain." Sutherland thought that analysts should share their problems and failures to reach a more profound understanding and to contribute to the development of theory that would help those who are suffering, and so he was generous in putting forth his ideas and experience for discussion.

To Sutherland, this paper is a set of tentative working notes. To me it is a remarkable synthesis of the writings of others whose views he valued, and proof of his commitment to understanding the self as a dynamical matrix, an object for others, and an object in its own right. This paper, like his final paper "The Autonomous Self" (1980), is preliminary to the full realization of his views, which could not be completed before his death. But I think that it stands on its own as a contribution to be preserved, and a worthy companion to the 1979 and 1980 papers.

Chapters from Britain by Clarke and Singh deal with the philosophical roots of Sutherland's views, and show how personal his object relations theory was. Brearley follows in the Sutherland tradition of consulting to community organizations, helping people to see how their organizations reflect their need to defend against anxieties that can be dealt with more productively. McCluskey addresses the regulation of affect in group situations. From the United States, Aviram deals with a particular kind of internal object that he calls the social object, an internalization of the experience of being a member of ingroups and outgroups. Bagnini expands Sutherland's socio-intrapsychic model to his work with a complicated family structure. Lastly, Setton and Varela from Panamá join the editors in describing a model for teaching and learning object relations theory that is based on object relations principles and draws in part from group relations training events of the kind to which Sutherland consulted.

Chapter 19

The self and personal (object) relations

John D. Sutherland

Challenge to classical metapsychology

Psychoanalytic theory is manifestly in the melting pot. In Kuhn's (1962) terms, the paradigm of classical metapsychology was successfully challenged by Hartmann (1958) and his school, and though the changes in theory were initiated largely on general biological considerations of the problem of adaptation, they gave rise to a rich stream of clinical and developmental studies. Simultaneously, an independent challenge was emerging from the clinical work of a few British analysts with patients commonly regarded at that time as unsuited for psychoanalytical treatment. For many years the special social and political factors surrounding the development of psychoanalytical theory and practice kept these trends apart. The merging of them which is now taking place has inevitably widened the base from which theory is being appraised; and of particular importance have been changes outside of psychoanalysis, in the philosophy of science and in general biology. The new scene can be characterized by the rise of interest in such personalized concepts as "the self" or "identity", compared with the traditional theoretical issues couched in the language of nineteenth-century science; that is, in the impersonal terms of forces and energy transformations.

Clinically, a concept of "the self" has very real value in our understanding of certain fundamental aspects of personal functioning (see Khan 1974), especially when problems are presented as disturbances of total personal behaviour. Having a concept of the self is essential for working with patients whose whole commitment to living is seriously impaired as indicated by such phrases as: "I go through the motions of living but I am not in it"; "I am not the self I feel I should be"; or "I do not feel I know who I really am." These, and similar descriptions are commonplace. What is striking is the emergence of these states of mind in persons who have previously had lengthy periods of analysis. British analysts who have either explicitly or implicitly made extensive use of concepts of "the self" have been much influenced by such cases, written about by Balint, Winnicott, Fairbairn and Guntrip.[1] The need for further treatment was not attributed to inadequate work on the part of the previous analysts – in fact they had mostly been treated by senior analysts – but was regarded as due to a pervasive disturbance at the core of the person which only became accessible some time after more superficial layers of defences and conflicts, often in classical Oedipal terms, had been worked through. The nature of the self and its theoretical position therefore merit much more attention than has been given.

Ego and self

To what, then, does the concept of "the self" refer? There is most prominently the person's sense of his self – his "I" – as a free agent in the creation of what is meaningful to him. What is it that is sensed? Chein (1972) in his examination of the question "Who is the Actor?" notes that although the self cannot be observed directly, seeing the self is not a requirement in the proof of its existence. The self can be present transcendentally as the intervening subject self which gives identity to past and future object selves. Chein states: "The most significant aspect of the self is the appearance of the object self as actor." All such observations, all referable to a continuing self-identity, make up a complex *self-concept* which embraces many constituents, such as the relation to one's body, the observation of the behaviour that accompanies that relationship, and the attributions, explicit and implicit, made about one by others. Society contributes in a basic way to the development of the self-concept through the behaviour it rewards. Nevertheless, although the self-concept construes the subject of the person's actions, *a concept cannot be the actor*.

   Since he cannot readily find the real referents of the self, Chein appraises the ego as the actor. Within the ego system, many motives are concerned with doing things for "the self" and so the self as the object of these motives must be a structure which interacts with them. There are also motives that are not within the boundaries of the ego, but are subsumed under the terms superego and id. Chein has been found guilty of anthropomorphism in attributing to these subsystems humanoid characteristics, but he rejects the criticism. He maintains that the attribution is appropriate; for these systems function in action as human beings would. For Chein, then, there is a functional significance of the self in the ego structure, and that accounts for the interchangeability of the terms "self" and "ego". Psychotherapeutic work forces upon us the view that the ego has many structures with varying degrees of interrelatedness ranging from a relative unity in function to such extremes of

---

1 Ed: see Sutherland (1980).

disorganization as multiple personalities. Its organizing and controlling functions are concerned with maintaining adaptedness and anticipation, through the effectiveness of mapping the person's world. The ego is thus the system in which options are considered and decisions made.

Chein therefore concludes that the person or actor is an overall system constituted by the ego, superego, id, along with the self and the body. The first three combine to give a motivational system within which there are subsystems; and within the general system are the unfulfillable goals of seeking to anticipate the contingencies of an uncertain world. The essential psychological human quality is not one to be accounted for in energy terms; for it is one of commitment to a developing and continuing set of unending, interacting, interdependent, and mutually modifying long-range enterprises.

I have quoted Chein because his contribution to our topic from the standpoint of a sophisticated humanistic psychologist has so much of relevance to what we have to consider. It cannot be pretended, however, that the position of a self is unambiguous in Chein's views. A central integrative role appears to have been given to the self, not only in its transcendental function, but concretely. He observes: "Self-preservative, self-enhancing, and self-determining motivation is directed to the self *per se* rather than to our concept or image of it . . . it is as if all the syntonic behaviors of the actor (that is, all the spontaneous directed activities in which he engages and with respect to which he at least subconsciously assents or accepts responsibility) emanate from it." We are then surprised when we find decision making located within the ego – one system, even if a highly complex one, that has not been allocated a supraordinate role. Further, in multiple personalities each one acts like a person encompassing at least part of the functions of all; the constituent systems of the person. Yet Chein takes these to be disruptions in the ego. Where are we then to place the origin of the splitting? Who or what splits whom or what?

The self as a supraordinate system

Are we not back in the same dilemma that confronts all attempts to build up the person in his wholeness from his parts, whether we are dealing with the organization of motives or even of behavioural systems as studied by the ethologists despite the hierarchical organization they allow on the basis of the components? A bold answer to this question has been provided by Saperstein and Gaines (1973) who insist that a psychological explanatory theory must rest on the personal phenomena of clinical data. Apart from Erikson's (1959) concept of identity, they conclude that most metapsychological approaches to the self such as those of Hartmann (1958), Sandler and Joffe (1969), and Jacobson (1964), emerge with a presumably *scientific* description of the activities of the person resting on parts, and so avoiding the question of the self-as-agent. These authors, as did Lichtenstein (1961) come back to the persistent influence of the Cartesian dualism of mind and body in which there is no place for such a self. Taking a stance on modern philosophical, biological and psychological considerations, they view it as a necessity to conceptualize a supraordinate self-as-agent which can be explored as a natural phenomenon without resorting to a mystical model to account for intentionality, purpose and freedom of choice. They then quote Langer (1967) on the dynamic whole of living organisms whose activities are integrated within a *matrix* which, though having various degrees of coherence and persistence, is a system that is "self-sustaining, and self-propagating, wherein every event is prepared by progressively changing conditions of the integral whole. Every distinguishable change arises out of the matrix, and emerges as an act of an agent; for such a vital matrix is an agent" (Langer, quoted in Saperstein and Gaines 1973: 421). Saperstein and Gaines take this vital matrix as a supraordinate self which is independent from, and more than the sum of its parts though affected by them. In other words it is the system at the highest level of the cybernetic hierarchy that the organism requires for the integration of its subsystems. Though similar to the biological organizing principles postulated by Spitz (1945) and by Sandler and Joffe (1969), there is here a clearer base for subsequent organization being developed by differentiation within an original supraordinate dynamic system concerned with the organism as a whole rather than having to find ways of bringing parts together. And all general systems theorists assume this kind of view.

Psychoanalysis increases the freedom of choice available to this self; and, though it is not knowable directly, its structure can be investigated through self-representations. It too is a hierarchically ordered system with its own structure so that its nature and functioning can only be understood by genetic reconstruction.

The views of Saperstein and Gaines have been stimulated by the gap between modern philosophy and biology on the one hand and the outmoded science available to Freud as much as by that between metapsychology and clinical work. It is all the more striking then that the explicit attempt to bridge this latter gap made by Fairbairn over 30 years ago, and hence without the help of the advances made in science and general biological theory during this period, should result in a theory of the self and its development so closely in agreement.

From pristine ego through object relationship to self

Fairbairn postulated the existence of a unified ego from birth. As Ernest Jones (1952), with quite exceptional perspicacity, stated in his preface to Fairbairn's (1952) book, Fairbairn started at the centre of the personality in contrast to Freud's working in from the periphery. Writing years before systems theory had become prominent, Fairbairn thus adopted a view of development as proceeding by differentiation within an overall dynamic integrative matrix, which is the carrier of the experience of the infant and within which structuring inevitably takes place according to the emerging patterns of experience.

The pristine ego he takes to be lacking in complexity because it is lacking in experience; but it is the active organizer of experience from the start and its experience in a state of total dependence is entirely centred on its interactions with its mother. At this stage there is no difficulty in substituting "self" for "ego". (Fairbairn's terminology does not do full justice to his position. He wanted to get theory on to a quite definite personal level because he considered that was the only level at which clinical phenomena could be discussed. At the same time, he had no wish to be thought of as setting up a new school; he regarded his work to be entirely a continuation of Freud's. The radical nature of his theories is therefore somewhat covered because of his using as far as possible a "classical" mode of expression, with terms such as "ego" for "self", and "object" for "personal" relations, so that the old and the new could be related. By the time Guntrip and Winnicott were writing, the word "self" raised few eyebrows!)

Like Hartmann, Fairbairn rejects the id as a separate area of the mind from which the ego is developed. Instinctive activity is merely one mode in which the self-matrix can be activated, this self-matrix being a highly dynamic system concerned in its earliest stages, with making relations with the mother. These interactions bring satisfaction of bodily needs and provide a creative impetus towards growth constituted by the various maturational developments.

The innumerable subordinate functions and specific behavioural systems all serve as they mature to root the matrix in relationships in an extremely complex way. To simplify considerations, we can restrict ourselves to what Fairbairn conceived as the central self. We can ignore at this state the inevitable splitting in the self-system which arises from incompatible qualities and goals within the mother–child relationships. Within the system, the self pole differentiates from the object and, with ordinary good mothering as the necessary setting, the external world is mapped and created in the first instance internally. In this process, all the "ego-autonomous" functions play their part along with fantasy and the more specific behaviours. Winnicott (1971) stresses the appropriately responsive role of the mother in allowing the experience of the self as creating its objects, an experience which appears to be his way of describing the establishment of basic trust (Erikson 1950). He gives particularly sensitive accounts of the kind of relationship experience that permits the growth of a secure and *creative* self. For him the role of play is of the greatest importance in this development, and the capacity to play freely has to be founded on a quality of interaction with the mother that generates the enjoyment of play.

The formation of this mother imago is stressed by Sullivan (1953). For

Klein (1935), working through the depressive position represents achieving an imago of the mother as a whole person who is reliably supportive. Within the ego psychology tradition, Spitz (1945), Mahler *et al.* (1975), Anna Freud (1946) and many others have confirmed this process of successful individuation resting on the good mother–child relationship, while the invaluably comprehensive studies by Bowlby (1969, 1973) have underpinned the relationship requirements definitively. Lichtenstein (1965) has commented on Erikson's concept of epigenetic phases as implying the continuity of a central developmental principle such as identity.

There is wide agreement that future development into adaptive and creative adulthood is governed by what happens in the interactive experiences of these earliest phases. The quality of the personal relationships at all subsequent stages through adolescence affects the form of the adult personality, yet deprivation of certain kinds and degrees at the first formative phase can be only partially compensated with later good experience. To put it in diagrammatic form, the first phase of interaction normally creates a self-pole with a good mother imago which gives to the self-matrix a capacity to interact joyously with the world. The role of affect in such a relationship-seeking matrix is to monitor and reinforce the selection and organization of the activities that preserve good relationships.

When the good mother–child relationship is followed by experience with other family relationships of similar quality in which the child experiences mutual trust and a reliable and consistent concern for development of his independent creativity, the child passes through the phases that Erikson describes, and emerges as a young adult with an established identity. Identity is thus the pattern of relationships the self is able to make with others along with the patterns of creative activity in work and play. From an original interaction matrix structured when the self separates from the imago of the good mother, the course of development adds the content of the relationships with the father and other significant figures in fostering self-reliance. Experience is expanded and new understandings and skills are acquired to give a range of competences. Adulthood merges what were originally the personalized imagoes into the ideals and values that direct spontaneous creativity and sustained commitment to giving something back to life. For many, the life space in which their maturity is expressed may be a restricted one compared with that which richer talents and opportunities have given to others, yet the essential psychological processes are the same.

Living is about making relationships – loving and contributing to the environment by working, as Freud said (1930: 80 fn.). The growth of the self towards achieving the capacity for love and work has been tracked in long-term studies of development. Bowlby summarizes a sample of these researches, which show the positive correlation between the future effectiveness of the personality and the quality of care within the family from the earliest phase through adolescence. Although Bowlby favours a theoretical position which builds the integration of the personality from separate behavioural systems – and he takes great pains to get the language for his approach – nevertheless the terms he uses in his discussion of the happy outcome to the child's development are interestingly "secure attachment" and "the growth of *self-reliance*"!

Clinical examples: Sources of difficulty in love and work

The effects of early failures can be illustrated from some of the statements made by two analysands in the course of their analyses which had been sought following a feeling of virtual breakdown. The first had had a mother whose attitude, since ever she could remember, was a rejecting one. She never felt she could do anything right. Throughout her later years at home her emergence into womanhood was perpetually denigrated. Any attempt to show affection was regarded by her mother with a suspicious "what-are-you-up-to" attitude and any need to get it was repulsed with a "don't-be-silly" comment and emotional withdrawal. It took years of analytic work before affection towards me could be admitted. After one such admission following a period of anger and despair with me, she experienced a sense of relaxation in marked contrast to a state of anxious tension that had lasted for months. Accompanying this relaxation, there was also a change in attitude to work. Her work, which had been greatly blocked during this period of tension – her working capacity had always been unreliable – began to flourish, and she brought to it a new feeling of confidence and commitment. Because of her high abilities she had been able to achieve considerable success, though always there was a sense of never using her potential. She now had a feeling of greater freedom to work as well as to love – a markedly different feeling within herself.

The second, a man, had had consistent reliable mothering but from a mother who was a rather controlling, inhibited, religious person. He too had considerable difficulty in making close relations and his output of work varied. He felt that his mother had never accepted his spontaneous liveliness, and this aura of mistrust of vitality still enveloped him. Well on towards middle-age, he had a vivid sense that this feeling had been present at his core throughout his life. As with the woman patient, his high abilities had carried him along but the despair about his relationships and an increasingly variable work performance brought him to the point of suicide.

With both patients, it required a few years of treatment for trust in their analysts to grow to the point where they could feel less defended against making the close relationships they wished to achieve. What was striking was the general increase in freedom to work, to play, and to have enjoyable relationships with others, as they relieved some of the feelings belonging to the earliest relationship. Equally striking was the language they used to describe the improvement: "I feel better in myself."

These examples are, of course, commonplace. I quote them to emphasize the dominant theme amidst a variety of more specific complaints, a recurrent motif of the constriction of *the self as an overall system managing their lives*. And, as mentioned earlier, breakdown in the self system as an overall manager is particularly striking in patients who have had lengthy analysis previously.

The sense of self

I have proceeded so far on a hypothetical "central", or even "unitary", self to simplify the discussion. What we have arrived at is the usefulness of postulating an overall integrative system that exists from the start to mediate the interaction of the person as a whole with his environment. Initially, its structuring is minimal in keeping with the prototaxic experience of the earliest phase, to use Sullivan's (1953) term. The main, the first, and the most critical development is the patterning of the system in terms of a self-pole at one end of the dynamic relation-seeking system with an image of a mother at the other end. With optimal developmental conditions, this imago (later the ego ideal) maintains in the system a positively toned affect and general attitude to the world that allows optimal maturational progress of innumerable behavioural systems. There seems to be no good reason for preferring the impersonal term ego to self for this system for which "self-feeling" or "self-esteem" are the terms that best describe its tone. What began presumably with the minimally structured feeling of being pleasurably or painfully real – and this quality of experience is obviously a product of processes in the nervous system – becomes differentially structured on the basis of these affective qualities. Affects would thus seem to be the "magnetic" force that coheres experience into patterns.

The sense of self stems from the whole matrix, and so it encompasses everything that goes on in it – from all the bodily sensations to the developing perceptual world, from outside the self to inner fantasy. Self-presentation and self-concepts become enriched rapidly, and, as has been stressed, are basically structured by the input from the early relations. This latter process has been described by various writers as the mirroring effect within the self of the image that the mother has of her child. The mother imparts through her responses, and especially through behaviour affected by her unconscious attitudes, a pattern of how she wants the child to be and to respond to her. It is to this primary patterning of the person-relating self that Lichtenstein (1977) gives the term "identity theme". Lichtenstein rejects the term "self" because of its confusing links with "sense of self" and other dynamic connotations. He responded to pressure to avoid this vague term, which Hartmann had declared unsatisfactory since in the current state of knowledge it was not easy to distinguish it from the much more "scientific" ego. The identity theme (or self-system as I would call it), patterned by the way in which mother and child relate, is an essential achievement if the person is to function at all.

Lichtenstein (1965, 1977) regards the identity theme as virtually unchangeable, rather in the manner of the first structuring of response systems that the ethologists have called imprinting. He sees this theme in the development of the person as a motif in music, which is carried on in a series of variations. Identity is accordingly the social objectivation achieved through subsequent experience. This is virtually the same as the basic patterning of the self-matrix in a relations-making system. What was the relatively unstructured matrix thus becomes the structured system that governs the mode and mood of all subsequent relationships. It is the governing centre required by any complex hierarchically ordered system. This does not imply a harmoniously effective control but it does mean that without an integrative supraordinate system the whole cannot survive. Subsystems can have ranges of autonomy in their functioning and can get out of balance to a disruptive extent. That kind of imbalance is a familiar occurrence at some time or other in all complex systems such as large businesses and organizations as well as in the individual. It merely emphasizes the point that the person needs a governing system, a system whose task is to plan, to make decisions, and to act for the whole. Consciousness and affect determine meanings and commitment, which are the essence of a self-system that is the actor.

The functions of the ego include the mapping of the environment socially and physically and the organizing of all the implications of action in response. The maintenance of the underlying commitment to action, however, seems to fall out with what we usually refer to as the ego, even though the latter plays a major role in the later development of long-term goals. It is in this way that there is an advantage in referring the final determination of action to the self. It is difficult to see how a group of functions could acquire the directedness of a self-system. The ego, as Chein says, needs a self. The ego, however, is the organization of the transactions with the environment under the "direction" of the self-matrix.

Splitting and the structure of the self

To revert now to the more ordinary circumstances in development, we have to look at the phenomena of splitting. Painful experience with the mother, when persistent enough, builds up a bad imago related to a self that also feels bad. Many different outcomes arise in the structuring of the self according to the degree and the quality of the frustration or mismatch between the needs of the infant and the input from the mother. The infant is so made that attachment to a mother is a necessity for survival, and since separation is the source of great anxiety – the view taken by the object relations analysts – the need to attach is intensified, as Bowlby's evidence confirms. The imago of mother is thus installed even more dominantly when she provides less security. The child simply has to evolve ways of coming to terms with the particular patterns of the mother. Two main effects are encountered in clinical work. The child withdraws internally to lock up part of its response potential and so relates with an attenuated part of its resources. The metaphor of the self being locked behind fortress-like doors is a typical descriptor for the resulting schizoid personality. What then appears is a conforming or "false" self and a denuded, hidden personality.

A confusion from Fairbairn's terminology may arise here. What he describes as the central self normally forms in relation to a central core of the good mother which is normally more potent than other aspects. But this is not always the case. The mother may be experienced as over-exciting or rejecting of the child's needs for relationship, and the child is then deprived of the opportunity to take in a good mother experience at the core of the self. What the deprived child evolves is a self-system by which life under these circumstances is made possible. The child develops an *adapted* self, adapted to the mother's excessive influence whether this be from intensive over-control, or neglect, or unreliable, inconsistent responsiveness, rather than an *adaptive* self which good mothering fosters. (In passing we may ponder on whether the voices of criticism of psychotherapy as producing adaptedness rather than greater personal freedom may be loudest in those whose experience was largely one of an enforced adapted development.) When the patterning of early deprived relationships is reinforced in later years, especially during adolescence, then there is a high likelihood of failure to reach a viable living capacity.

The persistence of "life" in the withdrawn part of the self gives to the person the fantasy of what might have been; and experience outside the family helps to keep alive the hope for something better in his or her relationships. Even when the dominance of the "bad" mother is excessive, when hope is in danger of a complete replacement by despair, it is remarkable how such people retain sufficient hope to seek psychotherapeutic help, though the therapeutic task is then formidable. At the self-pole there may be despair and hate of near overwhelming intensity: then there is increasing danger of a move to identification with the hated mother to preserve the status quo lest a freer self lead to the terror of fresh abandonment or to unbearable humiliation and vulnerability if the withdrawn good self be rejected again.

It is not my purpose, however, to go into all the common patterns arising from splitting within the self. That could only be covered by a volume on psychopathology. My aim has been the limited one of advocating the replacement of the impersonal terms we have adopted and, in particular, to suggest that the self is a more useful concept than the ego as the actor and hence is the location of choice in regard to strategic decisions. Whatever the pattern of subsystems within the self, it is more appropriate to keep these in mind as modes of action of the self system even though restricted or distorted. Schafer's (1976) plea for a language that locates responsibility is certainly one to be supported.

The self matrix and its subsystems

The concept of relationships with internal objects has evoked surprising difficulty in some theorists. Conscious relationships with fantasy objects, however, have long been recognized, for instance, in the imaginary companions of childhood. Unconscious relationships have long been accepted in regard to the superego. The concept of an overall proactive matrix can readily include the functioning of a range of inner relationships as ways of dealing with "unsatisfactory" aspects of significant figures.

By placing subsystems within the self matrix when they are in action, all subsystem action then involves the self as actor. And when we think of all sub-self relationships within the overall system we can readily understand repression arising from the pressure of a dominant relationship to keep an incompatible one out of action. Instinctive activity operates within the self matrix even though it may be pressed largely into one subsystem, for instance, in repressed sexual fantasies.

It requires no great upheaval to adopt the notion of a supraordinate self-system within which the phenomena associated with what we have termed the ego, superego and id can operate. It does offer the great advantage of bringing theory close to practice, and it may well help with our clinical understanding. Analysis has been very much under scrutiny in regard to its therapeutic results. As a treatment for conflict of certain depth, mainly involving the Oedipal conflicts, it brought great rewards. The status of the Oedipus complex, however, may well be a derivative of earlier splitting and structuring, as Fairbairn suggested, rather than a fundamental etiological situation. Most important, our whole conception of what is involved in diagnosis and treatment could be influenced by a better grasp of the part that deprivation plays in the earliest structuring of the self.

Analytical psychotherapy has appealed to many analysts who prefer a freer more personalized setting. There is a tendency to regard this as a somewhat inferior procedure, despite the fact that, as the Blancks (1974) state, structural change can be greater in psychotherapy than in psychoanalysis because structure building is the very purpose of treatment when borderline and psychotic structures are the focus. The difficulty we so often encounter occurs when psychotic structures emerge from underneath the neurotic pictures that present initially.

Technical problems in the development of analytical psychotherapeutic practice are bound to occur if deprivation syndromes are to be met with a more personalized approach. The British object relations analysts adopted a warmer, more spontaneous attitude in their treatment of severely schizoid patients than that of orthodox psychoanalysis. Schafer criticizes Guntrip for apparently advocating "kindly" theory as better than the orthodox concepts. These British analysts do not, however, revise theory or practice for *kindly* reasons. They are advocating a different view for *scientific* reasons, namely that the self-system in these severely disturbed patients was crippled from the start because there had been a grossly inadequate experience of being loved for themselves. At this level of disorder, if an experience of personalized concern is needed, before progress can be made, then theory has to account for this; and, as I have mentioned already, many of the patients with whom they worked had already had long spells of analysis.

These problems can only be settled with more research. A difficulty in the evolution of psychotherapeutic theory and practice has always been the problem of appraising the state of a personality at one point in time in such a way that changes can be assessed. The more our theory fits practice, by using variables that can be related to practice, the better our chances of achieving more sensitive diagnostic instruments. By using a theory explicitly linked with the self and its subsystems it seemed to Gill and myself some years ago that language might be used to make such an instrument (Sutherland and Gill 1970). Our own efforts in this direction were little more than a first tentative attempt but, even so, they showed possibilities.[2]

One possible implication for clinical work focusing on the self is a greater impact on the analyst. The existentialists stress the importance of the "encounter" for personal relations and development. Weisman (1965) emphasizes that analysis and analytical psychotherapy are essentially the study of encounters. As he puts it: "Being in analysis is the analysis of Being." Countertransference is an inevitable complication. Levin (1969) suggests that analysis of the self all the time may be too painful a task for the individual analyst and that groups of analysts might work together on problems of self–object differentiation. Publication of findings under the authorship of the psychoanalytic society to which the group belonged would protect the individual analyst from the consequences of revelations about his or her own self. We all have difficult cases, and we do not work together enough on those problems situations in which we have reached a block or a failure. If we could do so, we could capitalize on the opportunity to advance our understanding of the nature of the self and the problems in its functioning brought to our attention so vividly at the centre of an analysis.

Conclusion

There is a growing body of opinion that the tripartite structural theory, id, ego and superego, is not adequate as a theoretical framework for clinical

---

2 See also Chapter 27.

work. Many theoreticians and most clinicians use the term "self" freely. Clinicians tend to use it as synonymous with the ego and, although theorists explicitly state that the self is a separate "concern", there is disagreement as to whether to refer to it as a structure. There is considerable reluctance to conceptualize it metapsychologically.

Existential considerations (as Weisman remarks, all analysts have an existential attitude though they may in no way share the views of existential philosophers) would certainly point to a foundation structure in the personality that establishes a pattern of relationships that mediates a commitment, or lack of commitment, to the social and physical environments. Thus primary anxiety would seem to be a prototype in itself for whatever causes the experience of self to become meaningless existence; it cannot be restricted to the image of a hungry or a frightened infant. Its antithesis is unconditional love or *agape*, and a similar antithesis is seen between hope and despair. Despair can put almost any or every psychic process and drive out of action, whether we prefer to think of these as located in the id, ego or superego, and it is one of the most difficult problems to treat. This indicates that it has a specifically central origin and a pervasive role in the structuring of the despairing person.

I believe the notion of a dynamic matrix in which affect is located from the start of psychic life and which then embodies a dominant pattern of relationships to others is one well worthy of further study. It would seem that it is to the properties of this basic pattern that we refer when we try to appraise our therapeutic task. Thus an established pattern of self in relation to an imago of a good enough mother as a differentiated object may be what makes psychoanalysis in the classical sense possible, for it is in this situation that the person has a stable enough core with sufficient autonomy and responsibility for his behavior. Kohut's (1971) work has brought out some of the complex ways in which the self-system can be stable and effective when the internal object within the self-system is not differentiated from the self-pole, though with this narcissistic structure analysts have to be ready to modify their approach.

In view of these lines of thought, it would seem that all the differentiated conflicts of specific phases, especially Oedipal conflicts, may be the focus of much effective analytic work yet they may be only the prelude to more fundamental problems.

It will be readily seen that around this whole subject a number of viewpoints are converging. While Hartmann's autonomous functions of the ego introduced new factors to give a necessary independent complement to the role of the instincts from the beginning of psychic life, his theoretical views, as Schafer demonstrates too convincingly, got virtually aborted by his adherence to energy concepts. M. Klein (1935, 1946), as Guntrip (1968) has stressed so often, really introduced the notion of dynamic relationships within the psyche from the start, but she and her colleagues have not provided an adequate account of the "permanent" structuring of these relationships.

Moreover, her view of development on the basis of part objects is difficult to reconcile with Spitz's (1945) findings that adequate feeding in the absence of mothering is no guarantee of healthy development. What has been referred to as a self-system here, however, could be related to what happens when the "depressive position" is worked through.

Mahler et al.'s (1975) views on the emergence of the separate self in parallel with object constancy obviously overlaps as do Erikson's (1950) phases of Basic Trust proceeding to Autonomy and Initiative. It is noteworthy, too, that Erikson (1959) later dropped the word "ego" from its early bracketing with "identity". Through the concept of epigenetic phases, identity implies a supraordinate core system. These writers and many others appear to be moving in the same direction as the British Object Relations theorists.

As Freud (1937) remarked in "Analysis Terminable and Interminable", the way through certain blocks to therapeutic success must rest on metapsychological speculation and theorizing. The clinical situations of therapeutic impasse, despair, and false self functioning are now attracting considerable psychoanalytic attention. To meet these clinical challenges, our theories require substantial metapsychological revision. At the centre of this task, is the study of the phenomena of "the self".

References

Blanck, G. and Blanck, R. (1974). *Ego Psychology*. New York: Columbia University Press.

Bowlby, J. (1969). *Attachment and Loss*, Vol. 1. London: Hogarth.

—— (1973). *Separation Anxiety and Anger*, Vol. 2. London: Hogarth.

Chein, I. (1972). *The Science of Behaviour and the Image of Man*. New York: Basic Books.

Erikson, E. H. (1950). *Childhood and Society*. New York: Norton.

—— (1959). Identity and the lifecycle. *Psychological Issues* 1(1): 1–171.

Fairbairn, W. R. D. (1952). *Psychoanalytic Studies of the Personality*. London: Tavistock, Routledge & Kegan Paul.

Freud, A. (1946). *The Ego and the Mechanisms of Defence*. New York: International Universities Press.

Freud, S. (1930). Civilization and its discontents. *Standard Edition* 21: 64–145.

—— (1937). Analysis terminable and interminable. *Standard Edition* 23: 216–253.

Guntrip, H. (1968). *Schizoid Phenomena, Object Relations and the Self*. London: Hogarth.

Hartmann, H. (1958). *Ego Psychology and the Problem of Adaptation*. Original 1939, trans. D. Rapaport 1958. New York: International Universities Press.

Jacobson, E. (1964). *The Self and the Object World*. New York: International Universities Press.

Jones, E. (1952). Preface. *Psychoanalytic Studies of the Personality*. London: Tavistock, Routledge & Kegan Paul.

Khan, M. (1974). *The Privacy of the Self*. London: Hogarth.

Klein, M. (1935). A contribution to the genesis of manic-depressive states. In *Love*

Guilt and Reparation and Other Works: 1921–1945, pp. 262–289. London: Hogarth, 1975.

—— (1946). Notes on some schizoid mechanisms. In *Envy and Gratitude and Other Works: 1946–1963*, pp. 1–24. London: Hogarth, 1975.

Kohut, H. (1971). *The Analysis of the Self. Psychoanalytic Study of the Child Monogr. 4.* New York: International Universities Press.

Kuhn, T. (1962). *The Structure of Scientific Revolution*, 2nd edn. Chicago: University of Chicago Press.

Langer, S. K. (1967). *Mind: An Essay on Human Feeling*, Vol. 1. Baltimore: Johns Hopkins Press.

Levin, D. C. (1969). The self: a contribution to its place in theory and technique. *International Journal of Psycho-Analysis* 50: 41–51.

Lichtenstein, H. (1961). Identity and sexuality, a study of their interrelationship in man. *Journal of the American Psychoanalytic Association* 9: 179–260.

—— (1965). Towards a metapsychological definition of the self. *International Journal of Psycho-Analysis* 46: 117–128.

—— (1977). *The Dilemma of Human Identity.* New York: Jason Aronson.

Mahler, M., Pine, F. and Bergman, A. (1975). *The Psychological Birth of the Human Infant.* New York: Basic Books.

Sandler, J. and Joffe, W. G. (1969). Towards a basic psychoanalytic model. *International Journal of Psycho-Analysis* 50: 79–90.

Saperstein, J. L. and Gaines, J. (1973). Metapsychological considerations of the self. *International Journal of Psycho-Analysis* 54: 415–424.

Schafer, R. A. (1976). *A New Language for Psychoanalysis.* New Haven, CT: Yale University Press.

Spitz, R. A. (1945). Hospitalism. *The Psychoanalytic Study of the Child* 1: 53–74.

Sullivan, H. S. (1953). *The Interpersonal Theory of Psychiatry.* New York: Norton.

Sutherland, J. D. (1980). The British Object Relations theorists: the contributions of Balint, Winnicott, Fairbairn, Guntrip. *Journal of the American Psychoanalytic Assocation* 28: 829–860.

Sutherland, J. D. and Gill, H. S. (1970). *Language and Psychodynamic Appraisal.* London: Karnac.

Weisman, A. D. (1965). *The Existential Core of Psychoanalysis: Reality Sense and Responsibility.* Boston, MA: Little, Brown.

Winnicott, D. W. (1971). *Playing and Reality.* London: Tavistock.

Chapter 20

The legacy of John D. Sutherland

Self and society

Jill Savege Scharff

John D. Sutherland, known to all as Jock, was a remarkable person, with a great capacity for moving freely between levels of scale from self to society, building bridges between points of view, and integrating psychoanalytic and social theories (Kohon 1996). The main part of his work was devoted to managing staff, teaching and supervising trainees, developing programs, and working with the community to build a caring community of mental health service providers, yet, at the beginning and end of each day, he found time for six analytic patients to keep himself in touch with clinical work. For his contributions to mental health he received the order of Commander of the British Empire, an honor given to only two other analysts, John Bowlby and Anna Freud.

Sutherland had broad influence on the young trainees in mental health and on his peers through his editorial work and writing, which was remarkably extensive. He served as editor of the *British Journal of Medical Psychology*, the *International Journal of Psycho-Analysis*, and the International Psycho-Analytic Library (producing more than 100 books). He was the co-founder of the Scottish Institute of Human Relations, Director of the Tavistock Centre, in London; and in the United States, Sloan Professor at the Menninger Clinic, and a distinguished guest lecturer at Austen Riggs, the Institute of Contemporary Psychotherapy, and the Washington School of Psychiatry. He was not only the co-founder of the Scottish Institute – that was actually a late life activity – but prior to that he had been Director of the Tavistock Centre in London, where he had indirectly influenced many students, not just in England, but in other European countries.

Sutherland was particularly interested in Fairbairn, his life, and his ideas on human development starting from the centre of the personality (Fairbairn 1952; Sutherland 1989). He took Fairbairn's ideas on the endopsychic situation, and worked with them, extending them to suit his own needs, and clarifying certain points. He admired Fairbairn's systematic, philosophical argument, which emphasized internalization of the bad object as the basis for the structuring of the self. Sutherland agreed with that, and was particularly aware of the self's need to control the bad object or be controlled by it, but he was critical of the lack of specificity in Fairbairn's theory concerning the good object. Given that Fairbairn believed that the ego was object seeking, he was obviously interested in the desired object, but how did that goodness of the desired object get into the self? Sutherland thought that Fairbairn had taken for granted the fact that the good object fills the self automatically. Sutherland used to say that the good object suffuses the self, giving it a warm glow. He emphasized the role of affect in connecting each part of the ego with the corresponding part of the object, a point also emphasized by Kernberg, and validated by current findings on the neurobiological basis for affect regulation (Schore 1994).

Sutherland could argue metapsychology with the best of them, but in clinical practice, and in supervision with trainees, he talked in everyday language. For instance, I had not heard the terms "object relations theory" or "projective identification" until I came to the United States. He liked to keep it simple. He would say, only half-joking, "I only deal with four-letter words – love, hate, milk." He talked in terms of bits of the self. For instance, when dealing with the persecutory object, he would say, "There's this part of the self that fills you with a dreadful feeling, an angry kind of father figure." Did he do away with the drives? No, he thought that the drives are normally inherent in the self and object relationship (Padel 1995). He believed that at those times when the drives are expressed in raw intensity and seem to validate Freudian drive theories, they are actually the breakdown product of a failed connection between the self and the object. He taught that the internal object relationships bind the drives, express the drives, color them, give them meaning, and invest them with interpersonal significance.

Sutherland was respectful of Freud's enormous contribution to society, but it was not Freud's theories that mattered to him. He felt that Freud's lasting legacy was his "method for exploring the unconscious processes in our inner worlds" (1994a: 368). Sutherland turned away from classical theory and embraced Fairbairn's theory as a truly radical revision. Nevertheless, he was invited to London to give the Freud lecture at University College in London. To every honor, he brought a pawky Scottish sense of humor, and in this case, referred to himself as "the Frood Professor." When lecturing in his eighties, going off on fascinating tangents concerning the development of the self, he would end with a self-deprecating taunt: "Where have you got to tonight, my wandering boy?" To get back to Freud, Sutherland agreed that Freud's structural theory was a great improvement over his topographical theory because it took into account the child's selective identification with aspects of the personalities of both parents in the Oedipal phase. But, for Sutherland, the problem with Freud's structural theory was that it was still built on drive theory and was not adequate to explain the wholeness of the person in relationship.

Sutherland appreciated the fact that Hartmann was particularly interested in the ego, but he could not accept the way he tried to divide up the self from the instincts. Sutherland thought that instinct was subsumed by ego. Sutherland did not follow Kleinian theory because, like Freud's, it was a dual instinct theory. Yet he appreciated the value of Klein's theory for dealing with hate in the transference, and he found her emphasis on aggression clinically useful, even though he disagreed with her idea that aggression stems from the death instinct. Sutherland has his own ideas on aggression, which I will come to at the end of the chapter. In general, he thought that Klein gave too much emphasis to unconscious fantasy and not enough attention to structure. He was influenced by Chein's (1972) view of the person as the actor in a "continuing set of unending, interacting, interdependent and mutually modifying long-range enterprises" (1980b: 43) and by Lichtenstein's (1977) view that the self-structure is whole from the start, expects to be treated like a person, and evolves its identity in interactions.

Sutherland admired Kohut's (1971) focus on the self. He thought that study of the self was the way forward for psychoanalysis. But he regretted that Kohut did not acknowledge Fairbairn's contribution. Some report that Sutherland thought that Kohut had had access to Fairbairn's writing and did not give him credit. I think that he kept an open mind on that, realizing that both of them may have been picking up the same ideas from working with the same type of schizoid/narcissistic patient in the same period of time. Kohut's sustained empathic connection is a quality of great importance to Jock who, for instance, made empathic connections with group members in therapy groups by making a point of referring to them by name and remarking on each individual contribution to the group process. He thought, however, that Kohut overused his empathy to block aggression, failed to elicit it, and did not want to deal with it. He thought that Kohut's concept of the bipolar self was a simplification.

In Sutherland's view, following Fairbairn, the self was much more complex than that, consisting of many parts. So Sutherland much preferred the work of the British object relations theorists among whom he included Balint, Winnicott, Guntrip, and Fairbairn (Sutherland 1980a). Balint was aware of the whole self when he worked with the basic fault of his regressed patients. Sutherland liked Guntrip's focus on the self, rather than on the ego, and his preference for the term personal relations theory. To Sutherland, the ego was a mechanistic concept left over from drive/structural theory, and retained by Fairbairn in respect of Freud. Sutherland much preferred to think in terms of the self and its many functions and processes. Winnicott's concept of the false self was helpful in thinking about aspects of self-functioning that covered and protected the true self. But even these theories were disappointing in the end, in that they could not account for growth over time.

Sutherland wanted a view of the self that continues to grow and develop, a self that is open to learning and to being modified in the light of future experience. That is why he needed other theories to take his ideas of the self and its object relations a bit further. His primary concern was always the self, not the self in isolation but the self in relationship. He studied how the self develops in its contexts – in the family and in the culture – and how it is sustained in interaction with others throughout the lifecycle in work, in play, and in connecting to the institutions of society (Harrow *et al.* 1994). The self must have a central place in our thoughts about who we are and how we are to move on to more experience and more knowledge. To develop this way of thinking, he needed other theories – to which I will return.

Sutherland said that the self is constructed of internal object relationships based on its relations with important people (external objects) in the outside world, which are taken into the self and become the building blocks of psychic structure. The self is not a linear entity created of instincts seeking expression across prearranged developmental stages, and eventually having structure imposed on them at the time of the resolution of the Oedipus complex. Instead, according to Sutherland, the self is a gestalt, and it takes a gestalt to relate to a gestalt. The self is made up of a shape that is prewired to build itself up from external experience, and as a shape it relates to the shapes that are encountered as the self moves through the lifecycle being reshaped by them. The self is central, but it is made of its relationships. The self is always the agent of action, and it expresses its endopsychic structure in action in its relationships. From day one the pristine ego, which Fairbairn referred to, is a managing, organizing ego. It is not instinctually based. It does not arrive out of the id, out of the mists of time. It is there, ready, prewired, ready to interact, needing to interact, and seeking meaning in relationships.

Sutherland needed other theories to make his theory of the self relevant to the late twentieth century. He needed open systems theory, evolution of biology, and holograms. Nineteenth-century science, current when Freudian theory was invented, held that all organisms seek homeostasis; they receive negative feedback and move towards a state of equilibrium. Sutherland said that this rule does not apply in the living organism. The living organism is in a state of non-equilibrium, always interacting with the environment, taking in further feedback, adapting, changing, growing, and moving forward. The living organism, such as the human being, is characterized by unpredictability and complexity (Prigogine 1976; Jantsch 1980). Sutherland saw the self as "an open system that both moulds and is moulded by the caretakers" (Averill 1992: 427).

Fairbairn's theory had emphasized the structuring of the self, and the interaction between the conscious part of the self and unconscious parts of the self through processes of splitting and repressing. Sutherland was more interested in these *processes* than in the *structures* themselves (Padel 1995). He emphasized the fact that the self is an open system. All parts of the self are in dynamic relation, the repressed and split off parts always seeking to rejoin the self, which can then become a whole interacting self. He emphasized that the unconscious parts are always seeking to expand that central ego so as to have it not be shorn of the excitement, rejection, and abandonment that had had to be repressed. The healthier self is infused with these elements which gives color and fullness to experience, possible only when these elements have not been so painful or rejecting as to have overwhelmed the immature ego, and so necessitated severe repression. The self is always in a state of dynamic relationship, and the central ego is not fixed. Its boundaries are shifting, depending on the security of the relationships and the cultural context that it finds itself in. Sutherland's is a process-oriented interpretation of the development of the self.

Now, what about holograms? In his writings as far as I can see, Sutherland never actually defined what a hologram is, assuming perhaps that the reader will know what it is. Negroponte (1995) defined a hologram as "all possible views of a scene collected into a single plane of light-modulating patterns." Sutherland applied this idea to conceptualize the self that develops out of its being viewed from many angles, as the different people to whom the self relates mirror the self. Thus the self is built from these many encounters and relationships, built and rebuilt, modified, and developed over time. Sutherland also looked to evolution and biology, which describes the behavioral change of organisms as they develop. Before Schore's (1994) compilation of research findings on neurological development and affect regulation, Sutherland had the idea of affects as a "monitoring system that could deal with all kinds of stimuli, and could set in motion internally a reactive mechanism" (1994c: 419). He thought that the structures of the self are constantly being built on the basis of affect-driven shifts in the neurological system of the brain. These shifts show up as behaviors of the self, which become structuralized in the self, and so determine particular ways of child rearing. The child may identify with, or against, the aspects of the parents that are associated with these behaviors. Affect-driven processes lead to psychic structure that affects the next generation. Sutherland gives a view of the self with processes of self-regulation, self-organization, self-renewal and self-transformation going on all the time. It is a positive view that brings hope for improvement and development for the individuals, the next generation, and culture.

This leads to the definition of the self that Sutherland came up with: "The self is a dynamic organization of purposes and commitments whose behavior is governed by conscious and unconscious motives, and whose developments and functioning are inseparably linked to the social environment" (Harrow *et al.* 1994: xxv). To be true to this definition, any psychoanalytic endeavor cannot focus only on the individual's wishes and fears and conflicts, but must consider the self in society as well. Sutherland believed that psychoanalysts must leave the ivory tower and take psychoanalytic knowledge to those who are responsible for the structures of society as well as to the professionals who treat the individuals, couples, and families suffering from mental distress. Sutherland took his knowledge and experience to disadvantaged communities, and he encouraged colleagues to take their psychoanalytic insight and share it with the social workers, family doctors, and clergy dealing with symptoms of social distress, such as high rates of teen pregnancy, drug addition, and domestic violence. These problems are indicators that the community is not able to hold and support its members. Sutherland went further to say that such a community may be the repository for troubled and unwanted parts of the self in a society that is unable or unwilling to deal with these overexciting and under-metabolized aspects of human experience.

I learned this working with Jock as his senior registrar back in the 1970s where he was consulting to a disadvantaged area of Edinburgh, formed after inner-city residents from slums in central Edinburgh were shipped out to the periphery where Edinburgh society would not have to see them, or think about them (Savege 1973). The city then fixed up the vacated slums as attractive flats for young professionals. But there can be no repression without a return of the repressed. Split off and repressed parts that the self cannot bear to keep in consciousness see re-integration: The displaced people expressed their connection to the center of the city by causing the city agencies trouble. In the community itself, there was a high index of social distress, including gang violence, graffiti, and destruction of public telephones, which interrupted essential means of communication for those who could not afford their own lines. In a forward-thinking move, it was agreed that the funding from Westminster for this disadvantaged community should be administered locally by a community board. This board was set up to use the expertise of locals who were already working together in a community organization called the Craigmillar Festival Society that put on a yearly festival at Craigmillar Castle in celebration of their long history. As the locals worked to put on the show, they developed skills for collaborating, cooperating, managing money, getting out publicity, and dealing with visitors. Professionals in community agencies – social workers, ministers, general practitioners, and consultants – worked with these neighborhood organizers to spend the government allocation of funds as the neighborhood saw fit, and so become the society that the residents themselves envisioned. Sutherland pointed out how the split off parts of the self are echoed in the societies that people form, and he helped the professionals to think together, work together, and look for ways to support individual selves to grow in a healthy environment, and create healthy environments in which individual selves could grow.

Sutherland's view of the self is very flexible – fully intrapsychic and at the same time, entirely social. The self is a dynamic system open to feedback, learning from experience, and available for regeneration by self analysis. Sutherland does not mean self analysis with a hyphen, in which an analyst interprets his own dreams in terms of repressed instincts, wish fulfillment, and latent content, as Freud did. By the term self analysis, Sutherland means analysis *of* the self *by* the self. He is referring to the self reflective activity of a person looking at his various behaviors in various situations and his dreams – in the light of Sutherland's definition of the self. People doing self analysis would observe how they act in social situations with various people so as to detect the various aspects of their self in action, and they would read their dreams as "shorts" – film clips of the personality in action, as Fairbairn suggested – rather than as fulfillments of wishes or repressed impulses. And then they would use the insight gained to understand and monitor the self, provide new experiences for learning, and make changes.

Sutherland came across as a healthy, integrated person, who had been effective and productive as a teacher, therapist, editor, writer, and administrator. At the same time, he always felt that he had a block against abstract thinking, a quality he admired in others, and found deficient in himself. Even though he disagreed with Hartmann's conceptual model, he envied Hartmann's capacity to conceptualize (personal communication). He worked in institutions where he created a facilitating environment for colleagues at the Tavistock to produce brilliant ideas, for psychoanalysts to publish in the journals he edited, and for colleagues to bring psychoanalytic ideas to a reluctant public in Scotland. At last he was able to provide the same facilitation for himself, and he did it through his self analysis (1994c). He was inspired to a transformative insight in the course of writing about Fairbairn's splitting of his mother and father figures, when he noticed that the same splitting was going on in his own self, and subjected it to self analysis. He realized that all his life he had been identified with his busy and ambitious mother, a woman who got lots of things done, and even though his editing took him into the business realm of his publisher father, he said that he had been ignoring his father, a more relaxed, laid-back man who enjoyed pottering in his garden and wearing the kilt. He realized that he had been keeping these two figures apart in his mind, not letting them come together, out of envy and hatred for their union. With this insight, he was then able to allow their coming together in his mind and this opened him to his own creativity. This became his evidence for the value of self analysis, about which he also joked, "the perpetual problem is the countertransference!"

After this piece of self analysis, he reached a more integrated state of mind, and became aware of a tremendous upsurge in creative, abstract thinking. He wrote the insightful Fairbairn biography when he was in his eighties. He used to say of the beneficial effects of self analysis, "There is hope for you all. Start at 70!" At the age of 86, he was still working towards a book on the self. Sadly, he did not live to finish it, but some of his preliminary thinking is recorded in Chapter 19. His final paper "The Autonomous Self" (1980a) goes quite a long way to pulling his ideas together.

Sutherland's view of the self as a system operating in an environment where it gets positive feedback from others, a self in dynamic relation, a self as a structure that develops across the lifecycle, culminated in his theory of the autonomous self. *Autonomous* does not mean operating independently of others. It means being whole, integrated, able to relate, able to take in, and able to put out. The self must be, it must do, it must relate. The self is not only being, but it is always becoming, always growing into a shape that lies ahead of it. The self is capable of conceiving of itself as a self. It has a continuity of self feeling. It provides an inner space for reflection. The autonomous self has a capacity to conceive, symbolize, communicate, share, plan, and negotiate. The autonomous self keeps the needs of self and other in balance and builds relationships of mature interdependency.

I would like to make the obvious addition that adult sexual intimacy brings together the inner self and social self in an expression of desire and committed companionship (see Chapters 6 and 7). It does so in a physical setting of high arousal which is a necessary condition for learning and making links. Mind and body, individual and other, come together in a union which is creative and productive as well as playful and physically pleasurable. Physical pleasure ensures that sex will be repeated, and this promotes and maintains the physical and mental union of the couple. In each member of the couple, their union facilitates the integration of parts of the self including the internal couple, a construct based on experiences with the parents over the developmental years, and one that affects and supports the current couple relationship.

In his later years, Sutherland became more interested in, and aware of, the need to analyze aggression. He knew that Klein's emphasis on aggression was important, but when he would recommend her approach he usually did so with a joke: "to understand this patient you need to enter darkest Melanesia." He found the Kleinian women a formidable group, but he valued their contributions especially when his drive to establish the Scottish Institute in a non-analytic climate confronted him with hatred and envy. Even so, he did not accept Klein's ideas on the source of aggression, because he thought that aggression arises from the frustration of attachment needs, as Bowlby had said, and the frustration of being in a satisfying relationship, as Fairbairn had said, but certainly not what Klein said – a desperate defense against annihilation of the self. He said, "I don't think we need Klein's death instinct. What we need is a protesting organism" (1994b: 389). Sutherland had his own ideas as to what the protesting is about, and this is where he goes beyond Bowlby and Fairbairn. It is not just protest about the fact that proximity and security of attachment and a meaningful relationship are not being offered. In Sutherland's view, aggression results from, and promotes, the struggle to pursue autonomy when the infant is frustrated by prolonged dependence. In his own words, "Far from being undifferentiated as Freud described it at birth, the self is being formed steadily and only interference with the self determining dynamic elicits intense aggression" (1980a: 330). To me, this is the crucial point. Where Freud saw sexual and aggressive drives, where Klein saw life and death instincts, Sutherland sees an autonomy drive leading the self to become the self that is inherited and that will be developed in interaction with others.

Applying the theory to ourselves, the autonomy drive is the drive to achieve our potential, to be what we can be, and become what we can become. If we allow ourselves to benefit from many opportunities, learning situations, experiences in relationships, and social groups, we will grow as integrated, self-actualized, productive, well-related people. We will then have an autonomous self "a highly integrative structure, which can permit us to internalize the world, play with it inside, and make innovating possibilities" (1994b: 389).

Sutherland was the epitome of an autonomous self – a very personal man, warm, respectful, and in his own way quite private, although socially engaging, intellectually independent, and astute. He was interested in clinical work, teaching, supervision, consultation to communities and businesses, writing, editing, institution building, and community outreach. A fantastic span, and it gives us an inspiring view of what we can accomplish if we work together to realize his vision of a truly multidimensional psychoanalysis, one that is built from the sharing of experiences of clinicians working across the modalities of psychoanalysis and psychotherapy with other professionals working in the caring system, and one that therefore also applies across the modalities of treatment and social intervention.

References

Averill, S. (1992). Epilogue. In J. S. Scharff (ed.) *The Autonomous Self: The Work of John D. Sutherland*, p. 427. Northvale, NJ: Jason Aronson.

Chein, I. (1972). *Science of Behavior and the Image of Man*. New York: Basic Books.

Fairbairn, W. R. D. (1952). *Psychoanalytic Studies of the Personality*. London: Routledge & Kegan Paul.

Harrow, A., Leishman, M., Macdonald, M. and Scott, D. (1994). Introduction. In J. S. Scharff (ed.) *The Autonomous Self: The Work of John D. Sutherland*, pp. xv–xxv. Northvale, NJ: Jason Aronson.

Jantsch, E. (1980). *The Self-Organizing Universe: Scientific and Human Implications of the Emerging Paradigm of Evolution*. New York: Pergamon.

Kohon, G. (1996). Review of *The Autonomous Self: The Work of John D. Sutherland*, ed. J. S. Scharff. *Journal of the American Psychoanalytic Association* 44, 4: 1261–1262.

Kohut, H. (1971). *The Analysis of the Self. A Systematic Approach to the Psychoanalytic Treatment of Narcissistic Personality Disorder*. New York: International Universities Press.

Lichtenstein, H. (1977). *The Dilemma of Human Identity*. New York: Jason Aronson.

Negroponte, N. (1995). *Being Digital*. New York: Random House.

Padel, J. (1995). Review of *The Autonomous Self: The Work of John D. Sutherland*, ed. J. S. Scharff. *International Journal of Psycho-Analysis* 76: 177–179.

Prigogine, I. (1976). Order through fluctuation: self organization and social system. In C. H. Waddington and E. Jantsch (eds) *Evolution and Consiousness: Human Systems in Transition*, pp. 93–126. Reading, MA: Addison-Wesley.

Savege, J. (1973). Psychodynamic understanding in community psychiatry. *Psychotherapy and Psychosomatics* 25: 272–278.

Scharff, J. S. (ed.) (1994). *The Autonomous Self: The Work of John D. Sutherland*. Northvale, NJ: Jason Aronson.

Schore, A. (1994). *Affect Regulation and the Origin of the Self: The Neurobiology of Emotional Development.* Hillsdale, NJ: Lawrence Erlbaum Associates, Inc.

Sutherland, J. D. (1963). Object relations theory and the conceptual model of psychoanalysis. *British Journal of Medical Psychology* 36: 109–124.

—— (1980a). The autonomous self. In J. S. Scharff (ed.) *The Autonomous Self: The Work of John D. Sutherland*, pp. 303–330. Based on unpublished paper, "Hate and the autonomy of the self". Also published as "The autonomous self", *Bulletin of the Menninger Clinic* 57, 1: 3–32, 1993.

—— (1980b). The British object relations theorists. In J. S. Scharff (ed.) *The Autonomous Self: The Work of John D. Sutherland*, pp. 25–44. Northvale, NJ: Jason Aronson.

—— (1989). *Fairbairn's Journey to the Interior.* London: Free Association Books.

—— (1994a). An object relations view of the great man. In J. S. Scharff (ed.) *The Autonomous Self: The Work of John D. Sutherland*, pp. 350–371. Northvale, NJ: Jason Aronson.

—— (1994b). On being and becoming a person. Lecture at the Washington School of Psychiatry, 1993. In J. S. Scharff (ed.) *The Autonomous Self: The Work of John D. Sutherland*, pp. 372–391. Northvale, NJ: Jason Aronson.

—— (1994c). Reminiscences. In J. S. Scharff (ed.) *The Autonomous Self: The Work of John D. Sutherland*, pp. 392–423. Northvale, NJ: Jason Aronson.

Chapter 21

Personal relations theory

Suttie, Fairbairn, Macmurray and Sutherland

Graham Clarke

John D. Sutherland called for a comprehensive theory of the self. To take up this challenge, I think we need to go back to the work of Suttie, Macmurray and Fairbairn, with Fairbairn's psychology of dynamic structure at the centre. I think it will help us to pursue this project if we give the distinctive body of work from this group of Scots a unique name. Object relations theory comes to mind, but it has become a catchall phrase that can be seen to include Kleinians, contemporary Freudians, a variety of independents at the very least, and maybe self psychologists and intersubjectivists too, many of whom share little in the way of fundamental ideas with Fairbairn, whom I take to be the exemplar of an object relations viewpoint. So I suggest using "personal relations theory" – a term invented by Fairbairn already.

It was in Sutherland's synoptic last paper, "The Autonomous Self" (1980/1993), that I first read that Fairbairn wanted to call his unique development of object relations theory "personal relations theory". I had just spent some time looking at the parallels between the thinking of Fairbairn and Macmurray. I had read Andrew Collier's *Being and Worth* (1999), which commends Macmurray's Spinozist view that rationality and irrationality are qualities of emotion, a view on reason and emotion that is similar to Antonio Damasio's (2003). In response to Collier's book, Wesley Shumar's (1999) review in *Alethia* (relaunched as the *Journal of Critical Realism*) suggests that Macmurray's work might form a theoretical basis for the object relations approach to psychoanalysis.

One person that provides a link between Macmurray and Fairbairn is their Scottish contemporary Ian D. Suttie, who was still active at the time when both men were formulating their later thinking. Macmurray explicitly acknowledged Suttie's influence on him, and Sutherland acknowledged Suttie's influence on Fairbairn. At a conference on Fairbairn in New York a few years ago, Alan Harrow (1998), of the then Scottish Institute of Human Relations, drew attention to the connections between Sutherland, Fairbairn and Suttie, mentioning Macmurray in passing. Harrow also noted the religious dimension to the theories of all these men: Sutherland argues that there is an innate capacity for empathy (as does Trevarthen); Suttie, Fairbairn and Macmurray argue that in our early infancy we depend totally upon an all-powerful, all-knowing and loving personal other who has the power of life and death over us. Suttie and Fairbairn believe that separation anxiety is the major problem we face as we grow up. Fairbairn holds that our original object is constitutive, to some degree, of our ego ideal. Taken together, the ideas of Suttie, Fairbairn and Macmurray could furnish us with a felt relation to the world that is akin to the positive notion of a loving personal god. As a secularist I have some difficulties with the religious dimension to this body of thought, but I appreciate that it provides an object relations account of the widespread belief in God or gods, without implying anything about the actual existence of gods.

In 1935 in his introduction to *The Origins of Love and Hate*, Suttie wrote presciently:

> English psychologists, who remain unattached to any "school," suffer a great disadvantage in lack of cooperation or even of common under-standing. Further (largely in consequence of this), they suffer in pres-tige and publicity and are stigmatised by psycho-analysts as half-hearted, eclectic and individualistic plagiarists of the Freudian discoveries. Neither their criticisms of psycho-analysis nor their own positive views had suf-ficient unity to lend each other support or to serve as a basis for further cooperative development.
>
> (Suttie 1935: 4)

Sadly, this might be seen to apply to the fate of three of the men I have cited: Suttie, tragically, because he died on the day of his book's publication; Fairbairn, because he remained an independent thinker in Scotland, far away from London, the centre of psychoanalytic development in the UK; and Macmurray because of his communitarian and action-based philosophy. Yet the three men are connected by their shared cultural roots. In a recent essay on Macmurray, Trevarthen (2002) locates the origins of the views that he and Macmurray share in the Scottish Enlightenment. Indeed, I think it is the legacy of the productive confrontation between idealism and common-sense thinking in eighteenth-century Scotland, from which, by the 1930s, these three distinctively different thinkers, two educated at Glasgow and one at Edinburgh, came to develop strikingly similar ideas concerning the nature, origins and development of the self.

What I am hoping to do is to use something from all four men – Sutherland, Fairbairn, Macmurray and Suttie – to sketch in the characteristics of a per-sonal relations theory approach. I could have taken Sutherland's paper and extracted the required characteristics from there, commenting upon their antecedents in the work of these other thinkers, but since I have been struck by the way in which each of the three develop similar ideas in similar terms, I thought it would be interesting to share that aspect of their family resemblance.

Maybe by bringing together their individual strengths and trying to combine them as part of a personal relations theory, their own singular contributions will come into greater and more positive relief.

Fairbairn

David Scharff and Ellinor Fairbairn Birtles (1997) have already pointed out the degree to which Fairbairn's thought has been appropriated by a number of strands within contemporary psychoanalysis without that appropriation being properly acknowledged. At the level of university education in the UK, in the various new psychoanalytic studies courses that have developed over the past decade or two, Fairbairn is sadly under-represented relative to his real importance in the development of psychoanalytic theory. Object relations has become almost synonymous with Klein in many people's minds and few other thinkers are properly recognised: Winnicott being the exception perhaps. However, as we know from synoptic studies of the development of object relations thinking, neither Klein nor Winnicott ever achieved the level of clarity or consistency that Fairbairn, with his training in philosophy, was able to achieve (Mitchell and Greenberg 1983; Hughes 1989).

Macmurray: the primacy of action

Let us start with one of the distinguishing characteristics of Macmurray's philosophy, the primacy of action. As Bevir and O'Brien (1999) put it:

> In modern philosophy, the self appears first of all in a contemplative realm, withdrawing from action to attain certain knowledge of itself and thus the world. Macmurray, in contrast, privileges action over thought. Action is the fullest expression of our human nature because it involves both mind and body whereas thought involves mind alone.
>
> (Bevir and O'Brien 1999: 3)

It should perhaps be pointed out that action is, at the very least, felt action. As Macmurray says:

> The infant's original consciousness, even as regards its sensory elements, must be feeling and feeling at its most primitive and undiscriminated level . . . the most we have a right to assert . . . is an original capacity to distinguish in feeling between comfort and discomfort. We postulate therefore; an original feeling consciousness with a discrimination between positive and negative phases.
>
> (Macmurray 1998: 57).

The baby then employs the only means open to communicate a feeling of comfort or discomfort to the mother. This recalls Fairbairn's account of infantile dependence and the pristine ego and Suttie's conclusion that: "We need only suppose the child is born with a mind and instincts adapted to infancy, or, in other words, so disposed as to profit by parental nature . . . Instead of an armament of instincts . . . it is born with a simple attachment to mother who is the sole source of food and protection" (Suttie 1935: 12). The infant is born adapted to being unadapted, as Macmurray puts it.

Trevarthen noted that Macmurray's Gifford lectures published in the late 1960s "were read with gratitude by a group of observers of infancy . . . who felt that they had independently discovered innate human abilities of a kind that had escaped attention by the authorities of behavioural and cognitive development in children" (2002: 82). This group included Daniel Stern. Published in the early 1950s, Fairbairn's book, which met with a hostile reception, may have been simply too early to trigger a similar reaction of recognition. After all, the research of John Bowlby on separation and loss and his development of attachment theory were significantly influenced by both Suttie and Fairbairn. According to Trevarthen:

> Modern naturalistic research has brought proof that infants are born as human beings who express personal powers of consciousness. Macmurray's view of human nature has been confirmed and extended . . . Their researches give support to a rich common-sense understanding of the "personal powers" born in humans and developing rapidly in the young child. Our assessment of Macmurray's theory of the infant's mind to the mother's care and teaching opens the way to an examination [of] what this psychology implies morally and politically.
>
> (Trevarthen 2002: 105).

All of this echoes ideas common to Fairbairn, Suttie and Sutherland and raises questions concerning the moral and political dimensions of this viewpoint. Is this a land fit for mature dependence?

Bevir and O'Brien (1999) argue:

> Macmurray . . . defends a thick concept of the self as embedded in inter-personal relations: "The Self is constituted by its relations to the Other" – "it has its being in its relationships" (Macmurray 1998, p. 17). This dependence upon others appears most forcefully in the relationship of the child to the mother . . . Such dependence "the mother–child relation" represents "the basic form of human existence", that is "a 'You and I' with a common life" (Macmurray 1998, p. 60) . . . it is inherently communal.
>
> (Bevir and O'Brien 1999: 2)

This is a view common to all of them.

So far we have an active self, which is innately geared to suckling and to making and sustaining relationships with a personal other. The overriding importance of the success of this earliest of relationships is stressed by Suttie, Fairbairn, Macmurray, and Sutherland. According to Fairbairn, it is failure in this early relationship that lies at the heart of all psychopathology. Sutherland and Trevarthen on the basis of recent infant research argue that the infant is more active than the others realised in making and sustaining this crucial relationship, but this is merely a degree of difference rather than an absolute disagreement, and all accept the foundational nature of this early relationship.

Macmurray's disillusionment and Fairbairn's tripartite structure

What happens when this earliest relationship fails to some degree or another, as it inevitably must, when in Fairbairn's terms it becomes unsatisfactory to some degree? For Fairbairn, this is the point at which the basic endopsychic structure is formed in order to be able to sustain the necessary relationship with mother. When Macmurray comes to deal with this process he chooses a phenomenon that he may have encountered in Winnicott, the process of disillusionment, the refusal of the mother to continue doing things that she judges the child is now ready and able to do for itself. This is clearly a benign situation and thus simpler to analyse than the random shortcomings of everyday life that lead to unsatisfactory situations which generate the basic endopsychic structure. However, there is a striking parallel between Macmurray's analysis of the possible consequences of disillusionment and Fairbairn's tripartite endopsychic structure. Macmurray suggests one positive and two negative possible outcomes to any attempted disillusionment characterised by the dominance of one or other of two motives, love and fear. Macmurray derives these basic motivations from Suttie and they need to be carefully considered against Fairbairn's choice of love and aggression as the underlying motive forces in any attempt to properly order a personal relations theory. For Suttie and Macmurray, fear produces aggression and hatred as a response to having love threatened or withdrawn. I think it would be fair to say that the libidinal and antilibidinal subsidiary selves of Fairbairn's theory of dynamic structures that form to bind aggression are based upon responses to fear. So the gap between these different formulations is not necessarily substantial.

In Macmurray's account of the negative response to disillusionment, based upon the continued existence of fear, we see something very similar to the development of Fairbairn's subsidiary libidinal and antilibidinal selves. One response is characterised by Macmurray as being "good", or over-compliant, and the other as "bad", or aggressive and rebellious:

> Both types of attitude – submissive and aggressive – are negative, and therefore involve unreality. They carry over the illusion of the negative

phase of withdrawal into the return to active relationship. They motivate a behaviour in relationship which is contradictory and therefore self defeating. For the inherent objective – the reality of the relationship – is the full mutuality of fellowship in a common life, the only way in which the individual can realise himself in person. But both the dispositions are egocentric, and motivate action that is for the sake of oneself, and not for the sake of the Other, which is therefore self-interested. Such action is implicitly a refusal of mutuality, and an effort to constrain the other to do what we want. By conforming submissively to his wishes we put him under an obligation to care for us. By aggressive behaviour we seek to make him afraid not to care for us. In both cases we are cheating: If it succeeds in its intention it produces the appearance of mutuality, but not the reality. It can produce, at most, a reciprocity of co-operation which simulates, even while it excludes, the personal unity which it seeks to achieve.

(Macmurray 1961/1998: 105)

Fairbairn's subsidiary selves and transitional techniques

We all start oriented towards reality and are deflected from that by our experiences of the world and others. The attempt to achieve mature dependence is the attempt to achieve a real relation to others and to see things clearly as they are. Our subsidiary selves operate exactly like these negative motivations based upon past object relations and prevent our acting realistically or really sharing our world. This naturally raises the issue of how one can overcome these negative aspects of the developing relationship between self and the world, which leads into the wider world of self and other. This is the world of Fairbairn's transitional techniques. Their terminus for some is in the achievement of mature dependency, which on this account has a substantial social and political dimension. For Padel (1991) the motor of psychic growth is bringing to consciousness object relations from the subsidiary selves and transforming them, so that the powers of the central self are enhanced at the expense of the subsidiary selves.

Suttie: sociocultural influences on the self

Suttie is particularly strong in his recognition and understanding of the contingent nature of the social world. Apart from his grounding in biology which leads to his trenchant criticism of the death instinct and instinct theory, in general he seems to me to be the first to develop the view that the Oedipus complex is a social and not a psychological situation, as Fairbairn later put it. Suttie says: "The Oedipus Complex, being largely contingent on particular modes of rearing and forms of family structure, culture and racial character must vary within wide limits" (1935: 5). In a wider context he also notes that "Freud and Adler ... naively regard as 'human nature' or 'instincts' traits and dispositions which may turn out to be the product in subtle ways of certain factors in our particular culture" (p. 7). Suttie even suggests that a properly matriarchal culture may not require repression at all given that it is the renunciation of the mother under patriarchy that is the motor of repression in Freud. This is a radical perspective indeed and would repay further investigation. Like Suttie, Fairbairn and Macmurray both recognise the contingent nature of our social existence, which accounts for the existential aspects of their thinking. Indeed it can be regarded as foundational to the view that this is a tragic rather than a fallen universe.

Towards a personal relations theory

The personal relations theory that I am proposing is based upon the work of three Scottish thinkers, Suttie, Fairbairn and Macmurray, and takes account of the recent work on human development and infant research identified by Sutherland and spelt out in detail by Trevarthen. It recognises that we are active, reality oriented, personal and social beings from the start, instinctively geared to suckling and to forming and sustaining relationships. It argues that we can only develop to our fullest if we are part of a joyful and loving dyad in our earliest relationship. It asserts that our overall motivations are love and fear and that it is fear that generates splitting and repression within inner reality. Finally it stresses that our fulfilment is in personal relationships within a community, and that the form of our social and political reality is contingent, but the great obstacle is fear. Each new life is a new possibility for love to blossom into mature dependence, organising and sustaining a common world for the benefit of all.

References

Bevir, M. and O'Brien, D. (1999). *The Philosophy of John Macmurray*. University of Newcastle (www.psa.ac.uk/cps/1999/bevir2.pdf).

Collier, A. (1999). *Being and Worth*. London: Routledge.

Damasio, A. (2003). *Looking for Spinoza: Joy, Sorrow and the Feeling of Pain*. London: Harcourt.

Harrow, J. A. (1998). The Scottish Connection, Suttie – Fairbairn – Sutherland: the quiet revolution. In N. J. Skolnick and D. E. Scharff (eds) *Fairbairn Then and Now*, pp. 3–16. Hillsdale, NJ: Analytic Press.

Hughes, J. (1989). *Reshaping the Psycho-Analytic Domain*. London: University of California Press.

Macmurray, J. (1961/1998). *Persons in Relation (1961)*. Vol. 2 of *The Form of the Personal*. London: Faber and Faber.

Mitchell, S. A. and Greenberg, J. R. (1993). *Object Relations in Psychoanalytic Theory*. Cambridge, MA: Harvard University Press.

Padel, J. (1991). Fairbairn's thoughts on the relationship of inner and outer worlds. *Free Associations*. 2(24): 589–615.

Scharff, D. E. and Birtles, E. F. (1997). From instinct to self: the evolution and implications of W. R. D. Fairbairn's theory of object relations. *International Journal of Psycho-Analysis* 78(6): 1085–1103.

Shumar, W. (1999). Beyond anthropocentrism in ethics. *Alethia* (recently relaunched as *Journal of Critical Realism*) 2: Part 2.

Sutherland, J. D. (1980/1993). The autonomous self. *Bulletin of the Menninger Clinic* 57(1): 3–32.

Suttie, I. D. (1935). Introduction. *The Origins of Love and Hate*, p. 4. London: Pelican, 1961.

Trevarthen, C. (2002). Proof of sympathy: the scientific evidence on the personality of the infant in Macmurray's *Mother and Child*. In D. Fergusson and N. Dower (eds) *John Macmurray: Critical Perspectives*, pp. 77–117. London: Peter Lang.

Chapter 22

Autonomy, the autonomous self, and the inter-human

Philosophy and psychoanalysis in the teaching of Sutherland

Neville Singh

Introduction

The concept of autonomy is well known in the literature of the philosophy of mind, the philosophy of action, and moral philosophy. David Rapaport, who attempted to systematize Freudian theory, introduced the concept of relative autonomy into psychoanalysis many years ago (Rapaport 1960). In his seventies, Sutherland became increasingly concerned about – not just interested in – the Self, both theoretically and practically as a psychoanalyst and teacher of psychoanalysis, which culminated in the posthumous publication (1993) of his last paper, "The Autonomous Self" (1980). My emphasis on the Inter-human acknowledges the influence on Sutherland of the great Jewish social and moral philosopher, Martin Buber, famous for his religious-ethical concept of "I and Thou" which is echoed in object relations theory. Like Buber in the late 1950s and early 1960s, Sutherland had links with the Washington School of Psychiatry in the late 1970s and 1980s.

Sutherland originally taught science and psychology before he studied medicine, psychiatry, and psychoanalysis. Like the American psychologist Isidor Chein who wrote *The Science of Behaviour and the Image of Man* (1972), which neatly integrated science and philosophy in psychology, Sutherland in his own lecture "The Psychodynamic Image of Man" (1979) approached personal being in terms that integrated science, psychoanalysis and philosophy. Sutherland was an impressive teacher, one of broad scope who taught beyond his designated subject matter, and was therefore in a league with teachers like Philip Rieff, the sociologist, and psychiatrists Robert Coles and Robert J. Lifton. Like his psychoanalytic colleague, the late Tom Main, Sutherland believed that psychoanalysis went beyond the consulting room but he cautioned that applied psychoanalysis in the broad field of care needs to be relevant and useful.

Sutherland as philosophical psychoanalyst

I will now proceed to lift out those philosophical themes inherent in Sutherland's teaching though not fully developed or articulated. It is striking that none of Sutherland's psychoanalytic writings are exclusively clinical. He never failed to be aware and mindful of adjacent subjects and disciplines, and he maintained a close association with the social scientists Eric Trist and Fred Emery. Sutherland's psychoanalysis has always been inclusive of contemporary ideas, with particular reference to social and moral thought. He distinguishes between morality, morals and moralizing. Morality is a vital necessity for a caring, healthy society whereas morals and moralizing can lead to social exclusion.

I have selected three of Sutherland's papers which articulate particularly well his views on the person embedded in society, on the person in relation to other persons, the self in relation to others, and the self in relation to oneself. These papers are: "The Psychodynamic Image of Man" (1979), "On Becoming and Being a Person" (1987), and "The Autonomous Self" (1980 in Scharff 1994).

The Psychodynamic Image of Man

"The Psychodynamic Image of Man", subtitled "A Philosophy for the Caring Professions", is replete with social and moral philosophical observations and principles. Sutherland sets his focus early in the paper:

> I want to focus on care devoted to the development and well-being of the person – to those factors that equip and maintain the individual in the business of living with a sense of wholeness and responsible autonomy . . . My interest is care related to what goes on at the centre of the person, where he is, or should be, in himself as a responsible free agent.
>
> (Sutherland 1979: 268)

"Responsible autonomy" and "responsible free agent" are social and moral philosophical concepts, which bring the two branches of philosophy together by way of human agency and action or praxis. Later, Sutherland would conceptualize what he refers to here as "what goes on at the centre of the person" as the Self. Further on, he declares: "I shall confine myself to the professions because I believe that they must constitute the vital core of our overall endeavour to provide *articulated knowledge* and *responsible practice*" [my emphases] (1979: 269). In addition to the social and moral philosophical concept and principle of "responsible practice", Sutherland, who had also trained in the sciences, stresses the vital importance of "articulated knowledge". Later on he would speak of the serious need for "validated knowledge", a principle inherent in the philosophy of science (p. 281).

Here's Sutherland again: "We cannot expect to foster responsible adults for instance, if we treat people as such in one sector and at the same time deny *responsible participation* in another" [my emphasis] (1979: 273). The very word "deny" in that sentence brings social and moral philosophy into contact with politics and society and raises the issues of social justice and social inclusion. From when he was at the Tavistock Institute after World War II, Sutherland was concerned about the consequences of exclusion of persons from purposeful participation in society. His was an inclusive, social psychoanalysis.

The following passage points to Sutherland as both humane philosophical psychoanalyst and rigorous scientist: "The psychodynamic image of man thus puts care for the person as essential for growth and our maintaining well-being. We are not dealing with a sentimental value. Care is a necessity in our philosophy and a necessity established on scientific evidence" (p. 277). He conceptualizes man as a "progressive organization of relatedness". He holds that "the foundation layer of the system, the primal organizer that holds the developmental differentiation together, is established effectively only when the relatedness is of love and care and, without a later input of that kind in maturer patterns, it becomes difficult to maintain the system as a whole" (p. 276).

On Becoming and Being a Person

At the very beginning of this paper Sutherland announces: "In recent years, I have got rather obsessed with the problem of the self because of what I feel to be the clamorous need for a new paradigm in psychoanalytic theory" (1987, in Scharff 1994: 372). I really do think that had Sutherland lived for a few years longer and remained physically fit he would have articulated the beginnings of a coherent metapsychology of the self. Like Freud, he was convinced that "without metapsychological speculation and theorising . . . we shall not get a step further" (Freud 1937: 326, quoted in Reisner 1991: 439).

The following passage shows Sutherland the psychoanalyst who is knowledgeable about the new biology and Sutherland the social thinker:

> Each organism contains an organising principle that determines the potential shape of the adult organism. Development within an organism, which is an open system, necessarily demands an autonomous urge to maintain this wholeness of the shape; otherwise, the organism dies. A threat to the autonomy of the organism is tantamount to a threat from a lethal predator. To survive it has to assert itself autonomously at all times with varying degrees of force, up to the point of maximum ferocity. Paradoxically, its resources for doing so, however, have to be developed – and to an increasing extent as we ascend the evolutionary scale – from its relatedness with the adults. The organism's life becomes the dynamic

process of preserving its autonomy within the heteronomy of relatedness with its social group and the physical environment.

(Sutherland 1987, in Scharff 1994: 376).

Sutherland's inclusion of the external environment is quite unusual in psychoanalytic theories.

Further on he repeats: "It is characteristic that, as we go up the evolutionary scale, the innate potential has more and more plasticity, more of a potential, rather than an inherited specific pattern. And the potential to reach adult development has to be realized within the framework of relationships with adults" (p. 376). You will have noticed Sutherland's preference for the idea of innate potential over inherited specific pattern. This is a very important distinction. Sutherland's is a psychology of progressive, organized becoming, rather than of overdetermination.

Here's Sutherland again: "The function of the self, or the person, is to integrate a developing series of differentiated sub-structures within what has been an integrated whole to cope with various specific needs, but a structure that retains its holistic quality. I postulate an autonomous self" (p. 379). I suggest that this condensed passage contains the ingredients for a coherent metapsychology of the self: depth psychology meets biology.

The following quote from the same paper shows Sutherland actually using the word metapsychology, a word he seldom uses in his writings: "All I want to stress is that we've simply got to take as the basic feature in metapsychology the autonomous struggle of the self. Rather than the vicissitudes of instinct, let's think of the *vicissitudes of the self* in the relationships it finds" [my emphasis] (p. 382).

Further on he writes: "A critical feature of working with the self as the agent in its presenting difficulties, is that we deal very little in metaphors. The self's experience is an ultimate factor, the thing in itself, and not requiring hypothetical realities other than itself" (p. 389). This phrasing recalls that of Edmund Husserl, the father of phenomenology, whose famous philosophical call was "to the things themselves" (1966: 3). I never heard Sutherland mention Husserl, but might he have heard of Husserl in the 1930s and 1940s from acquaintances in the Department of Philosophy at Edinburgh University?

Here's Sutherland's interesting observation on Melanie Klein's emphasis on the death instinct as the primary motivating engine of ego development: "I don't think we need Klein's death instinct. What we need is a protesting organism" (1987, in Scharff 1994: 389). There is so much potential in that all-too-brief comment. Sutherland was impressed with the self-actualizing potential of the self, and the idea of a self driven by mere instincts was anathema to him. He wanted more psychoanalysts to devote their attention to understanding the self in terms of relationships and potentialities, not putative constitutional givens.

At the end of the paper he predicts: "I think that the future of psycho-analytic theory will certainly rest on getting the self properly conceptualized" (p. 389). Here Sutherland is laying the foundation for a coherent developing theory of the self; work that will have to be continued by others.

The Autonomous Self

The last paper that I have chosen is closely related to the second of my trilogy. "The Autonomous Self", written in 1980, was originally submitted for publication in 1993 in the *Bulletin of the Menninger Clinic* by Sutherland's widow, the late Molly Sutherland, who followed closely the broad scope of his thought and work, especially in the issues of social care. I cannot do better than quote the editorial comments on the paper:

> Although the nature of the self has become a central issue in psycho-analysis, a comprehensive theory of its origin and development is needed. In an effort to elaborate one such theory, the author first reviews the history of psychoanalytic conceptualisations of the self. He then examines extra-clinical evidence from literature, philosophy, and the social sciences to gain additional insight into the persistent features of the self. Finally, he outlines some unique characteristics of the human self in light of new insights from modern evolutionary biology.
>
> (Averill 1993: 3)

This important paper needs to be read and re-read in its entirety in order to fully understand and appreciate its significance for psychoanalysis. I will quote a few passages from it. Sutherland, the astute observer of the history of psychoanalytic ideas, writes:

> What Erikson described as identity was the objectification of the self into a person with a sense of being a "somebody" aware of personal history and whose self had been organized into patterns laid down by peer social groups. The person recognized by others was the identity objectified, while the inner sense of being this person reflected this identity, although the existential awareness was absolutely unique to the individual.
>
> (Sutherland 1993: 9).

Sutherland's use of the term existential drew from his reading of a landmark publication *The Existential Core of Psychoanalysis* by Avery Weisman (1965). Returning to the concept of social being, Sutherland writes: "We refer to the human consciousness of being a unique person aware of one's own identity and boundaries in relation to others" (1993: 25).

Regarding the early development of the self, Sutherland notes:

At first, the self does not need to be conscious of itself in the manner of the adult. In an environment that is actively anticipating and providing for the needs of the self, the organization of experience can proceed by a sentience that monitors and distinguishes what feels "right" or "good" from what does not meet the tensions of need and so is affectively frustrating – that is, "bad" or "wrong". The growth of self awareness, however, must begin early to develop the capacity to be alert to the attitudes of others by recognizing their emotional states.

(Sutherland 1993: 27)

Intersubjectivity: philosophy (phenomenology) meets psychoanalysis

Interestingly, the intersubjective school of psychoanalysis has become increasingly influential in the last decade. Sutherland was always ahead of the curve as shown in the following excerpt:

Intersubjective sharing . . . is the means through which individuals can relate with rapid appraisals of intentions and affects in others. This sharing develops from the simultaneous acquisition of self-awareness and the knowledge of the self-states of others. In short, the person is created from interchanges with other persons.

(Sutherland 1993: 31)

Like the phenomenologist and social-moral-political philosopher Paul Ricoeur (1970), Sutherland enjoys an intellectually discerning, rigorous yet open approach and attitude to the life of the mind and its depths (Cohen and Marsh 2002). Quoting and commenting on Ricoeur, Richard Kearney (1996) writes: "The shortest route from self to self is through the other. This dictum of Paul Ricoeur expresses his central conviction that the self is never enough, is never sufficient unto its self, but constantly seeks out signs and signals of meaning in the other" (p. 1). Sutherland's philosophy of psychoanalysis precisely.

References

Averill, S. (1993). Preface: The autonomous self. *Bulletin of the Menninger Clinic* 57, 1: 3.

Chein, I. (1972). *The Science of Behaviour and the Image of Man*. New York: Basic Books.

Cohen, R. A. and Marsh, J. I. (eds) (2002). *Ricoeur As Another: The Ethics of Subjectivity*. New York: State University of New York Press.

Freud, S. (1937). Analysis terminable and interminable. *Standard Edition*, 23: 209–253.

Husserl, E. (1966). *The Idea of Phenomenology*, trans. W. P. Alston and G. Nakhnikian. The Hague: Nijhoff.

Kearney, R. (ed.) (1996). *Paul Ricoeur: The Hermeneutics of Action*. London: Sage.

Rapaport, D. (1960). *The Structure of Psychoanalytic Theory: A Systematizing Attempt*. New York: International Universities Press.

Reisner, S. (1991). Reclaiming the metapsychology: classical revisionism seduction and the self in Freudian analysis. *Psychoanalytic Psychology* 8, 4: 439–462.

Ricoeur, P. (1970). *Freud and Philosophy: An Essay on Interpretation*, trans. D. Savage. New Haven and London: Yale University Press.

Scharff, J. S. (ed.) (1994). *The Autonomous Self: The Work of John D. Sutherland*. New York and London: Jason Aronson.

Sutherland, J. D. (1979). The psychodynamic image of man. In *The Autonomous Self: The Work of John D Sutherland*, ed. J. Scharff, pp. 268–282. New York and London: Jason Aronson, 1994.

—— (1980). The autonomous self. *Bulletin of the Menninger Clinic* 57, 1: 3–32, and in *The Autonomous Self: The Work of John D. Sutherland*, ed. J. S. Scharff, pp. 303–330. New York and London: Jason Aronson.

—— (1987). On becoming and being a person. In *The Autonomous Self: The Work of John D Sutherland*, ed. J. Scharff, pp. 372–391. New York and London: Jason Aronson, 1994.

Weisman, A. (1965). *The Existential Core of Psychoanalysis: Reality Sense and Responsibility*. Boston: Little, Brown & Company.

Chapter 23

The social object and the pathology of prejudice

Ron B. Aviram

Prejudice and discrimination have been in evidence throughout history, and efforts to minimize their manifestations have not been successful. In the last 20 years, social-cognitive approaches have been brought to bear on understanding how social conditions influence psychological processes that contribute to prejudice. These theories provide important information about intergroup functioning, but they do not adequately address individual differences in prejudiced behavior, nor do they offer an intrapsychic model that can help identify developmental precursors for prejudice. I propose that developmental theory enriched by a relational perspective drawing on Fairbairn can address the gaps in our understanding of the origins of prejudice in individuals and societies.

The relational perspective on developmental theory (Bowlby 1969; Chodorow 1978; Stern 1985) has its roots in object relations theory. Human infants seek contact and affiliation with caregivers (Fairbairn 1952), and a sense of self evolves in relationship with others (Rubens 1994). In contrast to this expectation of development, a rigidly held focus on differences and separateness to the extreme may be regarded as pathological. Given that object relations theory addresses the normal relational development of persons, as well as the psychopathology associated with poor relational abilities, it stands to reason that object relations theory may be able to offer the theoretical foundation needed to integrate developmental and intrapsychic phenomena with the social cognitive emphasis on interpersonal and intergroup processes as they pertain to prejudice (Aviram 2002).

Prejudice is an attitude of mind in which a person, or a group, highlights differences that justify remaining separate from, or downright hostile to, certain others. One definition for prejudice is: "an unfair negative attitude toward a social group or a person perceived to be a member of that group" (Dovidio *et al.* 2000: 137). Favoring one's own group (the ingroup), and simultaneously perceiving some other groups negatively (the outgroups) may be a manifestation of particular intrapsychic needs that reflect idealized and disparaged social object representations, based on incorporated aspects of culture and identity. These social objects have dynamic energy in addition to the dynamic energy of the object representations associated with important early figures.

During certain periods in history, or in certain contexts, we all function at a level that involves group-based identity, known in the social psychological literature as *collective identity*. Collective identity becomes salient in response to an external threat that forces perceptions of self and other into categories of affiliation, such as race, religion, or nationality. When this occurs many people are likely to favor the ingroup, and to show prejudice to outgroups. Even when there is no threat, some individuals depend upon their collective identity to maintain or enhance self-worth and self-esteem (Tajfel and Turner 1979). These individuals, who are overdependent upon their ingroup remain prejudiced against certain outgroups all the time, regardless of social conditions. This is the kind of person that I will describe in a clinical vignette, later in this chapter. Individuals who harbor prejudiced (negative) views of certain outgroups, regardless of social conditions, establish an overidentification with a social group, which must therefore reflect an intrapsychic dependence on the group to compensate for a psychological threat to the self. Furthermore, it is a compensation that eliminates differentiation between self and group.

Object relations theory provides a developmental and intrapsychic explanation for normal identity formation of self in relation to affiliative groups and for overdependence on group identity in connection to pathological prejudice. Blos (1962) stated that, during the identity formation process, "the significant emotional needs and conflicts of early childhood must be recapitulated" (p. 11). Early object relations have implications for the development of identity formation. Identity formation is dependent upon the interrelationship of self and the social group, and so is prejudice. The object relations viewpoint provides a framework from which to understand prejudice as a pathology of individual differences.

The pathology of prejudice and overidentification

Fairbairn's early papers about the relationship of the individual with the social group indicate his awareness of the influence of a social object. Extrapolating from these early papers, I will develop an object relations theory of prejudice. Writing about war neuroses in 1943, Fairbairn identified some soldiers who were as strongly identified with the military as with their early objects. In other words, they had a persistence of infantile dependence. He stated that they are "so consumed with military zeal that they itch impatiently to be in the forefront of the fray" (p. 278). They had a predisposition to establish a strong psychological identification with a social group (in this case the military). Their pathology was revealed, however, because they had nervous breakdowns when the military did not reward their enthusiasm. As long as their value to the idealized ingroup compensated for their weak sense of self, they were able to function. However, when the idealized internal object could not be maintained, their psychological health deteriorated, their use to the ingroup diminished, their value dropped, and their sense of self and competence evaporated.

Further evidence that Fairbairn recognized the importance of the social object is seen in his discussion of totalitarianism. He suggested that totalitarian regimes such as Nazi Germany and the USSR developed state-sponsored propaganda to foster an overidentification with the regime in the population as a whole, while directing aggression at outgroups (1943: 284). They promoted connection to the state as a substitute for familial bonds, and fostered infantile dependence at the macro-social level. In these regimes, belonging to the ingroup brought not only psychological safety, but actual physical safety.

Totalitarian regimes foster overidentification in as many members as possible, along with a clear description of an enemy toward which to direct prejudice. The process of finding categories to fear and hate promotes stronger identification with the idealized ingroup. In a mutually reinforcing relationship, the state gets the idealizing members it needs to survive, and members feel safe in the state they need to idealize as good and protective. The world beyond the boundaries of the state is feared and either avoided or attacked.

Fairbairn's object relations theory: developmental precursors of prejudice

The precursors of the social object lie in object relationships as described by Fairbairn. Fairbairn (1952) described the development of object relationships as "a process whereby infantile dependence upon the object gradually gives place to mature dependence upon the object" (p. 34). The earlier stage of infantile dependence is characterized by incorporation, and later by primary emotional identification with caregivers, such that there is minimal psychological differentiation between infant and caregiver. A transition from infantile dependence to mature dependence is facilitated when caregivers offer genuine love, and accept such love back from their child. Under these conditions, healthy development is a process whereby relationships become more differentiated, yet continuously involve a mutual dependence. The more differentiated stage, called mature dependence is characterized by the capacity to have "cooperative relationships with differentiated objects" (1952: 145). Given that this transition is never perfect, cooperative, differentiated objects coexist with more primitive objects of attachment. The healthy need for attachment with caregivers (Bowlby 1969) persists in adulthood as a relationship with the social structures of their culture and society.

The significance of this early unavoidable interdependence of infants and their caregivers is that it foreshadows developmental needs in early adulthood when identifying with groups in society becomes one of the primary tasks. Blos (1962) stated that the identity formation process in young adulthood recapitulates early object relations as individuals begin to establish relationships with groups in society that symbolically represent parents. If this occurs, then during transition into adulthood the degree of emotional identification with early objects may influence the degree of emotional identification possible, or necessary, with some group in society.

Fairbairn suggested that psychopathology in adulthood stems from "a persistence into later life of an exaggerated degree of that emotional dependence which is characteristic of childhood" (1952: 259). Importantly, such an infantile dependence is associated with primary identification, which blurs the boundary between self and other. This defensive process may have served a protective function in early life, but if it is recapitulated in early adulthood it interferes with the identity formation process during the establishment of psychological and emotional relations with social groups. The tendency to overidentify with some groups and minimize differentiation between self and other groups (ingroups and outgroups), leads to the potential for pathological prejudice. Treatment of prejudice would have to involve treatment of social object relationships, where the social object incorporates culture and identity groups.

The social object in Fairbairnian terms

Fairbairn (1952) suggested that, to various degrees, identifications become the emotional experience of self. He recognized that early in life these identifications relate to familial attachments as the original social group upon which the child is dependent. However, he was aware that these early family attachments extend to clan, tribe, and nation (Fairbairn 1935). I understand his representation of the original love objects as proceeding toward progressively supra-ordinate identity structures in society. As individuals develop and their insufficiently met dependence needs are directed outside the family, primary identification with these parental substitutes may continue, with a resulting lack of differentiation between self and group. In such cases, primary identification continues to function as a defensive operation promoting an overidentification with the group as a compensation for the experienced inadequacy of the infantile character. At this point, the group represents the self.

Writing in the social cognitive literature, Smith and Henry (1996) found evidence that self-identification with group attributes was possible and identity groups do become perceived as part of the self. During intergroup conditions, group members become depersonalized, and ingroup attributes become part of the psychological self (Verkuyten and Hagendoorn 1998). These attributes may involve religion, gender, work roles, and numerous additional social structures with which one could identify, including antisocial gangs. It is when these affiliations become overidentifications with ingroups, and have low tolerance for outgroups that the risk of pathological prejudice increases.

Idealization and projection play an important part in this process. Sutherland (1994) discussed an intrapsychic process that has relevance to this discussion of object relationships and group affiliations. He suggested that inner tension due to unconsciously perceived attacks arising from inner objects leads to the need for self-defence achieved by projecting these bad objects outward, which permits a fantasy of safety. He goes on to say that this process is "perhaps reinforced by a clinging to the idealized internal object, as well as by the development of the defense of avoiding the objects onto which the frightening figures have been projected" (p. 113). Sutherland stresses that the cost of such a defense is a world that is filled with dreaded objects that thereby restrict potential interactions. Extrapolating from his description, I suggest that a sense of safety is established by idealizing the ingroup, blurring the distinction between the self and the ingroup, and projecting bad social objects onto outgroup members.

Clinical example

Shifting now to discussing clinical aspects of these ideas, I will describe a clinical case to illustrate the usefulness of considering the social group affiliations (the collective identity in socio-cognitive terms) with a patient who discussed the experience of others in terms of idealization and devaluation.

Ms A is a single, college-educated, Caucasian female in her mid-forties. She was raised Jewish, but converted to become Episcopalian Protestant several years prior to beginning her current treatment. Her parents divorced when she was 4 years old, and her father rejected any contact thereafter. Her mother married her stepfather soon after the divorce. The stepfather provided well for the family, but he was physically abusive toward Ms A and her mother. Ms A tends to focus on her experience of an idealized upper middle class lifestyle of that period, rather than on the abuse. When she was 13 years old, her mother divorced her stepfather, and since then Ms A and her mother have lived a life of poverty. Ms A's mother had a series of failed relationships with verbally and physically abusive men, who treated mother and daughter equally poorly. Now in her forties, Ms A admits that she is both financially and emotionally dependent upon her mother.

During early sessions, Ms A complained about her life as it is currently and as it was in the past. She was dismissive of any effort I made either to empathize or to seek change. She was frustrated with her longstanding struggle, and she tried to fill her days with productive tasks, but in reality she only appeared to be productive and did not expect to change anything in her life. I felt excluded from participating in sessions with her. She told me that I had unrealistic expectations for her to return to work or to have a satisfying relationship with a man. I noted a parallel between my inability to be a participant in our sessions, and her inability to participate in satisfying ways in her life. Ms A tended to engage in a monologue that was difficult to break through, about things like her neighbors making noise, or her difficulty getting a free computer from Dell, or the stupidity of men in general. She did not appear to be in therapy for the purpose of change.

As I began to consider her experience as one that pertained to identity, I hypothesized that one aspect of her identity was that of being one of a group of patients, distinct from me, a therapist. She said such things as, "We are stigmatized and therapists do not want to work with people like us," and "We borderlines are not understood," and "People like us are unique and things don't work out for us." I became curious about her identification with a patient group, particularly one that she perceived as having little chance of success or change, and little hope of being tolerated by others in the world (except for the therapist who was paid to sit with her). I acknowledged my awareness of her hopelessness about change based on her feelings of who she is. She agreed she felt hopeless, and moved on to other complaints.

A second identification, or perhaps overidentification, was associated with gender. Ms A was a virgin until she was 25 years old, when she began her first affair with a married coworker. She began two other affairs with married men before finishing the others, and this series of sexual encounters continued for three years or so until they gradually dropped off. By the end of the three years she was perplexed as ever about relationships with men. She has not had a relationship with a man since, sexual or otherwise. Nevertheless she saw herself as one of the beautiful and extremely intelligent women. She rationalized her rejection by men on the grounds that they were intimidated by her qualities, weak, stupid creatures unable to understand her.

Shortly after beginning therapy she reported that she was interested in a new married man who flirted with her at a community meeting. She was becoming extremely aroused by him, and after about a month, decided to invite him to go out for a drink, refusing to discuss the pros or cons of such action with me. Her effort failed and the man withdrew, at which point she espoused the utter lameness of men, calling all of them confusing, unreliable, and dishonest, "stupid pussies" who never say what they want. She was left feeling angry and devastated, more aware than she had been of a loneliness that now seemed permanent. I asked her if she had a reaction to being in therapy with a man, given that she had little faith that men could understand her. She dismissed my comment as irrelevant. She said that she had no such reaction to me as a man. I was not in her personal life, and anyway, she did not feel understood by her former therapist either, a woman.

Ms A clung to her identity as a person carrying a diagnosis of borderline personality disorder, which justified and organized a defiant, angry stance toward relationships. This stance kept her from feeling vulnerable and overshadowed any hope that things could be different for her. She experienced the world as hostile and rejecting. Her diagnosis provided an identity that permitted her to retain a hostile adversarial position with other people, and kept her isolated and feeling as if she does not belong in a community. In relation to me, she maintained her distance, and saw me as the doctor who could not understand her and might even damage her by trying to fix her according to my cultural values, such as valuing her returning to work and having more satisfying relationships.

By attending to aspects of her collective identity it became evident that she perceived considerable difference between herself and the surrounding community. Although she would refuse to address this directly in sessions, her perception of our differences in terms of social categories was stated as she devalued groups of which I was obviously a member, such as men and therapists. This was associated with a narcissistic maintenance of her self-esteem, a rigid rejection of needing to change something about herself, and certainty about the faults and inadequacies of others.

The social object in Ms A's inner world

For Ms A, identity reflects an overidentification with idealized social objects of the female and patient categories. These categories remain internal and provide a safe self-experience, as she confronts dreaded objects in the external world. She projects her hatred onto external social objects that represent social categories of males and non-psychiatric patients who she experiences as rejecting, denying her opportunity, acceptance, and power, and lacking the power of understanding themselves. All these object relationships are in association with the antilibidinal self and, as Sutherland showed, are projected onto social groups as well as individuals. These social objects reflect her experiences with her neglectful father and her abusive stepfather.

Additionally, Ms A clings to the idealized patient identity that she uses defensively to avoid the objects onto which her projections are directed. Although this social object with which she is identified is defensive, it does provide opportunities to interact with therapists, or treatment programs, but with serious limitations. The diagnosis as an identity provides purpose and entitlement, in that she can demand to be treated, and she can seek financial compensation from the state in the form of disability insurance. Ms A draws strength from her position as "a member of a group of the most difficult patients." With this self-knowledge she battles with state agencies, therapists, and corporations, while simultaneously she gains legitimate avenues for relationship and affiliation, though these are of limited potential.

Unintentionally, Ms A causes hatred to be directed at herself. The projection of hatred at outgroup members may provide an attachment to the bad object in the external world, but also may lead to hatred being directed back at the self. The provocation of hatred from others further justifies her own conscious experience of prejudice.

Social objects and prejudice

It would be very rare for patients to declare that the therapeutic task is to understand how their prejudice affects their life. However, prejudices exist in all patients and therapists and should be a subject of inquiry in therapy. Prejudices may first emerge as rigid perceptions about social categories that pertain to their own collective identity. For instance, substituting other categories for those raised by Ms A's case, such as Jew, or Caucasian, requires the same intrapsychic maneuvers in the service of self-protection by directing prejudice at certain social categories more commonly considered to be targets of prejudice. Overidentification with an idealized social category, and simultaneous devaluation associated with projection of frightening objects onto other social categories, leads to a perception of hate and rejection. Furthermore, the unconscious need to be hated, and the subsequent experience of threat from the hated and now hateful outgroup members, appears to justify the prejudice consciously.

Rubens (1994) suggested that the relationship between self and other forms the unit for consideration in object relations theory (p. 154). I propose expanding the realm of object relations theory to recognize the social group as a psychologically meaningful unit for consideration. Individuals have emotionally invested social object relationships that can distort perception. Their incorporation of cultural norms and identification with social groups is dependent upon the degree of self–other differentiation established during early development. During identity formation in early adulthood the level of maturity established earlier is recapitulated. Differentiation of self and social group reflects progress along the continuum between infantile dependence and mature dependence. Perceptions of the external world are determined by idealized or impoverished objects with which the central self relates. The degree to which these objects have been distorted determines the extent of pathology (Rubens 1994). Affiliation with and rejection of social groups in life currently is determined by this developmental process of perceiving social groups. When they have been idealized or impoverished, there is a likelihood that the adult will simplify their reality into one perceived as an idealized ingroup to belong to, and an outgroup to reject.

Future considerations

Individuals who become prejudiced against certain outgroups may be pathologically overidentified with the ingroup and yet within that ingroup have satisfying relationships. The question that comes to mind is whether they are pathological, given that they do have positive and supportive relationships. For example, extremely prejudiced Nazi officers who persecuted Jews might be loving toward ingroup members, or policemen who showed contempt or brutality toward suspects might be respectful to other officers and kind to family members.

For these individuals there is little differentiation between their ingroup and their experience of self. The group is representative of themselves and therefore other group members are extensions of themselves. The idealization of the ingroup, and themselves, is strengthening enough to allow them to function effectively in interpersonal relations within the ingroup. As with Fairbairn's overzealous soldiers, or citizens of a totalitarian regime, when the illusion of the idealized social object is threatened or destroyed, people find that their defenses are inadequate. As such, these individuals may appear healthy within a limited range of their own ingroups, but it is a temporary, fragile solution to compensate for their deficit. Overidentified individuals who are strengthened enough to have healthy relations within their own family may provide appropriate parenting so that their children need not struggle with infantile dependence and are not saddled with limited psychological development. Given that different cultural opportunities may then develop for these children in school and work, they may not be limited in similar fashion as their parent, and may not therefore live by the prejudice of the previous generation.

Conclusion

Fairbairn (1952) wrote that the functional aim throughout development is the establishment of satisfactory, cooperative relationships that represent a mature dependence which is not characterized by objects incorporated during the earlier stage of infantile dependence and primary emotional identification. Mature dependence is established between "two differentiated individuals who are mutually dependent" (p. 145).

Object relations theory complements empirical findings of social cognitive psychology. Both perspectives suggest that identification is an important psychological process, which leads to both adaptive and problematic outcomes. I suggest that early development can predispose some individuals to overidentify with ingroups as they recapitulate emotional needs of earlier periods in an effort to compensate for an infantile dependent character. Object relations theory helps explain why some people may overidentify with groups and as a result become prejudiced toward outgroups, even though social conditions do not warrant intergroup conflict. They merge their experience of self with the ingroup, such that there is no differentiation between self and group, and project hated and dreaded bad objects onto outgroups and their members. This allows for some attachment with the bad object to continue, and may satisfy the unconscious wish to be hated in the external world, thereby justifying one's own conscious experience of hatred. When infantile dependence persists in adulthood, there is overidentification with the ingroup. Understood in terms of object relations theory, which holds that healthy development involves satisfactory and cooperative relationships, prejudice is an expression of pathology. Prejudice can be addressed in psychotherapy by extending Fairbairn's object relationships to include the social object in connection with the object relations set.

References

Aviram, R. B. (2002). An object relations theory of prejudice: defining pathological prejudice. *Journal for the Psychoanalysis of Culture and Society* 7: 305–312.

Blos, P. (1962). *On Adolescence*. New York: Free Press.

Bowlby, J. (1969). *Attachment and Loss. Vol. 1: Attachment*. New York: Basic Books.

Chodorow, N. (1978). *The Reproduction of Mothering*. Berkeley: University of California Press.

Dovidio, J. F., Kawakama, K. & Gaertner, S. L. (2000). Reducing contemporary prejudice: combating explicit and implicit bias at the individual and the intergroup level. In S. Oskamp (ed.) *Reducing Prejudice and Discrimination*, pp. 137–164. New Jersey: Lawrence Erlbaum Associates, Inc.

Fairbairn, W. R. D. (1935). The sociological significance of communism considered in light of psychoanalysis. In *Psychoanalytic Studies of the Personality*, pp. 233–246. New York: Routledge, 1952.

—— (1943). The war neuroses – their nature and significance. In *Psychoanalytic Studies of the Personality*, pp. 256–288. New York: Routledge.

—— (1952). *Psychoanalytic Studies of the Personality*. London: Routledge & Kegan Paul.

Rubens, R. L. (1994). Fairbairn's structural theory. In J. S. Grotstein & D. B. Rinsley (eds) *Fairbairn and the Origins of Object Relations*, pp. 151–173. London: Free Association.

Smith, E. R. and Henry, S. (1996). An ingroup becomes part of the self: response time evidence. *Personality and Social Psychology Bulletin* 22: 635–642.

Stern, D. N. (1985). *The Interpersonal World of the Infant*. New York: Basic.

Sutherland, J. D. (1994). Small groups, their disorders and treatment. In J. S. Scharff (ed.) *The Autonomous Self*, pp. 111–122. Northvale, NJ: Jason Aronson.

Tajfel, H. and Turner, J. C. (1979). An integrative theory of intergroup conflict. In W. G. Austin and S. Worchel (eds) *The Social Psychology of Intergroup Relations*, pp. 33–47. Monterey, CA: Brooks-Cole.

Verkuyten, M. and Hagendoorn, L. (1998). Prejudice and self-categorization: the variable role of authoritarianism and ingroup stereotypes. *Personality and Social Psychology Bulletin* 24: 99–110.

Chapter 24

Application

Organizational consultancy

Judith Brearley

In this chapter my focus is on the life and work of Jock Sutherland, with particular reference to the part he has played in the development of psycho-analytically-informed organizational consultancy in Britain. My main teacher of method was Harold Bridger, but I learned the full potential of consultancy from various experiences with Jock Sutherland, and then developed it in practice in the Scottish Institute of Human Relations and elsewhere. I want to give a picture of this sort of consultancy from my own experience of working with organizations in health, education, social work, and the churches, inter-weaving relevant theoretical ideas developed by Sutherland and his colleagues with case illustrations and reflections.

It is almost impossible to speak of Jock's influence without including in the frame those professional "significant others" with whom he was work-ing. Much of his conversation and teaching conveyed, as does his writing, his enthusiasm for, and exceptional skill in, collaborative working, and indicated that his values, theories, ways of working, and institution building were almost always developed jointly. He demonstrated cooperation, mutual valuing and shared play in whatever he did. He had many close colleagues when he was director of the Tavistock Clinic in London – Wilfred Bion, Eric Trist, Harold Bridger, A. K. Rice, Eric Miller, Isabel Menzies, Michael Balint, and John Bowlby – each independently a brilliant researcher or clinician. Sutherland made it possible for them to work together. When he returned to Scotland he found in Edinburgh a group of senior people in the caring professions, and established the Scottish Insti-tute of Human Relations with them. His unobtrusiveness and valuing of others were demonstrated in the way the Scottish Institute began, and in the way he described its founding. He never claimed that he set it up. In a similar way he generously enabled many people to develop ideas and pub-lish their work, never jealously guarding his own part in this theory building.

Jock Sutherland's burning interest in organizations can be seen clearly from the 1940s onwards. His earliest published work included topics such as group problems in the British Army, morale in young textile workers, selection of management trainees, and social therapy. He described himself as "having learned to think socially about the issues, really to see the social dimensions in a realistic way" (1979 in Scharff 1994: 395). He consistently gravitated towards active involvement in consulting or leadership roles, creating and developing new institutions, conceptualizing the processes, and underpinning values as he went along. According to Eric Trist: "Experience during World War II had shown that psychoanalytic object relations theory could unify the psychological and social fields in a way that no other could" (Trist and Murray 1990: 30). And as Jock Sutherland (1965) said: "Object relations theory sheds light on the way in which individuals distribute their needed personal relationships in the groups to which they belong. It therefore bridges the gap between personality theory and group process" (Scharff 1994: 122). As Medical Director of the Tavistock Clinic from 1947, he was particularly instrumental in integrating the psychological and social fields of inquiry into a distinctive Tavistock approach encompassing both the clinic's mental health focus and the institute's study of wider social problems.

My approach to organizational consultancy

It is not surprising that I should find Sutherland's dual integrated approach attractive and eminently applicable, having initially studied sociology, psychology and social policy before moving via social work into the psychoanalytic field. Much of the work I do involves responding to requests from the leadership of organizations for help with the inevitable tensions which occur within and between working groups, especially at times of transition when processes of interaction result in stress, dysfunction and demoralization, even breakdown and chaos. It has made me deeply aware of both the destructive power of institutional dynamics and of the therapeutic potential of intervention by an invited outsider. This links precisely with some wise remarks of Jock Sutherland:

> If we remind ourselves that the characteristics of each system have been evolved to deal with the threatening tensions within it, then we will be prepared for the consequences of trying to change it. All of us are familiar with the anxieties aroused within the individual when he begins to alter his defense systems. It is inevitable that such alterations within the defensive patterns of a social system will also release anxiety and a degree of acting out. Social systems, like therapeutic groups, can create special difficulties during the change process, but it is also true that they offer considerable positive features in the support that members can give each other . . . New satisfactions have to be experienced and accepted before the old ways can be given up, and during this process the role of

the consultant has a close parallel with that of the therapist for the individual.

(Sutherland 1965, in Scharff 1994: 121)

It is important to have an initial period of careful negotiation to see what is going on and find out which are the main concerns. Only then is it agreed what sort of intervention might be appropriate. There has to be sufficient voluntary commitment from everyone to give it a try at least. Questions about which people to involve, the frequency of meetings, and the duration of the work are best kept under review and decided by consensus. The consultant avoids fostering too much dependency, and is certainly not the all-knowing expert with a magic wand or a ready-made solution, despite participants' wishful thinking along these lines! Advice giving is kept to a minimum. Instead, the consultant acts as a catalyst, facilitator and commentator, fostering the participants' self-understanding and skills in evaluating and resolving their own dilemmas, and enabling the organization to find its own way forward. It is akin to Edgar Schein's definition of process consultation as being "to help the client to perceive, understand and act upon process events which occur in the client's environment" (Schein 1969: 9).

The "outsiderness" of consultants is crucial in giving them an advantage because it allows them to see the situation with fresh eyes. Not having a vested interest in the outcome is essential. Objectivity and even-handedness foster the trust necessary for people to begin to explore difficult experiences. On the other hand there is a significant subjective element; I find that monitoring processes of projective identification, especially my own countertransference, is the most useful tool. It is vital to be open to the tone of what is being said at different levels, verbally and non-verbally, picking up the music behind the words. Consultancy is often highly intuitive, playing it by ear, depending on slow and painful development of new insights. I will now give a fragment of the beginning stages of a session to illustrate some of these points.

Case illustration: The start of a consultancy session

I was asked to work with a small group of people who shared responsibility for a voluntary organization offering family support. As a result of previous work, they had a realistic understanding of my approach and some trust in it. This group had become painfully stuck in their dealings with one another as a result of misunderstandings over time, the impact of profound change in the organization as they tried to adapt to new external needs, and what can best be described as a leadership vacuum. They had set aside one day for sorting out their respective roles and relationships.

Before the structured work began, there was a period of informal interaction. It was a miserable wet day, and as people arrived from all over Scotland, they commented on the weather, parking difficulties and so on. The common theme in the informal chat was confusion and mystification. One person had been convinced the meeting was in Glasgow, and had then gone to the wrong place in Edinburgh. The chairperson arrived late, having mistaken the time of the meeting and an arrangement about meeting a colleague. Yet she herself had sent clear letters to everyone explaining time, place, and purpose! Others talked in a similar mixed-up way. Gradually another note crept into the discussion. One person had just heard she was to become a grandmother. News of exciting developments in some work was shared. People did constructive bits of business with each other.

In the formal meeting with participants, I described what I had observed, and suggested that the various aspects were symbolic of the problems we were to work on. I told them that I had sensed depression, grimness, and apprehension about likely painful exchanges; an understandable wish to avoid such difficult work, and communication problems, expressed in all the confusion and misunderstanding. Balancing these, I noted the commitment expressed in attending, a degree of optimism, and some capacity to be constructive.

My comments were met with recognition and relief. We had a shared view, something that helped people tolerate looking together at the difficulties rather than perceiving one another as the difficulty. This is akin to the need in psychotherapy for a therapeutic alliance to be established, a pact between the critical egos of both parties. In consultancy there is limited time to achieve this. It is vital to create a facilitating environment before the consultation begins, so that people can begin to feel some trust in each other and in the purpose and process of the meeting. This is where skill in designing the event ensures programming of time to give a sense of direction, space to express feelings, enough but not too much structure, a logical sequence of areas to be explored, and sufficient flexibility to accommodate the unexpected!

Towards the end of a session like this, I would normally allow time for them to review and evaluate the work done in terms of the task they set themselves, the ways they were able to work, and their affective responses, and also to think about where they might go from the point reached.

Aspects of social science and psychoanalytic theories relevant to organizational consultancy

I want to highlight two imperatives. Consultancy takes place in an arena where the structure of social systems and the unconscious motivations of individuals are inextricably entwined. Therefore, it is essential that the social and psychoanalytic perspectives are used in tandem. If a psychoanalytic perspective alone is used, one risks increasing people's awareness of the unconscious factors but leaving them frustrated, lacking the conditions in which they can apply any insight gained. The social perspective alone might produce a plan for change, but this will probably fail because it does not take account of the psychic determinants of the situation (Mosse 1994).

The second imperative is that the concepts used must make sense to the practitioner experientially as well as intellectually. Exactly as in psychotherapy, it is impossible to practise at any depth without continually refining one's own self-awareness. The consultant needs to be thoroughly familiar with human responses to the most primitive anxieties, and able to recognize all sorts of unconscious defensive manoeuvres, particularly splitting and projection, and resistance to change. Detailed observational skills and understanding of the therapeutic process are vital. That is why most consultants in this tradition have analytic training and intensive experiential group relations learning, which combines psychoanalytic influence with systems thinking. This enables them to manage the boundary between their own inner worlds and the realities of the external environment, learn about leadership and authority, function in role; manage complexity, and to be less captive to group and organizational processes. The Tavistock–Leicester group relations training conferences emphasize study of the group's own behaviour in the here and now, the so-called *single task*. Harold Bridger developed Transitional Working Conferences with a *double task*, in which groups work on concerns from their own organizations, periodically suspending the agenda to review and reflect on the emotional and conflictual elements impeding progress. Jock Sutherland was involved in designing these conferences from the very start – integrating the models of work in the Tavistock Clinic and the Tavistock Institute of Human Relations and applying them in group relations training.

Open systems theory has provided an exceptionally strong underpinning for organizational work, entirely congruent with object relations theory, which conceives of the self as a system of parts in dynamic relation. Systems thinking stresses the interrelatedness of the organization and its environment, and concepts such as boundary and task definition. Boundary management is seen as the task of leadership. Boundaries need to be clearly demarcated to support the identity of what lies within the boundary and distinguish it from what lies outside it. At the same time, boundaries must be flexible and permeable to allow interchange of information, influence, and resources.

These ideas relate closely to what is now known as the transitional approach to the management of change. Jock Sutherland worked closely with three people who have contributed to our thinking about transitions, namely, Donald Winnicott, Eric Trist and Harold Bridger, and he kept in frequent touch with Trist and Bridger to the end of his life. Winnicott's (1971) concept of transitional phenomena – teddy bears, play, art, religion, culture – refers to an intermediate domain of illusion, in which inside and outside, subjective and objective, become joined together. In this potential space for transitional experience, a person can be inventive, envisaging new possibilities in a creative way.

At the time Winnicott was writing about this, Eric Trist was coming to think of transitions as a core issue through his work with Fred Emery. Together they coined the term turbulent environment. It has been said that we are now on a continuous change gradient, like a kayak that is moving in white water, always in transition. Times of rapid change require more open systems to respond to more turbulent environments. Roles, structures, and procedures need to be more fluid (Emery and Trist 1965).

Trist saw that relations among people at work deteriorated rapidly when the organization was perturbed by changes in its wider context. The level of aggression increased; the internal world of the organization became a more savage place. He wrote: "Socially amplified regression brings exceedingly primitive defenses into play, whether in the form of hostile projection or of alienated withdrawal. Once legitimated structures begin to give way, anxieties are unbound with the likelihood of catastrophe" (Trist 1989: 51).

Harold Bridger (1990) developed the organizational and societal implications of transitional objects in the adult world. Following Winnicott's aphorism that there is no such thing as a baby without a mother, so Bridger asserts there is no such thing as a group without a task; it is in the context of the task that we can make sense of conscious and unconcious processes operating within the working group. During any transition process, he viewed participants as grappling with several difficult interrelated tasks. They have to cope with the instability and insecurity of the changing conditions both in the organization and in the outside world. As they relinquish earlier, valued but now dysfunctional, ideas and practices, they discover or create new, more adaptive ways of thinking and acting. Good management would take account of these experiential difficulties, avoid change by directives, value and collaborate with staff, and provide the conditions needed to enable them to become committed to making needed changes (Amado and Ambrose 2001).

I now propose to offer a lengthier example from practice which I hope will highlight the application of some of these ideas and also convey the flavour and challenge of the work.

Case illustration: School closure

A secondary high school in a disadvantaged area heard that it would be closed at the end of the school year. The reason for closure was political rather than educational. Students and some staff would be transferred to another school not far away, unfortunately one with which the young people had acrimonious rivalry. It was not clear when and how decisions would be made about staff members' futures. Having consulted to a similar situation previously, I was asked by the head to work with him and his senior management team. Later, I also shared with a colleague the task of working with all the principal teachers as a group. The consultancy lasted about nine months.

From the start it was necessary to create opportunities for the senior group to express a range of very strong painful feelings; bewilderment and anger, distress and grief, uncertainty, fear and apprehension about the future, concern for the students, the staff and for each other. At the same time they had to get on with their normal work and, over and above that, make detailed plans for the transition. Previously the management team had been relatively cohesive, achieving a lot they could be proud of. But now, threatened with the loss of their collective identity, the trust and positive working relationships between them gradually began to disintegrate. This situation brought to mind Sutherland's observation: "The fact is that change processes within community institutions are apt to evoke the same kind of anxiety as arises in the individual who seeks to alter his established patterns of relating to himself and others" (1971: x–xi). As they shared out the responsibilities for different aspects of managing the closure, it became harder and harder for them to feel supported by each other and part of a common enterprise, tempers frayed, and recriminations began to be aired.

For example, the deputy head became engrossed in detailed and efficient planning for the future, the ways of achieving the shift into the other school, and the means of integrating the staff and students into the new entity, where he already knew he had a place. At times he seemed quite upbeat about it. In his single-minded focus he was not at all tolerant of looking backwards at past challenges and achievements, and grieving the loss of the school. In general, he was a man of action not given to much reflection or empathy.

On the other hand, the head was taking responsibility for closure aspects such as review and ending rituals. He was also relating to those in the school's wider environment at various levels; higher managers, advisers, politicians, the media, and people in the community, especially parents, some of whom had unsuccessfully fought the closure. Along with all this, he was dealing with the welfare of staff who were having to compete for jobs elsewhere, and listening to the students. It was difficult for him to look forward, as he knew he would not be moving to the other school, but did not yet know where he would be and what to expect in the future. He was a sensitive, thoughtful person, very much tuned in to the pain of others.

The rift between these two men was particularly stark; each felt desperately let down by the other. The more one of them focused on his areas of concern, the more the other felt abandoned. Their transactions had an either/or quality, rather than both/and; a sure sign of paranoid-schizoid functioning. I think there had been a father–son element in their relationship, with a benign mentoring quality, so there was sadness, often denied, at the prospect of going off separately, or coexisting with what I guess had become in fantasy an almost murderous rivalry.

Another team member, the only woman, had been supportive of her colleagues in the early months, but latterly had been increasingly opting out, not contributing much to the discussions or taking her share in the work. There was in each team member an equivalent unconscious wish to retreat and opt out, not to have to bother, and it was convenient for them that she expressed this in her behaviour on their behalf.

In these ways it became more difficult for them to provide the stable leadership the school needed, especially at this critical stage. Splits like this can be very quickly picked up and amplified throughout the whole system, with damaging consequences. Words of the poet W. B. Yeats came to mind: "Things fall apart; the centre cannot hold!" (Yeats 1924).

We had reached a crisis point. Not only were the team and the wider staff group affected by these destructive unconscious processes, but uncharacteristically, I myself also felt in danger of taking sides, blaming, or even giving up on them. I needed the wisdom of a trusted supervisory colleague to avoid becoming overwhelmed, and also to see a way forward.

I tried to offer containment to the team as they struggled with these inevitable tensions, not by facile reasssurance, but by helping them gradually to see what might be happening to them. Together we slowly worked out that these painful divisions happened when each one of them was actually undertaking something vital on behalf of the whole group. It was as Jock Sutherland (1979) said: "What supports the carer is not encouragement in the conventional sense. Instead, it is to be part of a learning system greater than himself. Anxiety from puzzlement and from feeling overwhelmed by human problems are best alleviated when we understand what is going on" (Scharff 1994: 277).

Their regular early morning meeting with me was the only time free from pressing practical matters for the team to share together, to have space to think not merely what they were doing, but how they were doing it, and to make sense of what they were feeling about themselves and the whole situation. Despite the tensions, the team did become again a "safe-enough" place, and the team members could once more listen, empathize, and think coherently rather than panic. This in turn enabled them to keep working effectively with the wider systems as well as internally, and to prepare well for the ending. One measure of their ultimate success was that sickness and absenteeism rates remained below the regional average throughout the process. I will now give two further theoretical reflections on this experience, first, on the delegation of functions, and second on containment.

Delegation

There were perfectly good task-effective reasons for them to delegate particular areas of the overall task to each other, and they did so appropriately on the basis of skill and experience. However, at a different level, other motivations were apparent, some of them unconscious. Each had a personal valency towards certain activities and styles of functioning. And each cast the others in particular roles, projecting onto colleagues unwanted, disavowed, threatening aspects of their own personality. Object relations theory makes sense of what was going on here. To quote Ashbach and Schermer (1994):

> *The differentiation of a group into the specific functions carried out by each member is a group equivalent of inner divisions of the personality* . . . Fairbairn stated such a theory of groups when he proposed that "the nature of group relations is . . . determined by the externalisations or projections of an internal object" (1952). The group-as-a-whole, including organizational systems, can come to represent aspects of the self and of object relations.
>
> (Ashbach and Schermer 1994: 58)

Containment in work groups

Bion's (1962) concept of containment is as useful with work groups as it is in individual therapy, and it was just what this situation would need. We made it explicit from the start that our purpose was for the participants to feel sufficiently contained to be able to offer similar containment to others in the system. In the face of extreme anxiety, the managers were often losing their capacity to think. Thinking requires the difficult task of tolerating and engaging with painful emotional conflicts in oneself. Inability to do this can lead instead to projective identification, in which unmanageable feelings are disowned and expelled into other people who then experience and enact the conflict. Only when that which has been projected (the contained) and then modified (contained) and so handed back in a less toxic form, can a sense of security, coherence and meaning be refound.

I next offer a shorter practice illustration to show how containment of an individual in the work context can restore the person's capacity to think and to make decisions, and also potentially influence the wider system.

Case illustration: Health care

An experienced health professional, not long in her present job, was bullied by her line manager. She experienced disparagement, covert aggression, and a capricious disregard for her job description. The company recognized this and transferred the manager, but the damage was done. Added to that, the investigation processes were handled insensitively, repeating the earlier damage and leaving the already traumatized worker even more vulnerable. She lost confidence in herself and in her employer, and became unable to work for a time.

A member of the directorate with responsibility for staff development asked me to offer consultancy to the worker in her role as she struggled to recover her competence. Some organizations merely send staff for counselling or therapy, thereby locating much of the pathology in the person and avoiding institutional responsibility. By contrast, this director shared her concern not only for the individual, but also for the troubled persecutory environment of the organization in which the abusive incidents had taken place when aggressive, demeaning behaviour had not been held in check. Despite the transfer of the aggressor, the worker had returned to a largely unaltered milieu with a destructive departmental subculture.

Having this awareness was helpful. We explored the impact of what the worker had faced, and identified strategies for managing the new and still extremely difficult situation. But we also kept in mind the whole context, and tried to make sense of what had gone on beyond the personalities and specific tensions involved. After a few months of one-to-one work, we had a joint session with the director, who affirmed the efforts being made by the worker to cope. She also suggested some creative possibilities for the worker's future role, and made it clear that many of the difficulties (still ongoing) were systemic ones which she was determined to have management treat seriously.

Not long after this, the worker decided that despite her best efforts she could no longer work in that environment, and handed in her notice. However, compared with the previous year, the contrast in her capacity to confront the situation was striking. She coped with the ending with dignity, giving detailed observations on the situation and clear reasons for her departure. She felt she had held on to her integrity, and left this job with the confidence and self-esteem to apply for other responsible posts.

Wider questions arise from this experience. The organization had recently been through several major reorganizations. Heightened anxiety meant that work difficulties had become personalized. I had worked with this director before, and greatly respected her commitment and perceptive leadership. But I wondered if her voice would be heard in a directorate beset by staff shortages, financial worries and performance targets. How could an adequate holding environment be offered to staff to prevent repetition of the damaging experience this worker had suffered? She was mature, had a lot of credibility, strong supports, and normally a good sense of identity. In a situation like hers, staff members without these assets are likely to be even more damaged.

These examples from health care and education demonstrate the tremendous difficulty of managing uncertainty and major change in complex organizations located in an increasingly turbulent environment. They also show how such change takes its toll in terms of less effective work, loss of commitment and goodwill, and threats to personal health and well-being.

Consultancy as professional development

I have emphasized the destructive aspects of problems in the workplace, and therefore the troubleshooting dimensions of consultancy. To correct the balance somewhat, I want to mention briefly the explicitly developmental and educational aspects of organizational consultancy. In fact some individuals and groups request consultancy in terms of developing their full potential, reviewing progress, or anticipating and lessening the impact of future challenges by good preparation. An additional aspect of consultancy is an educational function, in which the consultant helps staff in human services to understand the organizational dynamics of their particular field of work by learning about institutional processes.

Training for organizational consultancy

Psychotherapy training should include courses devoted to the theory of groups and organizations. To internalize the learning, therapist trainees need small application groups in which to study personal experience in a small group of peers and reflect on roles and dilemmas that present themselves in the organizations where they work. For instance, at the Scottish Institute for Human Relations founded by Sutherland and colleagues, course work on understanding institutional process has long been an integral part of the pre-clinical foundation stage of child psychotherapy training. Around 25 hours over two years are devoted to it.

Students learn to observe and give a coherent account of the complexities of interaction in their own organizations. They then use the resources of the group to understand and address a specific problem in which they play a part, and which has an impact on others. Also, during their clinical training, consultancy is offered every term to each cohort of students. This is a space for them to reflect on their role as psychotherapists in training, deal with aspects of their transition to the psychotherapy profession, and integrate an emerging view of themselves as psychotherapists. These cohorts of students strongly agree with Jock's oft-repeated phrase: "There's nothing so practical as a good theory!"

Jock Sutherland was passionate about disseminating psychoanalytic understanding to the wider community. I hope that the examples I have presented convey to you my belief that organizational consultancy is one effective way to do this. Finally, to quote him once more: "Since participation in work groups plays such a large part in our lives, we have to learn much more about making these contribute to the enrichment of the person" (Sutherland 1965, in Scharff 1994: 122).

References

Amado, G. and Ambrose, A. (eds) (2001). *The Transitional Approach to Change*. London: Karnac.

Ashbach, C. and Schermer, V. (1994). *Object Relations, the Self and the Group*. London: Routledge.

Bion, W. (1962). A theory of thinking. *International Journal of Psychoanalysis* 43: 306–310.

Bridger, H. (1990). Courses and working conferences as transitional learning institutions. In *The Social Engagement of Social Science: Vol. 1, The Socio-Psychological Perspective*, ed. E. Trist and H. Murray. London: Free Association Books.

Emery, F. and Trist, E. (1965). The causal texture of organizational environments. *Human Relations* 18: 21–32.

Fairbairn, W. R. D. (1952). *Psychoanalytic Studies of the Personality*. London: Routledge & Kegan Paul.

Mosse, J. (1994). Introduction: the institutional roots of consulting to institutions. In *The Unconscious at Work: Individual and Organizational Stress in the Human Services*, eds A. Obholzer and V. Zagier Roberts. London: Routledge.

Scharff, J. S. (ed.) (1994). *The Autonomous Self: The Work of John D. Sutherland*. Northvale, NJ: Jason Aronson.

Schein, E. (1969). *Process Consultation: Its Role in Organization Development*. London: Addison Wesley.

Sutherland, J. D. (1965). Small groups, their disorders and treatment. In *The Autonomous Self: The Work of John D. Sutherland*, ed. J. S. Scharff, pp. 111–122. Northvale, NJ: Jason Aronson.

—— (ed.) (1971). Introduction. *Towards Community Mental Health*. London: Tavistock.

—— (1979). The psychodynamic image of man: a philosophy for the caring professions. The Malcom Millar lecture, University of Aberdeen, 1979. In *The Autonomous Self: The Work of John D. Sutherland*, ed. J. S. Scharff, pp. 268–282. Northvale, NJ: Jason Aronson.

Trist, E. (1989). Psychoanalytic issues in organizational research and consultation. In L. Klein (ed.) *Working with Organizations: Papers to Celebrate the Eightieth Birthday of Harold Bridger*, pp. 50–57. London: Tavistock.

Trist, E. and Murray, H. (1990). *The Social Engagement of Social Science: Vol.1, The Socio-Psychological Approach*. Philadelphia, PA: University of Pennsylvania Press.

Yeats, W. B. (1924). The Second Coming. *Poetry 1900–1975*. London: Longman.

Winnicott, D. W. (1971). *Playing and Reality*. London: Tavistock.

Chapter 25

Object relations and attachment dynamics in group psychotherapy

Communication, regulation and exploration of affective states

Una McCluskey

Ronald Fairbairn (1952) took the view that we are born with a unitary psyche and that our primary desire is for a relationship with another person from whom we can receive support for our development. He noted that the psyche splits in response to pain and frustration experienced in that important relationship. The splitting of the psyche gives rise to a dynamic intrapsychic structure that is organised in such a way as to manage the painful affect generated by unsatisfactory experience in current and future relationships. The resulting endopsychic situation consists of a central ego in relation to an ideal object that is the trace of satisfactory experience with the caregiver. Split off from that and repressed, are the antilibidinal ego relating to the frustrating, rejecting aspects of the objects, and the libidinal ego relating to the unreliably exciting aspects of the object. The antilibidinal (rejecting self) secondarily represses the libidinal (needy self).

John Bowlby, bringing an ethological approach to the study of human infants, showed that, like all animals, human infants need a reliable relationship to the mother for survival. This is their actual secure base (or insecure if it is unsatisfactory) from which they develop internal working models of attachment as secure (or insecure). Bowlby's internal working model of insecurity is in line with Fairbairn's concept of the antilibidinal (frustrating/rejecting) and libidinal (unreliably exciting) internal object relationships, while the internal working model of security is reminiscent of central ego functioning in relation to a satisfactory object. Bowlby's research supported the theories that Fairbairn had arrived at from clinical experience.

Taking off from Fairbairn's theory of the endopsychic situation, and in close personal association with Bowlby, John D. Sutherland considered how the self grew in infancy and adulthood in the context of relationships. Over 40 years later, he integrated the infant development research of Daniel Stern (1985) and others into his understanding of personality development and the conditions that promote it (Sutherland 1980/1993). This chapter will build on Sutherland's concern with what constitutes care devoted to the development and well-being of the person, outlined both in his Malcolm Millar lecture "The Psychodynamic Image of Man" (1979) and his paper "The Autonomous Self" (1980/1993).

My training in understanding group processes started with Sutherland in Edinburgh in the early 1970s when I was a member of the first training course in analytic groups and associated applications conducted by him with Megan Browne OBE. My introduction to the work of Fairbairn started in earnest at that time. I have continued to work with groups in many different forms since then, particularly interested in carrying out research into empathic attunement (which I will illustrate later in this chapter). I have integrated the work of the attachment theorists, developmental psychologists, and systems-centred group psychotherapists into my understanding of individual behaviour in the group context and of the factors that promote change and development. I conceptualise groups as a series of transient dyadic relationships. Therefore I am interested in the relationships aroused between leader and member, member and member, and in the effect of context on defence, exploration, and integration.

In this chapter, I will show how Fairbairn and Sutherland's theories, and Yvonne Agazarian's exploration of different aspects of the self in subgroups within the context of the group as a whole, can illuminate the processes of interaction observed in therapeutic groups. The goal of groupwork is to integrate repudiated or spilt off parts of the self through collaboration in subgroups. My focus will be on affect attunement, identification, and regulation in the context of groups. I will start by looking at affect attunement and regulation in infancy. I will briefly consider the contributions of Bowlby (1969, 1982, 1988), Ainsworth (1991), Ainsworth and Wittig (1969), Ainsworth *et al.* (1974, 1978), and Heard and Lake (1986, 1997) to our understanding of the dynamics of attachment. I will refer to my own research into developing and measuring the concept of empathic attunement in adult psychotherapy (McCluskey *et al.* 1999) and will conclude with an example from my research on the effect of leader attunement and misattunement to member affect and its effect on the group as a whole from a systems perspective (Agazarian 1997; Agazarian and Gantt 2000).

Affect identification, attunement, misattunement and regulation and the early interactive experience between self and other

Research into infant development has provided evidence that infants imitate and respond to affective expressions on the face of a significant other. When they scan faces, they show more fluidity in their body movements than when they have no faces to respond to. Adults are programmed to understand and respond to infant communication and communicate with infants in similar ways across cultures. The language used has been described as "motherese" because of its tuneful and rhythmical quality. Researchers (Brazelton and Main 1974; Brazelton and Cramer 1990; Field 1981; Field *et al.* 1982; Meltzoff 1983; Meltzoff and Moore 1995; Murray and Trevarthen 1985, 1986; Papousek and Papousek 1979; Papousek 1994; Segal *et al.* 1995) believe that this mutuality of engagement and turn taking in vocal and gaze conversations is vital to physiological and affect regulation in very young infants. Hofer (1983) provides evidence from numerous animal studies which show that vital physiological systems, which the young are unable to regulate themselves, are regulated by contact with the parent. The physiological effects of separation from the parent account in large part for the distress expressed on separation. Schore (1994, 2000) and Siegel (1999) suggest that the early social environment "mediated by the primary caregiver, directly influences the evolution of structures in the brain that are responsible for the future socio-emotional development of the child" (Schore 1994: 62).

Schore's argument is that attachment patterns between infants and caregivers take place during the phase of development when the infant is dependent on the other for the regulation of their biological and neurological systems. Accurate affect identification, attunement, or misattunement on the part of the caregiver are crucial aspects of the process of engagement and regulation. Stern (1985) has provided numerous illustrations of these processes as they take place between 6-month-old infants and their caregivers. He also identified the role and function of vitality affects and distinguished between affect attunement and empathy. He described affect attunement as occurring largely outwith consciousness and being communicated cross-modally, whereas empathy is mediated through cognition.

Infants modify their affective displays and behaviours on the basis of their appreciation of their caregiver's affective response. In his 1989 paper Tronick summarised his 1980 observations of infants who chronically experienced miscoordinated interactions: "These infants repeatedly engaged in self regulating behaviours (e.g., they turned away, had dull looking eyes, lost postural control, orally self comforted, rocked and self clasped" (Tronick 1989). Cohn and Tronick (1987) came up with interesting associations between caregiver behaviour and infant expression of affect at 7 months of age. For instance, mothers who were disengaged had infants who expressed more protest; mothers who were intrusive had infants who tended to look away more; mothers who were positive had infants who expressed more positive affect.

Care-seeking and care-giving is an interactive process of great complexity. Affect regulation in the very young infant is clearly important to keep physiological arousal levels within manageable and comfortable limits. In addition, affect attunement, purposeful misattunement, non-attunement and empathy influence the process of establishing reciprocity in the caregiving relationship, for better or worse.

Affect regulation and the dynamics of attachment

Infants and children get attached to the person who accurately attunes to their state of being and who does what is required to keep their physiological and emotional arousal levels within comfortable limits. Bowlby (1969, 1973, 1979, 1980, 1982, 1988, 1991) postulated the existence of two instinctive biological goal-corrected systems – careseeking and caregiving. Careseeking is activated in times of stress, threat to life, hunger and fatigue; its function is to achieve proximity and get care. Caregiving is activated in response to careseeking. Both are goal-corrected in the sense that once the goal of the system has been met, the system shuts down until it is activated again by a trigger in the internal or external environment.

Following Bowlby's original work, there has been a great deal of research into attachment behaviour, starting with the seminal work of Mary Salter Ainsworth (Ainsworth *et al.* 1978) who devised what has become known as the Strange Situation test, which is used to make reliable classifications of the attachment status of young children, shown during reunion with the mother after separation. She described three categories of attachment style. After further analysis of the data by Carol George, Mary Main and colleagues, a fourth category was detected (see Cassidy and Shaver 1999). These four categories are labelled: secure, insecure ambivalent-resistant, insecure avoidant, and disorganised. The first three styles are based on anticipated and predictable caregiver responses. The fourth pattern occurs in response to caregiver behaviour that is unpredictable and sometimes frightening. Careseekers who feel secure have generally experienced attuned, accurate and sensitive responses from readily available caregivers, and as a consequence accurately identify their own and others' affect, and are direct and coherent in asking for help (Bretherton 1990; Grossmann and Grossmann 1991a, 1991b). Insecure ambivalent resistant careseekers have generally experienced a mix of responses. The insecure avoidant pattern tends to be in response to insensitive intrusiveness on the part of the caregiver. Whatever the pattern of behaviour, all experiences of failed careseeking will be accompanied by the arousal of painful emotion, sadness, anger, or despair. These affects are demonstrated in the group that I will describe presently.

In addition to the two instinctive systems identified by Bowlby, Heard and Lake (1986, 1997) have added three further instinctive goal-corrected systems to the formulation of attachment theory in order to account for what they consider to be the problems that bring people into therapy: interest sharing, sexuality and self-defence. The formulation of attachment dynamics presented by Heard and Lake is known as extended attachment theory. Their inclusion of interest sharing, sexuality, and self-defence links with the research into infant development referred to earlier. Their work on self and other regulation, and defensive postures associated with a failure of regulation, provides some evidence for the inclusion of an instinctive system for self-defence in the formulation of attachment dynamics.

Research into affect attunement and adult psychotherapy (McCluskey *et al.* 1997, 1999; McCluskey 2001) suggests that one can conceptualise the adult therapeutic situation as arousing the dynamics of attachment. As long as careseeking is active, the instinctive exploratory system will remain inhibited. Careseeking will shut down when met with effective caregiving. Effective caregiving not only requires affect attunement but also requires an empathic response that is sustained and goal-corrected. Subsequent research has identified nine distinct patterns of interaction that arise in the course of careseeking and caregiving, summarised in Table 25.1 (McCluskey 2005).

Object relations, extended attachment theory and systems

Analysis of a vignette from a group episode

I intend to look at the affect aroused by misattuned leader behaviour towards a group member, in the context of the early phase of development in a systems centered group. My approach to understanding and working with groups derives from Systems Centered® Therapy (SCT), developed by Yvonne Agazarian as a method of conflict resolution through functional subgrouping. In functional subgrouping, group members join in a subset on the basis of similar emotional resonance and they separate from a subset on the basis of difference; both strategies having the aim of identifying and integrating the similarity in the apparently different and the different in the apparently similar (Agazarian and Gantt 2000). In this way SCT attends to the different experiences of the self in relation to internalised and external others, which Fairbairn had identified, and provides a method for working with them. To put it in object relations terms, the method of subgrouping promoted by systems centered group psychotherapy allows people to explore

Table 25.1 Careseeking and caregiving patterns

- Careseeker and caregiver establish a relationship of mutual responsivity.
- Careseeker interrupts and diverts communications.
- Caregiver's interruptive stance is modified and becomes more responsive.
- Demanding careseeker meets intellectualising responses.
- Careseeker finds minimal responsivity and gives up.
- Caregiver emphasises verbal communication and misses affective cues.
- Caregiver is distracted by careseeker's profusion of details and misses the point.
- Caregiver pursues relentlessly until careseeker withdraws.
- Incoherent careseeker meets containing caregiver and is helped to communicate needs.

aspects of themselves in the safety of resonance with others. This can have an ameliorating effect on critical self-judgements and internalised feelings of shame that can get in the way of exploring what is known but not accepted.

Group example

The group consisted of 22 members and a leader whom I will call Matt. It was a closed group and attended by those who were already experienced in SCT methods but were not fully trained SCT therapists. This group experience was embedded in a five-day training. I have chosen the mid-week session for study. I reconstructed it from video footage made from two cameras placed in the group room. Using an Apple Powerbook and Final Cut Pro, I was able to examine the video, frame by frame (25 frames to the second). I looked at the interaction and inspected the spectrograph for affect matching and sound resonance.

The session went through nine distinct phases which could be understood as group processing responses to the misattunement to affect experienced by many members in the previous evening's large group. Even though the transcript is heavily edited due to space limitations, the sequence of phases of subgroup formation that I present is accurate. Members drawn together by emotional resonance do not switch seats to sit together in visible subgroups, but they feel close to one another as they explore different levels of emotional and physiological experience including intention movements, and so form a subgroup. Members of the whole group who are not experiencing the emotion being explored in this subgroup will either be in a different subgroup already identified, working along silently, or waiting to access their own experience in order to either join an existing subgroup, or start a new subgroup. The non-vocal subgroups maintain roving eye contact with each other until such time as there is space for them to work. I tracked the flow of the group session, noting who is speaking, about what, and with what affect.

A woman member angrily described her frustrating experience in the group the previous evening when she was prevented by the leader from making a connection by eye contact either with him or with other members of the group. Reflecting on the nature of early developmental processes and the importance of gaze interactions for sighted infants, I could see how not getting eye contact could be experienced as a withdrawal or abandonment by the caregiver, in this case the group leader. I knew from my previous research that various affects might be generated in response to lack of eye contact – frustration, disappointment, hurt, loneliness, protest – each of them typical for the person who, when their careseeking system is aroused, feels cut off by the attachment figure. The woman group member who reported the lack of eye contact responded with frustration and anger. Other members of the group responded similarly with anger, or differently with flat affect, withdrawal, despair, fear, sadness and revulsion, or with an integrating response.

They joined into subgroups based on shared affect. Some members were horrified by the level of sadism expressed. In another session of the group, these same members might well be working in a subgroup exploring sadistic impulses as the best behavioural currency. Membership of a subgroup is not fixed but shifts as affects change, and depends on which members are sharing them.

Reviewing the tapes of this session of the group, I monitored the leader's (Matt's) interventions and the responses generated in the members, particularly in the woman who had felt deprived of eye contact in the previous evening's group. I also monitored the group as a whole in order to see in what way the leader was attuned or misattuned to the various affects of the group members (McCluskey 2002). I recorded my observations on verbal and affective communications, and identified which parts of the self were active in each subgrouping as the group proceeded (Table 25.2).

Table 25.2 Sequence of expression of affect and formation of subgroups

Speaker	Verbal communication	Vitality affect
Female 1	I am very angry. I was in the large group last night and I brought in something, and did not make eye contact. I said I was drowning, and did not get eye contact.	**Anger**
First subgroup. Theme: Targeting the self. Agency: Antilibidinal self		
Female 2	I get mad with myself when I am waiting for resonance and I cannot get resonance, and I begin to wonder is there something wrong with me.	**Flat**
Male 1	I felt that big time. What is wrong with me that I cannot feel a connection? I am out there, but I cannot feel a connection.	**Flat**
Second subgroup. Theme: Sadistic anger at leader. Agency: Exciting-rejecting object		
Male 2	I feel it in my jaw. Bite! I want to bite the leader's head, wondering is he going to do the same thing to us – not let anyone else work.	**Anger**
Female 2	I want to move forward, push Matt and grab him by the shoulders and say 'LOOK AT ME!'	**Anger**
Male 2	My fist wants to go – right into Matt's face and just make a big hole in his face – blood in his face – a black hole.	**Anger**
Third subgroup. Theme: Resignation, giving up. Agency: Withdrawn self		
Female 5	I feel so resigned. I wish I were angry but I have the feeling I am so useless. I don't have the right to be angry really.	**Despair**
Male 1	I'm there. Giving up and feeling useless. I also feel unable to change what I am experiencing. Not being able to find anger.	**Despair**
Fourth subgroup. Theme: Solidity and connectedness. Agency: Central ego		
Female 8	I have the experience of not knowing where I am but feeling very solid. Feeling very much part of the group.	**Centred**

Table 25.2 (Contd.)

Speaker	Verbal communication	Vitality affect
Male 7	I can join you on that. I feel very solid and feel very present to the work of the group but not wanting to join.	**Centred**

Fifth subgroup. Theme: Disconnecting self and other. Agency: Withdrawn self

Male 1	I am working in the subgroup and I am scaring myself thinking that I will go away and won't be able to come in.	**Fear**

Sixth subgroup. Theme: Sadness about destruction. Agency: Central ego

Female 7	I didn't want to join the anger and I realise I felt tremendous sadness about the destruction.	**Sadness**

Seventh subgroup. Theme: Sadism. Agency: Antilibidinal ego

Male 3	My anger is white.	**Anger**
Male 5	It is good to hear your anger is white. I begin to bristle.	**Anger**
Female 2	I am angry with Matt.	**Anger**
Leader	And your experience?	
Female 2	Push him out of the room.	**Anger**
Male 2	My fist is going into him over and over again – smash the body.	**Anger**

Eighth subgroup. Theme: Revulsion. Agency: Antilibidinal ego

Male 11	Can the group make room for another voice? I am feeling a really sickening feeling almost nausea – revulsion – over the rage – feeling very heavy.	**Revulsion**

End of whole group. Theme: Saying goodbye with eye contact. Agency: Central ego

Male 7	I have a wish before we end to say goodbye by making eye contact.	**Centred**

Brief analysis and conclusion

I suggest that this group research shows the way in which relationship with self and other becomes fragmented when not regulated by an empathic, attuned, effective leader. The impulse then is to regulate the self (Tronick *et al.* 1982) or coerce the other to provide a regulating context, even though the other may be in a self-centred, unempathic, and exploitative place, based on fear and insecurity. Subgroupings form to express and bind shared affect. When the group acknowledges the character of the various subgroups, a view of the whole emerges. In resonance with this, splits within each group member's personality can hope for a similar degree of integration on the individual level. In this way the closed internal systems of experience of self in relationship, identified by Fairbairn (1952), can become permeable to influence. Groups provide companionship and interest sharing at the very least. But when they can be helped towards an empathic stance towards self and other, groups can promote change and development "at the core of the person" (Sutherland 1979).

References

Agazarian, Y. M. (1997). *Systems-Centered Therapy for Groups*. New York: Guilford Press.

Agazarian, Y. M. and Gantt, S. P. (2000). *An Autobiography of a Theory*. London and Philadelphia: Jessica Kingsley Publishers.

Ainsworth, M. D. S. (1991). Attachments and other affectional bonds across the lifecycle. In C. M. Parkes, J. Stevenson-Hinde and P. Marris (eds) *Attachment Across the Life Cycle*, pp. 33–51. London and New York: Routledge.

Ainsworth, M. D. S. and Wittig, B. A. (1969). Attachment and the exploratory behaviour of one-year-olds in a strange situation. In B. M. Foss (ed.) *Determinants of Infant Behaviour*, Vol. 4, pp. 113–136. London: Methuen.

Ainsworth, M. D. S., Bell, S. M. and Stayton, D. (1974). Infant–mother attachment and social development. In M. P. Richards (ed.) *The Introduction of the Child into a Social World*, pp. 99–135. Cambridge: Cambridge University Press.

Ainsworth, M. D. S., Blehar, M. C., Waters, E. and Wall, S. (1978). *Patterns of Attachment: A Psychological Study of the Strange Situation*. Hillsdale, NJ: Lawrence Erlbaum Associates, Inc.

Bowlby, J. (1969). *Attachment and Loss: Vol. I, Attachment*. London: Hogarth.

—— (1973). *Attachment and Loss: Vol. II, Separation, Anxiety and Anger*. London: Hogarth.

—— (1979). *The Making and Breaking of Affectional Bonds*. London: Tavistock.

—— (1980). *Attachment and Loss: Vol. III, Loss: Sadness and Depression*. London: Hogarth.

—— (1982). *Attachment and Loss*, 2nd edn. *Vol. I, Attachment*. Harmondsworth: Penguin.

—— (1988). On knowing what you are not supposed to know and feeling what you are not supposed to feel. In *A Secure Base*, pp. 99–119. London: Routledge.

—— (1991). Postscript. In C. M. Parkes, J. Stevenson-Hinde and P. Marris (eds) *Attachment Across the Life Cycle*, pp. 293–297. London and New York: Routledge.

Brazelton, T. B. and Cramer, B. G. (1990). *The Earliest Relationship*. Reading: Addison-Wesley.

Brazelton, T. B. K. B. and Main, M. (1974). The origins of reciprocity: the early mother–infant interaction. In M. Lewis and L. A. Rosenblum (eds) *The Effect of the Infant on its Caregiver*, pp. 49–76. New York: Wiley.

Bretherton, I. (1990). Communication patterns, internal working models, and the intergenerational transmission of attachment relationships. *Infant Mental Health Journal* 11: 237–252.

Cassidy, J. and Shaver, P. R. (eds) (1999). *Handbook of Attachment*. New York: Guilford Press.

Cohn, J. and Tronick., E. Z. (1987). Mother–infant face-to-face interaction: the sequence of dyadic states at 3, 6, and 9 months. *Developmental Psychology* 23: 68–77.

Fairbairn, R. (1952). *Psychoanalytic Studies of the Personality*. London: Tavistock.

Field, T. (1981). Infant arousal, attention and affect during early interactions. In L. P. Lipsitt (ed.) *Advances in Infancy Research*, Vol. 1. Norwood, NJ: Ablex.

Field, T. N., Woodson, R., Greenberg, R. and Cohen, D. (1982). Discrimination and imitation of facial expressions by neonates. *Science* 218: 179–181.

Grossmann, K. and Grossmann, K. E. (1991a). Newborn behaviour, early parenting quality and later toddler–parent relationships in a group of German infants. In J. Nugent, K. and B. M. Lester and T. B. Brazleton (eds) *The Cultural Context of Infancy*, Vol. 2. Norwood, NJ: Ablex.

——(1991b). Attachment quality as an organiser of emotional and behavioural: responses in a longitudinal perspective. In C. M. Parkes, J. Stevenson-Hinde and P. Marris (eds) *Attachment Across the Life Cycle*, pp. 93–114. London and New York: Routledge.

Heard, D. and Lake, B. (1986). The attachment dynamic in adult life. *British Journal of Psychiatry* 149: 430–439.

——(1997). *The Challenge of Attachment for Caregiving*. London: Routledge.

Hofer, M. A. (1983). On the relationship between attachment and separation processes in infancy. In R. Plutchik & H. Kellerman (eds) *Emotion: Theory, Research and Experience*, Vol. 2, pp. 199–219. New York: London: Academic Press.

McCluskey, U. (2001). A theory of care-giving in adult life: developing and measuring the concept of goal-corrected empathic attunement. Unpublished DPhil thesis, University of York Library.

——(2002). The dynamics of attachment and systems-centered group psychotherapy. *Group Dynamics: Theory, Research, and Practice* 6: 131–142.

——(2005). *To Be Met as a Person: The Dynamics of Attachment in Professional Encounters*. London: Karnac.

McCluskey, U., Roger, D. and Nash, P. (1997). A preliminary study of the role of attunement in adult psychotherapy. *Human Relations* 50: 1261–1273.

McCluskey, U., Hooper, C. and Bingley Miller, L. (1999). Goal-corrected empathic attunement, developing and rating the concept. *Psychotherapy, Theory, Research, Training and Practice*, 36: 80–90.

Meltzoff, A. N. and Moore, M. K. (1995). Infants' understanding of people and things: from body imitation to folk psychology. In J. Bermudez, A. J. Marcel and N. Eilan (eds) *Body and the Self*, pp. 43–69. Cambridge: MIT Press.

Murray, L. and Trevarthen, C. (1985). Emotional regulation of interactions between two-month-olds and their mothers. In T. M. Field and N. A. Fox (eds) *Social Perception in Infants*. New Jersey: Norwood.

——(1986). The infant's role in mother–infant communications. *Journal of Child Language* 13: 15–29.

Papousek, H. and Papousek, M. (1979). Early ontogony of human social interaction: its biological roots and social dimensions. In M. V. Cranach (ed.) *Human Ethology*. Cambridge: Cambridge University Press.

Papousek, M. (1994). Melodies in caregivers' speech: a species specific guidance towards language. *Early Development and Parenting* 3: 5–17.

Schore, A. N. (1994). *Affect Regulation and the Origin of the Self: The Neurobiology of Emotional Development*. Hillsdale, NJ: Lawrence Erlbaum Associates, Inc.

——(2000). Attachment and the regulation of the right brain. *Attachment and Human Development* 2: 23–47.

Segal, L. B., Oster, H., Cohen, M., Caspi, B., Myers, M. and Brown, D. (1995). Smiling and fussing in seven-month-old preterm and full-term black infants in the still-face situation. *Child Development* 66: 1829–1843.

Siegel, D. J. (1999). *The Developing Mind: Towards a Neurobiology of Interpersonal Experience*. New York: Guilford Press.

Stern, D. N. (1985). *The Interpersonal World of the Infant*. New York: Basic Books.

Sutherland, J. D. (1979). *The Malcolm Millar Lecture*. The psychodynamic image of man: a philosophy for the caring professions. Aberdeen: University of Aberdeen Press.

—— (1980/1993). The autonomous self. *Bulletin of the Menninger Clinic*, 3–30.

Tronick, E. Z. (1989). Emotions and emotional communication in infants. *American Psychologist* 44: 112–119.

Tronick, E. Z., Ricks, M. and Cohn, J. F. (1982). Maternal and infant affective exchange: patterns of adaptation. In T. Field and A. Fogel (eds) *Emotion and Early Interaction*. Hillsdale, NJ: Lawrence Erlbaum Associates, Inc.

Chapter 26

Extending Fairbairn and Sutherland's socio-intrapsychic model to assessment and treatment of a stepfamily

Carl Bagnini

Introduction

My thoughts on families branch out from two object relations concepts: Fairbairn's idea that the object in which the individual is incorporated is then incorporated within the individual; and Sutherland's concept that the mind is an open system in which development establishes order through fluctuation (Fairbairn 1952; Sutherland 1983; Scharff 1994). Their ideas fit with the way infants interact with others within and across generations in their families – a social basis for object seeking. The infant experiences, internalizes, and projects into the family group. This process shapes the internal object relationships in the endopsychic structure of the self. Impingements from the family environment on the infant's autonomous strivings foster non-thinking and lead to aggression, or dissociated forms of it, and they affect the nature of the internalized objects. But this is true not just for infancy. Object construction is a lifelong, cybernetic process of reconfiguring the self (Scharff and Scharff 1998).

When I work with families, I use these ideas and extend them to understand individual conflicts and the dynamics of the family group. I will illustrate the family therapy application of object relations by describing a complex treatment arrangement for relationship difficulties and problems with self-regulation in the family of a divorced couple and their two adult children – 28 years after the parents' divorce.

The object relations family therapy approach

As a family therapist, I can see firsthand how current symptoms are the reliving of the problems of earlier relationships, which prevent authentic individual and family relatedness. I help the family toward a healthy acknowledgement of the limitations of the past, with hope for the future. I join with the family as a special witness to their living history by a process of careful and attentive listening and empathic responsiveness. Identifying the defensive patterns, and noting the countertransferences that they evoke, I experience the family transferences and underlying anxieties about disappointing relationships, and I am then in a position to interpret them from inside my own experience. The therapeutic process of holding and containing allows for the painful aspects of the disturbed unconscious family conflicts to emerge and be detoxified by discussion and reworking. The aim of this therapy is to enable the family members to relocate and heal lost aspects of themselves and others.

The specific approach taken with the divorced family I will present is highly controversial, for it involves reassembling a family that had dissolved 28 years before. This unusual therapy arrangement took place with the generous cooperation and occasional participation of the members of the parents' new families because their current spouses recognized that the unresolved issues of the originally divorced partners had continued to haunt the development of the two adult children.

I developed this flexible treatment approach after experience in early sessions with the divorced family. There the parents' discussions concerning the two adult children were repeatedly pulled into a long-standing undertow of unresolved marital and child-rearing issues that remained from earlier years. I realized that intensive subunit reconstruction of the original family's relationships would be needed to release the emotional logjam preventing individuation of the adult children in meaningful post-divorce relationships.

The family

The parents, to whom I will refer simply as Father and Mother, are both in their fifties, divorced, and now in their third marriages to others. The adult children from Father and Mother's first marriage were the focus of the treatment. These adult children are Megan, 29, and George, 32. George has temper tantrums, and gambling issues; Megan has severe depression, anxiety, employment problems and interpersonal difficulties; both have serious credit card debt. George and Megan continue to relate to their parents as helpers and draw them into unsuccessful situations. This has drained their parents financially and emotionally, and angered their respective spouses, especially Mother's husband, whose three children barely endure Megan and George's extended dependencies on Mother.

The stepfather's children, who live independently, have accepted Mother and him as a couple but Father and Mother's children cannot adapt to stepfamily life. The tension between Father's commitment to his stepfamily, and the children's escalating demands grew, fueled by unconscious fantasies of a return to a nurturing nuclear family that in fact they had never known.

The complexity of the family situation called for an expanded, flexible approach, alternating between 12 sibling sessions for Megan and George, 18 parent sessions for Father and Mother, family sessions for the four of them, and extended stepfamily sessions to include the stepparents, and at times the stepfather's three children. After giving the history of the treatment, I will present material from a late session with the divorced Father and Mother and their two adult children Megan and George.

Expanding the approach to treatment of a stepfamily

Extending the psychoanalytic object relations approach to family work, the Scharffs recommend a combined and conjoint model in which the children are seen alternately with each parent to help them integrate and differentiate their dual family experience (Scharff and Scharff 1987b). The approach includes repairing the bond with the alienated parent, grieving the loss of the wished-for family, accepting the custodial parent's new marital partnership, and moving on (Scharff and Scharff 1987b). With adult children of divorce and remarriage I enlarge the frame by alternating sibling sessions, sessions with both biological parents, and the original nuclear family as a whole. I study sibling connections too, because they reveal particular internalized object representations (Bank and Kahn 1982) paralleling and reflecting the nature of the parents' marital relationship. Expanding the frame accommodates and recognizes the subgroups. Attunement to their needs builds safety and trust – a vital requirement.

A flexible treatment approach

The need for flexible treatment combinations in this case was determined by the ambiguities and ambivalences within the current group of the multiply remarried adults and the two adult children of the primary parents. Though 28 years had elapsed since the primary family went through divorce, much emotional reactivity remained, with little understanding of how to deal with it. The nuclear fallout was impeding everyone's abilities to move ahead. Father and Mother's third marriages were improvements over their first and second choices. Even so, Megan and George were in turmoil and had trouble bonding with their current stepparents. They felt left out of the loop concerning their parents' choices about whom they married, and the reasons for divorce. Both parents expected the children to adapt to their new spouses and deal with the loss of prior ones. At the same time they both expressed concern and caring for their children, but felt frustrated about helping them feel better. The family could not remember a time when caring was adequate for any of them to move through life's challenges with confidence.

George and Megan made attempts at bonding with others outside the family but only alienated everyone, none more desperately than each other. They shared an apartment, but could not get along. Megan clung to the living arrangement, and George wanted to move on – a pattern of disruption stemming from early childhood, similar to the entering and leaving of their father and then their stepfather. George maintained a close and consistent relationship with his mother, but at the price of listening to tearful confessions and complaints by her about her depressing life, and absolving her of guilt. As adults the children still had insecurities in trusting themselves in a world that forces adjustment after adjustment, with little recognition of what has been lost.

Intergenerational trauma and neglect

The couple's divorce had occurred when Megan was 18 months and George was 3 years old, respectively. Father and Mother had met at university in the early 1970s, and each was seeking independence and a higher power for understanding themselves in relation to the political and social world. They lived together in a religious commune for some months. As soon as they married, they realized that they differed with respect to security, with Mother being the more serious about preparing for a family and financial stability, and Father so involved with the religious movement that he gave up an academic fellowship to maintain his commitment. The couple elected to move ahead in having children, despite considerable tension between them regarding Father's freedom to find his own way, and Mother's nesting requirements. They moved east and Father took up a lowpaid but steady teaching job in token adherence to Mother's family values. The children were born, arguments intensified about money and family versus individual values, and the relationship deteriorated further. Mother got depressed and Father, unable to cope, became violent towards Mother. Father's physical abusiveness led to the separation and continued to prevent co-parenting for many years after the tumultuous divorce.

The children hung on to whatever nurturing was available, largely from Mother, even though she was usually depressed and enraged at Father's irresponsibility in failing to maintain child support payments through periods of their greatest dependency. Nevertheless, they had managed, and the children, who were bright, had had a good education. George was in a dental residency, while Megan was a college graduate. They had been able to apply themselves academically, which gave a sense of accomplishment.

In the assessment sessions, George and Megan listened attentively, but said little, often looking down when Mother revisited Father's hurtfulness and neglect. Each parent acted as though their lost marriage was the only issue even now, and still minimized the impact on the children. Father showed almost no regret for the suffering of Mother and the children. George's gambling and credit card debt, and Megan's depression, underemployment, and intermittent periods of clinging to her brother and mother when unable to live on her own did not claim sufficient attention. The children seemed insecure and helpless because they were not able to defend themselves by thinking. I found myself empathizing with the children more than with the parents, a countertransference wish to supply the missing attention to the least nurtured members with whom I identified.

I learned that Father had been physically abusive to George during bitter arguments with Mother, beginning at age 3 and continuing during visitation after the divorce. Even though she was physically spared herself, Megan, a terrified witness to this abuse, erected a mental fortress in which anger in any form was intolerable. George felt that she had been spared because she was their father's favorite. Unmet longings for parental nurturing had been displaced onto each sibling in the form of rivalry and demands that could not be met. The resulting high levels of frustration caused major regressive pulls between depression and aggression. The children didn't understand that their parents' rejecting behavior was related to events, not to them, and so they placed themselves as a couple at the center of what caused their rejection (Fonagy 2001).

Examining the sibling bond (Bank and Kahn 1982; Kahn and Lewis 1988) unlocked and treated the secret ways that sibling couples were caught in the web of their parents' marriage. Working back and forth with the sibling unit, across the generations, from past to present, subunit to subunit, and from parts to the whole, I understood the "reactive identities" (Horner 1999) introjected by the brother and sister. Then in whole family sessions, the siblings could share this understanding of what they were carrying for their parents, and so release themselves from the grip of the parental projections.

This was more easily thought than done. Father was unwilling to admit that his aggression and inconsistency had contributed to the children's future difficulties. From the parents' standpoint they, not their children, were at the center of their hurt feelings. From each child's point of view, the parents were emotionally lacking, overinvolved, or unavailable. Megan was currently hateful of George, but remembered being protective of him when his father was punishing him. She did not fully understand how these events and feelings helped to shape their lives, and often went blank when approaching the subject.

I saw this as Megan's dissociation from her emerging affects and from her mother's and brother's repressed rage at their father, and as her identification with the helpless mother, who clung to George, but who did not protect him or Megan in the early years. The parents each took on the victim's role, projected the blame, and evacuated the shame. In this way they had little emotional space to take in the children's needs or experiences, and little recognition of inner and outer aspects of reality or of their own part in the situation.

The children were huddling *inside* their own experience as a sibling couple in which they felt the attributes of each parent projected on each other. Everyone suffered the divorce fallout. The children could not learn to master thoughts and feelings in relation to their parents' unexplained states of depression or disengagement, and so resorted to clinging and identification. There were no conversations to clarify what things meant, and, due to their individual narcissistic hurts and angers, each parent ignored the significant communications of each child.

Working with the family unit

My impression was that what they all wanted was not so much to be understood, but to be agreed with. Megan and Mother expressed being hurt by the tantrums that George and Father rationalized as outbursts justified by not being understood. George saw the link between his father's corporal punishment of him and his own quick temper; but this was not so much an insight for his own benefit as it was a way of placating Megan and his mother. Megan felt that she had to make up for her mother's loneliness and lost love and to quell her mother's depression so that it did not engulf Megan and make her feel helpless. Mother and Megan saw that their mutual clinging was connected to making up for deprivations across three generations of women, all of whom thought that the way for a woman to get love from a man was to give in to his demands. This family assumption exacerbated Megan's difficulty in decision making, and in finding a proper partner.

More recently, however, Mother became annoyed that Megan was not making an independent life for herself, while she herself was in the midst of trying to salvage a troubled third marriage. Mother's turning away brought out Megan's strained relationship with her neglectful father and revealed her abandonment anxieties. She felt that she couldn't expect anything at all from a man. The parents began to express disappointment openly with the children about the way they were sucking them dry. Persecutory feelings increased family defensiveness, and made discussions tenuous and emptied the atmosphere of all hope.

Treating separate subunits

Working separately with Mother and Father in parent sessions, and with Megan and George in sibling sessions, I enabled both pairs to work on the historical derivatives of the current problems.

The parents

The parents more fully located the unconscious bases for their selection of each other. Father realized that he had been attracted to Mother's selflessness and commitment to his lofty spiritual pursuits. In this way she was like his own mother who had given in to his father's demands, and she was compliant in the face of his temper. Father was hungry for a woman who would not only make his wishes her priority and submit to his temper outbursts, but who would also take his side, something his mother had not done for him when he was hit by his own angry father. Mother's father was aloof, and she sought the opposite, a man who would supply her with closeness, even if she felt controlled by his temper. Recognizing these projections brought Father and Mother in touch with the needs that they each carried into the choice of partner, and that led to unsatisfied longing, rage, and eventually despair.

Father and Mother addressed their fears of opening up further. Father was afraid of losing control, as he was in such a rage at Mother's attachment to the children's needs. The intensity of his reaction stemmed from his hatred of his parents' relationship in which his father demanded and received undivided attention from his mother, and so as a boy he had to go without. Father's own father abused his wife, while he, as a small boy, could do nothing. Mother could relate to these dynamics as they were repeated in the current situation when George abused her verbally during family get-togethers, and Father did not intervene. Each parent expressed anger at the other in relation to the children's adult problems.

Mother brought her frustration over money into the present, challenging Father to own up to being a wimp about George's debts. Father responded with the accusation that Mother had had no compassion for the financial problems that interfered with his child support, and in retaliation had prevented Father from seeing the children. Thus the children had seen their father for only one week in each of two summers, and infrequently during the elementary school years.

Father and Mother realized that their relationships with their own parents in childhood were filled with childhood fears of physical and emotional punishment, which meant that they didn't dare complain. Therapy was different. Having experienced my empathy, they stopped justifying their mistakes, and became able to allow Megan and George to voice their grievances. They were on their way to establishing a more effective, responsive parental attitude.

The sibling subunit

I then expanded the treatment to allow sessions for the siblings to separate from the parents. This opened up a more comfortable space for full sharing of each child's hurts and conflicts. Until then, the parents had blocked each child's interpretations of current and childhood difficulties, any time either parent was criticized for inflicting emotional pain, whether by neglect or intrusiveness.

Megan and George's sessions focused on the ruptured sibling bond, and its origins. George revisited his assumption that Megan was his father's favorite. In tearful sessions Megan recounted how, when terrified of her father's treatment of George, she used to fear for George, and cry in hopes that Father would stop. All the while George had believed that she was spared because she was her father's princess, and he had been made the scapegoat. George's attitude to Megan softened when he realized how his sister had felt for him, but being the younger child, Megan had had no option but to cling to her mother, and submit to her father.

George and Megan each recognized that neither of them was the special one, and both had suffered in their own ways. The sibling work reduced the rivalry and provided them with a means for uniting to confront their parents with what they had learned when nuclear family sessions resumed. Competitive feelings had modified enough to make this possible.

Expanding the frame to include the stepfamily

In the expanded family sessions, the two current spouses and the stepfather's children encouraged the four original family members to face up to each other and deal with the past.

The effect on the divorced family as a whole

My benign attention softened the pain of prior deprivations. The sibling pair and the parental pair separately developed a trusting relationship with me. Each pair expressed curiosity about what the other pair was doing, and then empathy. The parents' good faith efforts offered renewed hope to George and Megan that at last they could mend their relationship as parents, and bring the children a unity of concern. If the children could get along better, the parental burden of obligation might be lessened. However the road continued to be bumpy.

The family was frustrated that Father had shown no remorse in therapy over physical violence to Mother and George years ago. Father had made it clear that he would have to have a safe forum for telling his own side of things first. Mother and the children saw this as his rationalizing, but they were all capable of denial like that, and they went along with him for a time. It amazed me that they were so patient. There were moments where I was filled with an angry countertransference as Father's refusal to be accountable continued the destructive denial at the center of their lives. They hoped that a full hearing of his experience might set the stage for forgiveness, but he hadn't found the right time for it, and they didn't force the issue. Violence not acknowledged or repented, cast a long shadow on this family's ability to rework the past.

Example of a family session

Father and Megan had not been getting into anything deep, as Megan put it, and so she was not feeling close to him. Single, feeling unattractive, soon to turn 30 and underemployed as a youth worker, Megan had no real prospects in her love life or career. She had failure after failure in independent living, and was hard pressed to afford remaining in the apartment on her own when George left.

As the session began, Megan tearfully related examples of being cut off from her father. Father said that because of her long-standing depression and her rejection of him over the years, he felt cautious about finding his way back to her, and was not about to expect too much too soon. Mother insisted that Father had always feared Megan's need for a genuine relationship with him, and his elusiveness left Megan disposed to choose only those men she thought she could control. Megan said that she lost her father before the age of 3, and then she tried to please him by putting up with his inconsistent visits, his "bad mouthing" her mother, and never having separate time for her. She was in deep pain, crying openly, and communicating freely with me, but unable to look at him, or at her mother or brother.

I asked if in addition to these early losses and longings there were fears as well. George said that he was scared when his father punished him physically, and he felt protected when Megan had cried. At this, Megan could no longer speak! I told her I would pay attention to her pain and continue looking at its causes and trying to find words that might help label the experience.

My attention turned to Mother. I thought of the terror of a little girl whose safety was falling apart. Mother and Megan shared the assumption that a man would not stay, and if he did he would turn violent. Megan could not express the anger associated with her torment, and so she trivialized men, by selecting those she could control, but never love. I surmised that she desperately needed her father to own up, in order to be angry with him safely. Otherwise there would be no possibility of forgiveness.

I asked if Mother could validate Megan's childhood experience. Mother was able to recount the instances of her own depression, and her anger at Father in the years lasting through the children's adolescence, but she couldn't acknowledge Megan's pain. George had done so in his own way, but not Mother. I felt irritated with her use of time for her own purposes, although I knew that she needed a forum for her hurts as well. I worked with my countertransference, realizing that I was identified with the child who needs sympathetic parental understanding of her deep anguish. I would, if needed, go to Father, George, or Mother for a bridge back to Megan if she could not speak for herself as yet.

The direction of the therapy had to be towards mourning the lost needed objects, recognizing the hurts and how they occurred, and creating a space for shared experiences of denied affect. With the family array of narcissistic wounds, much work would be needed if taking responsibility for past injuries were to be accomplished. Experiencing shared sadness might be a modest step in that direction.

Father had been quietly listening to Mother's account of the separation and the divorce's tumultuous effects on her. As Mother spoke, his facial expression was one of disbelief. I noticed that Megan had recovered and was listening attentively to Mother. I asked Megan to tell me about any scary time in the past. Megan said, "I used to be terrified when Dad gave it to Mom. I had to hide under the bed."

Father remained pensive for a few moments, lowered his head, looked over at Mother, and said, "I'm sorry for what I did to you in my helpless rage." This was far from a full apology to his family, but was as close to remorse as he could get, and the others acknowledged his healing step.

Progress

Over the course of the treatment there was a gradual improvement in the family's holding capacity. The members engaged in a complete accounting of their many hurts and losses and a full expression of their sadness. Appropriate boundaries, with decreased clinging and ambivalence were established. Mother and Father continue to respect each other's input as they work together to help the children continue their adult development. Megan's self-esteem improved, her depression lifted somewhat, and she found a better job. George's finances came under control due to a creative debt consolidation and budgeting arrangement that Mother, Father, and he came up with. Mother and Father continued to work on improving their relationship as parents of their adult children, and their current marriages improved. Sibling conflict lessened in intensity.

Conclusion

Even though 28 years had elapsed since the first divorce, this group experienced tremendous difficulties in adapting to stepfamily life after multiple remarriages. The expansion of the object relations family therapy frame to include various subgroupings at significant points in the process provided a holding environment for addressing individual, couple, family, stepfamily, and intergenerational problems. The parents' inability to address the children's needs during the marriage and since the marital break-up had prevented them from achieving satisfying relationships with each other, and compromised their attempts at bonding with others.

The custom-made design demonstrates the flexibility of an object relations approach, but remains controversial. I arrived at an unusual frame for the treatment in response to Mother and Father's investment in their children and in each other as their parents, the long-standing nature of the problem, and their current families' support. The wisdom of the approach seems to be validated by the resulting therapeutic process. The family translated the emotions and psychic structures derived from the prior disturbed relationships into a shared language. Competing demands gave way to more satisfying compromises and relative improvements within the parental pair, sibling pair, and stepfamily.

Expanded object relations family therapy with a stepfamily requires us to move gradually and thoroughly, back and forth, from past to present, interpersonal to intrapsychic, individual to group, family to stepfamily. Ample time for therapeutic attention to the pathological underpinnings, reworking conflicts, and accepting the new reality propels post-divorce movement into the potentially healing embrace of stepfamily life.

References

Bagnini, C. (2003). Containing anxiety with divorcing couples. In J. S. Scharff and S. Tsigounis (eds) *Self Hatred in Psychoanalysis: Detoxifying the Persecutory Object*, pp. 165–178. London: Routledge.

Bank, S. and Kahn, M. (1982). *The Sibling Bond*. New York: Basic Books.

Fairbairn, W. R. D. (1952) *Psychoanalytic Studies of the Personality*. London: Tavistock.

Fonagy, P. (2001). *Attachment Theory and Psychoanalysis*. New York: Other Press.

Horner, A. (1999). *Being and Loving*. Northvale, NJ: Jason Aronson.

Kahn, M. and Lewis, G. (eds) (1988). *Siblings in Therapy: Life Span and Clinical Issues*. New York: Norton.

Scharff, D. E., and Scharff, J. S. (1987a). *Object Relations Family Therapy*. Northvale, NJ: Jason Aronson.

—— (1987b). Families of divorce and remarriage. In *Object Relations Family Therapy*, pp. 367–393. Northvale, NJ: Jason Aronson.

Scharff, J. S. (ed.) (1994). *The Autonomous Self: The Work of John D. Sutherland*. Northvale, NJ: Jason Aronson.

Scharff, J., and Scharff, D. (1998). *Object Relations Individual Therapy*, pp. 219–236. Northvale, NJ: Jason Aronson.

Sutherland, J. D. (1983). The self and object relations: a challenge to psychoanalysis. *Bulletin of the Menninger Clinic* 47(6): 525–541. Reprinted in *The Autonomous Self: The Work of John D. Sutherland*, ed. J. S. Scharff, pp. 285–302. Northvale, NJ: Jason Aronson, 1994.

Winnicott, D. W. (1952). Anxiety associated with insecurity. In *Through Paediatrics to Psychoanalysis Collected Papers*, pp. 97–100. New York: Brunner/Mazel, 1992.

Chapter 27

Teaching and learning object relations theory with the Group Affective Model

Lea de Setton, Yolanda de Varela, David E. Scharff and Jill Savege Scharff

The Group Affective Model (Scharff and Scharff 2000) is an innovative teaching method, using the principles of object relations theory to facilitate participants' learning about object relations theories. In addition to the traditional combination of lectures, readings, discussions, and case presentations, the Group Affective Model uses the study of personal reactions to the material and of the resulting group interaction so as to illustrate the psychoanalytic concepts and clinical problems being studied. The group provides an affective, interpersonal matrix that functions as a laboratory for examining the concepts in vivo. For instance, participants studying Fairbairn and Klein can see a variety of Fairbairn's endopsychic situations displayed in the group process, and can learn Klein's processes of projective and introjective identification as they are created.

The group affective model is based on the group analytic theory of Bion, the individual object relations theory of Fairbairn and Winnicott, Sutherland's (1979) concept of the caring community chaos theory, new research on affect regulation and neurobiological development (Schore 1994), and action research on the processes of teaching and learning (Scharff and Scharff 1979).

New findings on affect regulation and neurological development confirm that the mind is interpersonally constructed – as Fairbairn thought. The infant needs a mother who is sensitively attuned at crucial moments of development if satisfactory neurological growth is going to occur. Cognitive functioning of the left brain is grafted on an affective base in right brain functioning. So it follows that learning will occur more effectively in situations where affects are welcomed and responded to as part of the teaching task.

Applying the ideas taken from chaos theory, we see the mind as a non-linear system, which shows fractal similarity to the family group in which the person was raised. The infants mind is "entrained" (brought into conformity) with the more organized system of the mother's mind. At the beginning of life, where the potential for chaos is extreme and life threatening, the mother sensitively takes a turbulent situation and moves it into a state of adaptation. She operates as a strange attractor that continually moves the infant to higher and higher states of development closer and closer to her own. Similarly, a therapist through years of training and treatment becomes a more organized self system. When a patient meets a therapist, the patient experiences turbulence in the patient's level of adaptation, and the transference to the therapist as a strange attractor moves the patient toward disorganization and then reorganization in a healthier way. Similarly, participants in affective learning groups experience turbulence personally and in relation to other small group members as they all try to learn unfamiliar concepts that deal with primitive anxieties. In relation to the institution's holding and containment and in response to group interpretation of these anxieties, participants arrive at a new adaptation in relation to new concepts.

The small group integrative task

The small affective learning group is characterized by its integrative task. The group exists as a place to integrate cognitive and emotional aspects of the learning process at the intrapsychic and interpersonal levels, observing the resonance of the there-and-then in the here-and-now. The group enables its members to carry out the integrative task. Group members explore the group process and its relationship to the group leader, and they examine how the theme of the institution is reflected in the small group.

The role of the group leader

It is the leader's job to maintain a triple focus on the didactic material, its dynamic implications for the individuals and the group, and its clinical application. The leader functions in terms that Winnicott uses to describe good parenting – as the environmental mother who provides a good holding environment, and as the object mother toward whom direct transferences are experienced in core affective exchanges. The group provides a transitional space in which to play, discover, and create new knowledge from current experience. The group has a containing function transforming anxiety and the unthinkable unknown into narrative and thinkable experience.

The leader embodies an attitude of teaching and learning, sets the tone, balances investment in cognitive and emotional work, and tracks coverage of the presented material. The leader focuses on the group as a whole and commutes between that group as a whole and the individual within it, actively seeking the voice of each member to build the whole, monitoring silences, hesitations and non-verbal communications, and keeping a good balance between giving to the group and frustrating group longings. The leader senses the atmosphere, follows the affect, follows the unconscious theme, contains anxiety, notes defensive patterns, uses confrontation, contains and interprets underlying anxieties of the group as a whole, and interprets the group's use of the leader as an object of attachment, desire, hatred, contempt, neglect, denigration, envy, admiration, idealization, spoiling, and so on. The transference to the leader may be a maternal, paternal or sibling transference. The leader interprets these transferences in the light of countertransference experiences with the group.

Affective learning groups have some aspects in common with therapy groups. The leader works with group process, transference and countertransference, follows affect, and makes interpretations. However, the goal of the affective learning group is growth, not healing. Discretion is offered but confidentiality is not guaranteed. The leader's responsibility is educational not clinical.

Premises of the Group Affective Learning Model

1   Affects are the motivating and integrating engine of self-object organization at all levels – in the mind, in the neuro-psychological functioning of the brain, in relationships, and in groups.
2   The internal relationship of self and object is the basic unit of the structure and functioning of the psyche as the organizer of external relationships.
3   Individual psyches communicate with others through unconscious processes of projective and introjective identification. Unconscious processes lead individuals to combine spontaneously with others to form subgroups that express shared unconscious concerns.
4   Following the affective landmarks of subgroupings, and learning from the experience, is more effective than cognition alone in arriving at understanding.
5   The processes of learning in the group provide illustrations of the psychoanalytic concepts that are being learned.

Multi-channel teaching in the large group

The Group Affective Model uses multi-channel teaching – lecture, video, powerpoint, small and large group discussion – in order to reach a variety of therapists with a range of learning styles and to reinforce the learning by coming at it from various vertices. In lecture events, narratives and visuals are used together because some people learn through their eyes and others through their ears. Others take in the concepts best when they experience them in action, and for them the groupwork will be more meaningful than the lectures and case presentations. The more intellectual student finds the lecture an effective, orienting experience, and that is where we start. Affectively oriented students tend to tune out a lecture unless they know that they will be able to express their feelings and digest the material later. Whatever their learning style, participants benefit from active engagement in discussion during the lecture and from reinforcement of the learning in the small group.

The large group also meets in a plenary format to get the total picture of what the small groups are learning and how they reflect aspects of the institution and the learning task (Turquet 1985). This prevents splitting and compartmentalization which would otherwise interfere with the integrative task. At designated times, the large group may meet as a process group to explore the life of the large group and to study and illustrate processes of merger, chaos, aggregation, and massification and the role of basic assumption life in the large group (Bion 1961; Hopper 2003). The focus of the large group is on the cognitive aspects of learning. The group process that develops may further the learning task or it may be a resistance to it. In general, the large group makes intellectual sense of emotional experience.

Small groups meet afterwards to carry forward the integrative work. Where the large group translates emotional processes into intellectual content, the small group works principally to imbue intellectual content with emotional meaning. For the purpose of this chapter, we will focus our remarks on the activity of the small affective learning group, and on a pilot research project using the object relations technique to assess the effect of learning with the Group Affective Model.

A closer look at learning in the small affective learning group

In the small group, members share their comments, questions, and responses, and the group engages in discussion. Interpersonal interaction amplifies each individual's intrapsychic response, and the group dynamic that emerges demonstrates the concept. Associations to life and clinical experience in the there-and-then are connected to experience in the here-and-now of the group. The small learning group may regress at times and look more like a therapy group than a learning group, but this is in the service of internalizing the concepts being taught, and then the group moves back to a more mature level.

The small group task is to facilitate the participants' learning. It offers a safe space that is more intimate than the large group. Powerful emotional reactions occur when members resonate unconsciously with the concepts they are trying to understand. The small group process that develops as members interact demonstrates the concepts in action and so facilitates the members' internalizing the concepts through the process of valuing their emotional aspect, a step that is a prerequisite for their useful clinical application.

The leader ensures that the group reviews the concepts; focuses on individual emotional reactions, interpersonal interactions, group process, and clinical examples; and keeps in mind the small group's relation to the institution as a whole.

The student's job is to think about the concepts, share emotional reactions, study the group process, and think about cases, and then review the concepts in relation to what has been said and experienced, all in order to internalize those aspects of the concepts that are most useful clinically.

The leader guards the boundaries of the group by starting and stopping each group session on time and maintaining the same group membership over the life of the group without intrusions and absences, as far as possible. Group leaders hold the many facets of the learning task in mind, and maintain an integrative intention. They interpret resistances to working with the complexity of the task, and they foster the learning for themselves and for their groups. They have the authority of their faculty status, but they are also there to learn and re-learn the concepts themselves.

Leaders are responsible for ensuring that their small affective learning groups are addressing the concepts actively, which is especially necessary when the group processes takes on a life of their own. They focus on the individual and the group as a whole, and on the cognitive and emotional aspects of the learning experience. They balance the need to give information and interpretation with the need to hold back and leave the group room for discovery.

Like group therapists, leaders of small affective learning groups support communication from each member of the group to widen the field of participation in the learning experience. They listen to the words, the non-verbal communications, and each individual's way of telling the story. They recognize defensive patterns like those that Bion (1961) described – dependency on the leader, fight against the task, flight from the group, and pairing with the hope that the newly formed couple will produce a leader who meets the group's needs. They notice their countertransferences, which help them to interpret the group's transference. They monitor the atmosphere, follow the affect, and in general keep in touch with the group at a deep unconscious level. They offer firm empathic psychological holding, creating the safe space within the secure frame. They provide containment by processing anxiety so that it becomes thinkable and manageable, instead of getting in the way of learning. Learning to process and review is essential for participants who are learning to become better clinicians.

If you looked at only one session of an ongoing small affective learning group, you might think that it is like a therapy group. You would notice a free expression of affect, conflict, and distress. The group might attend to a member who is overwhelmed by feelings in reverberation with one of the concepts and is functioning more like a disturbed patient than a therapist in training. You would see the group leader dealing with transference and countertransference. But if you examined the group over time you would learn that the group moves between regression and progression. The primary task is education not treatment. The group process is reported at faculty meetings where the faculty members extend their learning by examining the effect that the teaching and learning of the concepts have at every level of learning, from the individual to the whole institution.

Research into the effectiveness of the Group Affective Model

We take an action research stance while we are teaching. A learning institution must be concerned with credibility. We are constantly evaluating our methods and their effectiveness and assessing the need for change. We think of our institution as a dynamic system of parts – programs, courses, lectures, small groups, faculty, participants – all influencing one another. We subject our impressions to process and review in faculty meetings and plenary meetings of faculty and participants. We publish our process and our conclusions from time to time, and subject them to critical reading. A few years ago, we looked for a research method that, while still suitably qualitative, gives results that can be measured against standardized norms. Yolanda de Varela brought an updated version of the Object Relations Technique to the task.

The Object Relations Technique (ORT) is a projective test somewhat like a cross between the Thematic Apperception Test and the Rorschach. It was devised by Phillipson at the Tavistock Centre for assessing change in psychotherapy. Sutherland knew and valued the ORT: indeed, he wrote the introduction to its first edition. The ORT fell into disuse for a time, but now, with permission, it has been reissued with new plates, and a new scoring system by Martin Shaw (2002). In a pilot research project, Varela applied the ORT to study change, not in psychotherapy patients, but in participants after a course of study in object relations theory and practice, of which an essential component is their attendance at small affective learning groups the purpose of which is to integrate cognitive and affective aspects of their learning (as we have described more fully above).

The research sample came from mental health professionals who volunteered to participate anonymously. They were enrolled as (a) second-year students at a week-long course of instruction in object relations theory and practice; or (b) first-year students at a week-long course of instruction in object relations theory and practice; or (c) first-year students in object relations couple therapy; and (d) mental health professionals who are not enrolled in a program. So, three groups of test subjects drawn from programs using the Group Affective Model were formed, and were tested before and after a week of instruction and participation in twice daily small affective learning groups, and the fourth group of test subjects who were not in the programs were tested at the beginning and end of the same week.

- Group A: Four (4) second-year students in object relations theory and practice, attending classes on infant observation, attachment and research.
- Group B: Four (4) first-year students in object relations theory and practice, attending classes on infant observation, attachment, and research.
- Group C: Four (4) students of object relations couple therapy, studying

the object relations of unstable couple relationships and marriages on the brink of divorce

- Group D: (the control group): Four (4) mental health professionals who were not enrolled as students and did not participate in any part of the above courses.

Before the participants attended the first lecture of the week, they were given a pre-test. They were shown three of the plates that comprise the ORT, each of which depicts a group situation in a slightly hazy way that lends itself to multiple interpretations. These were Plates AG, BG, and CG. Participants were asked to look at each plate for a few minutes, and then write a story about each situation. The test was repeated at the end of the week. Important elements of each narrative were isolated, and reduced to a single sentence, which could then be coded against standards developed by Martin Shaw. Varela tested two hypotheses, concerning change in the use of defenses before and after a week's immersion in the group affective model in each category of participant being tested. We will not attempt to explain the complicated implementation of the research methodology or present the coded results, which can be studied in the ORT manual and in Varela's (2004) thesis respectively. For the purposes of this chapter, we are not trying to be true to the research study. We are taking a qualitative approach instead. We are simply selecting one of the ORT plates, called Plate AG, and highlighting the pre- and post-test responses given by one representative of each of the four groups from which Varela, attending to unconscious themes in that data, builds a picture of the learning experiences of the four individuals, relates three of them to the progress of their small affective learning groups, and compares them to the experience of the group that did not use the group affective method.

Group A (in Year 2 of affective learning program)

Plate AG: Pre-test story of participant A1

The services ended half an hour ago. John felt himself drawn to stay. He wondered how it had all come about. He stood quietly, looking over the grave, as if looking at the bottom of a deep hole in the earth. He knew he needed to turn away shortly to ascend the stairs behind him – but he found that he needed to stay there to think about the relationship with his lost friend, to feel his feelings about his friend, for just a few more moments. They had been such good friends, he and Frank, for so many years. Things will be very different now – but how?

Participant A1, a second-year student, had been in the same small affective learning group for a year already. That small group, now at the beginning of its second year, had to deal with the loss of one of its members. The group is aware that the member who withdrew was carrying some of their individual projections. Participant A1 is capable of dealing with loss and with contemplating the void. He is getting ready to re-own projective identifications placed on the lost student. A reworking of similar issues in each member's internal world is depicted in A1's individual story.

Plate AG: Post-test – A1's story

> It's growing very late in the afternoon, late enough that the fire is glowing and shining on the faces of the men sitting around it. White Cloud becomes a man today. He brought down the largest buffalo in the herd, enough to feed the entire clan for many days. The chief stands behind him and begins the chant, opening the ceremony. White Cloud is full of thoughts and feelings. He is wondering what life will be like now? How should he react to his peers? He is tired and sad, but ready to move on.

Tracking the progression in themes from the pre-test to the post-test, we hypothesize that reworking infant attachment issues in the affective learning group has secured his base and propelled this student toward a more potent view of himself as a provider, a leader, and a man. If his story correctly represents the learning of the members of his group, we may assume that his group has moved to take up group issues and group responsibilities. There is a change in the expression of affect from pre-test emphasis on detachment to the post-test emphasis on the individual feeling part of the group and feeling valued by the group members. The endlessly deep hole mentioned on the pre-test seems to have been filled, and the affect is in the depressive position. The main character feels enriched and strong in the group. He is also detaching and getting ready to go back to other relationships, not knowing how they will react to him after this experience.

Group B (in Week 1 of 2-year affective learning program)

Plate AG: Pre-test story of participant B1

> It is very foggy out – perhaps it is dusk. They are in a cemetery as someone has recently died. There are six figures in the scene, three in the forefront, and three in the background. The three figures in the background are bystanders witnessing the scene in the forefront. The three people in the forefront are at the gravesite and are very sad. The larger figure is the father who is standing over his two sons. They are not speaking but are deep in thought – each in his own world of reflection, memory, and love for the person who has passed. Though they are separate, they are connected in their grief and mourning. They will hold this moment for the rest of their lives, as if frozen in time.

Participant B1 is joining a new group. Each participant comes to the program carrying their own personal issues in a private, silent space. The story indicates that B1 recognizes the universality of feelings of loss and may find similar feelings among peers in the group, but takes an observing stance from which he sees people as separate, representing defenses that will maintain emotional distance from the group's affects.

Plate AG: Post-test – B1's story

It is a very cold foggy day in San Francisco in a park. There are men in the scene who appear to be looking downcast. It is misting lightly, not a full rain. None of the men know each other, and they each seem lost in their own preoccupations. They seem to be thinking deeply but are disconnected from one another, barely aware of one another but each of them somehow a little less lonely because of the presence of another. In a moment they will leave the park and go about their day, missing an opportunity to connect with another human being.

B1's story shows a slight movement from the isolation in the pre-test to a stage where he is reconnecting with his feelings. The frozen affect of the pre-test has given way to a light mist, not a full rain, not fully in touch emotionally. Not there yet, but functioning in a more depressive mode, he is beginning to realize his need to relate and to recognize the missed opportunities to do so. Despite some movement from the pre-test to the post-test story, he still turns to his past defenses of isolation before joining the world outside the course. Still, there is the awareness of the presence of another, possibly standing for the group leader, in whom he is placing the responsibility for maintaining attachment.

Group C (in a 1-week affective learning program)

Plate AG: Pre-test story of participant C1

There are two people, no, six people contemplating their thoughts and feelings related to a recent event. They are in a city park, with buildings in the background. Two of them are whispering about their ideas and reactions. The others are separated from them and from each other. Their posture shows that they are being introspective. The mood is quiet. Soon they will join together to listen to the music in the park.

C1's story calls attention to the confusion about whether there are two figures or six figures. C1 will participate in a group of approximately six participants who will study the functioning of couples on the brink. Already, issues about a couple and a group, perhaps standing for a family group, are on C1's mind.

C1 positions herself as an observer, projecting issues into the group and isolating her affects. She defends herself by predicting entering into a dependency state of listening to other people's music.

Plate AG: Post-test – C1's story

> There is a group meeting in an outdoor area. The individuals had to walk down steps to find a platform which was their meeting place. It is dusk. The atmosphere is ill-defined but gloomy. The members have no agenda. Some are sitting, others are standing and wondering who will start the meeting or who will present the first topic of discussion. They are making decisions for the town.

C1's defense mechanism of isolation of affect is still in place, and the main position is that of the observer. However, the people are to be involved in decision making, not just listening to music. Walking down to a gloomy atmosphere may refer to new aspects being discovered about the internal world or may refer literally to the fact that the affective learning group of which she is a member meets in a basement classroom. In contrast to the pretest, in the post-test the subject is not withdrawing from the task, being more able to contain doubts and confusion.

Group D (not in any affective learning program)

Plate AG: Pre-test story of participant D1

> There are many people in this scene but we can see only about six. They are sitting at a memorial service at New York harbor. There are boats in the harbor. The World Trade Center was hit last week by terrorists, and this is one of the services being held at the site. The smoke is still in the air rising from Ground Zero. The mood is somber and everyone is in mourning. There is a leader to the right – a clergyperson, a speaker, or a singer – and they are focusing their attention there. In the future there will be more such events. The smoke will eventually clear but the mood will remain the same.

D1 is not going to be a member of an affective learning group, and yet finds a group to belong to, those attacked on 9/11. The story conveys shock and the mobilization of defenses such as introjection, identification, displacement, and idealization. Superego figures come to the rescue but a sense of emotional paralysis permeates the story.

Plate AG: Post-test – D1's story

> Three people on the left are sitting at a 9/11 memorial service in lower Manhattan, a week after the attacks on the World Trade Center. The mood is somber and the service has just ended. The three people on the right are standing up, ready to depart. They are drifting off to watch the smoke from the buildings and the boats on the harbor. The two on the right have come together and are talking with each other; the other one is alone. Everyone is in a state of shock after the disaster.

From pre-test to post-test story of this participant in the control group, there is a striking lack of movement, and only the slight difference of two people walking away together. This participant has had no space in which to work on these shared issues, and therefore no space for internalizing the lecture material.

Conclusion

The pre-test stories reflect internal turmoil in anticipation of joining or re-joining a psychoanalytic program to study object relations. The post-test stories reflect the mobilization of defenses, and new ways of understanding theory and relating to others. The progression between the themes in the pre-test and post-test stories of one person is not offered as proof of value of the Group Affective Model, any more than one clinical case presentation proves the value of object relations theory. The vignettes from the research project are offered to show the way of working on the question of what effect the small affective learning group has. Differences were shown in the level of functioning before and after a week of learning. However, the most striking result was the strong contrast between the degree of difference between the pre- and post-test stories in the first three groups and the lack of it in the control group. These results show the impact of the instrument on the internal world of the participants in Groups A, B, and C, and the lack of change in Group D when a person does not have the opportunity to learn in a group.

Summary of the Affective Learning Model

The processes of learning in the group provide vivid, tangible illustrations of the psychoanalytic concepts that are being learned. Unconscious processes reverberating with the concepts lead group members to combine spontaneously in subgroups that express shared unconscious concerns. The individual psyches of these group members communicate with others through unconscious processes of projective and introjective identification to create these combinations. So the relationship of self and object that determines the structure and function of the individual psyche at the neurological and psychological levels is also the organizer of external relationships and of group and institutional process.

The motivating and integrating engine of this self-object organization is affect. And affect is the marker of self-object activation in the small affective learning group. Following the affective landmarks of subgroupings, learning from individual and group experience, and exploring transference to the group leader are together more effective than cognition alone in arriving at understanding of psychoanalytic concepts. Students report major change in their professional and personal lives. Learning in an affective learning program enhances the participants' use of mature defenses, which opens them to responding more fully in clinical situations.

References

Bion, W. (1961). *Experiences in Groups*. London: Social Science, 1968.

Hopper, E. (2003). *Traumatic Experience in the Unconscious Life of Groups*. London: Jessica Kingsley Publishers.

Scharff, D. E. and Scharff, J. S. (1979). Teaching and learning: an experiential conference. *Journal of Personality and Social Systems* 2, 1: 53–78.

—— (2000). *Tuning the Therapeutic Instrument: Affective Learning of Psychotherapy*. Northvale, NJ: Jason Aronson.

Schore, A. (1994). *Affect Regulation and the Origin of the Self: The Neurobiology of Emotional Development*. Hillsdale, NJ: Lawrence Erlbaum Associates, Inc.

Shaw, M. (2002). *The Object Relations Technique: Assessing the Individual*. Manhasset, NY: ORT Institute.

Sutherland, J. D. (1979). The psychodynamic image of man. In J. S. Scharff (ed.) *The Autonomous Self: The Work of John D. Sutherland*, pp. 268–282. Northvale, NJ: Jason Aronson.

Turquet, P. (1985). Leadership, the individual and the group. In G. Gabbard (ed.) *Analysis of Groups*. San Francisco: Jossey Bass, 1974. Reprinted in A. D. Colman and M. H. Geller (eds) *Group Relations Reader, Vol. 2*, pp. 71–87. Washington DC: A. K. Rice Institute.

Varela, Y. de (2004). Defences against learning: a statistical research. PhD thesis, Southern California University for Professional Studies.

Index

abandonment 80, 125, 126, 265; borderline pathology 134, 136; child therapy 145, 146; engulfment–abandonment 129, 130, 131, 132; fear of 171; relationship addiction 162, 163, 165; schizoid conflict 130

Abraham, K. 50, 52, 89, 133

abuse: bad objects 141; conditional badness 6; family therapy 263, 264, 266; negative transference 140; relationship addiction 159, 162–3, 164–6; sexual 3, 44, 140, 148–57, 161; *see also* trauma

acting out 102, 103, 136

action 45, 214

action research 271, 276

addiction 158–9, 207

aesthetic experience 178

affect: attunement 250–1, 253; child therapy 154, 156–7; Group Affective Model 273; group therapy 254, 255–6; as motivator of self-object organization 282; naming 174; object constellations 7–8; regulation 251, 252–3, 271; relationship-seeking 192; role of affects 3; Sutherland 194, 199, 203, 206; *see also* emotions

affective learning groups 272–3, 274–5, 276–81, 282

Agazarian, Yvonne 250, 253

aggression 10, 13, 94, 115, 141, 160; borderline pathology 136; couple relationship 169–75; family environment 260, 264; Klein 13, 204; Macmurray/Fairbairn comparison 216; organizational change 242; as reactive tendency 3, 14; Schreber case 12; sexual 73, 74, 78; Sutherland 209;

Suttie 26, 31; workplace 245, 246; *see also* anger

Aiello, Theresa 140–7

Ainsworth, Mary Salter 252

alcoholism 165

Alexander, F. 106

alienated structure 92–3, 95

allergic object relationship 91

ambivalence 5, 69, 89, 129, 133, 172; borderline personality 135, 136; couple therapy 173; hysteria 100; mature dependence 131; schizoid conflict 131, 135, 136

anality 5, 12, 52, 162; anal fixation 56; anus 82; sadism 76

analytical psychotherapy 197, 198

André, Jacques 53

anger: antilibidinal ego 69, 76; family therapy 264, 268; group therapy 254; Imago perspective 171; *see also* aggression; rage

anorexia nervosa 93

antilibidinal ego 7–9, 10, 66, 117, 172, 249; dominance of 108, 111; fetishism 77; Freudian transferences 64; group therapy 255, 256; hate towards rejecting object 69; Macmurray/Fairbairn comparison 216; masturbation 74; repression of 115, 141; sadism 74, 76; splitting 91; *see also* endopsychic structure; libidinal ego

anxiety: annihilatory 170; groups 238, 243, 272, 275; von Minden 62; pathology 16; primary 199; projective identification 81; puzzlement 244; separation 63, 129–30, 132, 134, 136, 160, 195, 213; sexual 83; Suttie 26, 27, 28, 31; work difficulties 246

situation 130; German psychoanalysis
66; hysteria 98; loss during oral phase
134; repression 11, 34, 122–3, 132;
trauma 121; *see also* splitting
Dodes, L. 159
domestic violence 161, 163, 164, 207, 267
Dovidio, J. F. 227
DPV *see* German Psychoanalytical
Association
dreams 10–11, 34, 84, 135; dissociated
material 127; Freud 177, 179;
hysterical patients 11–12; murderous
166; self analysis 207–8; sexual 73
Drever, James 117
drive theory 13, 122, 123; Fairbairn
refutation of 54, 55, 56–7, 58, 89;
Heising 62; Sutherland 203
Dutton, D. 163, 164
dyspareunia 85–6

Edinburgh 207
ego 7, 44–5, 46, 113, 118, 141; art 178;
dreamwork 177, 179; dynamic
structures 62, 64, 66; as endopsychic
structure 129, 130; functions of 195;
hysteria 102; inadequacy of structural
theory 198–9; number of object
relations 133; post-traumatic structure
126; primary 55; pristine 89, 191,
205, 215; projection 130; regressed 94;
schizoid conflict 132; splitting 4, 43,
61, 80, 89, 115, 123; Sutherland 188–9,
203–4; tactile interactions 68–9; *see
also* antilibidinal ego; central ego;
libidinal ego; self
Emery, Fred 221, 242
emotional unconscious 124–5, 126, 127
emotions: bodily state relationship 44,
82; Imago therapy 169; Macmurray
21, 22; psychopathy 31; small affective
learning group 274; Sutherland 34;
Suttie 25, 28, 31, 35; *see also* affect
empathy 204, 251, 253, 256
enactments 125, 126, 143
encopresis 145, 146
endopsychic structure 7–11, 14–16, 34,
40, 89, 115; aggression 114; as art 181;
channelling of energy 118; child
treatment 140–1; dependence 47;
dynamic aspects 46; engulfment–
abandonment 129; family influence on
260; German psychoanalysis 66;

hysteria definition 103; Lacan critique
of Fairbairn 51; Macmurray/Fairbairn
comparison 216; Pontalis 51–2;
psychosis 13; as series of repetitions
45; splitting 91, 249; Sutherland 202,
205; *see also* ego
engulfment–abandonment 129, 130, 131,
132
envy 30, 55, 82
epigenetic phases 192, 200
episodic memory 124
erectile dysfunction 83–5
Erikson, E. 95, 189, 192, 200, 224
erogenous masochism 55–6, 75–6
erogenous zones 56, 57, 90, 91
evil 6
evolutionary biology 205, 206, 222–3,
224
exciting object 34, 45, 74, 108, 115;
borderline organization 134;
cumulative trauma 92; endopsychic
structure 7–8, 9–10, 11, 15–16, 141,
249; fetishism 79; group therapy 255;
Heising 62; hysteria 102; internalized
relationships 105; libidinal ego 69;
masochism 75; model scene 146;
Oedipal situation 101, 102; sexual
desire 69; sexual dysfunction 81, 85,
86; splitting 91; *see also* object
relations; rejecting object
existentialism 198, 199, 218
eye contact 254

Fain, Michel 56
Fairbairn, W. R. D. 1, 19, 188, 190, 260;
aggression 172–3; ambivalence 89;
analyst as real person 93; analytic
relationship 106, 107; art 176, 177–82;
bad objects 6–7, 132, 159; contingent
nature of social existence 218;
contribution of 33–5; development of
his theory 3–18, 113–16; dissociation
121, 122–3, 127; dreams 208; early
infant experiences 80; endopsychic
structure 7–11, 14–16, 34, 140–1;
France 50–60, 113; Germany 61–7;
Group Affective Model 271; groups
245; hysteria 11–12, 97, 100–3;
integration of the self 87; internal
demons 167; internal process of his
theory 116–18; Klein comparison
13–14; Lacan critique of 50–1; libido

differentiation 234; sexual activity 68; social object 229; transitional stage 55, 100, 114
memory 42, 48, 123–4
men: fetishism 77–8; hysteria 99
Menninger Clinic 202
Menzies, Isabel 237
metapsychology 200, 203, 222, 223
Miller, Eric 237
Miller, J. 164
von Minden, Gerald 61–2, 66
mirroring 142, 173, 194
Mitchell, Stephen A. 69, 130
Mitscherlich, Alexander 61
Mitscherlich, Margarete 61
model scene 142, 143, 144–5, 146
moral defence 72, 74–5, 115, 158, 160–2, 166
morality 33, 221
mother: alienated structure 92–3; antilibidinal ego 7–8; Aulagnier 57; child dependence on 215; daughter relationship 162; early infant experiences 80; Freud 57; "good enough" 11, 54–5, 199; hysteria 98, 99, 102; imago 191–2, 194, 195–6, 199; intuitive position 90; lack of attention to infant needs 58; mirroring 194; Oedipal situation 11; as part object 5; projective identification 81; pseudo-separation from 97, 98; as sexual object 57–8; as strange attractor 271; Suttie 26, 27, 28, 29; Winnicott 54–5, 91–2, 191; see also breast; family therapy; Oedipal situation
motivational systems theory 140–6
Müller-Braunschweig, H. 61
multi-channel teaching 273–4
multiple personalities 189

narcissism 52, 62, 233; mind-object children 143; narcissistic seduction 56, 57; primary 56, 132; psychic retreat 106; relationship addiction 162, 163, 166
Nazism 229, 234–5
Negroponte, N. 206
neurology 206, 271
neuroscience 44, 124
neurosis: defensive techniques 100; mature dependence 132; object situation 129; obsessional 94; Oedipus concept 95; psychopathology of 4; sadism 74; "super-neurotics" 102, 103
neurotic hysteria 97, 102

object constancy 68, 69, 131, 161, 200
object relations 3, 7–8, 39, 44–5, 113–19, 212; analyst as new object 105–11; art 4; bodily locus of 86–7; Buber 220; Chasseguet 52; as core of Fairbairn's theory 63; developmental theory 227; Fairbairn critique of drive theory 56–7; family therapy 260–1, 262, 269; France 53, 54; functional subgrouping 253–4; Germany 61, 62, 65, 66; Group Affective Model 271, 281; group relations 244–5; Imago relationship theory 171; internal/external 5–6, 135; Klein 214; Lacan 50, 51; moral defence 160; naming the affect 174; negative transference 140; number of 133; persons-in-relation perspective 35; prejudice 228, 229–30, 235–6; schizoid conflict 129, 130–2; separation 195; sexual dysfunction 80–7; sexuality 68–79, 81; social object 234; subsidiary selves 217; Sutherland 186, 187–200, 203, 204, 205, 238; therapeutic focus of 172; warm treatment of schizoid patients 197; Winnicott 55, 91–2; see also bad objects; exciting object; objects; personal relations; rejecting object
Object Relations Technique (ORT) 276–7
object situation 129
objective position 94–5
objects: affect as motivator of self-object organization 281–2; alienated structure 92–3; allergic object relationship 91; bivalency 133; conscious relationships with 197; early infant experiences 80; Fairbairn/Klein contrast 66; Group Affective Model 273; ideal 8–9, 15, 45, 75, 91, 249; internalization 89; intuitive position 90–1; mature dependence 47, 48; memory 42; oscillating structure 93–4; social object 186, 227–9, 230–1, 233, 234, 235, 236; splitting 4; transformational 106, 107; transitional 5, 51, 131, 242; see also bad objects; exciting object; object relations; rejecting object

of 4; Schreber case 13; structure
building 197; trauma 122
psychotherapy: analytical 197, 198; child
therapy 140–6, 148, 149–57; criticisms
of 196; diagnosis 198; family therapy
260–70; growth in demand for 24;
organizational consultancy 247; as
reconciliation 25, 32; Suttie 25, 31–3;
therapist as strange attractor 272; *see
also* group therapy; psychoanalysis;
therapeutic relationship

Racamier, Paul-Claude 57, 58
Racker, H. 66
rage 8, 80, 98, 169, 171, 172, 173
Rangell, L. 99, 100
Rapaport, David 220
reactive tendencies 3, 117
regression: depressive 94, 95; hysteria 99;
organizational change 242;
psychopathy 31; schizoid conflict 132;
therapeutic 106
Rehberger, Rainer 1, 61–7
rejecting object 34, 45, 74, 115, 117;
antilibidinal ego 69, 108; cumulative
trauma 92; endopsychic structure 7–8,
9, 11, 15–16, 141, 249; father 101;
group therapy 255; Heising 62;
hysteria 102; identification with 106;
internalized relationships 105;
masochism 75; model scene 146;
Oedipal situation 101; sexual
dysfunction 85, 86; splitting 91;
trauma 127; *see also* exciting object;
object relations
rejection: family therapy 264; by father
100–1; by mother 196; sexual
dysfunction 82; traumatization 127
relationship addiction 158, 159–67
religion 20, 22–3, 171, 212–13
repetition 41–2, 43, 45, 48, 141
repression 6, 10, 15–16, 63, 80, 89; child
abuse 148, 153; dissociation 11, 34,
122–3; emphasis on 37; external
relationships 105; Fairbairn's works
114; German psychoanalysis 66; as
horizontal defence mechanism 126;
hysteria 10, 98, 100; of libido 179;
Oedipal situation 101; part objects
132; patriarchal 218; primary 43;
sexual dysfunction 85; superego 3;
Sutherland 205–6

research methods 276–7
restitutional principle 4, 177
Rey, Henri 103
Rey, Ricardo Juan 89–96
Rice, A. K. 237
Ricoeur, Paul 225
Riedesser, P. 121
Rieff, Philip 220
Rinsley, D. 141
role playing 78
Rosenberg, Benno 55–6
Rosenfeld, H. 125
Rosolato, Guy 52
Rost, W.-D. 62
Roussillon, René 58
Royal Edinburgh Hospital 185
Rubens, R. L. 234
Rupprecht-Schampera, Ute 66,
97–104
Rycroft, C. 46

sadism 74, 76, 255
sado-masochism 108
sameness 40, 41
Sandler, J. 189, 190
Saperstein, J. L. 189, 190
Sartre, J.-P. 40, 46, 47
Schafer, R. A. 197–8, 199
Scharff, David E. 1, 3–18, 34, 64, 67, 69,
81, 214, 262, 271–82
Scharff, Jill Savege 1, 34, 80–8, 185–6,
202–11, 262, 271–82
Scheidt, C. W. 121
Schein, Edgar 239
Schermer, V. 245
schizo-affective disorder 129, 131, 133,
134–5
schizoid conflict 76–7, 78, 129, 130–2,
134–5, 136
schizoid personality 4, 51–2, 61, 92, 117;
alienation 141; development of
Fairbairn's theory 114, 115;
endopsychic situation 91; fetishism 76;
Kohut 140; mind-object children 143;
von Minden 62; object relations
analysts 197; splitting 123; Sutherland
196
schizoid withdrawal 75–6
schizophrenia 131, 133, 134
Schore, A. N. 206, 251
Schreber case 12–13, 52–3, 116
Scotland 19, 213, 237